T0301461

STAYING AFLOAT

SOCIAL SCIENCE HISTORY

Edited by
Stephen Haber and David W. Brady

STAYING AFLOAT

Risk and Uncertainty in Spanish
Atlantic World Trade, 1760–1820

JEREMY BASKES

STANFORD UNIVERSITY PRESS

Stanford, California

Stanford University Press
Stanford, California

This book has been published with the assistance of Ohio
Wesleyan University.

Printed in the United States of America on acid-free,
archival-quality paper

Library of Congress Cataloging-in-Publication Data

Baskes, Jeremy, 1961– author.
    Staying afloat : risk and uncertainty in Spanish Atlantic
world trade, 1760–1820 / Jeremy Baskes.
        pages cm.—(Social science history)
    Includes bibliographical references and index.
    ISBN 978-0-8047-8542-6 (cloth : alk. paper)
    1. Spain—Colonies—America—Commerce—History.
2. Spain—Commerce—America—History.   3. America—
Commerce—Spain—History.   4. Risk management—
Spain—History.   5. Merchant marine—Spain—History.
6. Marine insurance—Spain—History.   I. Title.
II. Series: Social science history.
    HF3685.B37 2013
    382.0946'01821—dc23   2013011195

    ISBN 978-0-8047-8635-5 (electronic)

Typeset by Westchester Publishing Services in
10.5/13 Bembo

To Noah and Ethan, my best buddies

CONTENTS

*Appendixes: For referenced Appendixes, please see
Web Appendix tables at: http://www.sup.org/stayingafloat*

Figures

Tables

ACKNOWLEDGMENTS

In the nearly ten years since I began this book, I have benefitted from the generosity of a number of organizations and people. Ohio Wesleyan University has provided me repeatedly with grants from the Thomas E. Wenslau fund to conduct research in the Archive of the Indies in Seville, Spain. I have also been fortunate to have received a Fulbright scholarship from the Council for the International Exchange of Scholars as well as a year-long NEH Fellowship from the National Endowment for the Humanities. Both of these grants permitted me needed time to research and write.

While many friends and scholars have assisted me by reading and commenting on the manuscript, special thanks go to Xabier Lamikiz of the University of the Basque Country (Euskal Herriko Unibertsitatea). In addition to his valuable comments, he has been a lifeline, responding to my many esoteric emailed questions with detailed information about a wide variety of issues. Others whose comments and assistance have been especially important include Kenneth Andrien and Richard Salvucci, both of whom have been tremendously helpful and generous to me throughout my career. The book has also benefitted from the reading and comments of Herb Klein and Lyman Johnson. In the final stages of the book, Amy Bodiker provided much support and companionship.

A number of scholars have read portions of the book and have given me appreciated advice and commentary. I thank Carlos Marichal, Javier Cuenca Esteban, Richard Garner, John Kicza, and Alfonso Quiroz for their input. Anonymous reviewers at Stanford University Press and *Colonial Latin American Review* issued useful comments as well. I am grateful to Steve Haber, one of the editors of Stanford University Press's series on Social Science History, who has been incredibly supportive of me and my scholarship. I also thank John Coatsworth, Kris Lane, Matthew Restall, Julia Sarreal, and Gail Triner.

Several colleagues at Ohio Wesleyan University have helped and encouraged me during the production of this book. Bob Gitter of the

Economics Department gave me many hours of help and instruction in multivariate regression. He is a better teacher than I am a student. I have spent many hours talking with David Walker of the Geography Department about our common interests on Mexico, Latin America, and Spain. My history colleague Michael Flamm has always been a great dispenser of advice. Jody Forman, former office manager of the History Department, helped in many ways, including with analysis of data.

Thanks go to the many people I have run into or befriended at the AGI over the years. These include Bradley Benton, Asmaa Bouhrass, Kathryn Burns, Scott Cave, Sarah Chambers, Ashleigh Dean, Esther González, Saber Gray, Douglas Ingles, Cameron Jones, Jane Landers, Jane Mangan, Carmen McKee Rocha, Michel Oudijk, Amara Solari, Camilla Townsend, Spencer Tyce, and David Wheat. Discussions of our respective research projects were always enriching. I cannot adequately express my gratitude to and affection for Michael Francis and Annie Francis, who, in addition to providing advice and encouragement, have for years adopted me as their dining and carousing companion in Seville. Our friendship is one of the very best things to have come out of this project.

At Stanford University Press I thank my editor Emma Harper for her assistance and patience. I am also grateful to Norris Pope, Director of Scholarly Publishing, who oversaw production of both this and my previous book. At Westchester Publishing Services I thank Hillary Danz and Michael Haggett for their meticulous copyediting. Last, I appreciate the assistance of David Spadafora and the staff of the Newberry library for their help in identifying the map that graces the book's cover.

My parents, Julie and Roger Baskes, have been an inspiration to me for most of my fifty-plus years. They are also two of the best readers and editors I know. Without Jane Erickson helping me in the archives and home-schooling our children in Spain, this book might not have been written. My greatest projects and proudest accomplishments are my boys, Noah Alexander Erickson Baskes and Ethan Curtis Erickson Baskes. It is with boundless love that I dedicate this book to Noah and Ethan.

Chapter 1

Introduction: Risk and Uncertainty

Risk was pervasive in early modern, oceanic commerce. At virtually every juncture of a long-distance venture, merchants encountered risks that threatened to sink their investments and generate painful losses. This ever-present danger was even reflected in the basic language of trade: to engage in a commercial transaction was expressed in Spanish as *correr un riesgo*, "to take a risk." Given the prevalence of risk, it is not surprising that early modern traders were deeply aware and profoundly concerned about the many dangers that their business dealings might face and dedicated considerable energies to reduce or accommodate them. Despite the centrality of risk in governing commercial behavior, however, historians of the Spanish empire have virtually ignored its role.[1] This book seeks to rectify this omission by elevating risk and uncertainty to the center of analysis. Not only does this approach require the exploration of new issues, but analyzing familiar topics through the lens of risk management produces wholly different perspectives about the activities and behaviors of Spain's Atlantic traders.

Merchants engage in business with the goal of making profits. Risk represents an obstacle to the success of mercantile ventures, an event or danger that has a potentially negative consequence on the outcome of business deals. If not for risk and uncertainty, merchants could develop commercial strategies confident that all scenarios were known and that no surprises would arise. In classical economic theory entailing perfect

1

competition, "practical omniscience on the part of every member of the competitive system" is assumed. Entrepreneurs operate from positions of perfect knowledge in which "the future will be foreknown." Under such theoretical conditions, commerce would benefit from stability and predictability. In reality, however, business is always conducted with some degree of risk and uncertainty. Economic actors are not omniscient.[2]

In the early modern world, risk and uncertainty were pervasive, especially in long-distance, transoceanic trade. The central argument put forth in this book is that much of the commercial behavior of Spanish merchants should be understood as their responses to the ever-present riskiness of trade. Economic historian Peter Musgrave has argued that it is impossible to understand the early modern commercial world without considering the centrality of risk and uncertainty. In their efforts to mitigate risk, he argues, early modern merchants often engaged in "odd economic behavior," adding that "without [considering] uncertainty and its consequences, much of the economic and social history of the pre-modern world is, if not completely inexplicable, at least deeply mysterious."[3] To understand the behavior of Spanish imperial merchants, the historian must take into consideration the tremendously uncertain conditions under which they operated.

Early modern Spanish merchants did not accept passively the business climates that they encountered. Instead, they sought to shape or influence commercial environments and institutions. The Atlantic world was fraught with risks, any one of which could derail a merchant's plans or even devastate his financial empire. As a consequence, merchants engaged in risk-reducing strategies, developed risk-mitigating institutions, and sought whatever means possible to reduce the uncertainty and ambiguity that pervaded early modern trade.

Economists make an important distinction between risk and uncertainty. According to Frank H. Knight, an early twentieth-century American economist[4] whose pioneering work emphasized their difference, risk was "a quantity susceptible of measurement" whereas uncertainty was "unmeasurable." A risk was a phenomenon whose probability could be computed, allowing economic actors to pass it onto others, to buy protection against such a risk.[5] The Atlantic world mercantile community, for example, had some sense of the frequency of shipwrecks. While any individual accident was unpredictable, the law of large numbers[6] allowed the computation of the probability of a ship sinking. Knowing the probability of any one ship becoming lost in a shipwreck allowed shipowners to pool their risks so as to convert the danger into a fixed cost. Rather than bear the entire (albeit small) risk of having one's vessel wrecked, shipowners could eliminate the risk altogether by paying a small premium determined by the probability of a shipwreck. As such, no shipowner would suffer a total loss; instead, the cost of the premium would be known in advance. The consolidation (pooling) of risk is most often accomplished through the acquisition of insurance in which traders pass onto a company or partnership the risk that they prefer not to endure themselves.[7] By purchasing insurance, shipowners and merchants reduced significantly the riskiness of their ventures.

Far more problematic for economic actors, Knight argued, were unmeasurable risks, nowadays termed in the economics literature "Knightian uncertainties." These risks occur without any predictable pattern and thus cannot be addressed through insurance or other pooling mechanisms. "Business decisions," for example, "deal with situations that are far too unique, generally speaking, for any sort of statistical tabulation to have any value for guidance." To weather these risks and profit from his ventures, a businessmen had to rely on his judgment (experience, risk tolerance, business acumen, etc.) to guide his decisions. Obviously, merchants' judgment was highly imperfect and variable. Two veteran early modern merchants might employ their vast experiences to assess the multitude of factors that affected a potential deal and yet make wholly different decisions. The issues were so vast and unpredictable that merchants could not measure with much precision the probability of a venture's success. Put differently, long-distance trade entailed a notable element of gambling. Each transaction was distinct, the variety of influencing factors numerous, and its outcome thus uncertain. Merchants anticipated that their successful ventures would outweigh their failures, but the probability of success of any individual transaction was impossible to determine. Trade was uncertain.[8]

There are several ways to deal with risk and uncertainty. Again, measurable risks can be passed onto a third party, notably an insurer. Knightian uncertainties, however, were by definition too unpredictable or unique to be quantified and thus eliminated by finding others to assume them, to accept a payment to take them on. Long-distance commerce entailed many uncertainties that could never be eradicated, but merchants did attempt, with varying success, to limit their impact. While their unpredictability made them uninsurable, they could be minimized or reduced. No matter how greatly a trader sought to avoid risks and uncertainties, however, they were inevitably central factors determining the success or failure of long-distance trade. No merchant could ignore these factors.

• • •

This is a book about the ways in which merchants of the Spanish Atlantic world sought to deal with the endemic risks and uncertainties of long-distance commerce. Risk management (here understood to be the totality of efforts, individual and systemic, that aimed to reduce risk and uncertainty) was vital to the business decisions of long-distance merchants. Indeed, this book argues that managing risk was the principal concern of international merchants and that many aspects of Spanish imperial trade practices can only be understood fully when examined through the lenses of risk and uncertainty.

The riskiness (both measurable and unmeasurable) of early modern, Atlantic world trade arose from a multitude of factors, all of which a prudent merchant needed to consider. One major source of uncertainty resulted from the poor information that merchants inevitably possessed in the planning and execution of their business activities, an issue examined in Chapter 2. As Knight explains, "the fundamental uncertainties of economic life are the errors in predicting the future and in making present adjustments to fit future conditions."[9] One way that traders sought to reduce the uncertainty was by increasing their knowledge of the business and political climates that affected their interests. But good information was difficult and expensive to obtain in the early modern world as news traveled slowly and imperial politics were anything but transparent. As a result, business was most often conducted with only limited knowledge of relevant factors, what economists refer to as "bounded rationality," contributing greatly to the uncertainty surrounding long-distance trade, and complicating the already difficult judgments merchants were forced to make about the future. Few activities exhausted more of a merchant's time than writing letters to all corners of his business empire, trying to reduce the imperfection of his information. Knowledge of commercial and political conditions throughout the Atlantic world helped merchants penetrate the fogginess in which they engaged their trade. Although merchants understood the importance of good information, the communication technologies of the day were underdeveloped, especially so in the Spanish empire, resulting in the sporadic and slow movement of intelligence. Information received from the other side of the Atlantic was better than none, but it was always dated and might, if no longer accurate, even lead a merchant to make costly, ill-advised decisions. Long-distance trade moved at a snail's pace and required decisions about unpredictable markets and unknowable circumstances well in the future, and "the longer it is, the more uncertainty will naturally be involved."[10] Even the best informed long-distance merchants operated largely in the dark.

Imperfect information increased greatly the costs and risks of doing business. One of the greatest dangers emerged from unpredictable and changing market conditions. Merchants guided their commercial decisions on reports they received regarding existing supply and demand in markets throughout the Atlantic world and beyond. But given the slow movement of information and goods, market conditions could change radically between, for example, the dispatch of intelligence from America, its receipt in Spain, and the corresponding shipment and arrival of goods back to America. The danger of market risk plagued all early modern merchants, no matter from where they operated their businesses.

The cost of conducting business is influenced by the political, legal, economic, and cultural institutional framework in which such economic activities are undertaken. According to Nobel laureate Douglass North, institutions "determine transaction and transformation costs and hence the profitability and feasibility of engaging in economic activity."[11] These institutions, however, are not fixed. Indeed, institutional economists predict that when faced with elevated risk and other costly obstacles to economic growth, economic actors will design new (or adapt existing) institutions or economic practices to lower costs, reduce risks, and make feasible economic activities that would otherwise be too dangerous or expensive to undertake. "The major role of institutions in a society is to reduce uncertainty by establishing a stable (but not necessarily efficient) structure to human interaction."[12]

Merchants responded to the uncertainty of market risk, sudden fluctuations in supply or demand, by either creating new or adapting existing institutions. Chapter 3 examines market risk in the Atlantic world as well as the institutional responses designed to reduce such risks. Merchants throughout turned to economic institutions to lower the frequency or severity of market shifts. One institution that merchants outside of the Spanish empire relied upon heavily to reduce commercial risk was the vertically integrated trading company—for example, the English, Dutch, or French East India Companies, the Royal African Company, or the Hudson Bay Company. By concentrating trade in a single entity with sanctioned monopoly privileges, merchants benefited by exercising more direct control over supplies in distant markets, allowing them to reduce the likelihood of sudden saturation of markets. Trade became less volatile and risky, and thus more feasible. According to Knight, a larger business entity, such as a corporation, faces reduced risks due to "the extension of the scope of operations to include a large number of individual decisions, ventures, or 'instances.'"[13] Decisions and the intelligence informing them were aggregated, and thus uncertainty was lessened.

In the Spanish empire, monopoly trading companies did not develop for the most important routes. Instead, there emerged a complex array of regulations on commerce which had the consequence of performing some of the same risk-reducing functions as the chartered companies. Historians have failed to adequately appreciate these parallels; instead they have stressed only the negative, monopolistic aspects of the Carrera de Indias. Until commercial reform in the last decades of the eighteenth century, granting of trade licenses in Spain was tightly controlled and severely limited, restricting the total amounts involved in transatlantic commerce to quantities that could be reasonably consumed in the colonies. The number of open ports was also kept deliberately few. One explicit goal of regulated commerce was to match supply and demand, to prevent the glutting of markets. Until they were terminated in 1739 to Peru and 1778 to Mexico, the flotas and galleons that ran between Spain and the colonies helped to regularize trade, making supplies more predictable and reducing the degree of market risk. Limited licensing and organized fleets lowered risk by making trade less volatile. They functioned in a somewhat similar fashion to chartered companies in other Atlantic world empires.

Scholars have tended to view the regulated Spanish commercial system solely as a vehicle of the mercantile elite to garner excessive monopoly profits by excluding competition. Because this widely embraced view of the trade system is at odds, to some degree, with the risk-reducing rationale for regulation put forth here, it is also examined in Chapter 3. Monopoly, in this context, had two distinct features. First, monopoly was geographical; the Andalusian cities of Seville (until 1717) and Cadiz (thereafter) enjoyed Crown-granted, exclusive access to the Spanish American markets. Similarly, legal ports in the colonies were limited to a choice few, Veracruz and Callao (Lima) being the most important. Seville/Cadiz became an international hub with all of the financial and commercial institutions necessary to facilitate transatlantic trade, a concentration of trade institutions that provided certain economic efficiencies. Wealthy merchants from all corners of the Atlantic world migrated to Andalusia to partake in commerce. While non-Spaniards were excluded from trading directly with the colonies, a perfectly comprehensible policy given Spain's mercantilist goals, there were no obvious trade barriers to Spanish merchants of a certain size and wealth, assuming they relocated to Andalusia.

Spaniards from every region of the peninsula matriculated into the Andalusian *consulados*, the powerful merchant guilds of Seville and Cadiz. The dominance of Spanish-Atlantic trade by members of the *consulado* is a second monopoly characteristic identified by historians who argue that the wealthy *consulado* merchants exploited their political and economic power to earn excessive profits. Chapter 3 challenges this traditional argument, suggesting that there were far too many traders involved in Spanish imperial trade to have permitted even the largest and wealthiest to exercise monopoly and dictate commodity prices. Merchants engaged in Atlantic world trade were usually wealthy, and for good reason, but their individual interests trumped any class or institutional alliances that might have pressured them to collude on prices. In any event, there were too many of them to have functioned as a cartel. Wealth might have gained them a foothold in the commercial system, but once they entered, they faced considerable competition from similar traders.

Relative to its neighbors, Spain's continued decline throughout most of the eighteenth century led reformers to prescribe changes to the regulated Spanish commercial system. Indeed by the second half of the century, a Bourbon modernizing ideology that painted the commercial system as an obstacle to Spain's development had triumphed, making the *Carrera de Indias* a central target for restructuring. Initiated in 1765, the zenith of reform was the 1778 promulgation of *comercio libre* (free trade), which opened the Spanish imperial commercial system to many more ports and led the Crown to greatly increase the number of ships and volume of cargo licensed to trade in the Spanish Atlantic world. Chapter 4 examines the impact of trade reform. The 1778 legislation has traditionally been depicted as a singularly revolutionary transformation in Spanish commerce, one that led to a spectacular increase in transatlantic trade and the emergence of a more competitive, entrepreneurial class of traders. In fact, the period after 1778 has even been dubbed a "golden age" in Spanish trade.[14] All of these assumptions are scrutinized in this chapter. First, a new body of scholarship leaves little question that the actual growth of trade was a small fraction of that which historians have traditionally suggested. Deregulation of the commercial system did lead to commercial expansion, but nowhere near what has been accepted in the dominant historiography. Second, the still substantial growth of commerce after 1778 had both positive and negative consequences. Growing competition expanded trade, lowered prices for consumers, and increased Royal tax revenues, but also led to increasingly volatile markets and a major surge of commercial bankruptcies in the late 1780s and turn of the 1790s. The argument developed in Chapter 4 is that the promulgation of *comercio libre* altered the institutional arrangements that had helped regularize supply and mitigate uncertainty in the pre-reform era. It would be incorrect to paint the pre-reform era as risk-free, but the Bourbon reforms dismantled several of the practices that traders had relied upon to deal with pervasive uncertainty. Believing that the new post-1778 commercial environment of free trade was too unpredictable, some experienced Spanish traders withdrew from Atlantic world commerce, reinvesting into ventures perceived to be less risky such as land ownership, silver mining, and financial services, including the provision of insurance. In short, Chapter 4 argues that to term the fifteen years following the introduction of reform a "golden age" is misleading. Trade did experience growth to the benefit of Crown tax revenues and, perhaps, consumers, but the end of regulated commerce also led to increased riskiness, the growing unpredictability of trade, and corresponding financial dislocations. While the ensuing bankruptcies might merely have reflected less competitive merchants failing to adjust to the new, more competitive environment, the start of the wars of the French Revolution and Napoleon makes difficult any such long-term assessment. The wars finished off many of the merchants who had managed to adjust to the new trade regime.

Widespread reliance on credit had always been one of the major sources of riskiness in early modern trade. Atlantic world commercial ventures almost invariably took years to complete. Goods had to be acquired, packaged, shipped, and sold, and then the process was repeated on the other side of the ocean before the original merchant recovered his investment and calculated his profits. One consequence of the prolonged nature of commerce was that merchants often turned to financiers to help sustain their businesses. The dependence on credit, perhaps, was fueled by the endemic shortage of minted coins in the colonies; few traders had the liquidity to pay for the imported wares they bought in bulk. The Bourbon commercial reforms of 1778 might have exacerbated the situation. First, the termination of the convoy and the *feria de Jalapa* (trade fair of Jalapa) in Mexico caused a partial withdrawal of many of the wealthy Mexican merchants from international trade. No longer did they descend to Veracruz with large amounts of cash to buy imported goods at the trade fair. Instead, the Peninsular *flotistas* (import/export merchants) increasingly sold on credit to less well-funded Mexican traders, tying up their funds for lengthy periods and exposing themselves to significant risks of default.

Second, liberalization of trade caused a flood of imports into America as more traders were granted licenses to carry products. In the 1780s and 1790s, international traders in all corners of the empire complained of the growing need to finance sales and to do so for longer terms to increasingly less creditworthy consumers. Extending credit always exposed merchants to the potential for losses due to debtor insolvency, but as the quantities of imports and the uncertainties of trade grew after 1778, importers were forced to finance more and more of their sales, incurring additional risks. Bankruptcies were the most glaring consequence. Chapter 5 explores the role of credit in Spanish Atlantic world commerce and the rising incidence of bankruptcy in the years following the introduction of *comercio libre*.

The experiment in free trade was abruptly interrupted by the outbreak of war in 1793. For the next two decades, Spain was engaged in nearly constant hostilities alternately with France and Great Britain. Napoleon's defeat in 1815 did not spell relief for the Spanish empire; Spain remained engulfed in war as its American colonies fought for their independence. Of course, even the start of free trade was delayed by Spain's involvement in the American Revolutionary War. During peacetime, merchants encountered a multitude of potentially costly risks; warfare introduced a host of different, and even more devastating, dangers. The nature of commerce changed dramatically during wartime as an entirely different set of factors and risks influenced merchants' business decisions. Warfare always interrupted commercial sea lanes, but nations at war also contracted privateers to attack the commercial vessels of their enemies. The danger of losses from enemy corsairs was the greatest risk that merchants faced during wartime, but war also led to losses as commerce stalled and merchants failed to get their goods to market. Chapter 6 examines the economic and commercial impacts of war, and especially its impact on risk. While the examples used come from the second half of the eighteenth century, many of the effects were equally suffered in previous wars.

Merchants eliminated some of the risks that they encountered by purchasing marine insurance. For a fee, they could insure themselves against losses sustained from shipwrecks, inclement weather, flooding, fire, enemy encounters, piracy, or corsairs. In the last decades of the eighteenth century, a flourishing industry in the underwriting of risk expanded in the port city of Cadiz, replacing what had been largely a foreign-dominated business. Dozens of insurance partnerships were established in the 1780s and 1790s, and Spanish merchants turned increasingly to these local financial institutions to obtain insurance coverage for their international business dealings. Merchants paid insurance premiums and transferred to these companies some portion of the riskiness of Atlantic world trade. Ironically, the rapid emergence of this industry might have been partially the response to the escalation of market riskiness following the adoption of *comercio libre*. Some of the large merchants who had invested in the colonial trade withdrew from this increasingly unpredictable business, choosing to underwrite measurable (and more predictable) risk via insurance policies instead. Previously, Spanish merchants had either secured coverage abroad or obtained security through alternative financial instruments,[15] but now they increasingly acquired marine insurance directly in Cadiz. Chapters 7 through 9 examine the emerging late eighteenth-century Cadiz-based insurance industry. Chapter 7 focuses on the capital structure of these newly formed insurance partnerships as well as the business strategies devised to guide their operations. Firms consisted of financial partners who, in acquiring shares, guaranteed to assume any commercial risks underwritten. The typical firm subscribed forty individual shares of ten thousand pesos apiece for a total pledge of four hundred thousand pesos. Shareholders, most of them merchants themselves, agreed to share in the profits and losses of the underwriting business. Company charters outlined the firms' policies and strategies and offer a unique window into the perceptions of Atlantic world risk at the time. Chapter 8 provides a microeconomic analysis of nearly eight hundred insurance policies written in Cadiz between 1759 and 1818. A separate policy was written for each insurable event, whether the shipment of a cargo or the sailing of a vessel. Each policy stipulated in minute detail the particular terms—outlining the route, cargo, value, ship type, and premium, and usually appending additional conditions unique to the specific case. Insurance premiums, always expressed as a percentage of the insured value, were a function of the perceived (measured) risk and thus fluctuated with changing coverage or shifting circumstances. In determining rates, insurers considered a host of factors, including the nature of the item underwritten, the type of ship, the season of the year, and, most interesting to the historian, the political climate in all corners of the Atlantic world. Indeed, insurers developed ingenious ways to protect themselves against the unexpected outbreak of war or to discourage insured shipowners from acting recklessly. Despite their precautions and the extremely high premium rates that they charged during wartime, the insurance companies seem to have sustained hefty losses after 1793, shaking the foundations of the Andalusian economy and financial markets. The profitability of the firms and the financial stability of the Cadiz insurance industry during the wars of the French Revolution and Napoleon are the topics of Chapter 9. As war-related insurance claims mounted, the companies strained to indemnify their losses, placing financial pressures upon their shareholders, who were called upon to cover the shortages. An examination of the lists of shareholders suggests that many of the partners held multiple shares in numerous firms, exposing themselves to dangerously high losses. Such concentration suggests that risk had not been adequately spread, leaving vulnerable the financial security of the Cadiz mercantile community.

Geographical Focus

This book began specifically as a study of the riskiness of trade between Spain and Mexico, a large topic in itself. In the course of research, however, this narrower focus became increasingly difficult to maintain and gradually expanded to encompass the entire Spanish empire and, in some aspects, the entire Atlantic world. In the introduction to an edited volume on the Atlantic world, historians Jack P. Greene and Philip P. Morgan make the obvious but too often ignored point that "events in one place had repercussions in others."[16] Along with other Atlantic world historians, Greene and Morgan argue that taken as a whole the various empires that surrounded and were active in the Atlantic comprise a cohesive and illuminating focus of study. Or as Alison Games nicely puts it, "the ocean . . . was the unique space within which goods and people were created, defined, and transformed."[17] The Spanish empire did not exist in a vacuum but was profoundly influenced by the other empires that operated in the Atlantic. "Imperial boundaries were permeable and there was considerable crossing of imperial lines."[18] Spanish imperial trade, for example, was but one stage of the international trade linking America and Europe. Most traded goods merely passed through Spain en route to the colonies or northern Europe. Commercial circuits transcended imperial borders. Trade legislation, *comercio libre* included, was most often designed and enacted with Spain's Atlantic world neighbors in mind, as a partial response to rising contraband, for example. Warfare, naturally, erupted due to conflicts between Spain and its Atlantic world enemies. For these and other reasons, this book became geographically much larger than originally envisioned.

Atlantic world history has enjoyed considerable scholarly attention in recent years, but historians of the Spanish empire have been slower than their British counterparts in widening their focus. Instead, Spanish American colonial history has largely been written with a local focus, only rarely expanding beyond the level of a single viceroyalty. Even Spain, the "mother country," has often taken a back seat in colonial Latin American histories, existing in the background, a distant place from which edicts, often inappropriate or ignored, occasionally arrived to guide or irk the colonialists. This observation is by no means meant as criticism. In the past four decades the high-quality work of colonial Spanish American historians has provided a vivid image and profound understanding of the Spanish American world that Columbus's journey initiated. Historians' focus on the local is critical; one can hardly comprehend the interaction of empires without first expanding knowledge about each one individually. Atlantic world history is an attempt to enlarge and widen the scope of these more geographically focused studies.

To some degree Atlantic world history itself builds upon earlier historical schools that attempted to examine the broader implications and consequences of the interplay between the two sides of the Atlantic. The influential work of Alfred Crosby and others demonstrated the monumental effects on both sides of the Atlantic caused by the Columbian exchange, the movement of flora and fauna between the Old World and the New World following Columbus's voyage of 1492.[19] Blossoming in the 1960s, and building on the work of earlier economists such as Raúl Prebisch,[20] the dependency school embraced a global perspective designed to explain the disparity of wealth between the developed and "underdeveloped" worlds. While the broad claims of the dependency school have been increasingly rejected, this macro-approach and cross-oceanic focus was certainly an important precursor to the efforts of Atlantic historians.[21] Some of the best studies of the Atlantic world have been produced by scholars of the African slave trade. The notorious "middle passage" was, of course, the link between Africa and America and was critical in the making of the Atlantic world. A massive historiography examines the effects of the slave trade and slavery on both sides of the Atlantic.[22]

While Atlantic world historians have been influenced by many schools, their paradigm is clearly the work of Fernand Braudel, specifically his monumental *The Mediterranean and the Mediterranean World in the Age of Philip II*.[23] Just as Braudel's work broke away from the narrower focus on nations and empires to explore the entire "Mediterranean World," Atlantic world historians seek to write "history without borders," a "Braudelian Atlantic history."[24]

Atlantic world history, as it is now defined, is relatively young, but it has nonetheless begun to produce a wealth of new works, especially for the English-speaking Atlantic.[25] While recent studies have also made significant contributions to integrate the Spanish empire into the broader

Atlantic world history, the literature is comparatively slim. Encouragingly, in the last decade-plus excellent works have been published in a variety of different subfields of Spanish Atlantic history.[26]

Economic history is especially well-suited to examine the whole of the Atlantic world. By necessity, long-distance merchants, the focus of this book, dealt with their counterparts in other parts of the world. The market for commodities transcended imperial borders requiring constant communication with agents in other Atlantic world commercial centers. Spanish merchants specializing in the importation of colonial goods turned to commercial houses in France, Great Britain, Holland, or elsewhere for lines of credit, interlinking the finances and the fortunes of traders throughout the Atlantic world. Crisis in one region caused waves, or worse, in the others. The Atlantic world was an integrated market. Long-distance trade forced participants to operate beyond the boundaries of the nation or empire; leading Spanish merchants were indeed engaged in activities that encompassed the entire Atlantic world and beyond. Their far-flung commercial interests required merchants to engage in mercantile correspondence that reflected this geographical expanse; Cadiz-based merchants communicated regularly with mercantile houses in virtually every major port of the Atlantic world.

Spanish Atlantic merchants rarely specialized in the trade of a single colony or commodity. Instead they were generalists (diversifying trade and minimizing risks), shipping to whichever markets seemed to offer potential for profit, and buying whatever colonial goods were in demand in Europe. Spanish merchants procured, most often for reexport, silver and cochineal from Mexico, indigo from Guatemala, sugar from Cuba, hides from Buenos Aires, cacao from Caracas and Guayaquil, and silver from Peru, among many other colonial products. They paid for these imports with typical European exports—textiles, wine, liquor, and a host of other luxury items—produced in Spain or, more commonly, imported to Iberia from northern Europe and then reexported to the colonies.

Commercial exchange tied the Spanish colonies and their inhabitants into the wider world. African slaves in the Caribbean and Brazil labored on plantations, producing sugar for European consumers.[27] Indigenous Oaxacans tended and harvested cochineal for the markets of London, Amsterdam, and beyond.[28] Enslaved miners in New Granada collected platinum which found its way to the laboratories of British scientists.[29] Indians of the viceroyalties of Mexico and Peru produced the silver that permitted worldwide commerce to expand.[30] Indeed virtually every colonial region specialized in a commodity or two that linked its peoples to global markets and exchange.

Similarly, the Cadiz-based insurance industry underwrote risk for ships traveling to destinations in every corner of the world, whether in Spanish America, Europe, North America, Africa, or Asia. No matter where a ship sailed, underwriters had to consider factors that transcended Spanish imperial politics and economics. Events in British America, for example, affected the riskiness of commerce between Cadiz and Río de la Plata. Factors contributing to risk were rarely contained by imperial borders. Indeed war, the most destructive commercial hazard, was almost always international; the constant warfare of the late eighteenth century requires that a study of risk in the Spanish empire examine related issues in the broader Atlantic world. Even the wars of Spanish American independence that ended the period under study had international dimensions. Furthermore, insurance underwriting in Spain was not wholly independent from the same business in other Atlantic world ports. There were no regulations that prohibited Spanish merchants from obtaining their coverage in London or Amsterdam. As a result, the market for insurance was international, forcing Spanish insurers to compete with their rivals in other Atlantic centers.

While the examples employed in this book come from all corners of the Spanish-Atlantic world, Mexico still looms more largely than any other colony. The issues discussed are deeply influenced by the historiography on colonial Mexico. Furthermore, the discussion of politics, especially in connection to the liberalization of trade in the eighteenth century, remains more fully focused on Mexico.

Sources

Most of the research for this book was conducted in the Fondo de Consulados, located at the Archivo General de Indias (AGI) in Seville. The majority of this collection pertains to the Cadiz *consulado*, the merchant guild established in 1717 upon the relocation of the *Casa de Contratación* from Seville to Cadiz. Because of the *consulado*'s dominant role in the colonial trade, its papers were naturally central to this study. Virtually every sheet of its several thousand *libros* and *legajos* deals with economic issues, especially international trade, making it an indispensable source for the study of Spanish commerce. Primary information from other archives and other sections of the AGI were also collected and used in the research for this book, but the *consulado* sources were simply the most useful and relevant, meriting their special mention.

Among the responsibilities of the guild was to adjudicate commercial disputes. In this capacity, the *consulado* heard bankruptcy proceedings, one source of materials for this study. In its oversight of bankruptcies, the guild came to possess the private papers of many merchants, from their letters to their financial records, principal primary documentation utilized in the writing of this book. Merchants wrote copiously to their commercial agents and allies, and their correspondence provides an astonishing wealth of information about commerce and the risk-management strategies of their authors. One illuminating aspect of mercantile correspondence is that it was intended exclusively for the private consumption of the merchant author and his addressee. As a consequence, these letters spoke with tremendous frankness, revealing commercial secrets that traders guarded with great care. Mercantile correspondence sought to inform and guide merchants' and their agents' commercial behavior and as such aimed for clarity, the goal being to provide unambiguously and precisely the extant conditions affecting commerce.

In addition to being a tribunal, the *consulado* was a merchants' association, protecting and promoting the interests of its members. In this role, the guild was regularly consulted by the Council of Indies on all matters economic, preparing *informes* (official reports) about a wide variety of issues. More generally, the consular officials maintained regular correspondence with various Crown ministers and others about issues of perceived urgency. These reports and letters were an additionally indispensable source for this project. Especially useful were the numerous reports prepared by the *consulado* of Cadiz, and its counterpart in Mexico, regarding the adoption and effects of late-eighteenth-century commercial liberalization.

The *consulado* was also vested with authority over the insurance industry. Among insurance-related papers deposited in the Fondo de Consulados were the charters of eighty-four insurance partnerships established at the end of the eighteenth century. These charters provide a wealth of information about the commercial factors that merchants perceived as risky at the time. In addition, the charters list all of the company shareholders and are thus a useful source in identifying and understanding the financiers behind the underwriting business. Also deposited in the *consulado* are many hundreds of insurance policies. Rich in numerical information, these policies permitted the construction of a massive database, allowing the quantification of risk to complement the more qualitative information discussed in other sections.

. . .

Early modern commerce exposed merchants to a multitude of risks. The poor flow of information, slow transportation technologies, the uncertain and changing market conditions, the volatile political climate, and a host of other potential problems plagued Spanish merchants and threatened to ruin their long-distance commercial ventures. This is a book that examines how merchants of the Spanish empire dealt with and accommodated these risks and uncertainties. Risk management was central to the economic planning of long-distance traders, and only by examining their economic activities and behavior in light of these strategies can historians hope to fully understand early modern trade.

Chapter 2

Staying Informed: The Risks of Poor Information in Atlantic World Trade

Information was the lifeblood of the mercantile community. Merchants used it to guide their decisions of when to invest in one or another commodity as well as where and when to ship. According to economist Frank Knight, "the most thoroughgoing methods of dealing with uncertainty [entail] securing better knowledge of and control over the future."[1] Without adequate information, merchants operated in the dark, increasing enormously what were already very risky ventures. Unfortunately for early modern traders, the flow of communications was poor, even under the best of circumstances. The great distances and existing transportation and communication technologies of the era guaranteed only partial knowledge of the political or economic news that might have an impact on markets. Merchants were forced to transact without adequate access to good and reliable information. This obstacle was by no means unique to the Spanish commercial world; it was a fundamental problem that faced all long-distance merchants during this era, one that merchants recognized and took means to minimize.[2]

Correspondence between merchants in key ports provided the main source of intelligence that traders utilized to guide their commercial operations. One historian observed that "practically every letter of every merchant I have ever seen has a postscript telling the recipient the latest price for some commodity."[3] Stein and Stein observed that "personal market information formed the sole basis of business decision-making."[4]

Xabier Lamikiz has argued that due to the rising use of individual register ships over the course of the eighteenth century, the importance of such correspondence in governing mercantile decisions grew sharply.[5] To increase their access to information, wealthier merchants could place permanent agents or factors in principal ports throughout the Spanish commercial empire. As Jeremy Adelman explains, "the most successful operated on a large scale through a network of agents scattered around many trading centers . . . while smaller merchants had to rely on more specialized, and thus more risky and more precarious, businesses."[6] Such agents were often family members who could best be trusted to pursue the interests of their relations.[7] In this regard the Spaniards acted little differently than their counterparts in other corners of the Atlantic world.[8] A good example of such a familial network, one used extensively in this study, is the Marticorena y Laurnaga clan, natives of Echalar in the Kingdom of Navarra.[9] Beginning in the 1770s, four of the Marticorena brothers emigrated to important commercial ports within the empire. Juan Vicente de Marticorena took up residence in Cadiz, matriculating in its *consulado* in 1776. His older brother, Juan Miguel de Marticorena, matriculated in the Cadiz guild in the same year but established himself in Lima, Peru.[10] Their younger brother, Juan Bautista de Marticorena, received license to travel to Guatemala in 1782,[11] where he became a prominent merchant, ultimately marrying into the powerful Aycinena family.[12] In 1787 the youngest of the four, Miguel Jacinto de Marticorena, was granted license to Veracruz where for a number of years he helped manage the trade of his siblings.[13] This familial network also depended on cousins. Cousin Juan Francisco de Goyeneche was the trusted factor in Mexico City. Another cousin, Juan Bernardo Larrain, resided in Caracas, and his brother lived in Cadiz, for awhile sharing a house with Juan Vicente. Another cousin, Juan Phelipe Laurnaga, related to the Marticorenas through their mother, doña Maria Felipa de Laurnaga, was a resident of Veracruz. Last, Juan Vicente de Marticorena employed the services of another cousin, Pedro Fermín de Córdoba, who worked alongside him for a number of years in Cadiz. The extensive correspondence received by Juan Vicente de Marticorena of Cadiz reveals how his relatives attempted to keep him informed of shifting supply and demand as well as the changing political climate in these diverse corners of the Spanish empire in which Juan Vicente traded.[14]

Major Spanish merchants were international traders as well; they acquired luxury goods in northern Europe to send to America, and they reexported their colonial imports to commercial centers throughout

Europe and beyond. Naturally, none but the largest trading houses could station agents in all of the ports with which they conducted business. Instead most merchants established long-standing ties with their counterparts in principal trading cities, perhaps employing one another as commission agents to forge and strengthen ties. The correspondence of veteran Cadiz trader Francisco de Sierra reveals the international nature of his dealings. He engaged in regular communications with commercial houses in London, Genoa, Hamburg, Marseilles, Rouen, Amsterdam, Oostende, Bordeaux, Lisbon, and Philadelphia, among other locales, frequently receiving letters in French and sometimes in English, Italian, or Portuguese.[15]

Table 2.1 illustrates the geographical diversity of the correspondence received by Sierra during two years of the early 1780s, 1781 and 1784. In total for these two years, Francisco de Sierra received 1225 letters, 438 from correspondents in Spain and 787 from all other locations. Nearly half of the total, 703, were sent from Europe (excluding Spain). Just under a quarter, 280, originated in America.

Significantly, the European letters arrived from a wide diversity of Atlantic world locations. Sierra exchanged regular communication with trading houses in the large commercial centers of London and Amsterdam as well as the French port cities of Marseille, Bordeaux, Nantes, and Rouen. Sierra's correspondence with Genoa, Italy, was amongst his most extensive. Sierra also communicated with some regularity with Lisbon-based associates. Further afield, Sierra corresponded with traders in central Europe, Hamburg and Solingen in Germany and Gdansk in modern-day Poland.[16] Sierra's widely dispersed correspondence reveals the degree to which Sierra operated as an international merchant. His interests and commercial ventures required him to keep abreast of events and trends throughout the Atlantic world.

Of course, Francisco de Sierra's commercial prominence was critically connected to his Spanish citizenship and access to the *Carrera de Indias*. Sierra's business deals primarily entailed reexporting to principal European ports the colonial goods that he obtained from his factors throughout America. Cochineal from Mexico, indigo from Central America, cacao from New Granada, quina (quinine) from Peru, and hides from Río de la Plata were the main commodities in which Sierra dealt. To obtain these items required Sierra to communicate with his agents and factors throughout the Spanish America. As Table 2.1 illustrates, Sierra received letters from a wide variety of colonial centers, the greatest number from

TABLE 2.1

Geographical Distribution of Correspondence Received by Francisco de Sierra in 1781 and 1784

Letter Origin	1781	1784	Grand Total	Letter Origin	1781	1784	Grand Total
Amsterdam	9	66	75	Marseille	68	57	125
Bordeaux	47	2	49	Martinique	14		14
Buenos Aires	2	9	11	Mexico	6	1	7
Caracas		6	6	Montevideo	1	4	5
Gdansk	5	4	9	Nantes	17	3	20
Exon (Eng.)	1	3	4	Oostende	20		20
Ghent (Belgium)	4	2	6	Other America	1	3	4
Genoa	38	49	87	Other Europe	20	3	23
Guárico	5		5	Other Spain	7	3	10
(Cap-Haïtien)				Paris	14	13	27
Hamburg	4	24	28	Rouen	4	12	16
Havana	28	21	49	Santo Domingo	2	3	5
Lima	4	24	28	Solingen (Germ.)		4	4
Lisbon	1	13	14	Spain	242	104	346
Livorno (Italy)	6	2	8	Veracruz	19	31	50
London	23	65	88				
Madrid	50	32	82	**Grand Total**	**662**	**563**	**1225**

SOURCE: AGI, *Consulados*, legajos 421, 426–27.

Veracruz, Lima and Havana. Sierra also communicated regularly with associates in Río de la Plata and New Granada.[17]

To function in this capacity necessitated that Sierra be multilingual. Table 2.2 illustrates the linguistic diversity of the correspondence received by Sierra in 1781 and 1784. More than a third of the correspondence that Sierra received in these years was written in French, which seems to have been the lingua franca of Atlantic world merchants. Many of the letters written in Spanish were composed by native speakers, including Sierra's primary correspondents in Amsterdam, but the London-based Portuguese trading house of Mendes da Costa also communicated in Spanish . Letters that arrived from France or Genoa were generally written in French, as was the case for the majority from Germany. It is unknown whether Francisco de Sierra answered these letters in French since his outgoing correspondence does not survive. Presumably, however, he responded to his French correspondents in French.[18] In addition to French and Spanish, Sierra received a small number of letters in Portuguese and Italian, and in several years other than 1781 and 1784, he received letters in English from a firm in Philadelphia.

No matter in what language or from which location Sierra received correspondence, it all served the same purpose. Such information kept

TABLE 2.2

*Languages of Letters Received by Francisco de Sierra
in 1781 and 1784*

French	437
Italian	3
Portuguese	13
Spanish	772
Grand Total	**1225**

SOURCE: AGI, *Consulados*, legajos 421, 426–27.

him better informed of market conditions and helped govern his business decisions. Valuable was the data on prices or supplies that he received from distant markets, such as in January 1786 when he learned from his London informants that cochineal was fetching 13/9 to 14 shillings, indigo 9/6 to 10/6, and that hides from Buenos Aires were in very short supply.[19] Sierra's far-flung correspondence provided him detail about markets throughout Europe and America. Frequent letters from a Joséph Zengolio of Genoa delineated the prices and demand for Sierra's exports in that city and its hinterlands. Regarding hides, Zengolio reported in July 1784 that "this article is without demand, and I regret to inform you that the price is very miserable." While the demand for cochineal was improving, "indigo is calm."[20] Virtually every letter that arrived to Sierra apprised him of market conditions or extant prices. In theory, if not always in practice, such information permitted him to operate with less uncertainty, guiding his decisions and helping him more intelligently navigate a risky environment.

Possessing information about a distant market in no way eradicated the danger of a sudden market shift or an unexpected change in local economic conditions, but information at least provided a bit of direction, giving a merchant some basis with which to manage his business. Encouraged in 1776 to reroute his ship *El Jasón* to Louisiana, Francisco de Sierra refused, stating that Louisiana is "unfamiliar commerce and everyone flees from newness there being alternatives that experience has shown to be very safe."[21] Sierra's caution was not that of a pampered and privileged rentier who refused to engage in productive ventures; rather his reluctance stemmed from the knowledge that a smart merchant avoided operating in unfamiliar waters.

While each of the Atlantic world empires jealously guarded its national commercial interests from foreign interlopers by erecting mercantilist, protectionist trade policies, markets were nonetheless integrated, if imperfectly. The market for Spanish American commodities such as cochineal and indigo, to name only the most valuable, was widespread. The prices of these dyestuffs were watched closely by merchants in London, Amsterdam, and other commercial centers and were even quoted on the Dutch and English commodities exchanges.[22] News about these items, thus, affected their prices throughout the Atlantic world. Despite the hostilities of the American Revolutionary War, merchants in London and Amsterdam stayed informed, as best they could, of cochineal supplies arriving to Spain. On 1 November 1781, the Dutch commercial house of Echenique y Sánchez warned Sierra that the market for "cochineal is inactive and will probably be so until the convoy from Havana arrives there and a going price is established."[23] Just a week later, on 9 November 1781, the London house of Fermín de Tastet and Company informed Sierra that "the news of the arrival to there of the fleet from Havana suspends entirely any trade in cochineal. The vendors do not know what to ask nor the buyers what to pay, but we presume it will not be long before a price is set." Several weeks later, the impact was clearer and Fermín could advise Sierra that in fact "cochineal has not dropped as was expected with the arrival there of such a large portion."[24]

Traders sought to obtain the most recent information to permit them to operate with the least uncertainty possible. Agents thus sent their principals a regular flow of correspondence discussing any pertinent economic or political news. Experience dictated that multiple copies of at least important information should be sent, and so letters were sometimes sent in duplicate, triplicate, or even quadruplicate to ensure safe and timely arrival. Sending duplicate copies could be complicated from less busy ports since weeks or even months might pass without the arrival or departure of a ship. This problem could be minimized somewhat by dealing through an intermediary. When Juan Bautista de Marticorena wrote from Guatemala to his brother Juan Vicente in Cadiz, the letters often traveled by way of a third brother, Miguel Jacinto, who resided in Veracruz. Since ships departing from Central America to Spain were relatively few in number, Juan Bautista directed his brother Miguel Jacinto to open and make additional copies of the letters he sent via Veracruz whenever he felt that this might speed delivery. As Miguel Jacinto explained to Juan Vicente:

> [Juan Bautista] advises me that whenever there is opportunity to direct [letters] to you aboard two boats that I can open them and make a copy

or two if necessary . . . and as such it might arrive at that port at the same time or even earlier than the first, so that whenever I see two frigates departing 6 or 8 or 10 days apart from one another for that port (Cadiz), I will pursue the same course . . . because in this way I believe you might have news of [say] the arrival of your ship to Honduras more promptly than via the maritime mail.[25]

Certainly the erratic flow of information was inevitable given the great distances and existing technologies of the day, especially for transatlantic communication. Mail service within Spain and the continent was fairly ordered, although myriad interruptions might preclude its timely arrival. At the turn of the nineteenth century, Cadiz and other Spanish cities had regularly scheduled departure and arrival days for mail to and from a variety of locations. For example, Cadiz received mail from "Spain and foreign kingdoms" every Monday and Thursday at dawn; mail departed Cadiz for these destinations at midnight on Tuesday and Friday. Postal deliveries for Barcelona from "all of Spain, Portugal and the North" arrived at dawn on Tuesdays and Fridays; outgoing mail departed on the same days at 10:00 A.M.[26]

Mail service to and from America was far less predictable. Despite efforts throughout the colonial era to establish a more regular and reliable system of transatlantic *correos*, even in the late eighteenth century information from the other side of the ocean was stale, when available at all.[27] Regarding "correspondence to America," merchants in Barcelona were advised: "As this is conducted via the mail boats that depart from La Coruña on the dates determined by Madrid, subjects writing to these dominions should deliver their letters to this office at least fifteen days prior, so that it will arrive in time for the maritime mail [boats] of that city."[28] Clearly, this was no recipe for the rapid exchange of information. The viceroy of Mexico, Juan Vicente Güemes y Pacheco, the second conde de Revillagigedo, alluded to poor imperial communication in 1793 in a report about the "decadence" of Mexico's economy. According to the viceroy, Spanish merchants lacked adequate knowledge about consumer tastes (i.e., demand) and often exported to Mexico inappropriate items. The problem, he diagnosed, was due to the fact that mail boats made several stops en route to Mexico, allowing even merchantmen to make the voyage more rapidly. With experienced captains and direct service between Cadiz and Mexico, he estimated, mail would reach Mexico in forty to fifty days, about one-third faster than then occurred.[29]

Revillagigedo's proposal to reduce the length of mail service between Spain and Mexico to forty or fifty days would have represented a significant improvement, much more, even, than the one-third he estimated. This conclusion is based on evidence from the transatlantic correspondence carried out between Cadiz merchant Francisco de Sierra and his American factors. Sierra owned several ships and maintained regular communication with his captains and commission agents throughout Spanish America. The timeliness of information was critical to Sierra's business decisions, and so Sierra, like other merchants, dedicated considerable time to correspondence. Naturally, individuals dated their letters so that a recipient could understand the timing of the information, highly useful given that posts arrived on irregular schedules. Sierra also recorded the dates that he received most of his mail, a procedure that other merchants for which correspondence survives did not follow. This practice of recording the dates on which letters were received permits computation of the length of time letters took to travel from America to Spain.

Tables 2.3a and 2.3b show the number of days correspondence took to arrive to Sierra from a handful of Spanish ports from 1776 to the beginning of 1788.[30] The first of the two tables shows his correspondence during the years of the American Revolutionary War. Table 2.3b displays the roughly five years following the November 1782 signing of preliminary peace treaties that ended the hostilities.

As Table 2.3b indicates, correspondence moved quite slowly between Spanish American ports and Cadiz even during peacetime. The most

TABLE 2.3A

Time for Sample of Francisco de Sierra's Mail to Travel to Cadiz from Selected Ports (During American Revolutionary War)

Origin of letter	No. of letters	Min # of Days to arrive	Average # of Days to arrive	Max # of Days to arrive	Median # of Days to arrive	Standard Deviation	Coefficient of Variation
Buenos Aires	12	98	122	171	117	23	19.2%
Campeche	1	172	172	172		N/A	
Guárico (Cap-Haïtien)	1	155	155	155		N/A	
Guatemala	2	245	263	281		25	9.7%
Havana	18	47	93	252	70	54	58.3%
Lima	9	157	299	426	271	97	32.4%
Montevideo	6	94	102	115	97	10	10.0%
Sto. Domingo	5	103	166	230	142	54	32.4%
Veracruz	27	92	135	265	122	38	28.3%

SOURCE: Cartas a Francisco de Sierra, AGI, *Consulados*, legajos 420–28.

TABLE 2.3B

Time for Sample of Francisco de Sierra's Mail to Travel to Cadiz from Selected Ports
(End of American Revolutionary War to January 1788)

Origin of letter	No. of letters	Min # of Days to arrive	Average # of Days to arrive	Max # of Days to arrive	Median # of Days to arrive	Standard Deviation	Coefficient of Variation
Buenos Aires	10	100	130	167	134	20	15%
Caracas	5	65	83	103	86	16	20%
Cartagena	9	77	133	171	132	30	22%
Havana	17	55	88	176	73	34	38%
Lima	36	122	197	334	191	47	24%
Montevideo	8	77	123	226	107	48	39%
Sto. Domingo	13	96	118	165	109	21	18%
Veracruz	27	75	109	196	97	35	32%

SOURCE: Cartas a Francisco de Sierra, AGI, *Consulados*, legajos 420–28.

rapid letter from Veracruz, for example, took two and a half months to reach merchant Sierra in Spain. Even if Sierra responded immediately, a ship was ready to depart, and his own letter arrived as quickly, roughly five months would have elapsed before Sierra's response arrived in Mexico. And five months was under the best circumstances; the average correspondence from Veracruz during the era of peace required 109 days to Cadiz or just over seven months roundtrip.

Other routes experienced different delays. Mail in these peace years arrived from Caracas and Havana most quickly, the average duration from these ports being 83 and 88 days respectively, while letters to Sierra from Buenos Aires and Santo Domingo took a bit longer than those from Veracruz. Service from Montevideo was normally faster than from Buenos Aires, perhaps suggesting that ships from Buenos Aires stopped in Montevideo before continuing on to the peninsula. Not surprisingly, the slowest correspondence occurred between Lima and Spain, the average duration during peacetime being 197 days, about six and a half months, or well over a calendar year for information to voyage roundtrip.

International strife introduced additional hindrances to the already sluggish flows of information. Letters from Veracruz during the war years took, on average, an additional month to arrive to Sierra. From Santo Domingo the impact was even greater, adding nearly two months to the average voyage. Oddly and inexplicably, the correspondence from Rio de la Plata arrived more quickly to Cadiz during the war years. Finally, the data suggests that the war affected the Lima route most profoundly, adding a hundred days to the average duration of the Lima to Cadiz voyage.

Not only was the movement of information slow under all circumstances, but it was unpredictable, as indicated by the standard deviations of the data. The average number of days for a letter to travel during peacetime between Veracruz and Cadiz was 109 days, but most correspondence deviated substantially from this mean, suggesting that there was great risk that a letter would fail to take the expected (mean) duration. The standard deviation for this route was 35 days, meaning that roughly two-thirds of the mail took from 74 to 144 days, assuming normal deviation, an indication of how very difficult it would have been to rely confidently on the collection of timely information.

The coefficient of variation quantifies the relative magnitude of the deviation from the average or expected duration; the higher the coefficient, the greater is the deviation as a percentage of the average.[31] So, the risk that correspondence in peacetime would arrive extremely late (deviation from the mean) was much lower for letters sent to Buenos Aires. The riskiest or least predictable route was Havana with the remaining routes clustered between these locales. The unpredictability of mail was not unrecognized by merchants, who took measures to try to minimize this risk. Juan Bautista de Marticorena, for example, observed that sometimes correspondence that departed from Veracruz on a later vessel might still arrive to Cadiz earlier, a claim borne out by the data in online Appendix A. On 20 December 1782, for example, Miguel Ignacio de Miranda wrote to Sierra from Veracruz, but his letter took 192 days to reach Cadiz, arriving nearly a month after his subsequent post to Sierra, dated 10 March 1783, which only took 92 days. Obviously this created a potential problem since the information in the latter correspondence presumed knowledge of the former. Merchants sought to address this potential confusion by beginning letters with a duplicate of the prior dispatch. Regardless, the unpredictability of information flows reveal that traders could not enjoy absolute faith that their important correspondence would arrive to their destinations in time to have the desired impacts.

As noted, merchants attempted to overcome these potential disruptions by dispatching multiple copies of letters to increase the likelihood of the rapid arrival of at least one copy. On 11 October 1780, for example, Juan Joséf de Puch posted two identical letters to Sierra, presumably on separate ships departing from Veracruz. One of the pieces arrived on 6 February 1781, 118 days after Puch had sent it. The other one took an additional 52 days, arriving on 30 March. Even more extreme were the two letters posted 5 February 1781 from Lima by Antonio Sáenz de Texada, one of Sierra's many factors. One of the posts arrived to Sierra a full 102 days sooner than its partner. Certainly sending duplicate copies improved the effectiveness of transatlantic communication; at the very least it helped minimize the obstacles.

Principal-Agent Problem

The lengthy communication delays imposed significant risks to trade. Merchants could only act on the most recent information available to them, but conditions could change dramatically between the dispatch of a letter and its receipt across the Atlantic. By the time the recipient adjusted his trade according to the newest reports and, for example, shipped whatever commodities were reportedly in short supply, circumstances might have changed entirely. For this reason, merchants became doubly dependent on their agents. An agent had to be granted significant freedom to pursue the merchant's best interests. It made little sense for a merchant to prescribe too closely how he desired his factor to engage in trade since the merchant's knowledge of distant market conditions was necessarily limited. The need to depend so greatly on an agent suggests how critical it was that a merchant carefully select a trustworthy individual of good reputation.[32] Naturally, this necessity to relinquish considerable control to an agent reveals why traders built their commercial networks with as many family members or *paisanos*, folks from the same village or region, as possible.

Of course, relying heavily on agents and granting them needed autonomy exposed merchants to greater potential for fraud. Given the geographical scale of the Atlantic world market, trade naturally took place under conditions of profound information asymmetry; agents were better informed than merchants about conditions in the marketplace in which they operated, which allowed them space to defraud their employers. Furthermore, merchants in Cadiz were largely powerless to monitor their agents' behavior but had to simply place significant trust in them. Employing agents from within their immediate familial or ethnic circles undoubtedly helped instill trust, but even close relations could prove dishonest. Of course, merchants could not rely exclusively on relatives and *paisanos*, especially when dealing in foreign markets; some transactions inevitably were carried out with outsiders.

Economists often refer to a so-called principal-agent problem, the difficulty that merchants had in ensuring that their factors pursued their best interests under conditions of information asymmetry. Merchants sometimes introduced mechanisms designed to increase the honest behavior of agents.[33] In his recent book, Xabier Lamikiz deals extensively with the

question of "trade and trust" in Spanish long-distance commerce. He
identifies a variety of different strategies employed by merchants to increase the honesty of their agents. In the seventeenth and early eighteenth
centuries, for instance, it became common for Dutch and English merchants to reside for extended periods in the private homes of their Bilbao
counterparts. Upon returning to their countries, these *huespedes* (lodgers)
became the primary trading agents for their previous Bilbaíno hosts, having established close relations of mutual trust.[34] Ship captains were also
instrumental in helping merchants to deal with the "agency problem."
Captains and merchants often owned vessels jointly, and the former even
took a share in the cargo, both of which provided captains with direct
economic incentives to look out for the merchants' interests. Because they
traveled constantly from port to port, captains could not replace agents,
but they did come into direct contact with distant traders and agents, allowing for the closer monitoring of their behavior, all to the benefit of the
principal in Spain.[35] Last, Lamikiz emphasizes the growing role of communication between correspondents on each side of the ocean, especially
following the end of the galleon trade to Peru. Merchants cast their networks of correspondents widely so that they could more effectively monitor the actions of those in whom they had placed their trust. While a
merchant might transact with a single agent in a distant port, he might
nonetheless correspond with others in that port who could keep an eye on
the agent's behavior. Correspondents looked out for one another's interests, at the very least reporting general perceptions of the effectiveness or
reliability of each other's agents.[36]

Within the Spanish empire, conflict between economic actors might
lead to the intercession of the appropriate *consulados*, which were empowered with adjudicating commercial disputes. Settling disagreements in the
tribunal, however, was both expensive and cumbersome and would not
have been practical in most cases. But the *consulados* still played an important role in facilitating trust between merchants. Membership in a guild
served informally to certify a trader's legitimacy. Of course, *consulado*
members could be dishonest or financially strapped as well, but their association must have allayed some uncertainties. Membership in the guild
suggested reputability.

Even without formalized practices or institutions, however, merchants
and agents had great reason to behave honestly. Traders reaped what they
sowed, and so merchants in the Atlantic world had the incentive to act as
truthfully and honorably as possible with their clients since such behavior

would be reciprocated. This was a self-regulating system in which one's good behavior earned reciprocal treatment. In addition, a merchant of good repute was treated more advantageously and provided better opportunities. In contrast, once a bad reputation was established, it spread quickly and was difficult to shake. Traders castigated transgressors, if not formally through legal proceedings, then informally by refusing to transact with them.

As with all of their agents, merchants had to select their foreign agents with great caution. Fortunately, reputations even transcended imperial borders. When Francisco de Sierra needed a correspondent in the Austro-Hungarian empire, he consulted with an acquaintance in Vienna, Domingo de Yriarte, as to which commercial houses were most highly regarded. Yriarte provided Sierra with the names of three reputable Vienna trading houses—one Swiss, one Genoese, and one German. He further advised Sierra to send letters of introduction signed by well known Cadiz merchants who could vouch for his own good standing. In short, the goal on both ends was to establish a relationship of trust based on each party's good reputation established through networks of trusted acquaintances.[37]

Letters of recommendation also served to introduce agents to merchants within the Spanish empire. Lamikiz discovered a number of such letters written by individuals in Peru that were then carried across the Atlantic by the recommended subject who hoped to find a position in Cadiz. These letters were important in establishing reputations but, as Lamikiz argues, became somewhat formulaic. Indeed, the letter might be followed by a more candid commentary about the subject's character and abilities sent under separate cover.[38]

Information asymmetries, exacerbated by slow-moving communication and transportation, introduced an "agency problem" into long-distance trade. Merchants investing large sums and dispatching wares over long distances were forced to place their trust in individuals over whom they had no direct oversight, often encouraging them to employ the services of relatives or *paisanos*. As merchants' trade networks grew wider, however, they were inevitably compelled to depend on individuals or firms who were outside their ethnic circles, potentially exposing them to greater risks of agent malfeasance. Agents enjoyed innumerable opportunities to cheat their principals, skimming profits or absconding with capital altogether. Merchants pursued all avenues possible to reduce their exposure to dishonest parties, but some fraud was inevitable.[39] While traders did what little they could to keep their associates honest, the latter were restrained by their desire to maintain good reputations. The career of an agent or merchant caught cheating would have been irreparably curtailed.

Political Information

A merchant's correspondents became his eyes and ears in faraway corners of the globe. He relied on his network to inform him of any sort of news that might influence his commercial decisions. Especially important was news of shifting international political affairs. Spain and its empire could not easily escape the ramifications of political events in other corners of the Atlantic world. Even if Spain maintained its neutrality, which it rarely could, growing diplomatic conflict anywhere in the Atlantic threatened to rupture the peace upon which commercial prosperity so relied. Merchants thus sought recent and reliable intelligence on political affairs. When in April 1793 Juan Bautista de Marticorena of Guatemala wrote of the "ultimate iniquity that the French could have and did commit in taking the life of their King," his interest was more than that of a disinterested Spaniard commenting on the execution of Louis XVI. As a merchant, he undoubtedly comprehended regicide as a portent of commercial troubles.[40] Not surprisingly, then, mercantile correspondence often discussed the political affairs of the day, and especially how these events might affect trade.[41]

Throughout the autumn and winter of 1790, for example, merchant Juan Miguel de Marticorena discussed in his correspondence the concerns of the merchant community of Lima that the outbreak of war was likely, presumably in response to the Anglo-Spanish conflict centered upon Nootka Sound on Vancouver Island in northwest America.[42] According to Marticorena, many of the city's vendors were raising the prices of their stocks expecting shortages if hostilities were to erupt.[43] In the event, war did not erupt in 1790. But sluggish communications as well as the ambiguity of Anglo-Spanish relations kept Peruvian merchants in a state of uncertainty. In this case one sees how imperial trade was even affected by events beyond the confines of the Atlantic world, although the feared war would have almost certainly included an Atlantic naval engagement.

Rumors of war were again flying in 1796 in Guatemala. Indigo trader Pedro José de Górriz wrote to one of his correspondents in Spain that prices of goods were rising rapidly in that colony due to the anticipation that Spain would soon be at war with England.[44] In December of the same year, José Ramón de Ugarteche of Buenos Aires wrote to Antonio de

Artechea, his consigner in Cadiz, that he had withdrawn a shipment of wool from a vessel due to the rumors circulating that war with England had already begun.[45]

Despite poor communications, merchants tried to remain abreast of political events. Trader Rafael José Facio of Mexico demonstrated his keen interest in the evolving European diplomacy in a 1798 letter to his "*hermano*," Juan José de Puch. He wrote of the uncertainty circulating in the markets of Mexico owing to "the diversity of news about the reaching of peace treaties, [and] the Congress of Lille."[46]

There was good reason for merchants to be concerned about politics. Without adequate information about the state of war or peace, ship owners might send their vessels into peril. At the start of any war, it was always the case that many ships, unaware of the state of hostilities, were lost to privateers.[47] Understandably concerned about the costs to commerce, the *consulado* sometimes took extraordinary initiative of its own to warn potential victims. Twice in 1797 the guild dispatched ships to notify Spanish vessels and authorities in America about British Admiral Horatio Nelson's blockade of Cadiz. In April, the governing junta of the *consulado* met and agreed to dispatch ships to "go by diverse sea routes to whatever points and seaways that seem opportune to bring to Spanish vessels, whether warships or merchantmen, news of the formal blockade in which this port finds itself." The state of emergency stemmed from news having arrived to the guild that a warship called *El Ángel* had made port at Havana carrying from Veracruz five million pesos worth of treasure and goods to which cargo from Cartagena was to be added. Upon arriving in Cuba, *El Ángel* had taken advantage of the imminent departure for Spain of a mail boat to send notice of its cargo and anticipated schedule. The correspondence, however, had presumably fallen into the hands of the British since the mail boat had never arrived safely. The *consulado* reasonably feared that this information would encourage the British to target and more easily intercept *El Ángel*, which would not only be a victory for "the enemy" but a disaster for Spain's finances and commerce. The *consulado* hoped to avert this catastrophe by warning Havana of the military situation.[48]

In October, the *consulado* again ordered ships dispatched to spread news of the blockade, but this time to Montevideo. At a meeting of the guild, it was divulged that the interim viceroy of Río de la Plata had detained in Buenos Aires several cargo ships that had recently arrived from Lima until either the restoration of peace or the arrival of contrary instructions. The officers of the guild applauded this prudent decision and decided to dispatch two ships from Huelva to bring news of the blockade to the viceroy as well as to congratulate him on his wisdom.[49]

After four ships returning to Spain from Buenos Aires were seized by British corsairs in 1804, the *consulado* of Cadiz once more proposed outfitting fast boats to American ports to advise ship captains readying their departure that the war had resumed. Their plan entailed sending ships to Veracruz, Caracas and Cartagena, Montevideo, Puerto Rico, and Havana. They also proposed that two intercept ships be sent to "advise vessels *en route* from the Indies of the current news."[50] Merchants in possession of such vital intelligence might avert disaster. Too often, however, merchants operated in the dark about the state of the Spanish Crown's diplomatic relations, an inevitable consequence of the slow movement of information.

· · ·

Governments responded to war by contracting privateers to target their enemy's mercantile fleets; but merchants in the bellicose nations might still share diplomatic news and even conduct trade with one another. Francisco de Sierra had longstanding relations with the London-based commercial house of Hananel Jacob Mendes da Costa, with whom he exchanged frequent correspondence. Despite Spain's involvement against England in the War of American Independence, Sierra continued to dispatch cochineal to Mendes da Costa's firm and to receive textiles in return for his trade with the colonies. Given Sierra's commercial interests, he obviously sought to keep abreast of political shifts throughout the Atlantic world, especially those involving Anglo-Spanish relations. On 17 January 1783, Mendes da Costa wrote to advise Sierra that "some people who believe that peace is imminent have begun to buy woolens with a fervor which has caused the price of all wool clothing to rise." But the London commercial house was pessimistic about this speculation, adding: "we remain as always in the same uncertainty whether this exhausting war will soon come to an end . . . . We seriously doubt that the war is going to end soon."[51] In the event, Mendes da Costa proved wrong and only a week later advised Sierra that "last night our Secretary of State announced to the business sector that peace between this court and those of Spain and France was reached on the 20th of this month." Political affairs concerned these merchants primarily for the effects they might have on their economic decisions.[52]

Merchants throughout the Atlantic world undoubtedly held nationalist biases and certainly embraced the mercantilist policies that their respective monarchs pursued, but the commercial world also required transnational cooperation. Sierra's economic decisions were equally dependent on the information that he acquired from his American agents as his London or Amsterdam-based associates. Regarding the seventeenth century, Bernard Bailyn reasonably concluded that for British merchants "correspondences with foreigners were difficult to establish and maintain. To British colonials in this period, it seemed that little reliance could be placed on the bonds of Frenchmen who desired nothing more than the collapse of the British settlements in the New World."[53] The regular correspondence between Sierra and his factors throughout the Atlantic world suggests otherwise for the eighteenth century. Despite the hostilities between the monarchies of Spain and Great Britain, the mercantile communities of the respective empires found common interests. Sierra needed news from London just as Mendes da Costa relied on updates from Sierra.

Despite the best of efforts to remain informed, communication breakdowns sometimes caused traders to incur unintended risks. In April 1797 Buenos Aires merchant José Ramón de Ugarteche wrote angrily to his Cadiz partner, Antonio de Artechea, who had failed to secure insurance for his shipment of cargo to Spain. Apparently a misunderstanding had occurred, perhaps due to the failure of a message to reach Cadiz, and Artechea had failed to insure the risks as Ugarteche had requested. As the latter pointed out, the ships could have easily been seized by corsairs, and for lack of coverage, he would have sustained devastating losses. Ugarteche would probably not have dispatched his wares had he realized they were uninsured.[54]

Information and Market Conditions

Political news was valuable, but even more important was information about supply and demand in faraway markets and the prices being paid. Without such information, long-distance merchants could not make prudent commercial decisions. The commercial community of Barcelona emphasized the lack of such intelligence in guiding its economic decisions in a 1773 petition sent to the king. The authors of the document sought exemption from the requirement that they register to which Caribbean ports they intended to ship their cargoes, desiring the freedom to transport their wares to wherever they could best sell them. To indicate the final destination in advance was problematic, they argued, "not being possible that the owners know the abundance or scarcity that there might be in said islands . . . since from this knowledge comes the success of the expedition."[55]

Spanish merchants were at somewhat of a disadvantage relative to their European counterparts owing to the paucity of Spanish newspapers regularly updated with news about overseas markets. Cadiz *consulado* member Don Matías de la Vega proposed in 1787 the establishment of a monthly *Gaceta Mercantil* in which import and export data as well as commodity prices would be published, arguing that this would provide dependable and valuable information to all merchants. His proposal was made in light of a spate of bankruptcies that had shaken the Cadiz commercial community and which Vega partially attributed to the inadequate information with which traders operated. According to Vega, better data could be compiled by representatives of the various *consulados* of the empire to the benefit of businessmen everywhere. Equipped with reliable mercantile information, capable merchants would thrive. While some traders might still go bankrupt, "he who cannot speculate informed with such news, it little matters if he loses, because it will show that he was inadequate for commerce."[56]

Even with newspapers, merchants would have depended heavily on their mercantile correspondence, which, unsurprisingly, focused primarily on market conditions. Letters crisscrossed the Atlantic listing current prices or the existing stock of wares. Merchants even sent one another preprinted lists of frequently traded commodities with the existing prices penned in.[57]

Communication between merchants followed similar patterns, discussing the performance of past deals, the potential for new business, the evolution of consumer tastes, and the existing supplies and prices of frequently traded commodities. Typical was the information contained in an April 1782 letter addressed to Francisco de Sierra from the Lima merchant Diego Sáenz de Texada. In addition to listing the current prices of colonial items Sierra might like him to remit, Sáenz de Texada indicated in great detail "the articles that might be appropriate in the case that you want to make an expedition to this port of Callao with some of your ships." Especially prevalent on his list were textiles, a reflection of the centrality of this commodity in Spanish trade with the Andes. He also wrote to Sierra about the Tupac Amaru Rebellion, but his interest in these "civil wars" stemmed primarily from their impact on the trade in commodities.

Cacao is running at 7.5 to 8 pesos per load, an exorbitant price given the existing war, [but] should be worth much less given the lack of demand for this article . . . paper and knives are very abundant, and today have limited outlet due to the civil wars (*guerras intestinas*) which are destroying the Kingdom . . . but shirts will give to you a very good return. . . . Presently, medium thickness taffetas from Requena, heavy cloth from Sevilla (these without any black), all types of linens especially fashionable items being Royal Platillas, English baizes, blue plushes, some red ones of San Fernando . . . and women's silk stockings embroidered inside and outside with cypresses and little birds . . . or with small flowers, hand worked cambrics, and Dutch linens. With the current prices on these items, you can be very well compensated if you choose to take a risk.[58]

Mercantile correspondence universally attempted to alert merchants to the articles that they should send to match existing demand. The examples are endless; in 1798 Rafael José Facio of Mexico acknowledged his partner's (Juan José Puch) request that he rapidly dispatch a cargo of cochineal to Cadiz. Puch had previously written to advise Facio that the scarcity of cochineal in Europe had driven prices skywards.[59] Two weeks later Facio sent his own request to Puch urging him to "buy goods that appear on the list that I accompany taking notice of their good quality and likely fairness of the prices, and with the objective of remitting them to me in the first register ships."[60]

Sometimes the best advice entailed a warning against certain activities. In 1779, for instance, the wealthy Mexican merchant Francisco Ignacio de Yraeta sent a letter to his Guatemala factor stating that "under no condition are you to make purchases of goods with the idea of sending them here, as commerce is totally stopped as never before."[61]

Yraeta understood perfectly that the role of a factor was to maintain close and detailed correspondence with his principals. In 1779, Yraeta's mercantile prominence and good reputation won him the lucrative position of commissions agent for the Royal Company of the Philippines' operations in Mexico, a post that required him to represent the Royal Company in its business dealings in Mexico, buying and selling on its account. In a letter to the company's directors, Yraeta assured them that he would keep them informed of the prices in Mexico of Asian goods, "not only via maritime mail but also via the ships that sail from Veracruz for Cadiz and other ports." Consistent with his promise, Yraeta enclosed a list of the current prices in the marketplace of Mexico.[62]

Spanish merchants sought reliable information about markets throughout the Atlantic world. Francisco de Sierra engaged in monthly and sometimes weekly correspondence with commercial houses in leading ports throughout Europe. His extensive communication with Echenique Sánchez, director of his own Amsterdam commercial house, illustrated the interconnectedness of commerce and politics in the Atlantic world. Merchants like Sierra or Echenique were international traders whose interests and need for information transcended national or imperial borders. In a letter dated 30 January 1783, Echenique enlightened Sierra on the anticipated commercial impact in the Netherlands of the end of the American Revolutionary War.

> This news has not caused even the slightest alteration in [the market for] our American commodities which maintain the same prices, which we believe will be influenced by whether the convoy of Havana arrives early or late. Sugar has demonstrated some significant decline recently, but as they write from the French ports, as peace solidifies, the price of this item will regularize and the same will occur here. We will exercise care to keep you informed of what happens for the guidance [of your dealings]. We do not know the amount of cinnamon that our company will sell this year, but we presume it will be more or less the same amount as in the past, and that it will not be any cheaper because there is very little in Europe and it will be at least two years before any more can arrive from India. As the news of peace normally results in the outfitting of a flota for Veracruz, consider, your grace, whether you want to make a purchase in the next company sale, and send us the order that you judge desirable. The exchange rate has begun to turn in your favor as just today it is 84¼ to 84½.[63]

In subsequent correspondence, Echenique showed great interest in learning from Sierra when ships from Veracruz were expected to arrive to Cadiz, an event that would have direct impact on the prices of principal commodities traded in Holland, most notably colonial dyes, Mexican cochineal, and Central American indigo.[64] Like his Dutch counterpart, London merchant Hananel Jacob Mendes da Costa was concerned about the impact of Veracruz shipping on the English cochineal market following the American Revolutionary War, and he thus plied Sierra for information. "We anticipate [the price] to drop but it all depends on the quantities that come from there, and we would appreciate that you advise us for our guidance, if you can, when a quantity of this dye might be expected to arrive from Veracruz. Indigo continues at very high prices owing to its scarcity."[65]

Good information was itself an invaluable commodity, which is why merchants invested so much time and effort in corresponding. Without regular and reliable information about market conditions, merchants could not transact rationally, make good decisions about what products to buy or sell. Long-distance trade was always extremely risky; merchants in pos-session of reliable information could take comfort that they had reduced at least somewhat trade's riskiness. But the harsh reality was that the move-ment of information was simply too slow and lengthy to allow merchants adequate time to react to changing circumstances. Even the most dedi-cated or talented factor was unable to anticipate the nature of demand a year or more into the future when the shipment might finally arrive. So while they could inform their bosses about the current trends and prices, the market for the cargo that this information elicited might no longer be buoyant when the goods arrived.

This point was made in October 1784 by Antonio Sáenz de Texada, Lima *consulado* merchant and a rather frustrated correspondent of Fran-cisco de Sierra. According to Sáenz de Texada, shipments from Spain al-ways seemed to be imperfect, "even if informed of shortages by the latest arriving news. Because from what I have seen, in the present nothing is more excessive than the item that was previously in short supply because everyone asks for it."[66] In other words, agents in Peru all wrote back to their merchants in Cadiz urging them to send the same commodities, a reflection of scarcities existing at the moment of their letters. The result was that commodity shortages turned into market gluts. Sáenz de Texa-da's ultimate advice to withdraw from commerce and "free yourself from the losses that others will experience" was probably not too helpful to the veteran trader Sierra; at least it was not practicable in the short run.

No matter how well informed a merchant, long-distance trade entailed risky speculation. The inherent riskiness of long-distance trade encour-aged Atlantic-world merchants to adapt their dealings to avoid financial disaster. Unable to predict the profitability or even the existence of de-mand for any single commodity, prudent traders chose instead to "diver-sify their activities so as to run less risk."[67] Typical registers revealed the wide variety of commodities in which individual merchants dealt, hope-ful that the market would prove favorable for most.[68] Likewise, successful merchants operated in a variety of markets, driven by the hope that a downturn in Peru might be offset by good fortune in Mexico. As Adelman has argued, "the vulnerability to losses compelled merchants to diversify their enterprise . . . trying to make fortunes off a variety of transactions, not just one, in order to diminish the punishment from a loss in any one branch."[69]

The Oversupplying of Markets

Merchants sought information about myriad issues—political, economic, or other. Being well informed reduced, although in no way eliminated, the uncertainty that pervaded long-distance, transoceanic trade. Under normal circumstances, the most immediate danger to traders was neither war, piracy, hurricanes, nor inclement weather, but the potential catastrophe that resulted from the overly supplied markets referred to by Antonio Sáenz de Texada. Having invested large sums into the purchase, transport, insurance, Royal taxes, and other expenses needed to deliver merchandise to distant markets, merchants might find that these wares were already more than amply supplied. This market risk, as it is called, plagues all businessmen but was especially acute in the long-distance trade of the early modern era in which transport and communication moved slowly.

Transatlantic commerce was not well suited for the impatient merchant. Few ventures were concluded in less than a year; most took many years to complete. Referring to the seventeenth century trade to Mexico, Louise Hoberman observed that "the return on money invested in transoceanic goods easily could take two or three years to be realized."[70] Obviously merchants purchased commodities in one market with the hope of selling them at a much higher price in another. But markets were highly unstable, the consequence, to some degree, of the pool of consumers being small, the markets shallow.[71] The volatility of the market was all the more perilous given the long duration of commercial undertakings. Armed with the most recent information conceivable about consumer demand and existing supplies, there was nonetheless a major element of gambling when traders engaged in long-distance commerce. The arrival of even a small shipment of competing supplies had the potential to satisfy demand and depress prices.

Even the Crown recognized the enormity of this obstacle. Being in the Crown's fiscal interests to promote trade, the government occasionally attempted to assist the long-distance Spanish traders by supplying them with news of colonial markets. A Royal Order was issued for this purpose in 1779, commanding high colonial officials to "send to this ministry individual notices of the European goods that have the greatest dispatch in those dominions as well as their quantity and variety so that merchants with this information can manage their speculations more securely."[72] Well intentioned as it was, the Crown possessed no better means than merchants to acquire up-to-date information.

The risks and consequences of market saturation had concerned and affected Spanish merchants since the advent of the *Carrera de Indias*. Fisher notes that in the mid-sixteenth century the confidence of the commercial community was shaken by "the over-supply of the American market with luxury goods up to 1550."[73] In March 1624, a colonial administrator named Manuel López Peyrera identified the risk of oversupplying the American market as one of the gravest problems facing transatlantic trade.[74] The *consulados* of Seville and Cadiz frequently sounded this alarm in the seventeenth and eighteenth centuries, pointing to glutted American markets that threatened to destroy their members' finances.[75]

Importing European luxury goods into America did not guarantee a return. High demand for some commodity could evaporate overnight. All too frequently distressed agents wrote to their principals that markets were supplied in excess and that prices had plummeted. Having imported to Mexico liquor and other merchandise only to find the "greatest abundance of *aguardiente* ever," Tomás Ruiz de Apodaca wrote to Cadiz from Jalapa in 1760 complaining that "there is nobody buying anything."[76]

In 1771 an anonymous report identified the oversupply of the American market as the primary reason for a commercial recession plaguing Cadiz at that time. The author blamed the abundance on foreign merchants who operated through *prestanombres*, Spanish agents who claimed the foreigners' merchandise as their own so as to circumvent restrictions on the participation of non-Spaniards in Spanish colonial trade.

> It is from, as has occurred, the embarkation of merchandise in such abundance that it greatly exceeds what can be consumed in America that necessarily has followed the fatal consequences that we experience. Those who bring or send [goods] see themselves forced to sell them at a lower price [in America] than they are [worth] in Europe, and, failing to stop this continuous detriment within a couple years, there will be the total ruin of our Spanish merchants.[77]

The problem of oversupply became especially acute in the years following the American Revolutionary War, which were also the years in which *comercio libre* was newly in effect. In his memoirs, produced in the final decade of colonial rule, Nicolás de la Cruz y Bahamonde, the Conde de Maule, one of the wealthier merchants in Cadiz, attributed many of the commercial difficulties of the previous several decades to the shipment of excessive supplies of European goods to America, a process that escalated in the aftermath of the American Revolutionary War. According to the count, merchants greedily, and unwisely, dove into international trade after witnessing the arrival of peace and the "tremendously profitable sales that the merchants of Cadiz realized in '84 and the large fortunes that arrived to this port in the same year."[78] As a result of their enthusiasm, merchants shipped excessive wares to America, glutting colonial markets.

Wealthy Cadiz merchant Mariano Bernabe de Frías was one such victim of avarice. In 1786 he was forced to declare bankruptcy after nearly three decades as a member of the Cadiz *consulado*.[79] Having invested more than half a million pesos, much of it borrowed, to purchase and send merchandise to Mexico on his own ships, Bernabe de Frías found that supply of these goods in Veracruz far outstripped demand. In defense of his client, Bernabe de Frías's attorney, Licenciado don Francisco Xavier Peñaranda y Castañeda, explained at the bankruptcy proceedings that "the news from that continent, instantly changeable by any occurrence according to the vicissitudes of commerce, even if only rumored, did not confirm that sales were occurring as had been expected."[80] In other words, Bernabe de Frías's merchandise could not be profitably sold in Mexico.

Just two years later, in 1788, the merchant Mateo Bernal sought the Cadiz *consulado*'s protection from his creditors in the aftermath of a catastrophic transatlantic venture. Bernal was also a veteran of the colonial trade, having engaged in this business since 1746, but his experience did not protect him from the growing volatility of commerce. Several years earlier, Bernal had procured 183,000 pesos worth of woolens and other miscellany that his correspondents in America had erroneously suggested would sell profitably. In fact, markets in both Mexico and Peru had "an excessive abundance of European goods," and Bernal lost heavily on the venture.[81]

The joint stock company of Cinco Gremios Mayores de Madrid was equally vulnerable to the unpredictability of the market. Having initiated a plan to buy large quantities of cacao and sugar in the markets of La Guaira and Havana, selling peninsular goods in exchange, the house withdrew from the business in 1792 noting the abundance of "efectos nacionales" in America and the corresponding low prices. The company blamed the surplus on contraband.[82]

· · ·

Long-distance trade in the early modern era was a very risky business. The potential for profits was substantial, but the possibility of financial catastrophe loomed large as well. So pervasive were the risks of long-distance commerce that no trader could possibly ignore them. Indeed, operating a successful international trading house required constant attention to risk. Mercantile strategies were designed as much to manage risk as to pursue lucrative opportunities. Trading conservatively and taking all precautions might reduce the dangers of trade, but even then merchants faced the real possibility of losing large sums due to unpredictable or un-avoidable factors. Potential profits were large but so were the associated risks.

The poor or insufficient information used by economic actors to govern their activities was a major source of this riskiness. In long-distance, early modern trade, poor information was endemic; merchants in Europe possessed scant and outdated knowledge of events or markets in America, and, obviously, American merchants were equally ignorant of relevant factors in Europe. This poor information represented an enormous risk to their endeavors. Uninformed of conditions or in possession, even worse, of incorrect intelligence, merchants might unknowingly engage in activities contrary to their interests. The need for good information was not unique to the early modern era; modern consumers and producers also spend enormously to inform themselves. But in the early modern Atlantic economy, good information was simply less accessible. The lack of reliable, timely information magnified the uncertainty of business and increased the risk of bad economic outcomes.

Despite the obstacles, merchants sought the most current knowledge possible about commercial and political conditions throughout the Atlantic world. Long-distance merchants remained in regular contact with trusted correspondents throughout the Atlantic world in their efforts to remain educated about political and market conditions. Indeed, one can vividly imagine the long-distant merchant hunched over his desk for hours at a time recording to the best of his abilities the prevailing factors affecting his business or that of his partners. Such investments of time were critical.

To expand their access to information, large merchants stationed their agents, often relatives, in key colonial centers and forged alliances with their counterparts in ports throughout the Atlantic world. They wrote copiously to their correspondents, communicating in multiple languages. The great distances over which their commercial interests spread, however, hindered their attempts to remain fully informed. Letters were delayed for months; others failed to reach their destinations altogether, lost in storms or intercepted by privateers. The purpose of commercial intelligence was to help a merchant govern his operations. Even when information arrived without interruption, however, it was already months old, and before the news could be heeded and a corresponding response carried out, many additional months or even years had passed. By then, circumstances might have changed, much to the detriment of business; consumer tastes might have altered or supplies of a once-scarce commodity might have become abundant.

Merchants invested great time and effort to stay informed. They had no choice; information was the lifeblood of the commercial community. Early modern, long-distance trade entailed enormous risks, and merchants who were well informed were better able to manage them. No matter their efforts, however, breakdowns in communication were inevitable. Incompletely informed, merchants inevitably operated in a sea of risk and uncertainty.

Chapter 3

The Institutions of Trade and the Reduction of Market Risk: The Convoy System

Acquiring information from their correspondents throughout the Atlantic world permitted merchants to govern their commercial dealings with greater economic rationale, although the quality of such intelligence was often poor and the decisions thus informed imperfectly. As argued in the previous chapter, one of the primary risks of long-distance trade during the early modern era was the inability of merchants to react quickly enough to protect themselves against market volatility, the likelihood that a sudden increase in supply of a commodity might outstrip demand and cause a sharp decrease in price. The oversupply of shallow markets was frequent and devastating to merchants.

Economic innovation frequently arises to overcome market imperfections. The existing communication technologies in the early modern world produced substantial inefficiencies, often leading economic actors to engage unknowingly in activities contrary to their economic interests. Poor information encouraged merchants to make inefficient and costly economic decisions. Economists predict that such market imperfections will lead to institutional improvements that result in the more efficient allocation of resources. When faced with difficulties of trade, the unpredictability associated with market risk, for example, merchants devise institutions or embrace rules and regulations that aim to reduce such risks, to make feasible economic activities that might be otherwise unattractive.[1] Such institutions might reduce the role of the market in allocating resources but

43

with the goal of reducing risk so that economic actors will engage in activities that they would otherwise deem unworthy. In other words, the solution to market imperfections might entail embracing nonmarket modes of organization, including uncompetitive or monopolistic institutions. The result will be to expand overall economic activity even though certain individuals might be negatively affected by the new practices.[2]

This chapter explores the economic institutions of trade in the Spanish empire, especially the famous flotas and galleons that transported transatlantic goods for more than two centuries. The argument put forth is that the rigid commercial regulations that governed colonial trade, the fleet system among these, helped to overcome market imperfections, among them the problem of slow communication and the associated risks. This depiction indirectly challenges the conventional image of the *Carerra de Indias* as a monopolistic trade system designed to allow the wealthy and politically connected merchants to profit inordinately by engaging in anticompetitive practices.

This chapter begins by demonstrating certain weaknesses in the conventional historiographical depictions of the Indies trade. Specifically, it is argued that the evidence for monopoly profiteering is unconvincing. While trade was deliberately contained by the myriad regulations put in place, those merchants who did enter long-distance commerce were numerous and faced considerable competition, preventing one another from earning monopoly profits under most circumstances. Although by no means was the organization of trade characterized by perfect competition, fleet merchants were not able to dictate prices and collect monopoly profits as is customarily argued. Under most circumstances, individual traders lacked sufficient market shares to create artificial supply shortages sufficient to elevate prices; they were too weak to behave as monopolists.

After presenting evidence against historians' traditional rationale for the Cadiz guild's dogged support of the *Carerra de Indias*, the chapter proceeds to provide an alternative explanation of why regulated trade appealed and benefitted these long-distance traders. Regulation of the Indies trade did not regularly provide merchants astronomical profits but did lower significantly the uncertainty of long-distance trade by helping somewhat to mitigate the enormity of risk stemming from poor information. The regulated commercial system served to diminish the volatility of shifts in supply, which reduced, but did not eliminate, the dangers of financial catastrophe caused by glutted markets. Importantly, the Spanish commercial system was not unique in its design; all of the principal trading empires of the early modern era organized at least a portion of their long-distance commerce with economic institutions that served to minimize market risk.

Limits of Monopoly in the Spanish Commercial System

Historians of colonial Spanish America universally portray the *Carrera de Indias* as a "monopoly trade system" in which the port of Seville (Cadiz after 1717) and the *consulado* merchants who resided there enjoyed a "monopoly over the Indies trade."[3] In the words of Haring, upon whom so much of the contemporary literature is based, "Castillian exporters, by manipulating each year the nature and quantity of the merchandise to be shipped to the Indies, raised prices at will and reaped enormous profits, said to have amounted sometimes to 300 to 400 percent."[4]

Economists define monopoly as a condition in which one supplier has sufficient control over supply to dictate the terms of distribution. While noneconomists might use the term a bit more loosely, implied in both modern and contemporary assessments of the fleet system is that merchants earned profits that were excessive due to their capacity to operate under less than competitive conditions. It is indisputable that long-distance traders sometimes made fortunes; they might arrive to market fortuitously in possession of the only bundle of a highly desired commodity. Merchants did occasionally sell their wares for several hundred percent more than they had paid, but this reveals little about the overall profitability of their businesses. Historians' negative characterization is not surprising given the privileges afforded the merchant guild's members, the regulation of trade, and the requirements that colonial trade begin and end in Seville/Cadiz. But the nature of this "monopoly" (oligopoly[5] to be less imprecise) warrants closer examination.[6]

In depicting the Indies trade as monopolistic, historians point to the commercial dominance exercised by members of the *consulados*. There was, undoubtedly, a very high correlation between membership in a merchant guild and level of engagement in the Indies trade. In this regard, historians are correct in identifying the economic primacy of the *consulado* members. The question, however, is not whether the *consulado* merchants dominated trade but whether they did so because they were affiliated with the guild. In fact, there was also a strong correlation between wealth and engagement in long-distance commerce, at least until the introduction of free trade and the entry of less wealthy traders.

So while historians are correct that there was a direct relationship between membership in a guild and involvement in trade, it is equally clear that there was a correlation between wealth and participation in trade.[7] Indeed, the merchant guilds in Spain and America were composed of many of the wealthiest inhabitants of their respective communities. In his classic study of Spanish merchant guilds, Smith unsurprisingly identifies wealth and commercial experience as being qualifications for entering the guild.[8] Kicza notes that the Mexico City *consulado* members "were the most powerful and wealthy members of the colony."[9] The typical transatlantic trader, then, was a wealthy, male member of a guild.

There were very good reasons why the wealthy dominated long-distance trade. Wealth helped insulate traders from the inevitable volatility of commerce; it served as a cushion to help them overcome the riskiness and uncertainty of trade. Expressing the importance of an ample inheritance in facilitating a mercantile career, one early modern historian claimed with intended irony that "the most important rule for the would-be successful, risk-averse man of business was to choose his parents, even his grandparents wisely."[10] Long delays between the investment and the return, unavoidable losses from ventures gone badly, and a host of other factors meant that a merchant without adequate reserves was doomed to fail eventually.[11] This factor was well understood by contemporary merchants. In 1778, Francisco Ignacio de Yraeta, one of Mexico's leading international traders, grumbled to his Guatemalan partner that in "oceanic commerce one doesn't just need valor and persistence but significant sums, as the delays are unendurable . . . one needs three sums, one to have encumbered (*embromado*) here, one for the shipments to Cadiz, and one to attend to the business of the company."[12] Peruvian merchants' successes in business also hinged on their ability to quickly mobilize liquid capital, a necessity better fulfilled by deep-pocketed traders.[13] To survive in transatlantic trade, one had to begin with substantial assets because one's investment was inevitably inaccessible for lengthy durations.

Wars wreaked havoc on long-distance trade as exchange within the Atlantic world slowed sharply or even ceased until the return of peace. While some merchants benefited, if they were fortunate to possess a commodity whose price rose sharply due to its war-induced scarcity, most suffered losses from the suspension of commerce. Observing late colonial Argentina, Socolow concluded that "many marginal traders were wiped out at the beginning of each war . . . usually the wealthiest had enough liquid capital on hand to wait out the war while maintaining their economic position."[14] Even during times of peace, oceanic trade gave rise to long delays or unforeseeable events that might deny a trader access to his wealth for extended periods, even to the point of financial ruin. During the difficult commercial times of the late 1780s, a number of "diputados de comercio de Buenos Aires" explained to their viceroy, the Marques de Loreto, that merchants "of limited wealth have been entirely ruined; those of great [wealth] have been reduced to the formers' class, and one should fear that with the passage of time [these wealthy traders] will also be driven to [commercial ruin]."[15] Wise merchants recognized their limitations. In a 1794 letter to his Spanish colleague, Buenos Aires trader Vicente Antonio del Murrieta wrote: "I am not prepared to be owing large overdue sums as can easily occur if one becomes entangled; my capital is not sufficient to withstand large losses."[16]

The wealthy dominated long-distance trade because their greater resources gave them a comparative advantage over the less well-to-do. Likewise, the richest merchants matriculated in the *consulado* because they were most deeply engaged in long-distance trade. From these two truths does not automatically follow that merchants grew wealthier because they were members of the *consulado*.

This last point is important because conventional portrayals of the *consulados* suggest that their members had great success using the power of the guild to promote their private interests.[17] While transatlantic traders were not required to be members of the *consulados*, those matriculated in the *consulado* were more fully represented in oceanic commerce. Merchants desirous of sending goods to Spanish America were required to wade through a sea of red tape.[18] The volumes and values of merchandise had to be recorded and verified and licenses to export obtained from the *Casa de Contratación* (House of Trade). Cargo space on ships had to be secured and taxes assessed and paid. Along the way, would-be traders could be curtailed. Undoubtedly guild membership helped merchants navigate more easily the arcane and cumbersome trade bureaucracy. There is no question that the *consulados* looked out for the welfare of their members, but this did not mean that membership gave individual merchants a significant commercial advantage over the nonmatriculated traders, at least once the latter succeeded in gaining access to the semi-closed system.

Oligopolists can earn extraordinary profits when acting in collusion with one another and artificially elevating prices, although in practice such cartels are difficult to maintain.[19] While the *consulado* merchants might have occasionally found common ground to fight off legislation prejudicial to them as a group, it seems doubtful that they could have held together as a mercantile bloc, "profit[ing] from the scarcity and consequent high prices that the system created."[20]

The fewer the merchants, the more effective a cartel, since it is easier for a few suppliers to cooperate than for many. Given the rather large number of traders involved in oceanic trade, to describe them as an oligopoly is even inaccurate. It is possible to gain some sense of the number of participants in transatlantic trade by examining the membership of the *consulados*. For the period 1730 to 1823, Ruiz Rivera identified 3,252 merchants who matriculated into the Cadiz *consulado*, the majority of these during the period 1750–80. Membership at any given time in these peak decades must have been well above one thousand merchants, clearly too many to collude.[21] Lamikiz argues that the *libro de matricula*, the book recording guild members, was somewhat misleading since "many members traded only for a very short period of time." He instead estimates the number of active merchants at any given time to be in the range of only two to three hundred.[22] Even this reduced figure leaves far too many to collude.

In addressing the same question for Mexico in the seventeenth century, Louisa Hoberman estimates that the number of wholesalers (*mercaderes*), to whom membership in the guild was limited, ranged "from 252 in 1598 to 177 in 1689." These were Mexico's greatest merchants, she notes, but many others participated in international trade on a smaller scale.[23] In the late eighteenth century, according to John Kicza, the Mexico City *consulado* "regularly afforded membership to some two hundred merchants."[24]

Nor were large-scale traders the only ones engaged in international commerce, as Hoberman has amply demonstrated for the early seventeenth century. Examining the cargo of five flotas to Veracruz (1614, 1620, 1625, 1630, and 1639), Hoberman classified the shippers into three categories— small, medium, and large—based on the value of their cargoes.[25] In none of the flotas to Mexico did the large shippers exceed 15 percent of the total number of merchants; the overwhelming majority of those involved carried small to medium-sized cargoes. The number of large merchants averaged forty-four in the five flotas, and these controlled between 52.6 percent and 68.2 percent of the total cargo. The flota in which the cargo was most concentrated in the fewest hands was 1630 in which twenty-three investors controlled 68.2 percent of the registered merchandise.[26] Based on these findings, she concluded, although far too cautiously, that "the term *monopoly* must be accepted with reservations."[27]

For the *flotistas* to have succeeded in dictating prices would have required at a minimum the collusion of Hoberman's "large" investors. Even such collusion would not likely have been adequate, for while the larger investors controlled half to two-thirds of the cargo, the remainder would have been enough to subvert their price-gouging schemes. Furthermore, even in 1630, the year of greatest concentration of the cargo, the twenty-three merchants who controlled 68.2 percent held on average just 3 percent of the cargo apiece; they were hardly in possession of commanding market shares. Even if these larger merchants had acted in concert and increased their prices, the real beneficiaries would probably have been the small and medium merchants who would have slightly undersold them, taking advantage of the high demand for commodities that usually accompanied the fleet's arrival. By the time the colonial merchants showed any interest in the oligopolists' high-priced wares, the immediate thirst for European luxuries would have been satisfied and consumers' willingness to pay reduced.[28]

A methodology similar to Hoberman's sheds light on the degree of concentration of supply in Mexico during the mid-eighteenth century. The data comes from a November 1761 document analyzed by Richard Garner showing the still unsold cargo that had been introduced by *flotistas* to the Jalapa fair of 1760. Despite a year having passed since the fleet's arrival to Mexico, more than 14 million pesos worth of cargo remained unsold, still in the hands of the importers.[29] Unfortunately, the document does not indicate what percentage of the total convoy this represented, but given available evidence Garner estimates the value of the mid-century fleets to be approximately 18 million pesos apiece. While the calculations that follow depend indirectly on Garner's estimate of the typical fleet value of 18 million pesos, they clearly illustrate the lack of "monopoly" exercised by the importers.[30]

A year into the trade fair, the importing merchants still possessed the vast majority of the cargo they had imported, roughly 78 percent if we accept the estimated total value of 18 million pesos. Presumably, the *flotistas* had unloaded the first 4 million pesos' worth of goods quickly, perhaps to the Mexico City wholesalers who customarily descended to Jalapa to make their purchases. Indeed, Garner speculates that by the mid-eighteenth century the *consulado* merchants were spending approximately 5 million pesos at a typical fair.[31]

The ownership of the unsold goods warehoused in Jalapa was widely dispersed. In total, the document identified one hundred different owners of the 14 million pesos' worth of cargo. The largest share belonged to the "Señores Herraty e Ysturiz," who possessed merchandise valued at 819,771 pesos, equal to 5.84 percent of the total. Next came Manuel Rivero and Company, who held 720,000 pesos worth or 5.13 percent. The average merchant held around 1 percent or 140,470 pesos' worth of merchandise; the median was an even more humble 91,210 pesos.[32]

The fleet system is conventionally depicted as a "monopoly system," but this data suggests an entirely different story. Even the largest merchant controlled only a small percentage of the remaining cargo, less than 6 percent. That these merchants could have exploited their situation and dictated prices is implausible. Even if sales had been brisk, and clearly they were not, the importers were in no position to impose oligopoly prices given their modest market shares. This document strongly suggests that by 1761, and Hoberman suggests long before, the fleet was marked by considerable competition. Certainly the notion that the importers were in any position to collude and fix prices is baseless.

Furthermore, even if the *flotistas* had tried to hold out for better prices, a significant portion of them could not have afforded to wait too long, having arrived burdened with debts that had to be repaid promptly. Many of the *flotistas* financed their ventures by means of a sea loan, called in the Spanish empire a *préstamo a riesgo de mar* or *préstamo a la gruesa ventura*, a financial instrument that combined financing and risk protection. Sea loans typically required that the debtor repay upon arrival at port, at the very moment that the risk of sea had terminated.[33] Eager to make quick sales, repay their loans, and purchase cargo for the return voyage, the *flotistas* often preferred to sell their cargoes in large lots for cash.[34]

• • •

That the eighteenth-century *flotistas* operated from positions that might be more accurately depicted as weak than strong is supported by Brading, who argues that the tables had turned by this time and the colonial merchants of Lima and Mexico City, not the importers, had become the true monopolists, able to "lay down the law in prices."[35] According to Real Díaz, "the business of these merchants was easy and profitable, with a minimum of risk. It was reduced to buying wholesale the merchandise of the fleet and then distributing the European goods throughout the Kingdom . . . . leaving them a great margin of profit." The Mexico City merchants took advantage of their ready access to large quantities of silver to purchase large cargos from the Spanish *flotistas* who were eager to unload their wares.[36] As one observer claimed in 1771, the wealthy Americans simply waited until the importers "were bored from not being able to sell" before buying large lots at bargain prices.[37] Once in possession of the imported cargo, the *almaceneros* (wholesalers) operated with the knowledge and security that no additional supplies would arrive from Europe for several years, and they were consequently free to charge exorbitant prices. As Burkholder and Johnson argue, "these merchants had a monopoly over trade in their respective viceroyalties, [and] they were largely able to determine the exchange value of silver and other colonial products."[38]

Unfortunately, no serial data on market share held by Mexico City merchants has been located to allow analysis of the degree of oligopoly in the Mexican colonial marketplace. The issue can be indirectly addressed, however, with anecdotal evidence. During the debates over *comercio libre*, defenders of the fleet system pointed to the long-standing practice of the great *almaceneros* to hoard large amounts of cash in the months preceding the expected arrival of the fleet and the start of the Jalapa trade fair. Their purpose was to invest their capital into the purchase of the arriving wares. Writing in 1791, Gaspar Martín Vicario claimed that his fellow members of the Mexico City *consulado* each introduced 200,000 to 600,000 pesos to a typical fair. Given that Vicario's motivation was to impress the Crown with the large sums that could be mobilized during the pre–free trade era, it is doubtful that he would have understated the amounts.[39] Brading provides a similar, though slightly lower, figure of between 200,000 to 400,000 pesos invested per *almacenero*.[40] Even if, for the sake of argument, one were to assume that an entire fleet valued at Garner's estimated 18 million pesos were to be purchased by wealthy merchants investing 400,000 pesos apiece, and no evidence suggests that this was ever the case, this would still have meant there were forty-five well-stocked Mexico City merchants selling their imported wares in Mexico. As in the example of the flotistas, it seems untenable that such a large number of sellers could have somehow coordinated their marketing and held together as a bloc; their individual interests and financial exigencies would have encouraged them to "cheat" and sell rapidly. As noted, in such a cartel the greatest reward often accrues to the "cheaters" who easily sell their goods at a price slightly beneath the "oligopoly price."[41] To deal with this structural problem, cartels often monitor their members and impose stiff penalties on those discovered cheating, a means to ensure cooperation. No such system of penalties existed in colonial trade.[42]

Of course, this scenario was hypothetical. The Mexico City *consulado* merchants did not purchase anything close to the entire stock of imported merchandise. In the last several trade fairs of the eighteenth century, Garner found that the guild merchants left Jalapa with considerably less than half the imported merchandise. *Consulado* merchants took 40 percent of the 1769 flota, "just over one-third" of the 1772 imports, and about 25 percent of the 1776 fleet. Garner concludes that "more than half of each fair's merchandise almost certainly was sold to non-*consulado* members."[43] Even if the guild had been able to coordinate as a bloc, which seems dubious, non-*consulado* members would have undermined the strategies of the oligopolists.

"Oligopoly" seems no more accurate a description of the market in Peru in the first decades of the eighteenth century when the last of the galleons arrived in Panama. A detailed study of the final Portobello fairs demonstrates that the purchases made by the great Peruvian merchants gave them well beneath a commanding share of the goods introduced by their Spanish counterparts, although their proportion of the total exceeded their Mexican counterparts. Regardless, they would have been in no position to dictate prices upon their return to Lima. In 1726, the five largest investors "carried" back to Lima 19.5 percent of the merchandise sold at Portobello (see Table 3.1). The top 25 Peruvian traders accumulated just over half or 4.9 million pesos worth of Spanish imports. The remaining 49.1 percent of the imported cargo was acquired by 155 smaller merchants. Obviously, the significant share obtained by the less-well-financed merchants would have undercut any attempts of the larger merchants to fix prices. The next fair was celebrated at Portobello in 1730 and once again the case for oligopoly is weak. Five merchant houses bought a total of 24.2 percent of the galleon, and the top 25 carried 64.9 percent, a greater concentration than in 1726, but still not commanding. The remaining 35.1 percent was acquired by 92 smaller investors, a substantial market share distributed among many individuals. Last, in 1739, Portobello's final fair, the top 25 merchants took 52.8 percent of the galleon's imports, leaving nearly half of the cargo in the hands of 139 lesser traders.[44]

Spanish merchants engaged in Atlantic world commerce were the empire's elite, but there were far too many of them to have possibly colluded

TABLE 3.1

Concentration of Purchases at Portobello Fair: 1726–39

Year	Total number of merchants	Market share of 5 largest merchants	Market share of 25 largest merchants	Market share of all but top 25 merchants
1726	180	19.5%	50.9%	49.1%
1730	117	24.2%	64.9%	35.1%
1731–38	180	20.5%	61.2%	38.8%
1739	164	20.9%	52.8%	47.2%

SOURCE: Derived from Dilg, "Collapse of the Portobello Fairs," appendix B. (The disastrous 1731 fair was prolonged by the failure of the galleon imports to sell completely. For this reason, it is excluded from the above discussion. Dilg, "Collapse of the Portobello Fairs," ch. 6.)

in the sale of their goods in American markets. *Consulado* merchants did, however, have common interests, interests that encouraged them to cooperate. When the government in Madrid entertained implementation of policies that were generally prejudicial to *all* merchants, only then did the *consulado* members act in concert. Perhaps no better example can be found than the eighteenth-century debates over free trade, which pitted the *consulados* against modernizing government reformers. The *consulados* of Cadiz, Mexico City, and Lima maintained considerable cohesion, arguing, ultimately without success, for the preservation of commercial regulations.[45] The mercantile bodies joined forces to oppose legislation harmful to their members, but these same merchants would not have sacrificed their individual interests for the potential good of the collective. Kicza essentially made this very argument in reference to the Mexico City market when he noted that while *"consulado* members habitually formed themselves into consortiums and interest groups on grounds of consanguinity, affinity, and compatible economic interest, they composed too large a group of basically antagonistic competitors for any one subgroup to attain functional control over a major component of the city's trade."[46]

To refer to the *flotistas* of the *Carrera de Indias* or their colonial counterparts as monopoly merchants is inaccurate. Monopolists (or oligopolists) earn excessive profits (monopoly profits) by using their market power to charge elevated prices. But for such a market structure to exist, a small number of merchants would have had to have controlled the majority of the international cargo, a condition that was clearly not the case. There were simply too many merchants engaged in the fleet trade to collude, and none of them had sufficient market share alone to drive up prices.

To claim that colonial trade was not oligopolistic in no way suggests that it was characterized by perfect competition, that government regulations or *consulado* measures were inconsequential. For example, the allocation of limited space aboard the flota always involved the intercession of government functionaries who were potentially corrupt or inclined to favor the politically powerful. The size of the *Carrera de Indias* was always proscribed, which meant that some shipowners or traders failed to gain entry. In March 1775, merchants in Veracruz vied with one another to place their cochineal aboard one of two ships whose registries had just been opened. With the backing of the *consulado* of Mexico City, a number of traders who failed to win coveted space complained to the viceroy how quickly all of the ships had filled. Apparently in agreement, the viceroy nullified the Registry and ordered the process repeated. While the underlying politics are invisible, the dissenting traders certainly implied that something untoward had originally transpired.[47] Furthermore, permits to engage in commerce were sometimes granted to individuals as reward for serving the Crown or loaning money to the government, clearly a deviation from a purely competitive environment.[48] To express gratitude to the Conde de Reparaz, Juan Miguel de Uztariz, for his exceptional work since 1762 as director of the Royal Talavera Factory, in 1766 the Crown granted the count and his trading house, Uztariz y Hermanos, the right annually to outfit in Cadiz a ship laden with "ropas y frutas" to bring to Mexico. The firm was further allowed to return to Spain with cochineal equal in value to these goods plus any freight charges incurred. This annual concession, which in 1766 totaled nearly 670,000 pesos, reduced the cargo space available to other traders in the flota, demonstrating that access to the trade system was not uninfluenced by power or Crown favor.[49]

Merchants always needed licenses to place their merchandise aboard America-bound vessels, and membership in the *consulado* perhaps gave a trader an advantage in acquiring one of these limited concessions. Even after the promulgation of the *1778 Reglamento*, permits were required; only they seem to have been much more readily granted and widely distributed.[50] Gaining entry into the flota was not automatic, but once a merchant succeeded in placing his merchandise aboard an transatlantic-bound vessel, he faced a competitive commercial environment whether he was a *consulado* member or not.

The Port-Monopoly of Cadiz and Seville

In addition to *consulado* dominance, historians traditionally identify the port monopoly enjoyed by Seville/Cadiz as a source of merchants' monopoly and an obstacle to competition. The early sixteenth-century decision to require all imperial trade to pass through a single port was designed to facilitate the Crown government's control of the American trade and collection of taxes. As Bakewell states, "what concerned the government above all was that its silver—the royal fifth and other taxes—should not escape from its grasp, and that customs duties on the American trade should be collected. Both aims were more easily achieved if contact with the Indies were . . . funneled through a minimum of access points."[51] The selection of Seville made sense given its location, wealth, and the existing financial infrastructure provided by Genoese commercial houses. And, as Haring further notes, unlike Barcelona, another important mercantile center, Seville was located in Castile.[52]

An important question is how the Seville/Cadiz port monopoly affected commerce with America. There seems little question that the
development of these Andalusian cities occurred at the expense of other
Spanish towns. Had Bilbao or Barcelona been selected instead, these cities
would have prospered far more than they did. It is also indubitable that local
producers in Andalusia benefited from the proximity of the commercial
hub. The commercial monopoly, then, provided obvious benefits for the
Guadalquivir region and undoubtedly stifled the economic development
of other parts of Iberia, but the impact on commercial competition in the
American trade is less clear.

The Seville/Cadiz monopoly does not seem to have been an overwhelming barrier to participation in international trade of non-Andalusians.
If one examines the Cadiz *consulado*, for example, it is clear that membership, at least in the eighteenth century, was far from the sole prerogative of
southern Spaniards. Ruiz Rivera demonstrates that matriculated merchants
came from all regions of the Peninsula; nearly half originated from outside
of Andalusia, fewer than one third came from Cadiz. And if Cadiz was
overly represented, it probably had more to do with the fact that children
of merchants most often entered the family business than any geographic
prejudice in the favor of that city. In any event, many of the Cadiz natives
were the descendants of migrants from other regions of Spain.[53] While
exaggerating to make his point, *consulado* member Antonio de Vicuña y
Goenaga claimed in 1787 that "for every 10 Andalusian individuals, there
are 300 from the other provinces of the Peninsula."[54]

If an ambitious young Spaniard wanted a career in international trade,
he moved to southern Spain.[55] Juan Vicente de Marticorena, whose papers
are used extensively in this study, provides a good example. Marticorena
was born in 1755 in the small village of Echalar, in the Kingdom of Navarra. In 1776, at the age of twenty-one, he matriculated into the *consulado* of Cadiz and over the next three decades established himself as a
prominent colonial trader and active member of the merchant guild.
Marticorena was far from unique; many of his cohorts performed similar
migrations.[56] Cadiz's commercial monopoly was not an insurmountable
barrier to Marticorena or other northerners. While the requirement that
they move to Cadiz to matriculate in the guild and participate in the Indies
trade was undoubtedly a nuisance or even an obstacle to many northerners,
they did so frequently and enjoyed great success.

In contrast, the Andalusian monopoly did, theoretically, exclude non-
Spaniards from direct participation in the American trade since, by law,

foreign ships were prohibited from visiting Spanish American ports and all foreign goods destined for the Spanish colonies had to pass first through Seville/Cadiz to be then transshipped to America aboard Spanish vessels. Furthermore, only Spanish subjects were entitled to ship goods to the colonies. This exclusion, of course, was more fiction than reality. For much of the era of Spanish colonial rule, foreign capitalists succeeded in circumventing these regulations, supplying "the credits, capital, and merchandise" to *prestanombres*, Spaniards who lent their names to the venture and profited from the commissions.[57]

Whether effective or not, regulations barring foreigners from the Indies trade were consistent with early modern mercantilist notions that "accepted as more or less axiomatic . . . that colonial commerce should be the exclusive privilege of merchants of the home country."[58] Other Atlantic world empires imposed similar regulations designed to exclude nonnatives from their commerce. Most prominent, perhaps, were the English "Navigation Acts" of the 1650s and 1660s, which required all goods bound for the British colonies to pass first through England and then to be carried from there aboard English vessels manned by a largely English crew. In essence, the "Navigation Acts" imposed restrictions nearly identical to those of the Spanish empire. The point here is that restricted trade was the norm in the early modern Atlantic world. The Spanish commercial system was neither unique nor unusual.[59]

Importantly, while the granting of a trade monopoly to Seville reflected the Crown's desire to minimize administrative costs and reduce tax evasion, the concentration of mercantile resources provided certain economic efficiencies as well. Seville/Cadiz became an international trade hub where representatives of all of the commercial houses involved in the Indies trade, Spanish and foreign, opened offices. Southern Andalusia became an international trade center in which was concentrated commercial information from both the colonies and northern Europe, and from which this data was disseminated throughout the Atlantic world. The concentration of trade infrastructure in this single port also provided certain economies of scale that probably lowered transaction costs. While its smaller size might make comparison somewhat inappropriate, England's colonial trade was also overwhelmingly conducted through a single port, London, which was still receiving 68 percent of imports and dispatching 70 percent of exports as late as 1772–74.[60]

Even after the promulgation of *comercio libre* in 1778 opened all Spanish ports to trade with America, Cadiz maintained its "overwhelming" dominance. According to John Fisher, during the years 1778–96, 76 percent of exports to the colonies departed from Cadiz and 84 percent of imperial imports arrived at Cadiz, "and its share was growing rather than declining towards the end of the period." Fisher attributes Cadiz's commercial hegemony to "the availability of a complex infrastructure of shipping, insurance, banking, consular, and warehousing facilities."[61] Trade remained concentrated on this single marketplace, at least in the medium-run, because of its economic efficiency; Cadiz's greater institutional development reduced the costs of engaging in long-distance commerce.[62] While the continued importance of Cadiz after liberalization certainly reflected the fact that other ports' infrastructure was comparatively underdeveloped, Cadiz's continued centrality clearly illustrates the necessity of these very services. Establishing themselves in Andalusia, the commercial and financial center of the Spanish Atlantic trade system, enabled merchants to reduce the cost of conducting business (transaction costs) and benefit from the best information available about mercantile issues. While smaller traders in Barcelona or Cantabria might have resented their exclusion from direct access to the colonial trade, more substantial traders from those regions relocated their operations to Cadiz.

· · ·

The conventional historiography places too much emphasis on the monopolistic characteristics of Spanish imperial trade. There is no debating that the system was highly regulated and that these restrictions affected many aspects of the trade. Southern Spain experienced development beyond what would have occurred had it not been for the port monopoly of Seville/Cadiz. Smaller traders and producers in other regions of Iberia were excluded from access to the trade due to their inability to relocate. But, the emphasis placed by historians on the competitive impact of exclusivity seems overstated. Despite policies designed to limit the size of imperial commerce, from the fleets and galleons to the highly restrictive granting of licenses, many merchants still participated in colonial trade. Most important, the number of merchants engaged and the percentage of total trade that any single trader commanded precluded the exercise of price manipulation under most circumstances. While the Spanish imperial trade system was certainly not characterized by perfect competition, nor was it a case of effective monopoly or oligopoly.

While the overseas merchants did not extract monopoly profits, they did argue vociferously in favor of maintaining commercial regulations. Led by the *consulados* of the principal trading centers of Cadiz, Lima, and Mexico City, prosperous traders fought bitterly to preserve the fleet system and to prevent first the introduction and then the expansion of *comercio libre.* Indeed, the wealthy merchants even paid the Crown large "donations" to postpone reform. The question arises why these traders feared so greatly commercial reform if, as this chapter has argued, the existing commercial system already created competition sufficient to preclude them from exercising monopoly manipulation of the market. As the next section argues, existing commercial restrictions might not have generated monopoly profits, but they did serve to reduce the riskiness of market volatility, the dangers that supply would far outstrip demand and lead to devastating commercial losses. Regulations were probably more effective in preventing bankruptcies than in generating fortunes. The regulated commercial system served to make long-distance trade less uncertain and more predictable.

Trade Institutions and Long-Distance Trade

While there were barriers to entry into the Spanish commercial system for smaller (less capitalized) merchants, the larger merchants who did participate experienced considerable competition from their fellow traders. There were simply too many merchants engaged in Spanish imperial long-distance trade for organized collusion to succeed. Through much of the eighteenth century, reformists within the Spanish bureaucracy pushed for the dismantling of the fleet system, arguing that regulated trade benefitted a small number of privileged traders to the greater detriment of Crown interests. Reform, however, was heatedly resisted by the *consulados*, both in Spain and America. Historians have correctly interpreted the resistance of large Spanish and colonial merchants to reform as the attempts of monopoly merchants to guard their monopoly privileges.[63]

There is no question that *consulado* merchants fought hard against commercial reform. Large merchants viewed Spain's commercial system as beneficial to their interests, but not precisely for the reasons customarily asserted. Again, merchants could not, as historians have long argued, set prices arbitrarily, profiting from monopoly conditions. Instead, the appeal of the trade system to long-distance merchants was that it served to govern more predictably the flow of commodities to distant markets. The periodic fleet was a trade institution that served to lower the riskiness of exchange by reducing, somewhat but by no means entirely, the unpredictability of supply, thus giving merchants a greater ability to make informed decisions affecting their economic interests. Merchants still suffered from poor and inadequate information, but the knowledge that new commodity supplies would not repeatedly arrive in port and render their wares worthless provided valuable security under the very uncertain and risky conditions of long-distance commerce. Greater predictability allowed merchants to better forecast long-term market conditions. Given that most transatlantic ventures took many months and even years to complete, such a longer-term vision was essential.

Trading Companies

Market risk, the danger of a sudden shift in the price of commodities, was a problem that affected all long-distance traders of the early modern era. Faced with this obstacle, merchants everywhere formulated distinct strategies to mitigate the associated risks, to make less volatile long-distance trade. It is instructive to examine briefly the institutions and practices of traders from other Atlantic world empires, because in doing so light is shed on the Spanish commercial system.

One way the larger imperial governments of the Atlantic world responded to market risk was by establishing chartered trading companies with limited privileges that operated with some degree of protection from competition. A number of economic historians studying early modern trade have argued that one of the main purposes of these chartered trading companies was to reduce the problems associated with market risk, the danger that shipments would arrive to a glutted market.[64] According to Niels Steensgaard, the Dutch East India Company (VOC) used its government-granted commercial monopoly "not as a lever for short-term maximum profits, but as a guarantee against sudden fluctuations in supply or demand."[65] Unlike an individual merchant, the chartered company could respond to an oversupplied market by warehousing commodities rather that flooding the market and driving prices below a profitable level. In behaving this way, the VOC actually "enlarged the range of activities that might be calculated and planned rationally."[66] The Dutch company could even trade in goods that promised low returns since the ability to regulate supply reduced the risks of a minor price fluctuation making such activities unprofitable.

Steensgaard also discusses the integrated system of communications that facilitated the trading company to act in an economically more rational and efficient manner. The VOC stationed its information hub at Batavia (modern day Jakarta, Indonesia). There, the information collected from the Netherlands as well as the company's Asian factories could be compiled, reconciled, and disseminated so that the ship captains could make more informed commercial decisions. Of course, information was always old and outdated, but this hub system was more efficient than alternative communication means.[67] For the same reasons, the English East India Company operated its own internal postal system.[68]

In short, Steensgaard argues that the Dutch East India Company was organized in such a way as to reduce certain inherent risks of long-distance trade, especially, but not exclusively, the risk of sudden market fluctuations. This was only possible because of the firm's large scale; individual merchants or small partnerships would not have been able to replicate such stability. Furthermore, by reducing its risks, the company was able to trade in goods whose low profitability might otherwise have made them too volatile.

The "structural revolution" effected by the formation of the VOC and its English equivalent, the East India Company, is also emphasized by Peter Musgrave, who argues that these companies enjoyed a comparative advantage over smaller firms because of their greater ability to reduce the degree of commercial risk. Their sheer market size permitted these trading companies to gauge more confidently existing demand in a market and to ensure that the supply corresponded, to avoid flooding the market. By making trade less uncertain and more predictable, the chartered companies could better guarantee themselves a regular profit, and such diminished volatility "reduced the risk of total loss and the need to provide against this by high profits."[69] In other words, the company could more easily plan for the long term rather than worrying about the potential for commercial catastrophes in the short run. The company was able to sell goods more cheaply than they could have had they been forced to incorporate a premium into the price to reflect the riskiness of sudden market fluctuations.

In their comparative study of five early modern chartered trading companies, historians Ann M. Carlos and Stephen Nicholas similarly argue that because of the great distances and the imperfect information about market conditions, "domination of the market by many individual traders would have led to large fluctuations in both price and quantity." Comparing these "giants of an earlier capitalism" to modern multinationals, they argue that the early trading companies succeeded because they were better able to "have good information about the level of supply and demand."[70]

• • •

While large joint-stock trading companies with monopoly privileges were formed in Holland, England, and France to conduct long-distance trade, in the Spanish empire traditional monopoly companies were only established to minor ports or with limited rights. None was established to operate the main routes of Spanish Atlantic world commerce.[71] The failure of Spain to create similar companies cannot be explained by an absence of comparable risk. Spanish merchants were keenly aware of the dangers of market inundation and actively made efforts to avoid related losses. Nor did the Spaniards fail to understand that trading companies helped reduce this particular source of risk. As early as 1624, the Council of Indies was presented with three projects to create monopoly companies, two to the East Indies and one to the Caribbean. In proposing that a company be organized to trade with America, one petitioner, Manuel López Pereyra, argued that such an enterprise would overcome one of the greatest obstacles plaguing the trade, the recurring shipment of excessive stocks.[72] Several additional proposals reached the Council of Indies later in the seventeenth century.[73]

While a joint stock company might have helped alleviate the risk of market inundation in Spain's colonies, characteristics of the Spanish commercial system did, in fact, help to reduce this risk, although nowhere nearly as effectively as a trading company would have. Certain characteristics of the *Carrera de Indias* served a similar function to the chartered companies of Spain's northern neighbors. Indeed, at least one eighteenth-century observer recognized these parallels that have been overlooked by modern scholars. In 1777, Fernando Magallón, one of the ministers on the Council of Indies during the debates regarding the promulgation of *comercio libre*, observed that "the French West Indies Company resembled to a certain degree the corps of matriculated merchants in Cadiz." Perhaps the most ardent proponent of trade liberalization on the council, Magallón applauded the policies of "the great Colbert," who, recognizing the "decay and lack of prosperity" in the French empire, eradicated the old trading structures.[74]

Prior to reforms in the eighteenth century, the Spanish commercial system, as is well known to historians, was marked by strict regulation. For most of the period, ships departed *en masse* for America (or returned to Spain) almost exclusively in periodic sailings, the famous flotas and galleons, and traveled between just a few legal ports. This regulated structure performed a similar purpose to that of the chartered companies; the periodicity of the fleets served to make supply more predictable and diminish, but not eradicate, the risk of glutted markets. Even during periods in which convoyed shipping was suspended—after 1739 to Peru, and from 1737 to 1757 to Mexico—the parsimonious granting of register shipping licenses limited the flow of commodities to American markets, helping to reduce the total volume of traded goods.

Spanish Commercial System and Oversupply of Markets

Before examining how the Spanish commercial system reduced market risk, a brief summary of its organization is necessary. The origins of the colonial commercial structure date to the decade after Columbus's famous voyages. King Ferdinand and Queen Isabella initially envisioned a Crown monopoly on trade to the "Indies" modeled after the Portuguese system in which the *Casa de Contratación*, founded in January 1503, would manage the Royals' interests. Despite the Crown's initial intentions, private traders quickly came to dominate the transatlantic route, and the *Casa's* role evolved to overseeing the operation of this trade. In part due to its highly defensible port, Seville, Spain's largest and wealthiest city, was chosen as the location of the *Casa de Contratación*. By law, all trade to and from America was required to pass through the *Casa's* registry, which granted Seville a *de facto* monopoly on trade with the colonies.[75] To further consolidate Spain's control over this commerce and ensure the collection of Royal tax revenues, monopoly rights were granted to limited ports in America as well, the only open ports in America initially being Havana, Veracruz, Cartagena, and Callao (via Portobello).[76]

The creation of the fleets also dated from the early sixteenth century. At first ships sailed independently. But as the wealth extracted from Spain's colonies grew, piracy became an increasingly alarming problem, leading the Crown to issue a series of edicts designed to protect the valuable cargoes. In 1521 the Crown ordered "that a squadron be organized of four or five ships whose cost will be deducted from the silver, gold, and merchandise that arrives to the ports of Andalucía, as well as the Indies and the Canary Islands, and [belonging to] both the king and private individuals."[77] In 1522 the Crown ordered all merchant vessels to equip themselves with armament sufficient to defend against predators. Four years later, in 1526, ships were forbidden to sail alone, required to journey in convoy with others, the rationale being that together they could more effectively ward off attacks. In 1537, the Royal Armada escorted a fleet of trading vessels to the Caribbean for the first time. This convoy was replicated in 1542. Finally, in August 1543, at the behest of the Seville commercial class, the Crown decreed a permanent annual *flota* of merchant vessels to be accompanied by warships of the Royal Armada. [78]

Once established in the mid-sixteenth century, the basic structure, if not the regularity, of the *Carrera de Indias* remained intact for the next two centuries.[79] Each year, in theory, the fleets set sail from Spain in the early summer, often stopping in the Canary Islands en route to America. After

entering the Caribbean the fleet split, the flota ultimately sailing to Veracruz and the galleons heading to the trans-Isthmian crossing at Portobello,
with some ships diverted to Cartagena and lesser ports in the Caribbean. The
ships usually reconvened at Havana the following spring to commence the
return voyage to Spain.[80] The convoy was supposed to sail annually, but
by the seventeenth century it had become less regular. Already reduced in
number in the first half of the century, in the second half, only sixteen galleons were dispatched to Tierra Firme and twenty-five flotas to Mexico.[81]

The conventional wisdom maintains that the transatlantic fleet system
generated abnormally large profits for the merchants involved. As the
argument goes, the "monopolistic" *consulado* merchants of Seville, later
Cadiz, took advantage of the infrequency of the fleets to limit the flow of
commodities to colonial markets so as to create artificial shortages and
elevate prices and profitability. Their colonial counterparts colluded since
they too could manipulate the system to their advantage. Operating with
the knowledge that fresh supplies from Spain arrived infrequently, American merchants hoarded supplies, leaking them slowly onto the market at
exorbitantly high rates.[82]

There is no doubt that the *consulado* merchants on both sides of the Atlantic favored the convoy and resisted strongly any attempts to dismantle or
even tinker with it.[83] It is also beyond any question that the merchant guild
members perceived the system as beneficial to their interests. But the nature
of the benefit is debatable. Historians universally argue that Spanish merchants were wedded to regulation of the fleet system as it "enabled them to
drive up prices by withholding goods from the transatlantic market."[84]

While this idea undoubtedly contains some truth, merchants were not
regularly able to "drive up prices," as was argued earlier in this chapter,
because they rarely held large enough market shares to do so. The many
traders marketing virtually identical products provided ample competition
to prevent excessive price gouging. Instead, the primary appeal of the regulated system was that it reduced the risks associated with market saturation.
Having shipped goods across the Atlantic, often on borrowed funds, and
having endured months or years in anticipation of their sale and the re-
mittance of the revenues in goods or coin, merchants understandably
feared their financial ruin if they failed to sell their wares at favorable prices,
prices that at least covered their costs. Regulated trade lessened, although
it did not erase, this commercial risk.

That merchants were fearful of the glutting of markets is more than
amply demonstrated by the historical record. A handful of examples have
already been presented. There is also no question that merchants saw in

the fleet system a means to address this risk, to prevent the flooding of colonial markets. The process by which each fleet was organized provided the *consulado* merchants with a vehicle to control aggregate supply; they employed it to prevent, or at least attempt to prevent, the glutting of overseas markets. The scheduling of a fleet was, by law, initiated by the Council of Indies, which traditionally began by ordering the *consulado* of Seville (Cadiz after 1717)[85] to estimate the size of the cargo needed to satisfy demand in American markets.[86] With this information in hand, the *Casa de Contratación* began the process of issuing permits to register cargoes for the outward bound voyage. The goal of the *Casa* was to establish a balance between supply from Spain and expected sales in America, or as one anonymous source described the goal in 1771, "to remit what the Americans need such that neither shortage raises the prices excessively, nor surplus lowers them so much that this commerce [of Cadiz] is harmed."[87] That the Council of Indies instructed the trading house to determine the ideal size of the fleet shows that the Council accepted the need to balance supply with demand.

To assess the ideal size of the convoy, administrators attempted to take into account anticipated consumption in colonial markets. In preparation for Commander Antonio de Ulloa's 1776 flota to Veracruz, for example, the king ordered the interim president of the *Casa de Contratación* to produce an account of the imports he believed the economy of New Spain could absorb. Pointing to the varied successes and failures of the previous several fleets, the interim president produced a detailed response. In 1757, according to his report, the convoy to Mexico had carried merchandise in the volume of 619,505 palmos,[88] and these goods had sold rapidly leading to "a happy [trade] fair." The following flota (1760) transported 827,846 palmos "and it is well known the bad success that this fair experienced." In 1765 the cargo was reduced to 527,612 palmos, "and although it was so moderate . . . the fair achieved little happiness." The volume in 1768 was decreased still further to 458,202 palmos and "the fair was very happy." Finally, in 1772 Spaniards shipped 714,600 palmos of freight "whose success, although delayed, has been fairly happy."[89] Based on this data, administrators set out to determine the ideal volume for the 1776 flota, a level that would supply but not inundate colonial markets. By attempting to coordinate supply with demand, the *consulado* and the *Casa de Contratación*, in essence, were performing the type of analysis that one would expect from the board of directors of a large enterprise such as the Royal chartered companies of northern Europe. The purpose was to lower the risk of the financial ruin that would spring from traders transporting more commodities than the colonial markets could absorb.

At times, the *consulado* petitioned the Crown for the delay or suspension of the scheduled fleet, fearful that it would arrive before the stock of supplies in American markets had been fully exhausted. When in 1620 news from Mexico revealed that demand for European imports was depressed, merchants succeeded in reducing by two the number of ships scheduled to sail for that port, the excluded owners being compensated *pro rata* by those fortunate merchants whose cargoes sailed. This occurred again in 1622 and 1627. In 1636, the fleet to New Spain was suspended altogether due to news that the market was still well-stocked.[90] Certainly such requests reveal that imperial commerce diverged significantly from perfect competition, but the petitioners' motivations were to avoid the further inundation of the Mexican market and the corresponding losses that would naturally follow rather than to create an artificial shortage with the goal of profiteering.

The interests of the colonial merchants coincided with those of the Spaniards on this matter. When supplies were swollen in the colonies, American merchants who held large stocks feared great losses if fresh supplies arrived and depressed prices. An appeal written sometime in the mid-1730s by Juan de Berria, "deputy of commerce in Peru," warned the Crown that during the recent trade fairs "much abundance" of goods had been introduced, resulting in a severe drop in prices and growing stocks of unsold goods, all to the detriment of the viceroyalty of Peru's commerce. Berria urged the king to postpone the next galleon to Portobello to allow the Peruvian merchants to dispose of their warehoused merchandise before fresh stocks arrived.[91] The great distances and slow movement of information and transportation meant that long-distance merchants could not quickly respond to market fluctuations. Alternative institutional practices such as the convoys helped compensate for such market imperfections.

Employing a similar argument in a 1755 petition, the merchants of Mexico City joined their peninsular counterparts in convincing the Crown to postpone the convoy until 1757, pointing to the excess of unsold items in Mexico.[92] In November 1763, the *consulado* of Mexico City virtually begged Viceroy Joaquín de Monserrat to intercede on its behalf and ensure the delay of the upcoming flota scheduled for April 1764. According to the *consulado*, the Mexico City wholesalers still had enormous quantities in their warehouses and would suffer grave hardships and devastating losses if the fleet were to arrive with new supplies. Similar burdens, they argued, would be experienced by the *flotistas*, the Spanish importers who would find no buyers for their imports.[93] Perhaps owing to the *consulado*'s persistence, the fleet did not sail until the following year.[94]

At the same time that the Mexico City *consulado* was urging the viceroy to stall the flota, Fernando de Bustillo, Veracruz agent of the Cadiz trader Tómas Ruiz de Apodaca, wrote to his principal claiming that due to lack of buyers, he had been unable to sell Ruiz de Apodaca's wine and *aguardiente*. He ominously predicted that the next "fleet will produce intolerable bankruptcies" if it were not postponed.

> I will celebrate if the flota is delayed until the year of '65 or '66, because one foresees as inevitable the ruin of that commerce [Cadiz] without any benefit to this commerce [Mexico], because it is possible that all of the silver minted until the year '65 will be needed to pay for the many goods that are [still] existing in hands of the importers (Cadiz flotistas), who at present are very concerned.[95]

Petitions to delay the fleets were not uncommon. And the Council of Indies was often receptive, at least partially because these requests offered an opportunity for the Crown to exact a "voluntary donation" for its coffers.[96]

• • •

Not all Spanish imperial trade was conducted via convoys. The galleons serving the viceroyalty of Peru ceased in 1739, following the sacking of Portobello by British Admiral Edward Vernon on 21 November, early in the War of Jenkins's Ear.[97] In truth, the trans-isthmian route had outlived its usefulness anyway. For the rest of the colonial period, Peru was supplied by register ships sailing directly to Callao through the Straits of Magellan, a route that avoided the costly transportation of goods across the Panamanian isthmus. The attack on Portobello also led the Crown to temporarily suspend convoys to Mexico, a policy that was not rescinded until 1754, despite the protests of the Cadiz and Mexico City guilds. From 1739 to 1754, then, cargo was transported to Mexico exclusively on individual register ships.[98] Other ports, most importantly Buenos Aires, had never been part of the convoy, depending exclusively on licensed register ships. Excluded entirely from direct trade until the eighteenth century, a limited number of register ships began trading between Cadiz and Buenos Aires only in 1721.[99]

The substitution of register ships for fleets reduced the predictability of supply in final markets. With convoys, merchants operated with more information about the levels of supply and knew that additional imports were not immediately forthcoming. This greater predictability lessened the riskiness of long-distance trade. Register ships, in contrast, came and went on their own schedules and thus introduced goods more frequently. The possibility that competing imports would reduce the price of commodities increased uncertainty and made transatlantic trade riskier. But, very importantly, prior to the introduction of Bourbon commercial reforms in the 1760s and 1770s, the number of licenses granted to register ships remained very restricted; numerous requests to outfit register ships were denied. Permits continued to be distributed conservatively with the goal of balancing supply and demand. As the president of the *Casa de Contratación* explained in 1754 in justification of his decision to reject a requested license, "there is no reason to grant more *permisos* at least until there are news of the state of those provinces, for a multitude of them would be prejudicial to this commerce and that of the Indies."[100] While register ships provided less security than fleets did, the limits placed on the number of register ships still afforded merchants some protection from market volatility, thus lowering the riskiness of their ventures.

· · ·

Early modern trade operated under far from perfect conditions. The distances over which markets extended were expansive, and the extant communication and transportation technologies were slow. Merchants ventured enormous sums to buy commodities in one market and dispose of them, hopefully at a profit, in others at great distances across the ocean. The poor flow of information, however, meant that merchants made their commercial decisions under conditions of great uncertainty; they had to operate largely in the dark, hoping that more of their activities proved successes than failures. Nor could they quickly change course; deals took months and even years to complete, and traders had little ability to adjust to changing conditions.

Uncertainty cannot be measured; as a result, it cannot easily be eliminated through the pooling of risk.[101] It does, however, impose significant costs and obstacles to the transacting of business. Certain activities are avoided as too risky, and the outcome of others diverge significantly from the expected. Economists predict that economic actors will respond by devising or adapting institutions to reduce market distortions such as those caused by uncertainty. As Douglass North famously put it, "when it is costly to transact, institutions matter."[102]

Commercial regulations in the Spanish empire reduced the uncertainty and unpredictability of trade. Albeit far from perfect, the convoy and the subsequent strict limitation of the number of register ships helped to make more predictable and less volatile the stream of commodities between Spain and its American dominions. The periodic fleets allowed long-distance traders the ability to better gauge commodity supplies and thus to operate under less volatile conditions than would have existed had ships arrived to ports on a regular basis. Although not as effective, the limited distribution of register ship licenses was carried out with an eye on preventing the flooding of American markets. Both practices increased the predictability of trade, thus reducing the endemic uncertainties. In essence, regulated commerce meant merchants were better informed about existing and anticipated supplies. In possession of better information, merchants experienced less uncertainty and engaged in commerce that otherwise would have been far more speculative.

The rigid commercial restrictions imposed in the Spanish trade system provided some of the benefits of the chartered companies of Spain's neighbors.[103] Economic historians of the English and Dutch empires have closely scrutinized the operations of the joint-stock companies organized for the Asian trade and have concluded that the monopolies of trade granted to these northern European chartered companies were essential in providing "a systematic solution . . . to maintaining the equilibrium between supply and demand," mitigating commercial risk.[104] Though far less effective, the regulated trade in the Spanish system served a similar purpose by regularizing flows and matching supply with demand, reducing the risk that markets would be oversupplied when merchants' cargoes arrived.

Chapter 4

Comercio Libre and the Rise
of Commercial Risk

While supported by the large and experienced merchants, the regulated Spanish trade system had many vocal detractors. For more than a century, Spanish political economists (*arbitristas* and *proyectistas*) had criticized Spanish mercantilism and argued in favor of reform. While their justifications differed, their general thrust was that the closed system had retarded growth of the Spanish economy and that deregulation would expand trade, promote local Iberian industries, and benefit the Royal treasury. Limited reforms were introduced in 1720, but broader change was delayed, to some degree because of the organized resistance of the empire's dominant traders, the members of the *consulados*.[1]

Major commercial reforms were finally introduced in the last third of the eighteenth century. *Comercio libre*, as it was termed, had a significant impact on Spanish imperial trade. As predicted, Spanish Atlantic world trade expanded as did Royal tax collections. Free trade, however, also had consequences unanticipated by its authors.

Maintaining the focus on risk, this chapter explores the effects of free trade. While trade volumes did expand significantly, one result was the substantial rise in the riskiness of Spanish Atlantic commerce. The end of regulated trade led to rising competition and the unfettered flow of commodities within the empire. The expansion of export licenses led to more and more merchants shipping on growing numbers of ships. Merchandise arrived regularly to American ports, curtailing the ability of traders to gauge supplies and organize their businesses accordingly. Early modern trade had always been conducted amid tremendous uncertainty, but liberalization intensified its unpredictability. Markets, especially in the colonies, became flooded with imports, and the international traders, both old and new, found themselves sitting on large stores of unsalable merchandise. Many traders went bankrupt in the fifteen years between the 1778 promulgation of free trade and the 1793 outbreak of war. Others withdrew from commerce altogether, preferring ventures perceived to be less risky, among those the underwriting of marine insurance to traders and shipowners, the focus of Chapters 8 through 10.

The wealthy merchants of the *consulados* of Cadiz, Lima, and Mexico City criticized vehemently the new, more open commercial system, arguing that commerce had grown too unpredictable and that merchants could no longer govern their operations intelligently. They further tried to persuade the Crown to reintroduce the recently terminated convoy system to Mexico. Their cries were rejected, however, and free imperial trade continued unabated until the outbreak of war in 1793 severely interrupted shipping and hastened the long-term decline of Spain's commercial empire.

Promulgation of Comercio Libre

On 12 October 1778, the 286th anniversary of Columbus's arrival to America, by order of King Charles III, the *consulado* merchants were issued a devastating blow with the promulgation of the *Reglamento y aranceles para el comercio libre de España a Indias* (Regulations and tariffs for the free trade of Spain to the Indies).[2] Long proposed by modernizing reformers, this legislation granted freedom of trade to thirteen peninsular and twenty-four American ports. Excluded from liberalization until 1789 were Mexico, the richest colony, and Venezuela, to which the Real Compañía Guipúzcoana de Caracas possessed a monopoly charter. The story of the implementation of *comercio libre* is well known to scholars of colonial Spanish America. Historians point to the English navy's "humiliating" 1762 seizure and occupation of Havana during the Seven Years' War as a catalyst for finally implementing long-overdue commercial reform. The opening of Cuba to non-Spanish merchants led to a sharp rise in the importation of African slaves and English merchandise, and awakened the Crown to the trade potentially lost due to its rigid commercial regulations.[3] Accordingly, on 16 November 1765, shortly after Cuba's restoration to Spain, the Crown declared free imperial trade to Cuba, Puerto

Rico, and Santo Domingo from nine peninsular ports.[4] This initial, experimental step was followed by the more extensive reform of 1778.

The new free trade regime was far from absolute, for it still excluded foreigners and foreign ports from direct trade with Spanish America. The new system did, however, end the port monopolies enjoyed by Cadiz and Callao (Lima). Although the promulgation did not stipulate the termination of the flota to Mexico, it was canceled simultaneously, its counterpart to Peru having ended in the 1730s.[5] In contrast, Veracruz did retain its status as the exclusive Atlantic port for the Mexican market.

An aspect of liberalization at least as significant as ending the port monopolies was the concomitant policy of far more generously granting *permisos*, licenses to shipowners and merchants to participate directly in oceanic trade. As Lamikiz explains, "licenses were now granted by ministers who were determined to make colonial trade grow."[6] Within the rubric of Spanish mercantilist principles, the totality of reforms represented significant liberalization. Over the next decade, a rising number of ships set sail carrying a growing quantity of merchandise. John Fisher, who painstakingly collected the most complete sets of trade data for the period after 1778, describes the *reglamento* as having "promoted a massive expansion in the value" of trade, an impression widely embraced by scholars even before Fisher's series were published.[7] Analyzing the registers of nearly seven thousand ships that sailed to and from Spain in the years 1778 to 1796, Fisher found a "fourfold expansion in exports from Spain to America" relative to 1778. "Much more spectacular" Spanish American exports to Spain for the same period were "more than ten times greater than in 1778."[8]

Assessing the Impact of Comercio Libre on Trade Values

Comercio libre certainly led to an increase in Spanish transatlantic trade, at least in the short run, but the magnitudes reported by Fisher are dubious. First, from a purely logical standpoint, it is hard to believe that a single political reform could have so quickly generated such a monumental increase in international trade. Had there really been so much potential for additional commerce, then the "monopoly merchants" of the *consulado* would certainly have tapped at least some of it. Second, one wonders from where all of the tradable merchandise on both sides of the Atlantic could have so rapidly materialized, especially since historians have already established that the production of silver, the dominant colonial export, grew only minimally during this era. Fisher's series suggests that the share of precious metals in total imports into Cadiz maintained a fairly consistent level of about 55 percent per year throughout the entire period of growth. If Spanish American exports rose, as Fisher suggests, "more than ten times" over the period, then clearly bullion exports would have had to have risen at a comparable rate.[9] The problem is that no study of Spanish American mining indicates more than moderate increase in bullion production over the same years and certainly nothing in the order of 1000 percent. Silver production in Mexico, the leading producer by the end of the colonial era, grew 10 percent in the quinquennium 1780–84 relative to the period 1775–79, but lost most of this gain in the next five-year period. Its peak occurred during the French Revolutionary Wars, after the period examined by Fisher.[10] Nor does the evidence from Potosí make plausible massive increases in silver exports. In the last three decades of the century, silver output rose only marginally.[11] In summary, silver production, by far the greatest single contributor to total exports, barely sustained growth at a time when precious metal exports would have had to have grown by an order of ten to sustain the export growth suggested by Fisher. Arguing this same point from a slightly different angle, from the perspective of Mexican consumption, Garner states that "without an expanding silver industry, Veracruz could hardly have become the 'most important destination' for Spanish exports in the late eighteenth century."[12]

Fisher's work has been received with skepticism by several Spanish economic historians who have argued that his findings suffer from faulty methodology and incomplete data. Specifically, they argue that Fisher's use of 1778 as his base year against which to compare subsequent trade data has skewed his findings. Indeed, the growth rates that Fisher attributes to *comercio libre* depend entirely on the reliability of his 1778 figures; if import-export data for this year are incomplete, then his magnitudes of growth are exaggerated.[13]

Historian Delgado Ribas argues that 1778 was a poor choice to use as a base year because many merchants, concerned by the potential for war between Spain and Great Britain, had cut back their trade. This factor depressed aggregate trade in 1778, tending to exaggerate subsequent growth.[14] There is also evidence to suggest that rumors of the likely promulgation of *comercio libre* scared away certain merchants from participating in long-distance trade in the period shortly before 1778, rendering the amounts for this year to be unrepresentative of the pre-*reglamento* era. In September of that year Spanish *flotistas* in Jalapa complained to the viceroy of New Spain about the poor sale of Spanish imports since the arrival two years earlier of the 1776 flota. According to these Spanish traders, Mexican wholesalers were fearful of buying more than small sums due to the rumors that free trade might be extended to Mexico and that existing supplies might skyrocket accordingly. It seems plausible that many merchants would have preferred to await less uncertain times, choosing not to ship additional commodities to distant markets until the new rules of the game became clearer.[15] It seems doubtful, however, that fears of war or free trade alone explain Fisher's severely depressed figure for 1778.

Statistical evidence also strongly suggests that Fisher's figure of 3.7 million pesos for Spanish colonial imports in 1778 was atypical of the pre-1778 era. Official annual estimates of exports from Mexico, Central America, and Peru during the years 1757–61 were around 35 million pesos, nearly ten times Fisher's 1778 figure.[16] According to Garner, bullion exports from Mexico alone for the two decades 1752–71 totaled 225 million pesos, an average annual export value of more than 11 million pesos. And this figure excludes nonmetal exports and all of the rest of Spanish America.[17] These references, while somewhat random, cast further doubt about the reliability of Fisher's 1778 figure for Spanish imports.

Antonio García-Baquero seems to have solved the paradox, convincingly identifying the problem with Fisher's 1778 figure. According to García-Baquero, Fisher's figure only included ships sailing under the new *comercio libre* legislation, excluding both the 1778 flota from New Spain as well as *"registros sueltos,"* (ships granted licenses to sail individually). If these shipments are added to Fisher's data, the 1778 figure for Spanish imports is increased by 12.5 fold, from 3.7 million pesos to 46.5 million pesos.[18] Turning the argument on its head, the use of García-Baquero's revised 1778 figure suggests that average "imports in those years (1782–96) instead of increasing by 1011 percent relative to 1778, descend[ed] by 17 percent."[19] This revisionist bombshell has led García-Baquero to conclude that trade in 1778 was indeed uncharacteristic, but in the opposite direction; trade in 1778 was unusually robust. Given that the flota sailed in this year, the elevated value of trade is to be expected as it included goods anticipated for several years' consumption. Due to its abnormally high level, Garcia-Baquero smartly rejected the use of 1778 as the base year in favor of an average of annual imports for a number of years immediately preceding the *reglamento* of 1778. Employing, in a slightly revised form, data from his classic study of pre-1778 trade, García-Baquero constructed two import series, 1747–78 and 1765–78, which he subsequently averaged to use as his base to compare with Fisher's data from 1781 to 1796, which he accepted as accurate. The average annual import value for Garcia-Baquero's two periods was 21,798,164 and 24,526,608 pesos respectively, 5.85 and

6.58 times greater than Fisher's original 1778 figure, much more in line with the other estimates of pre-1778 trade values discussed above. They also suggest growth much less vibrant than Fisher contended.[20]

Since García-Baquero's revision of Fisher's figures, other scholars have entered the debate. Most recently, Javier Cuenca-Esteban has provided new estimates of Spanish imports from the colonies that he claims are more accurate, and thus better reflect the effects of *comercio libre*. For the most part, Cuenca-Esteban concurs with García-Baquero's revisions of Fisher's data, especially in regards to 1778. However, he further presents his own doubts about the quality of García-Baquero's revised data set. Critically, García-Baquero replaced Fisher's import data with figures that captured imports at Cadiz alone. Since one revolutionary aspect of the trade reforms was to allow many other ports to participate directly in Atlantic trade, this oversight was no small matter; García-Baquero ended up missing the effects on the very ports that the Crown aimed to benefit by the reforms. Second, Cuenca-Esteban notes that both Fisher's and García-Baquero's data were corrupted by the inconsistent manner in which certain commodity imports were valued during the era, most notably tobacco. In his revised data set, Cuenca-Esteban corrected these omissions and errors as well as several smaller issues.[21]

Table and Figure 4.1 illustrate the effects of *comercio libre* on private (non-Crown) imports using data derived from Cuenca-Esteban's study. The base used to assess growth during the era after 1778 was the average import value (in 1778 prices) for the years 1765–77, which equaled 146,401

TABLE 4.1

Value of Private Imports to Spain from Spanish America: 1765/77 to 1796

Year	Import Value (1778 prices) mns reales vellón	Index (1765–77 = 100)	Year	Import Value (1778 prices) mns reales vellón	Index (1765–77 = 100)
1765–77	146,401	100	1787	321,872	220
1778	234,623	160	1788	329,183	225
1779	108,494	74	1789	321,112	219
1780			1790	337,242	230
1781	154,691	106	1791	415,044	283
1782	94,593	65	1792	307,629	210
1783	227,006	155	1793	310,871	212
1784	377,577	258	1794	315,298	215
1785	379,388	259	1795	239,768	164
1786	294,088	201	1796	311,992	213

SOURCE: Cuenca-Esteban, "Statistics of Spain's Colonial Trade," 349, appendix table 5.

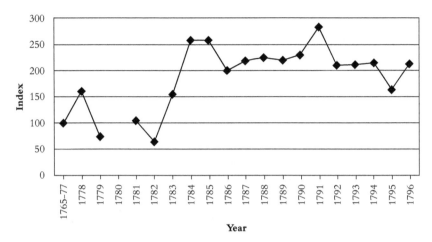

Figure 4.1. Effect of *Comercio Libre* on Spain's Private Imports from Spanish America
NOTES: 1778 prices. 1765–77=100=146, 401 mn reales vellon.
SOURCE: Cuenca-Esteban, "Statistics of Spain's Colonial Trade," 349, appendix table 5.

million reales vellón (7,305,050 pesos). As the figure and table reveal, the American Revolutionary War depressed private imports, but the end of hostilities led to a rapid recovery of international trade. For the rest of the period, 1784–96, imports hovered at slightly above double the base years' average. Cuenca-Esteban's revised figures, thus, show that while the 1778 *Reglamento* had a significant impact, it was much less profound than most historians have conventionally accepted. Certainly these revised figures suggest radically different conclusions than those put forth by John Fisher.

• • •

The reliability of Fisher's data on the export of commodities from Spain to the colonies has also been challenged by García-Baquero, who once again criticizes Fisher's use of 1778 as a base year. Unfortunately, however, neither García-Baquero nor anyone else has discovered alternative series for Spanish exports in the years prior to 1778. Consequently, scholars have been unable to construct a pre-1778 export value series against which to measure the impacts of free trade on Spanish exports. García-Baquero did, however, locate a Cadiz *consulado* document that estimated export values for all three years 1776 to 1778. While not as reliable as a longer series, he nonetheless used the average for these three years as a base to compare with the later data. This methodology provided him, one again, with a very different story to Fisher's estimate of "fourfold expansion in exports from Spain to America." Whereas Fisher used 3,725,798 pesos as his base, the value his data ascribed to 1778, García-Baquero employed a base of 18,242,149 pesos, the average for the three years 1776–78 reported by the *consulado* and a figure, once again, much more in line with other estimates. Obviously, García-Baquero's much higher base depressed greatly the subsequent appearance of growth. In fact, using his new base suggests that the average export value to America actually fell over the period in question by 16 percent.[22] Again, García-Baquero's revised export base was taken from a *consulado* document rather than computed directly from ship registers, which have not been located. As García-Baquero readily admitted, his analysis of Spain's exports was far less convincing than his assessment of imports. Regardless, Table 4.2 reproduces the revised Spanish export data presented by García-Baquero.

Unlike Fisher's data, García-Baquero's suggests that exports from Spain were depressed in 1782–83, the final years of the War of American Independence, a likely scenario given the interruption of trade caused by the hostilities. Both series show postwar recovery of Spanish exports, but their magnitudes differ dramatically. Using Fisher's 1778 figure suggests

TABLE 4.2

Effect of Free Trade on Spanish Exports to Spanish America

Year	Fisher's Data	Fisher's Index	García-Baquero's Data	García-Baquero's Index
1778	$3,725,798	100	$18,242,149	100
1779	N/A		N/A	
1780	N/A		N/A	
1781	N/A		N/A	
1782	$5,634,058	151	$5,634,058	31
1783	$6,837,515	184	$6,837,515	37
1784	$21,780,818	585	$21,780,818	119
1785	$22,883,784	614	$22,883,784	125
1786	$16,967,283	455	$16,967,283	93
1787	$12,936,265	347	$12,936,265	71
1788	$15,260,036	410	$15,260,036	84
1789	$16,325,057	438	$16,325,057	89
1790	$14,608,363	392	$14,608,363	80
1791	$18,514,143	497	$18,514,143	101
1792	$22,075,906	593	$22,075,906	121
1793	$15,364,893	412	$15,364,893	84
1794	$9,291,141	249	$9,291,141	51
1795	$14,104,068	379	$14,104,068	77
1796	$12,594,079	338	$12,594,079	69
Totals 1782–96	**$225,177,409**	**403**	**$225,177,409**	**82**

SOURCE: García-Baquero González, *Comercio Colonial*, 213.

export values in 1784 and 1785 nearly six times that sustained in 1778. Employing García-Baquero's base, the average for the years 1776–78, presents a much less dramatic, but more credible, figure for 1784 and 1785 of roughly 25 percent above 1778. Fisher's figures continue to indicate hefty exports throughout the era while García-Baquero's data suggest that this "golden age" was instead a period of commercial stagnation or even crisis.

The final word on the effects of *comercio libre* on trade values remains to be written, but Fisher's dramatic conclusions must be rejected. Cuenca-Esteban's import figures seem more credible and his methodology sound. García-Baquero's export revisions, however, should be accepted less confidently. By his own admission, his export database is based on less sound documentation. And, as is presented below, considerable anecdotal evidence makes it difficult to believe that Spanish exports dropped in the decade following the American Revolutionary War. Instead, merchants repeatedly wrote to one another complaining bitterly of the growing supplies of Spanish goods in American markets, complaints that seem hardly likely if García-Baquero's export figures are accurate. Indeed, recent studies have begun to challenge García-Baquero's export base, the average of 1776–78 as presented by the *consulado*. Employing a different source, one recent paper has revised his base downwards by about 38 percent which would yield average exports for the period 1782–96 of 33 percent above the base, a substantial increase over García-Baquero's estimate of 16 percent decline but still a far cry from Fisher's fourfold increase.[23] Quite clearly, the accuracy of Spanish export figures remains on shaky grounds.

• • •

The argument presented in this chapter to this point is that free trade's impact was nowhere near as great as most historians have been inclined to suggest. Fisher should be applauded for the monumental task of having collected the data without which historians would be unable to discuss intelligently imperial trade during this critical period. His use of what appears to be an unreliable figure for 1778 among other issues, however, calls into question his broad conclusions about free trade's impact. Historians' revisions convincingly show that the effects of *comercio libre* were much less revolutionary, although the precise impact remains somewhat unclear.

Assessing the Impact of Comercio Libre *on the Supply of Markets*

While the magnitudes of change might be open to further analysis, other evidence leaves little doubt that there was a significant rise in transatlantic commerce following the end of the War of American Independence. Contemporary observers commented repeatedly on the steep increase in trade within the empire. Consistent with the goals of the 1778 *reglamento*, unprecedented numbers of Iberian merchants received licenses to ship commodities to America, especially in 1784 and 1785, sending merchandise that had been warehoused during the war or contracting to ship newly acquired cargo.

Some merchants experienced with long-distance commerce were wary of trading in the new environment. Even before the *reglamento* was implemented, the partners Ygnacio Xavier Yanze and Juan José Puch decided to avoid engagement in Atlantic world trade until they could better judge the effects of the new trade regime. From Cadiz Yanze wrote Puch in Montevideo that:

> I do not consider it worthwhile to engage . . . especially in the uncertainty and fogginess that presently surrounds us, until such time as we see with greater clarity the state in which these matters are going to be resolved. Many of my friends are of this mind, and, like you and my buddy Suarez y Costa, have suspended their dealings for the time being until they see what course things take.[24]

Early modern merchants could not avoid operating under conditions of great uncertainty, yet they pursued whatever measures they could to reduce trade's unpredictability. The end of the more regulated trade of the pre-1778 era introduced unfamiliar conditions, entailing new and uncertain risks. Waiting for greater clarity, thus, seemed prudent to Yanze and Puch. It was better to miss an opportunity than to take unmeasurable and unpredictable risks. By September 1778, the effects of the pending reform were becoming clearer to Yanze, and he advised Puch not to make any shipments to Spain as the number of ships already arriving threatened to drown the city in a sea of unsalable merchandise. For what it is worth, the Basque Yanze, perhaps ribbing his Catalan partner, blamed the upsurge on "the plague of Catalans."[25]

While premature, Yanze's fears would prove correct. The growing conflict with Great Britain delayed the more profound effects of trade liberalization until after the cessation of the war. Only with the end of overt hostilities in late 1782 did the sharp surge in trade occur, quickly flooding markets and outstripping demand. Those who were lucky enough to be among the first after the war to place their goods in the market undoubtedly profited handsomely. Many of the traders who arrived later, however, found demand to be sated and were forced to sell at a loss or warehouse their goods until demand recovered.

Markets were already inundated barely a year after the signing of the Treaty of Paris that ended the American Revolutionary War. In January 1785 traders in Veracruz wrote regretfully to their principals back in Spain, complaining of the excessive imports. Francisco de Paula Carballeda, factor to Cadiz merchant and shipowner Francisco de Sierra, grumbled to his employer of the "enormity that there is of everything," adding that "the situation worsens continually as four well-stocked register ships from [Cadiz] and two settees from Malaga have just arrived. Presently, the only investment from which even a small return can be made is with an item of the highest esteem purchased at bargain prices with one's own funds."[26] Another of Sierra's correspondents delivered the same sobering news from Veracruz in March. Sebastián Fernández de Bobadilla reported that due to the arrival of numerous ships carrying a wide array of commodities "presently nothing will sell except at a loss . . . even if one wants to sell at cost plus expenses, forgoing even a small return, it cannot be done." The following month his assessment had grown worse, noting that "the buyers who appear offer a price that does not even cover the costs."[27] By late August and mid-September, the state of affairs had not improved as factor Carballeda informed Sierra that:

> things in the Kingdom are getting worse every day; there is not a single line of goods that is profitable due the abundance of everything . . . every day ships arrive from Malaga, Barcelona and even as far as Ferrol (La Coruña) and Santander . . . . The paltry amounts that are sold are done so on terms of up to a year, [but even so] one cannot always make the sale.[28]

In a similar vein the Catalán merchant and captain of a settee named *San Serafín*, Antoni Vidal, complained in mid-1786 of the flood of unsalable merchandise into the ports of Veracruz and Campeche. "There is nowhere to deal [it] and the worst is that every day registered ships arrive from Catalonia and Cadiz."[29]

Even the largest and most connected commercial houses became vastly overstocked. During the three years 1785 to 1787, the Cinco Gremios de Madrid imported large quantities of merchandise to Mexico but found that it was largely "unsalable." Ultimately, the House's Veracruz-based factors sent 266 *tercios* of the commodities back to Spain. Hoping to reduce at least somewhat the firm's "loss," the factors requested in 1791 that the Treasury refund the taxes (alcabala and almojarifazco) that they had previously paid on the merchandise.[30] Two years later the factors were again seeking a tax refund after returning thirty-two *tercios* of *"pintados,"* which, the petition complained, were "unsalable . . . even if one wants to unload them at a loss of fifty percent."[31]

Increased imports had also overwhelmed markets in Buenos Aires. In early January 1787 Francisco García de Gazeta wrote Francisco de Sierra of "the excessive abundance of sellers of goods and the lack of buyers" in the port of Río de la Plata. According to García de Gazeta, "all matters relating to sales or business are at present in an extremely fatal state in which one needs a year to sell on credit and then not even to upstanding people, giving terms of twelve months the way on other occasions [one gave] four."[32]

The news from Lima was no less discouraging. Joaquín Sorauren, captain of Sierra's ship *El Jasón*, first reported in August 1785 that Lima "offers nothing but losses, some days greater than others." The following June, almost a year later, Captain Sorauren returned to Peru from Buenos Aires to find that commodity prices remained "battered due to their great abundance."[33] Six weeks later he cursed the "deplorable state of this plaza and the depressed state of commerce. I can assure you that having the house loaded with goods, both yours and mine, I have not been able to sell anything but ten quintals of butter at 78 and 79 pesos apiece, a price that offers nothing but pure loss."[34]

Complaints by traders throughout the colonies about their inability to sell commodities in the overly supplied colonial markets continued unabated in the second half of the 1780s. Mathías Hernández of Cadiz, the uncle of trader Francisco Lerdo de Texada, wrote to the king on his nephew's behalf in November 1788. According to Hernández, Lerdo de Texada had traveled to Mexico in 1785 having been granted a three-year license to sell imported European merchandise. Three years had now passed, Hernández explained, but due to "growing remittances of goods by merchants of these dominions, and various bankruptcies occurring in that Kingdom, he has not been able to unload all of his cargo, nor collect the credit sales that he has made on different terms, for which the mentioned bankruptcies have affected him." Hernández requested a three-year extension for Lerdo, but the Crown granted him only two additional years. In November 1790, Hernández again petitioned the Crown for an extension since his nephew had still not completed his business. A final year was awarded on the condition that Lerdo not request more. By now five years had passed and still Lerdo had not unloaded all of his wares.[35]

In a nearly identical case, Joséf Andrés Rodríguez went to Cartagena de Indias in 1785 with a consignment of goods belonging to a merchant named Fernández Ximénez. By 1788 Rodríguez had not yet succeeded in selling all of the merchandise, forcing Ximénez to petition the king for a two-year extension. This was granted but proved inadequate since in 1790 Rodríguez still held some of the now five-year-old cargo and had not collected all of his debts; in September, Ximénez requested and received a second two-year extension.[36]

Sales of imported merchandise were also stagnant in Caracas, according to widow doña María Azucar y Mayo. Azucar wrote that shortly after her husband's death, she received a letter dated 30 October 1786 from the captain of their ship, *Nuestra Señora del Rosario*. The ship had been sent to Caracas with cargo to sell but due to "the fatal condition of that province's commerce" the captain was unable to unload the consignment at even "the invoice cost."[37]

The eastern coast of South America still remained buried under a barrage of imports late in the decade. Asked in 1789 by the viceroy of Río de la Plata to provide monthly statements of existing supplies in the port of Montevideo, the Royal Customs Administrator and Comptroller repeatedly reported that no commodities were lacking, that warehouses were abundantly stocked and prices correspondingly depressed.[38] Porteño merchants complained of the same to their colleagues in Spain. On New Year's Day, 1789, Gaspar de Santa Coloma advised his Spanish partner "to be patient and hold fast, for all we see is this Plaza full of unsalable merchandise, everyone in debt, and a lack of mind for anything."[39]

The start of the next decade provided little relief. In March 1790, Veracruz merchant Miguel Jacinto de Marticorena was unloading merchandise at prices that he had refused to consider only five months earlier. On 13 March he unhappily advised his brother: "yesterday I sold two bundles of plain cambric at 15 percent above principal on three months' term to a secure resident of this city."[40] Referring to another cargo, he estimated that while some of the items might sell for 16 to 17 percent above cost, for much of the rest "it is possible that I won't find anyone [to buy it] for even 10 percent above principal."[41] Even this pessimistic prediction proved unduly optimistic. By mid-July, he was complaining that business in Veracruz had altogether ceased. "We do nothing more than stand in the doorways of the warehouses waiting for buyers."[42] At the end of the month Miguel Jacinto wrote once more explaining that he had succeeded in selling a few items at "8 percent above principal, a price that I know is quite low but between the abundance and the current notorious season, one cannot do anything else."[43] It should be emphasized that sales at 10 to 20 percent above purchase costs almost certainly entailed steep losses, once insurance, freight, commissions, capital carrying costs, and other expenses were deducted.

Eventually, some merchants in Cadiz abandoned hope of profiting from the American markets. At least they chose to warehouse their goods in Spain and await more propitious economic conditions. The Conde de Maule, Cruz y Bahamonde, estimated that forty million pesos worth of textiles were warehoused in customs or private homes in Spain, not warranting the cost of sending them to America.[44] In sending goods to transatlantic markets, merchants incurred substantial costs beyond the value of the merchandise. Export taxes, freight, insurance and other variable costs could even cost as much as the commodity itself. With bad commercial news coming from the colonies, it must have seemed prudent to hold the wares in Spain or to sell them even at a loss, recuperating at least some of the principal. Delgado Ribas found that as warehoused textiles started accumulating in the 1780s, some traders began selling their goods in Cadiz at 60 percent of what they had originally paid.[45]

· · ·

Markets on the European side of the Atlantic also became inundated with Spanish colonial imports following the end of the American Revolutionary War, but, interestingly, the market seems to have adjusted and rebounded much more quickly than in America. Delgado Ribas found prices of colonial imports in Barcelona to be falling due to excessive supplies by the second half of 1785,[46] but elsewhere the downturn was even earlier. Not long after the restoration of peace, Spanish American colonial goods were beginning to amass unsold in northern European markets. In April 1784, the Amsterdam-based trading house of Echenique Sánchez and Company informed Cadiz merchant Francisco de Sierra that "sugar for which some demand and increase had emerged begins again to fall due to the considerable amounts that keep arriving from all over. The same is occurring with hides and to tell you the truth we do not see any sector nor any product from [Spanish] America whatsoever on which one could expect any return by shipping it here."[47]

Apparently Sierra had already taken possession of a large lot of Argentine hides and was determined to deliver them to Holland regardless. "You can count on us to get the best deal that the circumstances allow like anything that you might send us," Echenique Sánchez and Company assured him, "although with all truth . . . seeing the prices of everything here we are not eager to encourage you to do so, as for us there is nothing more disagreeable than to produce sales accounts that show a loss, and we do not know in what commodity to engage as all look bad due to the abundance that exists in all American products."[48]

Even cochineal, Mexico's second export commodity by value and usually the most dependably profitable American commodity, began arriving
in excess. In March 1784 the Cadiz *consulado* warned of the arrival of surplus levels of cochineal claiming that "with the immense portion that has
just arrived, bankruptcies will increase painfully." To avoid widespread
financial losses, the *consulado* urged the king to grant tax relief on cochineal.[49] Indeed, cochineal prices in Amsterdam, one of its principal markets, fell during these years, reaching a twenty-year low in 1784 and
remaining quite depressed for the remainder of the decade.[50] Cochineal
prices in England tumbled 43 percent in 1784 relative to the previous year
and remained at this lower plateau until the war years of the mid-1790s,
although the fact that published data in England only began in 1782
makes any longer-term conclusions difficult.[51]

The price of cochineal in Amsterdam had already plummeted by late
1783, according to reports from the commercial house of Echenique Sánchez. In March the firm had written hopefully about the possibility of
cochineal selling as high as 38 to 40, but in December had to report that
"they offer cochineal at the miserable price of 27/3 and no one buys."[52]
The surplus continued into the following spring. On 20 May, Echenique
Sánchez and Company wrote to Francisco de Sierra regarding ten sacks
of cochineal that the latter had shipped from Cadiz, reporting that for
the moment its market price held steady at 25. As with other American
commodities, however, the house was wary about dealing in Mexican
cochineal:

> We do not see any indication that [the price of] this product could increase
> because the amount arriving here is too great for [even its current price] to
> persist for much longer and while a lot of it is held in capable hands, there
> will always be those who from need are obliged to sell, and given that there
> is no shortage here to meet regular demand, we believe that those who
> hoard will experience nothing but losses and in the end decide to sell and
> subject themselves to circumstances of even greater loss.[53]

The house's pessimism persisted into the late summer. While the cochineal price remained where it had been in May, demand was limited
and the continued introduction of dyestuff unabated. "We do not think
that you will get too rich speculating. . . . From Veracruz there will soon
depart several thousand sacks and the quantity that there is in Europe is
[already] too great."[54]

There was no ambiguity whatsoever about the demand for Vicuña
wool from the Andes. In May, Echenique Sánchez informed Sierra that

there was surplus in Amsterdam. Furthermore, "we have inquired about it to Paris, Rouen, England and other parts, and they respond that we should not send it to them because in these cities there is more than what is needed, to which they add that the ships [in Cadiz] from the South Sea will bring still more."[55]

Echenique Sánchez and Company's guardedness toward the market for Spanish American exports seemed vindicated by the firm's news in December 1784 that one of its competitors in Amsterdam, a "casa Americana" called "Señores Moses Meyers," had suspended its operations on the previous Friday. Given the constant concerns expressed to Sierra during the previous half year, it seems likely that Moses Meyers's bankruptcy had resulted from speculating in Spanish American merchandise.[56]

The end of the American Revolutionary War caused a steep rise in the supply of Spanish American goods in European markets. Unlike the American markets, however, the glut seems to have been short-lived, and European markets seem to have largely adjusted and absorbed the growing supplies by the end of the 1780s. At least, this phenomenon is suggested by the evolution of prices in Amsterdam. The graphs in Figure 4.2 show for the years 1776 to 1793 the average annual prices in Amsterdam of four widely traded Spanish American commodities—Guatemalan indigo, Mexican cochineal, Buenos Aires hides, and Caracas cacao. As the graphs illustrate quite clearly, prices for these commodities rose during the American Revolutionary War, likely reflecting the difficulties of consumers in Amsterdam to obtain regular supplies. The restoration of peace, as has been shown, led to the flooding of the Dutch markets, causing a sharp fall in prices. Cochineal, indigo, and hides sold in the mid-1780s for only 66 to 75 percent of their wartime peak prices. Cacao suffered the greatest price decline, a full 50 percent. Over the remainder of the decade, however, prices gradually recovered. By the eve of the French Revolutionary Wars, prices for indigo, cochineal, and cacao had largely, if not completely, rebounded, suggesting that some market adjustment had occurred. The price of Buenos Aires' hides had reached new highs altogether.

Unfortunately, American price indices for imported goods comparable to those constructed from the Dutch data do not exist, and so it is not possible to analyze the evolution of American prices to the same degree. But the qualitative evidence pointing to the glutting of markets after 1783 is substantial; merchants continued to complain about market saturation throughout the 1780s and start of the 1790s. Only with the interruption of trade due to the outbreak of war in 1793 did demand finally catch up to supply.[57] The question as to why the American markets were unable to absorb the growing supply of commodities whose prices were even falling is dealt with directly in the following chapter.

For decades reformers had argued that the commercial system was detrimental to Spain's economy, suffocating Spanish industry, prejudicing producers and consumers, and reducing Crown tax revenues, all for the benefit of the vested interests of the privileged *consulado* merchants. *Comercio libre*, they argued, would rectify these ills. As reformers had expected, new traders entered an industry long proscribed, encouraged by the Crown's more liberal granting of export licenses. Proponents of free trade applauded the results; the initial evidence corroborated what they had long espoused. Trade expanded markedly and the Royal treasury benefitted.[58] But *comercio*

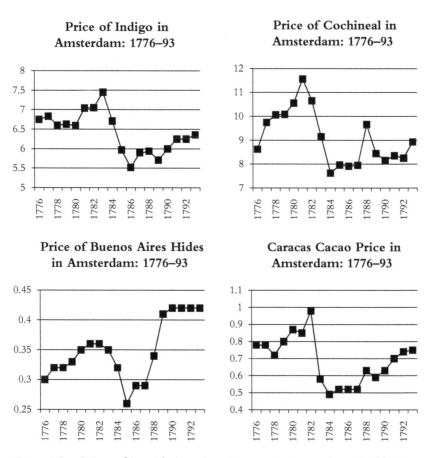

Figure 4.2.   Prices of Spanish American Imports in Amsterdam (Guilders): 1776–93

SOURCE: Posthumus, Inquiry into the History, 1:196–97, 356–57, 417–18, 422.

libre had additional effects as the *consulados* had long warned. Commercial liberalization led to a significant rise in international trade, exceeding the ability of markets, at least in the medium-run, to absorb the growing quantities of imports. Rising stocks caused prices to tumble, yet still markets remained oversupplied.

Trade officials had long intervened in the market to attempt to balance supply and demand. Indeed, this had been a central feature of regulated trade. Export licenses were distributed sparingly, members of the merchant guilds being especially favored to receive these coveted permits. Trade restrictions were critical to these traders since such practices helped compensate for the tremendous uncertainty that characterized long-distance exchange. *Comercio libre* dismantled these risk-reducing institutions and by doing so significantly altered the nature of trade within the Spanish empire. Many more traders now carried far more merchandise to the colonies. This caused rising competition for limited markets. Profits narrowed as imports amassed; merchants could no longer as easily compensate for a bad deal with a profitable one. Uncertainty rose as supplies became ever more difficult to predict. In short, *comercio libre* greatly increased the riskiness of long-distance trade.

"Lately One Cannot Engage in Any Business Without the Risk of Being Ruined"[59]

The issue of *comercio libre* was very controversial. For decades, discussions had ensued within official circles about the possibility of liberalizing trade. The large merchants who dominated long-distance trade remained unified in their opposition to dismantling the existing structures. Despite their concerted efforts, however, the *consulado* merchants of Spain and America failed ultimately to prevent its promulgation. The Cadiz institution exerted all of its efforts to prevent the initial experimentation with free trade in the Caribbean in 1765. Cadiz was joined by the *consulados* of Lima and Mexico City in combating vehemently the broadening of freedom to most of the rest of the colonies in 1778. Finally, the Mexico City and Cadiz guilds joined forces in resisting the extension of *comercio libre* to Mexico in 1789, although by then Mexico had, in effect, already experienced the most influential of changes, the sharp rise of licensed register ships. Even after their adoption, the commercial guilds regularly condemned the reforms, blaming them for a variety of alleged ills.

The merchant guilds missed few opportunities to express their displeasure with free trade. On numerous occasions, both before and after its promulgation, Crown officials sought the *consulados'* input about commercial reform. The responses of the various merchant guilds to official Crown interrogatories, the bulk of the sources used for the remainder of this chapter, illustrate in detail how these large merchants perceived *comercio libre*. Naturally, the *consulado* merchants were attempting to persuade the Crown of their position, and thus the historian must read these reports with attention to this bias. Obviously, these *informes* had to avoid topics that would have provided ammunition to their critics. The many historians who have examined these sources have presented them as the attempts of these privileged merchants to maintain their commercial privileges, an interpretation that is unquestionably accurate. However, a reexamination of these reports through the lens of risk management paints a more complex picture and provides a vivid and illuminating window into the economic strategies of long-distance Spanish traders in the late colonial era. These merchants consistently argued that trade liberalization would lead and had led to the imbalance of supply and demand; they further claimed that the new trade regime had increased uncertainty and thus the riskiness of engaging in Atlantic world commerce.[60]

· · ·

Even before the first reforms were introduced, the guilds began voicing their concerns. In late 1764, while a specially appointed *junta de comercio* explored the possibility of granting free commerce to the Islas de Barlovento, most importantly Cuba, the Cadiz mercantile body voiced opposition to the reform emphasizing the importance of maintaining balance between Cadiz's exports and imports (that is, avoiding the oversupply of either) adding, with undeniable hyperbole, that "the survival of the monarchy depends upon a balance between the two."[61]

Despite losing this first battle—the islands were indeed opened to trade— the *consulado* maintained this line of reasoning in 1778 in its opposition to extending *comercio libre*. On behalf of the commercial body, Antonio de Vicuña y Goenaga, Joséf Ventura Rubín de Zelis, and Joséf Antonio Gallego, who were all members of the *consulado* for twenty-five years or more, warned the king that "*libre comercio* will result in the abundance of goods above the many that already exist, and by necessary consequence . . . the ruin of commerce."[62] Having always preoccupied transatlantic merchants, this concern figured centrally in their defenses of the existing system. The fleets and restricted trade, they argued, helped lessen the perils of market saturation, reducing the riskiness of long-distance commerce.

A decade's experience with *comercio libre* only hardened their position. On the tenth anniversary of free trade's promulgation, the Cadiz *consulado* was asked by the Crown to respond to a series of questions about the state of trade to the Indies. In general, "the King desired that the *consulado* make clear what it believes ideal for the benefit of commerce, fomentation of our factories, agriculture and industry."[63] In late 1787, dozens of traders from the mercantile body submitted responses to the eight questions posed by the Crown; while virtually all acknowledged the expanded trade volumes since the promulgation of reforms, they simultaneously expressed unequivocally their resounding dissatisfaction with trade liberalization. Writing only four years after the end of the War of American Independence, most pointed to the inundation of colonial markets that had rendered international trade unpredictable and unprofitable.

Miguel Rodríguez Carasa, thirty-year veteran of the guild, commented that American markets were "superabundantly provisioned" and that "lately one cannot engage in any [transatlantic] business without danger of being ruined, as has occurred to many." Harkening to the familiar practices of trade in the pre-1778 era, he recommended, at the very least, temporarily halting transatlantic commerce in 1788 to allow the surpluses to be sold.[64]

Fellow *consulado* member Ventura de Imaña reported that "for more than three years now [commerce] in New Spain, as is well known, has been in such a deplorable state that no matter how well varied, one cannot sell a cargo without a loss . . . even financing the majority." Imaña admitted that *comercio libre* had produced an initial burst of commerce, but he believed that the situation had become unsustainable, that Mexico, for example, had adequate supplies of imported goods to last for the next year and a half.[65] Of course, *comercio libre* had not yet even been officially extended to Mexico. But the more critical issue was the quantities that were imported not from where the merchandise originated, Cadiz or Barcelona, for example. Officials in Cadiz had begun granting licenses far more freely, leading to the blanketing of the colony with imported goods.

Brothers Juan and Ramón Valiente attributed the rise in trade to undercapitalized traders borrowing large sums to finance their ventures. Merchants with assets totaling only 15,000 to 20,000 pesos, they claimed, were trading with 150,000 to 200,000 pesos' worth of borrowed goods, a recipe for disaster. The brothers recommend excluding from the Indies entrepreneurs who did not personally possess at least 40,000 pesos.[66] Their self-serving proposition sought to reduce the newly encountered competition, but, as will be discussed in the following chapter, they had, in fact, identified an increasingly pervasive problem, the recently swelling reliance on credit to facilitate trade.

In a similar vein, Diego Fernández Jiménez replied that the adoption of *comercio libre* had led to the entry of many traders who lacked both personal funds and commercial experience. As a consequence, the nature of trade to Mexico had changed, scaring off many of the veteran merchants who were wary of transacting in the increasingly unpredictable environment. Much of the immediate crisis originated with the end of the war when merchants shipped far more merchandise to America than could possibly have been consumed. The situation deteriorated "because the owners lack the funds necessary to weather the slack period they experience."[67] Indeed, in the next several years a growing number of heavily indebted traders did go bankrupt.

Free trade significantly increased commerce, Joséph Gutiérrez Palacio affirmed. But, he added, "although at first glance it seems beneficial to the State, I don't consider it so, in respect to the individuals that experience considerable detriment and significant losses to their wealth, proceeding gradually to their ruin." Too many individuals who engaged in trade were not financially prepared, and the result was catastrophic. "These merchants would be better off in the class of assistants to others, as before, and not slaves as such to their considerable arrears." Having criticized the business practices of these undercapitalized traders, Gutiérrez recommended the cessation of trade for a year so that the backlog of commodities in Mexico could be sold. His proposal, then, was to return to the regulation of commerce. In Veracruz, he further warned, "there is beginning to occur the same multitude of bankruptcies that we have seen in this marketplace [of Cadiz], and there will be the total destruction of honorable and industrious merchants."[68]

Sebastian Lasqueti noted that since the reforms Mexico's "*mercaderes*" were unwilling to purchase anything more than "the necessities for their consumption" since they had grown confident that "with the continued remittances from Spain, they will have the goods that they need in abundance, and with greater comfort, resisting any impulse to make purchases of greater consideration, as they did previously, of up to a million pesos by one subject and at one time." As Lasqueti argued, under the new trade regime merchants had too little capacity to govern their dealings along solid guidelines since supplies were too unpredictable. His "modest and sincere" recommendation that "without any infraction on the liberty of commerce might remedy the bad situation" was for the Ministry to "indicate a certain season of the year before which yes but after which no ship could initiate its departure for New Spain." In this way, he continued, importers to Mexico could sell their wares secure in the knowledge that no additional shipments would arrive too soon. With such a reformed system traders "informed of the internal situation of the Kingdom would have secure principals upon which to base their mercantile calculations and operations."[69]

These Cadiz merchants were naturally presenting arguments designed to impress the king about the negative consequences of *comercio libre*. Their policy prescriptions, if followed, would have encouraged a restoration of at least elements of the regulations recently dismantled. Under the earlier trade regime, it was these very same merchants who had benefitted from their privileged access to the less competitive conditions that had permitted the greater predictability of trade. For these reasons, one can understand historians' inclination to dismiss their complaints as merely self-serving. They were self-serving, but their reports still highlight the problems that plagued these early modern traders, problems that regulation had helped mitigate.

• • •

The commercial reforms were no more popular with the *consulado* merchants in Mexico City. Again, although Mexico was not opened to free trade until 1789, Mexico felt the effects of reform much earlier due to the expansion of licensed register ships. In 1776 the final convoy sailed from Spain to Mexico. Regulation continued to prohibit all ships from making port at Veracruz except those originating in Cadiz, but the Crown vastly increased the number of licensed *registros*, probably the most influential policy change during this era of reform. Indeed, as the reports below indicate, Mexican merchants viewed 1778 as the critical year, even referring to it as the year, erroneously, in which *comercio libre* had been implemented there. The result for Veracruz, as for all of the colonies, was an avalanche of imports.

Attuned to the commercial difficulties being experienced in Mexico, Spanish minister Diego de Gardoqui requested in 1791 that the viceroy, the Second Count of Revillagigedo, "investigate if there is decay in the commerce of those dominions and in the case that there is to find its causes and its remedies."[70] Viceroy Revillagigedo dedicated several years to the preparation of his *informe*, collecting numerous materials upon which to base his conclusions. Prominent among these were more than a dozen reports solicited in 1791 from prominent members of the Mexico City *consulado*, all of whom were longtime *mercaderes*, wholesalers engaged in the Indies trade. Asked to comment on the causes of economic "decay," nearly all of the respondents pointed to the rising uncertainty of oceanic trade attributable to trade liberalization.

Isidro Antonio de Icaza, matriculated member of the *consulado* of Mexico City and ex-*Regidor Honorario* of the *Cabildo*,[71] argued that the frequent arrival of ships to Veracruz since the last convoy (1776) had made long-distance commerce increasingly unpredictable. During the era of regulated commerce, he explained, merchants could make informed business decisions, but now one never knew whether an apparently promising venture one day could make a merchant a "laughing stock several days later." Icaza had not withdrawn from trade in 1778; instead he had invested upwards of two hundred thousand pesos over the following several years exchanging cochineal and silver for European textiles, ventures that had been unprofitable. Like many other "men of fortune" Icaza intended to reinvest his wealth into less risky ventures, such as haciendas and mining, leaving commerce in the hands of "novices who have little or nothing to lose, lacking the funds with which to manage their dealings and the related delays and difficulties that normally produce profits; wanting, as they regularly do, to sell quickly, very few will prosper, and there will be many who complain about the decline and bankruptcies that they experience in their commercial dealings."[72] In contrast, Icaza argued, the old system had been far more manageable because the three-year period between fleets had given merchants adequate time to dispose of their merchandise at a reasonable and more dependable profit. The new trading regime lacked the predictability of the flota system; uncertainty had risen.

Martín Gaspar Vicario also admitted that commerce had expanded dramatically since 1778, but he questioned whether to view this as positive. Prior to reform, merchants and producers alike enjoyed predictable and moderate returns, but since then there had been numerous bankruptcies. Traders who had once invested two hundred thousand to six hundred thousand pesos per flota had been frightened, choosing instead to place their capital in *inacción*. Those who continued investing in imports bought much smaller quantities than before, fearful that subsequent shipments would convert their investments into losses. The Spanish importers, unable to sell their merchandise, were forced to endure long delays in Jalapa or expose themselves to additional risks, selling their wares on credit to poorer traders who lacked liquid funds of their own.[73]

Lorenzo de Angulo Guardamino, another *consulado* merchant, had not withdrawn from commerce but had continued investing large amounts for which he had barely earned profits of 5 percent. The greatest difficulty, he suggested, resulted from the frequency of imports that led to sudden and unpredictable price shifts. A merchant might import commodities to Mexico only to find that another ship loaded with the same merchandise arrived simultaneously, producing losses for whomever held this item, no matter how "noble" a good. "A merchant does not have a firm idea of how to cast his lines due to the freedom that open commerce allows," Angulo Guardamino argued. He urged Revillagigedo to reintroduce the flota so that "merchants informed of the profitability that would come to them depending on supply and consumption can formulate ideas of what is convenient to buy and prices that they must pay for them with the object of gaining enough profits to remunerate their work and investment."[74] Merchant Angulo Guardamino desired a return to the reduced uncertainty that had existed during the era of regulated trade.

Manuel García Herreros pointed to the abundant influx into Veracruz of wool and silk as an example of how commerce had grown increasingly unpredictable since the end of the fleet system. The Cinco Gremios Mayores de Madrid, a joint stock firm composed of wealthy Madrid merchants,[75] had sustained heavy losses trading in the latter item, leading García Herreros to wonder how a smaller firm could survive if even the largest was suffering. The market was so saturated that experienced Mexican traders refused to buy European merchandise, forcing the importers to sell on credit to smaller peddlers, resulting in unpaid debts and rising bankruptcies. Like many of the respondents, García Herreros identified increasingly onerous taxes as a major cause of the economic crisis, feistily adding, "free trade . . . there is nothing free about it other than its name. . . . How about freedom from taxes? One can truly call it costly, oppressive and far-from-free trade."[76]

Claiming to be ambivalent about the reform, merchant Diego de Agreda suggested that the experiment with *comercio libre* had really only begun in 1784 after the end of the war. Due to the war, the Mexican market had faced shortages but was quickly replenished at war's end. New imports, however, did not abate and prices began to plummet, causing the catastrophes now being experienced by merchants. The problems, he argued, stemmed from the new system. To illustrate, Agreda discussed his own case, which was enviable, he admitted, in comparison to those of many other traders. While Agreda had a brother in Cadiz looking out for his best interests, enjoyed the liquidity to pay cash for items earning him more favorable terms, and succeeded in selling his purchases quickly, he still earned only 5.5 percent over seventeen months on his most recent venture. Unlike other merchants, Agreda did not recommend scrapping register ships altogether; instead he proposed only to limit the number and frequency of introductions of "foreign" goods, northern European items reexported from the peninsula.[77]

Because of the uncertainty arising from the frequent introductions of imported goods that began at the war's end in 1783 and 1784, the Mexico City wholesale merchants had ceased to buy imported goods in bulk, explained Juan Fernando Meoqui. With long-distance trade no longer profitable, these wealthy merchants withdrew their money, "the blood that before circulated through the veins of the mercantile body," reinvesting in mines, haciendas, or other ventures. Meoqui rejected the often-made claim by its defenders that *comercio libre* had merely spread out the profits among more traders. While a large number of traders had entered commerce, they had no funds of their own, forcing the "traffickers of the sea" to extend credit to unload their merchandise. This resulted in growing indebtedness, loan defaults, and bankruptcies. To remedy the crisis, Meoqui recommended a biannual convoy carrying twenty to twenty-two million pesos worth of goods, about double the amount, he estimated, Mexico could annually consume.[78] His proposal, then, was to once again attempt to balance supply with demand.

One of Mexico's wealthiest and most prominent traders, Antonio de Bassoco, provided a lengthy analysis of his own experiences in international trade since the promulgation of free trade, so that the viceroy could better understand why so many of the principal merchants had divested from commerce "so as not to risk losing in several years what they have acquired over the cost of many." From 1783 to 1785, Bassoco placed 500,000 pesos' worth of goods and coin in the marketplace of Cadiz hoping to secure a profit and a return cargo. He purchased 250,000 pesos' worth of commodities, most of which he had subsequently been unable to sell in Mexico despite reducing their prices and offering them on credit at favorable terms. What he did succeed in unloading had not generated profits. Rather than sink even more principal into commodities, he chose to make a 100,000 pesos sea loan to some Spanish merchants who were to repay him in Mexico in six to eight months. Another 156,000 pesos were sitting idle in Cadiz because Bassoco did not dare buy any more European luxury goods. Mexican exports fared no better, he added: "in the purchases that I have made during the same time in this Kingdom, I have experienced the same misfortunes, and these continuously bad results have obliged me to withdraw from mercantile concerns and make the decision to lend my capital at interest." Trade in Mexico had become so unpredictable, he added, that even when a commodity was in short supply, merchants refused to speculate for lack of knowledge of when another shipment might arrive and the price might fall. For all of these reasons, Bassoco argued, the flota should be reintroduced. Despite its negative image, he argued, the old system worked to the benefit of merchants on both sides of the Atlantic as well as consumers, although he did not explain how the latter benefitted.[79]

A slightly different perspective was presented by wealthy merchant Francisco Ignacio de Yraeta, who while acknowledging the commercial "decay" nonetheless believed that "*comercio libre* has been and is the best way to assist both kingdoms." Yraeta agreed that in recent years the Peninsular merchants had not "directed their shipments in the quantity or with the information necessary," but he believed that this was to be expected given the newness of free trade. Instead, the greatest obstacle to commerce, according to Yraeta, was the onerous and poorly designed tax system, which priced commodities too high and discouraged merchants from pursuing certain activities.[80] Yraeta suggested that prices would fall and consumption increase in Mexico if taxes were reduced, a position echoed by many of his counterparts.[81]

On both sides of the Atlantic, the wealthy merchants possessed similar opinions about the new trading regime. For them, the rising competition and the changing methods had increased dramatically the riskiness of trade. The old system had worked, in their minds, because it had served to restrict supply to levels consumable by the colonial markets. Furthermore, the regulations had created less volatile and more predictable conditions that allowed merchants to behave and transact with greater knowledge. *Comercio libre* had ruptured this balance and increased the uncertainty of long-distance trade. With virtually no exceptions, the great merchants sought a restoration of regulated trading.

•   •   •

It was with these Mexico City *consulado* members' *informes* that the viceroy of Mexico, the Second Conde de Revillagigedo, had intended to compile his report to the king. Virtually every merchant had proposed the restoration of restrictions as the only way to remedy the extant commercial crisis. The problem, though, was that the viceroy was ideologically persuaded that modernizing reform, and especially free trade, was inherently necessary and positive. As a consequence, the viceroy ignored the merchants' testimonies and "sought to justify at all costs the success of the reforms."[82] As a committed reformer, explains Ortiz de la Tabla, "the Viceroy was unhappy with the unfavorable opinion" of *comercio libre*, and thus proceeded to request additional *informes* from individuals who might be more sympathetic, thus delaying the compilation of his official report to the Crown.[83]

Viceroy Revillagigedo finally finished his report in August 1793, two years after the initial consular *informes* had been submitted. While he did mention that the merchants of the Mexico City *consulado* had expressed their negative opinions about *comercio libre*, he proceeded to defend the commercial reforms. The viceroy began by congratulating the king on the successes of his policy since "far from decay, there are very visible increases in commerce and happiness in these Kingdoms comparing the thirteen years of *comercio libre* with the final [years] of fleets." He then launched into a lengthy analysis of Mexico's economic conditions, in which the wealthy Mexico City merchants became the target of criticism, an impediment to the colony's modernization. "I found among the merchants of Mexico persons decidedly in favor of monopoly and restrictions on the importation of goods and the extraction of wealth, and in this way opposed to the true stimulation (*verdadero fomento*) of commerce."[84] The viceroy was correct; the merchants did favor the restoration of restrictions.

Consistent with the testimonies presented by the consular members, Revillagigedo acknowledged that many large merchants had withdrawn from transatlantic trade. The viceroy, however, presented their divestment as a positive outcome of reform since their capital had begun to develop underfinanced sectors of the Mexican economy, and, in any event, new traders had more than taken their place, entering Atlantic world commerce in large numbers:

> the old merchants upon seeing the commercial system changed and that no longer could they extract a large return on their money as they did before without caution, without calculation, and without risks . . . have withdrawn their funds . . . investing them in agriculture, finance and partly in mining, leaving commerce to the new speculators of lesser means but greater knowledge of the new methods of trade and less accustomed to excessive earnings with a perfect security and tranquility.[85]

According to Revillagigedo, the fleet system had offered "excessive earnings" to "subjects of immense capital." The new, more competitive environment had driven away the elite traders in favor of "many individuals of small fortune" who were "content to earn little more than their subsistence."[86]

The viceroy could not ignore altogether the evidence that had led to the official inquiry in the first place. As the *consulado* merchants in Mexico and Spain had repeatedly decried, and the government in Madrid knew, a not insignificant number of merchants on both sides of the Atlantic had been forced into bankruptcy in the years since the introduction of commercial reform. But Revillagigedo attributed these bankruptcies to those merchants' "ignorance, malfeasance or bad luck" rather than anything systemic in the new trade regime. Throughout his treatise Viceroy Revillagigedo remained unwavering in his position that *comercio libre* was succeeding and represented a profound improvement over the old system of convoys.[87]

Consulado merchants in both Cadiz and Mexico City argued in favor of the restoration of a trade system that had worked to their benefit by restricting competition. Reduced competition had created conditions that allowed the merchants to operate under less volatile conditions in which uncertainty was diminished, but by no means eradicated. Viceroy Revillagigedo of Mexico dismissed their reports, arguing that these were traders who were simply incapable of adjusting to the new, more competitive environment in which profits were smaller. The viceroy was certainly correct that the new conditions entailed greater competition. From the perspective of these experienced merchants, however, this was a major problem since it made an already risky business even more so. The old practices had not eliminated the risks of trade but had, by limiting competition, reduced some of the endemic uncertainty.

• • •

Once introduced, trade liberalization became permanent, despite the vociferous objections of the traditional traders. Yet the many sources of uncertainty that characterized long-distance trade did not disappear. The new merchants who took advantage of reform to enter into long-distance trade faced the very same uncertainties. In his recent study of Atlantic world commerce, Jeremy Adelman points to the irony that the promulgation of free trade led many smaller merchants in the colonies to begin clamoring to obtain their own protection from unfettered market volatility. According to Adelman, "In Venezuela, right after the Guipuzcoana Company was dismantled . . . merchants petitioned officials to create a local guild to monitor trading lest a commercial free-for-all wipe out their fortunes. No sooner was the Buenos Aires market opened to imperial traders in 1778 than local merchants . . . [became] worried about excessive competition."[88] Adelman's point is not to show that Spanish imperial merchants were anticompetitive or somehow lacking in entrepreneurial spirit. Instead, he argues that "an important line [had] to be maintained between domesticated competition and unbridled rivalry that might foster more uncertainty than opportunity."[89] In short, these smaller traders recognized that long-distance trade entailed extraordinary uncertainties that made such ventures potentially too risky. Their response to the unpredictability of long-distance trade was to seek protection or regulation to reduce such risk. The beneficiaries of free trade faced the same obstacles as their predecessors and sought similar devices to make trade less unpredictable.

Smaller merchants in newly opened Spanish ports responded with the same degree of trepidation about the uncertainties of Atlantic commerce. Shortly after the Crown's 1765 granting of free trade to the Caribbean, Juan Gálvez, deputy of maritime commerce for the Andalusian city of Malaga, lamented to the king that despite "the compassionate intention of Your Majesty in having wanted by means of this commerce to foment your vassals," Malagüeño merchants "have not made a single expedition from that port, so well provisioned in everything." According to this 1768 report, the traders:

> recognized that they could not do it without exposing themselves to great and inevitable losses . . . [due to the] difficulty in a commerce so distant to have dependable news nor the critical knowledge of existing supplies. When they arrive to the determined port and find that on that island it is not easy, or beneficial to sell their wares and fruits, or it is only in part, and not in total, or in some of the goods and fruits but not in all, they find themselves required to deeply discount them.[90]

Unlike the cases noted by Adelman, the deputy from Malaga made no reference to the merchants requesting protection for their commerce, but the case illustrates the same point that long-distance, early modern trade entailed great uncertainty and many risks that made prudent traders cautious to engage. The long-sought opening of additional ports to Atlantic world trade offered previously marginalized merchants new opportunities but did not provide them with any means to deal with the profound uncertainty that early modern, long-distance trade entailed.

One of the most important roles of economic institutions is to reduce uncertainty. Uncertainty is an impediment to commerce since traders, naturally, are reluctant to invest in activities that are too unpredictable or rely too heavily on luck. Institutional economists predict that obstacles and barriers to trade (i.e., market imperfections) will lead to the adaptation of institutions or the creation of new ones designed to diminish or eradicate such obstacles, and make possible economic activity that would otherwise prove uneconomical or too risky.[91] By controlling risk, institutions make certain economic activities more attractive.

The commercial institutions of the pre-1778 era had provided risk-reducing characteristics, thus allowing long-distance merchants to trade with greater security. The controlled flow of commodities helped lessen the likelihood of market inundation and thus reduced commercial risk. The more predictable supply of items helped compensate for the sluggishness of information flows, helping merchants manage their businesses more intelligently. The 1778 promulgation of free trade dismantled these risk-reducing institutions; as a result, post-1778 commerce was conducted in a much riskier environment. Perhaps it is no surprise that some of the smaller traders who engaged in imperial trade after 1778 sought similar institutional safeguards to reduce uncertainty. As Xabier Lamikiz well put it, "after 1783 making decisions in Cadiz was the nearest thing to gambling that anyone could imagine."[92]

Free Trade and the Rise of Commercial Bankruptcies in the Post-1778 Era

The dangers of financial loss had always been a prominent aspect of Atlantic world trade, but the old commercial system had served to reduce the risk of losses by making commodity flows less volatile and uncertain. The greater predictability of the old system was precisely the point repeatedly emphasized by the *consulado* merchants who were questioned by the Royal government. *Comercio libre* represented a radically new and more competitive business environment, one that forced veteran merchants to reconsider their participation. Many merchants long engaged in the Indies trade chose to withdraw from transatlantic trade because they believed that such investments had grown too risky, that expected returns did not justify the enormity of the risks. Reinvesting into agriculture, mining, or loans must have been perceived as safer than continuing to trade in the increasingly unpredictable Spanish Atlantic economy.

Merchants who continued in long-distance trade were aware of the growing unpredictability of commerce and contemplated divestment. A letter to Juan José de Puch sent by Pedro Gil de Texada in 1778 expressed this very sentiment. Texada began by expressing his gratitude to the merchant Juan Josef de Yriarte, who out of friendship had loaned him funds at 6 percent rather than the 7 percent he was charging others. Texada proceeded to contrast money-lending with commerce:

> you should consider that 6 percent is fixed, and business these days is so variable that it makes any man tremble to enter into trade due to the referred to [unpredictable] profitability which is so much more risky than in times of peace, while in the bank we have better information and are

less exposed than in other [activities] because there are lists of all of the Spanish and foreign commercial houses so that with these one operates with greater knowledge.

Commerce had grown so uncertain, he lamented, that one was probably better off lending one's funds at interest.[93]

Such risk aversion was not unwarranted. The fifteen years or so following the 1778 promulgation of free trade witnessed a slew of mercantile bankruptcies, an indication of the increasingly risky conditions of transatlantic commerce. Importantly, these bankruptcies occurred before the beginning of the French Revolutionary Wars; they occurred during the peacetime years preceding the 1793 outbreak of hostilities. These were financial failures that transpired during the height of free trade, not due to the war.

According to Stein and Stein, "bankruptcy proceedings . . . were all too common at Cadiz in the late 1780s."[94] Delgado Ribas found that a staggering 32 percent of the mercantile houses in Barcelona went bankrupt between 1786 and 1788.[95] Many of the Catalán shipowners who had only just recently won the right to trade directly in the Indies were forced to sell their vessels upon returning home to pay their accumulated debts.[96] The *consulado* in Lima protested to the king in 1788 that "commerce is very rapidly approaching its ultimate ruin."[97] The following year a Limeño merchant complained that "it is astonishing how much bankruptcy there has been in this marketplace."[98] Another Limeño merchant added in 1793: "we are seeing bankruptcies here every day."[99] Susan Socolow found that bankruptcies had reached Río de la Plata as well. In May 1790, Gaspar de Santa Coloma, a midsize merchant resident in Buenos Aires, complained to an associate in Cadiz that "this commerce grows worse each day for there's nothing but chicanery, overdrafts and bankruptcies; one no longer knows who to trust."[100] Indeed, the veteran trader Santa Coloma proceeded to withdraw most of his own capital from commerce over the next two years, preferring the less risky business of serving as commissions agent for other merchants. Socolow concludes that the persistent oversupply of markets led him "to believe that the market was too risky to warrant the investment of his own funds."[101]

When merchants declared insolvency, either voluntarily or as the result of legal pressure, their cases appeared before the *consulado*, which scheduled an assembly of creditors, known as a *concurso* or *junta de acreedores*.[102] At the meeting, presided over by appointed receivers (*síndicos*), creditors and debtors attempted to reach some type of accord, perhaps drawing up a feasible schedule for repayment of debts.[103] The practice seems to have been similar in both Cadiz and America, for when Joséf Carrillo, a merchant from Puebla, Mexico, declared insolvency in early 1782, a *junta de acreedores* was convened there and a schedule for repayment was hatched. In this particular case Carrillo's records indicated that he possessed wealth valued at 84,000 pesos and owed debts of 74,000 pesos. The agreement stipulated that Carrillo pay 8,000 pesos in 1782, 12,000 in 1783, and 17,000 in each of the next three years. The settlement allowed Carrillo to continue trading while he covered his obligations; his creditors were ordered to cease pressuring him for repayment and had to wait up to five years to collect their debts.[104]

Adjudicating bankruptcies was the responsibility of the *consulado*, but the guild also acted to prevent them in the first place by establishing and upholding commercial standards, ensuring that merchants engaged in proper business practices. In doing so, the guild aimed to protect its constituency, and nonmember traders indirectly, from the malfeasance of less honorable merchants. Sometimes this related to bankruptcy. When in December 1788 the Frenchman Esteban Laborde declared insolvency, the *consulado* petitioned the Crown to act harshly in cases such as his. The syndicate appointed by the guild had found Laborde's records to be in catastrophic disorder. Furthermore, Laborde had comingled funds between dealings, a practice considered grossly improper. Referring to its responsibility to protect the Cadiz mercantile community from the dishonesty of fraudulent traders like Laborde, the guild argued in favor of harsh treatment since such transgressions tarnished the reputation of all Cadiz traders. In punishing those who engaged in nefarious commercial practices, the *consulado* sought to create a less risky environment for the economic activities of other merchants.[105]

To help ensure the enforcement of contracts, the *consulado* was vested with the authority to arrest debtors or seize their belongings on behalf of creditors. Trader Domingo Labady fled to the Low Countries in 1791 beyond the reach of the *consulado* to avoid being arrested for the "enormous quantities" that he owed his creditors. When authorities entered the quarters that Labady rented in a house owned by another Cadiz merchant, Carlos Flore, they found a list of the debts owed by Labady as well as a letter explaining that he promised to return to Cadiz and face his debtors only after the order for his arrest was lifted. Labady requested that his creditors advise him that he had been granted safe passage by placing an announcement in secret code in the Leiden Gazette. Miguel Bernal and Pedro Galatoire, the *consulado* appointed receivers (*síndicos*) in the case, appealed to the Crown that the indictment against Labady be lifted, arguing that all they really desired was for Labady to satisfy his debts. They further requested that Labady be granted four months to appear in Cadiz and an additional four months to pay his obligations.[106]

In other cases, the *consulado* might exonerate insolvent merchants of any malfeasance. Mariano Bernabe de Frías declared bankruptcy in April 1786 after nearly thirty years of involvement in the Indies trade. Bernabe de Frías's attorney wrote a passionate defense of his client that attributed the financial catastrophe to numerous factors beyond Bernabe de Frías's control. "So honest, so sudden, so accidental, and guiltless was the bankruptcy of this loyal merchant. Who could condemn as unwarranted his speculations? . . . Nobody is the arbiter of luck, nor infallible in their judgment," the attorney argued.[107] The *consulado* apparently agreed, finding Bernabe de Frías innocent of any wrongdoing, a decision that infuriated several of his creditors, who accused the tribunal of bias, a charge rejected by the guild, which declared that it had no interests in the case beyond its institutional obligations.[108]

Despite its efforts to prevent bankruptcies, the *consulado* still presided over them frequently; unfortunately, no source of data permits a long-term analysis of how frequently. One source did list the *juntas de acreedores* scheduled in front of the Cadiz tribunal for the period June 1787 through March 1791. During this forty-six month period, the *consulado* held at least 125 *concursos*, an average of 2.7 per month. References to another thirty-four sessions were undated but almost certainly occurred during this same period, increasing the total to 159, or nearly 3.5 per month.[109] Figure 4.3 illustrates the number of *consulado* bankruptcy proceedings for each month for the 125 cases in which dates were available.[110] There do not appear to be any significant trends in the data beyond the fact that many *concursos* took place during these years.

The individuals declaring bankruptcy during these months seem to have come from a variety of socioeconomic levels. Most prominent was the Conde de Repáraz, Juan Bautista Uztáriz, whose *concurso de acreedores* took place on 11 March 1786.[111] A matriculated member of the guild since 1755, the count operated one of the largest Spanish commercial firms, Uztáriz y Compañía, which began as an offshoot of the powerful Cinco Gremios de Madrid.[112] The proceedings of Francisco de Sierra, another prominent merchant, took place on 12 October 1787. Owners of several ships, Sierra and his father José had both entered the *consulado* in 1768. Sierra's October *concurso* was not his first. He had been forced to suspend payments back in the late spring of 1786 as well, much to the dismay of one of his London-based creditors.[113] The 1786 agreement had allowed Sierra to continue

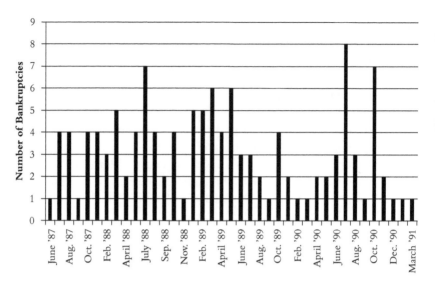

Figure 4.3. Number of Bankruptcy Proceedings Adjudicated by *Consulado* of Cadiz

SOURCE: AGI, *Consulados*, legajo 522, exp. 9, 1787–91, folios 892–1130.

conducting business, presumably with the anticipation that he could remedy his precarious financial condition if allowed to proceed. Indeed, in a February 1787 petition to obtain a license to outfit his ship, *La Nueva Paz*, for a voyage to Veracruz, Sierra noted that his creditors had "declar[ed] by general agreement that his arrears were the result of misfortune, and that they did not diminish his good faith . . . and as proof they left in his sole direction and care the collection and management of his debts."[114]

Many of the merchants who went bankrupt were members of the Cadiz *consulado*. In an effort to assess how many, the names of those for whom *concursos* were held were compared to Ruiz Rivera's list of matriculated *consulado* merchants.[115] It appears that bankruptcy proceedings for at least seventeen members of the Cadiz *consulado* took place in the period March 1786 through March 1791. These are displayed in Table 4.3.

Presumably, the majority of debtors appeared voluntarily before the *consulado*, undoubtedly desirous of preserving their honor by facing their creditors. Cooperation and the *concurso's* determination that the bankruptcy stemmed from bad luck might even win the individual some freedom to continue his dealings as occurred to Francisco de Sierra in 1786 or the Pueblan trader Joséf Carrillo in 1782. Some merchants forced to face their creditors were less compliant, or at least the authorities perceived them to be

TABLE 4.3

Bankrupted Merchants with Names Matching Consulado *Members*

Concurso Date	Name of Bankrupted	Name of *Consulado* Member	Matriculated
11 Mar 86	Conde de Repáraz	Juan Bautista Uztáriz	1755
22 Jun 87	Manuel Solsona	Manuel Solsona	1779
12 Oct 87	Francisco de Sierra	Francisco de Sierra	1768
17 Oct 87	Salvador Matheu	Salvador Mateu	1787
01 Jul 88	Manuel Laurel	Manuel José Laurel	1768
23 Jul 88	Jacinto Antonio Valdivieso	Jacinto Antonio Valdivioso	1774
17 Jan 89	Luis Costa	Luis Costas	1748
30 Mar 89	Joséph Feliz Canales	José Felix Canales	1750
12 May 89	Francisco de Pla y Mensa	Francisco Pla y Menza	1777
19 May 89	Juan Pedro Gazzo	Juan Gazo	1776
06 Jul 89	Joséph Guiaza	José Guiaza	1788
12 Sep 89	Martín Serra	Martín de Serra	1752
08 Oct 89	Matheo Rodríguez Sánchez	Mateo Rodríguez Sánchez	1784
22 Apr 90	Joséf Antonio Villora	José Antonio Villora	1775
14 Oct 90	Juan Estevan Lizardi	Juan Esteban de Lizardi	1770
?	Joséf Cerero	José Cerero	1769
?	Juan Oduyer	Juan Pablo Oduyer	1756

SOURCES: For columns 1–2, AGI, *Consulados*, legajo 522, exp. 9, folios 897–1130; for columns 3–4, Ruiz Rivera, *El Consulado de Cadiz*, 131–216.

greater flight risks. Juan Jardín was incarcerated in the royal prison prior to his *junta*.[116] It was likely to avoid similar fates that the debtors Joséph Cañelas and Joséph de Amores sought the protection of the church, the latter being listed as "secluded in the parochial church of Señor San Antonio."[117]

At least fourteen of the proceedings addressed bankruptcies occurring to specific ship voyages, most likely organized as partnerships, between captains and shipowners for example. On 10 July 1790, a *junta* met to review the records of the shipwrecked settee (*saetía*) *San Antonio de Padre*.[118] Shipwrecks, of course, occurred periodically and had no relation to the new commercial conditions. In contrast, the listings for the remaining thirteen *concursos* made no reference to navigational mishaps. On 29 June 1788, a *junta* examined the case of the frigate *El Principe de Asturias*, which had arrived from Honduras.[119] Similarly, the packet boat *La Purísima Concepción* entered bankruptcy proceedings on 24 March 1789 after its return from Havana.[120] The details surrounding these ships' bankruptcies are unspecified. Likely these were voyages that had failed financially and the proceedings were designed to ensure that creditors were at least partially compensated. Unfortunately, the documents listing these *concursos* contain only the names of the bankrupted, not any specifics about the cases.

The *consulado* oversaw 159 proceedings during the forty-six month period from June 1787 through March 1791. While this certainly sounds like a high figure, it is only meaningful in comparison to other time periods. The only other period for which similar lists were located was from January 1808 to March 1816, a ninety-nine month stretch. During this time, 106 bankruptcy proceedings (see Table 4.4) took place at the merchant guild, an average of just over one per month.[121] Clearly, there were far more bankruptcies in the much briefer period June 1787 to March 1791, leading one to imagine that this was a more financially volatile period.

The second decade of the nineteenth century, however, is not the ideal period to compare with the immediate post–free trade era. The argument put forth here is that commercial reform increased the riskiness of trade and contributed to the high incidence of bankruptcies in the 1780s and 1790s. Ideally, one would compare the proceedings with the period before 1778, which would help determine whether bankruptcies were less common during the pre-reform era. Using a different source, Antonio-Miguel Bernal was able to tally the number of bankruptcies adjudicated by the Council of Indies over a much longer period, from 1760 to 1799. Presumably, cases that reached the Council of Indies were extraordinary, as most bankruptcies would have been adequately addressed at lower bureaucratic levels, such as the tribunal of the *consulados*. As Bernal's data (Table 4.5) reveals, risk of bankruptcy always existed in long-distance trade, but there was a significant increase in the number of cases in the last two decades of the century. In the first two decades (1760s and 1770s), which correspond, for the most part, to the pre–free trade era, bankruptcies reached the Coun-

TABLE 4.4

Bankruptcy Proceedings in Front of Consulado: *1808 through March 1816*

Year	1808	1809	1810	1811	1812	1813	1814	1815	1816	Total
Number	13	7	3	10	13	19	24	12	5	106

SOURCE: Lista de los concursos que ha havido ante el tribunal de comercio desde el año de 1808, Cadiz, 5 April 1816, AGI, *Consulados*, legajo 522, folio 1131.

TABLE 4.5

Bankruptcies Brought in Front of the Council of Indies: 1760–99

Decade	1760–69	1770–79	1780–89	1790–99
Bankruptcies	34	43	64	113

SOURCE: Bernal, *Financiación de la Carrera de Indias*, 466.

cil of Indies infrequently, averaging 3.85 proceedings per year. In the 1780s, however, the annual average increased significantly to 6.4 and then rose to 11.3 in the 1790s.

The spike in the 1790s is partially attributable to the outbreak of the wars of the French Revolution and Napoleon, but, importantly, Bernal reports that the year of greatest incidence was the pre-war year of 1791 when twenty-four cases of bankruptcy reached the *Consejo* (Council of Indies). Unfortunately, Bernal does not provide annual figures, other than 1791, which precludes a closer temporal analysis. It would not be surprising, however, to discover that the bankruptcies clustered in the late 1780s and early 1790s.[122]

Certainly, the last years of the 1780s were remembered as a time during which many merchants declared bankruptcy. In the second decade of the nineteenth century the Conde de Maule, Nicolás de la Cruz y Bahamonde, recalled in his memoirs that "bankruptcies in '86 and '87 became so frequent in this plaza [of Cadiz], that their sum was believed to be twenty million pesos." Cruz y Bahamonde attributed the bankruptcies to the same factors as the critics in the *consulados*; with the end of the American Revolutionary War, markets in America were inundated with commodities and those merchants in Spain unlucky enough to have bought additional wares in 1785 were stuck with them. Unlike many of the *consulado* merchants, however, the count, who was decidedly pro–*comercio libre*, blamed the merchants who foolishly driven by "baseless greed felt compelled to solicit goods."[123]

Bankruptcies in these years also concerned contemporaries, who viewed their frequency as especially unusual and alarming. In December 1786, the Crown expressed growing distress with the number of financial failures, requesting the *consulado*'s opinion on the matter. In response to the Crown, a guild lawyer, Licenciado Juan de Mora y Morales, submitted a frank report that warned of "the ruin that might befall this commerce owing to the repeated bankruptcies." According to Mora y Morales, it was "undeniable" that Cadiz had suffered "scandalous" bankruptcies in the previous several years, threatening to tarnish the city's reputation, the "principal asset of any merchant body." He further expressed the widely embraced sentiment among the guild members that many of the bankruptcies stemmed from newer traders who, lacking sufficient personal funds, operated largely on borrowed capital. While they might possess "more or less feasible ideas and calculations," they could not weather the inevitable delays and were ultimately forced "to declare [what was] their original condition of insolvency." Mora y Morales distinguished between what he saw as "honorable" and "criminal" bankruptcies. The former entailed merchants who had at least partially invested their own funds and made "whatever sacrifice" necessary to meet their obligations. Other traders worked exclusively on borrowed capital, falsely passing themselves as men of means by "sustaining those external appearances that present the sharpest image." These swindlers only paid the creditors who pressured them the most, meeting their obligations by securing additional loans or "selling [merchandise] for cash for less than they have borrowed on credit," a Ponzi scheme of sorts. To protect the reputation of the mercantile community, the lawyer urged that bankruptcy laws be made less lenient, less predisposed to grant insolvent debtors generous moratoriums.[124] This report was produced about six months prior to the period corresponding to the list of the bankruptcy proceedings adjudicated by the *consulado* that was analyzed above. Clearly, the situation did not improve following Mora y Morales's report.

More than two years later the rash of bankruptcies had still not abated. In March 1789, representatives of the *consulado* lamented to the king that "never before has there been such repeated bankruptcies as in the present time nor more complicated litigations." Spain's commercial empire was at stake, they argued, for these bankruptcies "have introduced confusion in this commerce, and a general distrust among the individuals and the houses of commerce which are perceived in total discredit in Spain and foreign kingdoms." In reference to a previous communiqué, the *consulado* reiterated its belief that the king should establish a *lonja*, a public exchange where merchants could congregate and acquire better information about the "solidity" of Cadiz-based mercantile firms, both national and foreign. Reminiscent of Attorney Mora y Morales's 1786 report, the *consulado* also urged the king to introduce more clearly articulated bankruptcy laws, since insolvent merchants had come to expect generous treatment so long as their losses resulted from "unforeseen misfortunes or innocent mishaps."[125]

• • •

It is hard not to conclude that the slew of bankruptcies that began in 1780s was related to the implementation of commercial reform. Free trade unleashed a torrent of commercial activity as Crown officials liberally extended licenses to merchants to participate in the Indies trade. As experienced merchants had long warned, however, the growth in commerce resulted in the oversupply of markets. *Comercio libre* offered more and more merchants the opportunity to outfit ships or purchase cargo, perhaps leveraging themselves heavily to do so. When prices for their commodities plummeted, the result of rising competition, many, unsurprisingly, proved unable to repay their debts. Within several years of the end of the War of the American Revolution, merchants in Cadiz and America began declaring bankruptcy at unprecedented rates, much to the concern of the mercantile community. The dismantling of the traditional trade institutions reduced the predictability of what was already a highly uncertain business. The result was the escalation of risk and the rise of commercial failures.

Importantly, commercial difficulties were not exclusive to Cadiz; in the mid-1780s and after, bankruptcies began mounting in other Spanish ports as well. Delgado Ribas counted sixty-three Catalán firms that declared insolvency between 1785 and 1790 of which 62 percent (thirty-nine firms) were mercantile. Thirty-one of these establishments were totally ruined; only eight survived.[126] *Comercio libre* was designed to open trade to smaller merchants and new ports, to break the monopoly enjoyed by the *consulado* merchants of Cadiz. Bourbon reformers argued that the traditional merchants were pampered and inefficient, accustomed, to repeat the words of Revillagigedo, to earning "a large return on their money . . . without caution, without calculation, and without risks." These monopolists would be replaced by "new speculators of lesser means but greater knowledge of the new methods of trade and less accustomed to excessive earnings with a perfect security and tranquility."[127] Clearly, the reformers had oversimplified reality; the traditional merchants had never operated under conditions free of risk. Risk had been managed, but not eliminated, through the existing institutions that the reformers had targeted. In the newly unregulated trade environment, merchants, including the traders who reform was designed to benefit, encountered unfettered competition and an unbearably risky environment. There should be no surprise that so many traders failed.

Free Trade's Silver Lining

With the dismantling of *comercio libre* and the institutional practices that had long lessened the uncertainty of commerce, many merchants went bankrupt; but trade reform did accomplish many of the other goals envisioned by the Crown. For one, liberalization of trade expanded substantially Spain's imports and exports. While the figures remain deeply debated, the most reliable estimates suggest that imperial trade increased by 50 to 100 percent in the decade of peace, 1783–93.[128] Furthermore, reform opened colonial trade to merchants of greater socioeconomic diversity, and in doing so it created a more "enlightened" or "egalitarian" commercial system, increasing competition within the empire. Increased trade also brought about a notable rise in tax collections, one of the principal goals of the Bourbon reformers.[129] While Spanish industry as a whole did not enjoy the spurt of development for which reformers had wished, evidence does suggest that the growth in exports benefitted the burgeoning textile industry of Catalonia.[130]

While it seems unlikely that Crown officials anticipated that reform would effect so much financial turmoil, even the bankruptcies that so horrified the traditional commercial elites might be interpreted as a sign that the reforms were indeed working, that rising competition was pushing less-efficient traders out of the market. Had the market enjoyed more time to adjust to the reforms and to reach a new equilibrium, then the result might have been a more economically efficient commercial structure. In the event, the era of wars that began in 1793 ended the commercial boom, making any longer-term historical assessment difficult.

The primary cause of bankruptcies during the decade of the 1780s was the oversupply of American markets. Even market saturation, however, could be interpreted as having had the potential to bring about positive change. While the traders who entered the market only to see their ventures fail were distressed, the flooding of markets naturally drove prices down to the benefit of consumers. If one of the reformers' goals was to increase consumption in the colonies in order to stimulate Iberian manufacturing, then lower commodity prices were an obvious incentive. It seems doubtful, however, that lower prices alone would have increased sufficiently the number of colonial consumers. Profound socioeconomic and other structural obstacles, not to mention cultural ones, limited consumption in America to a small percentage of the population, an issue addressed in the following chapter.

The experiment with reform was resolutely interrupted with the return of war in 1793. For the next several decades, Atlantic world commerce was hindered by the disruptions of war. With time, the 1778 reforms might have accomplished all of the reformers' goals and ushered in a genuinely "golden era," but the post-1793 hostilities squelched any hopes of success.[131] Nor did the defeat of Napoleon revive Spanish commerce; revolutions in America continued the turmoil. In summary, there might have been some reason to be optimistic that the reforms would ultimately have produced a healthier and more buoyant Spanish imperial trade, but in fact, Spanish commerce never regained the stability of the pre-1778 era.

This chapter has proposed the thesis that the 1778 reforms dismantled commercial institutions that had managed to reduce risk and uncertainty.

The regulated commerce of the pre-reform era had succeeded in moving cargo throughout the Spanish Atlantic world for more than two hundred years. Free trade had the potential to expand trade, increase competition, and raise tax revenues, but under the new commercial environment, the uncertainty of trade grew dramatically. The traditional economic institutions had long provided an environment more propitious to long-distance trade under conditions of limited information and associated uncertainties. Their undoing provoked distortions to which the market failed to adjust before the commercially devastating wars erupted in 1793.

Chapter 5

The Rising Demand for Credit
and the Escalation of Risk
in the Post-1778 Era

Credit in Atlantic World Commerce

Free trade terminated the practice of balancing exports with expected consumption. Instead reformers desired the market to set an equilibrium supply and price and thus began liberally granting licenses to trade. But early modern long-distance markets could not respond rapidly to changing conditions. Oversupply of colonial markets and rising competition in the Indies trade increased risk to unprecedented levels, causing widespread bankruptcies within the commercial community.

Increasing supplies in colonial markets caused a general decline in the prices of imported goods which, according to classical economic theory, should have brought about a corresponding rise in demand, since imported articles became more affordable to local populations. Merchants might have been able to compensate for the lower prices, relative to those that the *Carrera de Indias* had generated, with a higher volume of sales. But expanding the market of consumers in America was not easily accomplished. Indeed, the glut of imports that occurred everywhere after 1783 resulted, in part, from the shallowness of colonial markets, the small percentage of populations adequately integrated into the market for European imports; at least this was one contemporary diagnosis. An anonymous detractor to *comercio libre* pointed to the paradox that while virtually every peninsular consumed at least some quantity of imports from the colonies, barely one-third of Americans were consumers of European wares.[1]

Low per capita consumption was partially due to the fact that the vast majority of Spanish America's inhabitants were part of the colonized underclass, economically and politically marginalized by colonial legal, political, and economic institutions. The colonies' masses consisted largely of subsistence peasants, slaves, and urban *castas* (free black and multiracial populations), whose poverty hardly made them a promising consumer class to drive Spain's economy, despite the wishes of reformers. To overcome the profound structural obstacles to the creation of a large consuming class would have required far greater reform than merely reduced prices, and obviously such redistributive policies would have been unthinkable to Crown policymakers, not to mention Creole elites.

The majority of Spanish Americans simply did not participate enough in the market to consume the large quantities of imported goods that *comercio libre* had unleashed. Adding to the structural obstacles, one can also point to the heavy fiscal burden born by Mexico's population, the largest and richest of the eighteenth-century Spanish colonies, a tax burden almost certainly comparable elsewhere in Spanish America. Carlos Marichal discovered that "colonial Mexicans paid perhaps ten times more per capita than taxpayers in the thirteen colonies." Perhaps even more relevant here, he noted that the tax system placed a particularly harsh burden on the low-income earning indigenous people. He posited that at the close of the eighteenth century, the "average working family" earned about sixty pesos per year yet paid eight pesos in taxes, "close to 15 percent of their extremely limited income."[2] Much of the potential disposable income of poorer Mexicans, then, was absorbed by the Royal treasury in the form of tribute and other taxes. Certainly, these impoverished peasants were in no position to absorb the growing quantities of European imports, and this assumes that they would have wanted them had they had greater disposable income.

• • •

In his 1793 treatise on *comercio libre,* Viceroy Revillagigedo of Mexico also complained about the colony's paltry consumption. In the previous several years, according to the viceroy, the average value of Mexico's annual imports had been thirteen to fourteen million pesos which, based on his estimate of the colony's population of around 3.5 million inhabitants, indicated a per capita import consumption of only four pesos. According to Revillagigedo, this level of consumption was far too low and should have been triple or quadruple this "very disgraceful quantity." He attributed low demand to a dozen factors, among them suppliers' inadequate attention to the tastes of consumers, elevated prices caused by steep taxes and poor roads, New Spain's lack of specie, and, in reference to the recently banned *repartimiento de bienes* (trade on credit between government functionaries and indigenous people),[3] the fact that Mexico's indigenous population was "accustomed to tak[ing] everything on credit and in advance," which he attributed to "custom [which] has much power over people, and especially the ignorant, in which category are the Indians."[4] Regarding this last point, the viceroy touched on an important issue, although his subsequent explanation fell back on the racism of the dominant Spaniards. Consumption in the colonies depended greatly on access to credit, without which many Americans remained outside the circle of potential consumers.

But it was not only the poor whose access to funds was limited; indeed, a major obstacle to greater consumption was the heavy reliance on credit of virtually all social groups in Mexico and other corners of the empire. Mexico's urban Spanish population, who consumed the majority of the imported items, relied on credit to afford luxury goods.[5] Marie Francois has shown that "middle-class" women of Spanish descent in Mexico City regularly pawned their personal belongings to allow themselves to afford the consumption of even small-valued items, part of their strategy of running their households and maintaining appearances appropriate to their perceived class status.[6] In the silver-rich city of Potosí as well, elites pawned their belongings to enlarge their capacity to consume, according to Jane Mangan.[7] The problem observed by Viceroy Revillagigedo was not simply that Mexicans consumed too little; rather, too few Mexicans participated extensively in the market for imports, at least without access to credit. Mexico's market was too shallow, a reflection of the colony's grossly unequal distribution of wealth. At the very least, the circulation of commodities in the colony depended on the flow of credit.

· · ·

Reliance on credit, of course, was widespread throughout the mercantile world, and nor was this unique to the Spanish empire. All merchants, no matter how wealthy, depended to a significant degree on credit to expand and facilitate their trade. At every level, its availability was one of the central factors determining the circulation of commodities. Merchants were constantly borrowing or lending capital to facilitate the extension of their businesses. And consumers' access to credit determined their levels of consumption. Historians of colonial Spanish America have long attributed the heavy reliance on credit to the shortage of specie. Brading, for instance, has noted that most silver minted in Mexico was quickly exported, and no alternative medium circulated widely. "The inevitable result of this situation was an almost universal reliance upon credit transactions."[8] A shortage of specie was undeniable, but the demand for credit had much deeper roots; credit augmented consumption and permitted traders to expand their business ventures. Even in modern economies with more than ample money supplies, credit is universal and instrumental.

Much of the merchandise shipped from Spain to America was acquired originally by the Spanish exporters on credit. As Stein and Stein argue, the Spanish *flotistas* were often no more than front men, *prestanombres*, for foreign commercial firms operating in Cadiz. Because commercial restrictions barred foreigners from direct participation in the Indies trade, European trading houses supplied Spanish commission merchants with merchandise on credit to transport to America for sale.[9]

To reduce the need to be constantly paying debts in specie, a burdensome requirement that would have greatly reduced the volumes of commerce, merchants depended on short-term commercial credit to allow their businesses to run more smoothly. One main credit instrument of merchants throughout the Atlantic world was the letter of credit, the *libranza*.[10] Letters of credit allowed merchants to draw funds from a commercial house with whom they enjoyed a relationship against their expected revenues from future sales. For example, Cadiz merchant Francisco de Sierra conducted most of his London business through the commissions house of Hananel and Jacob Mendes da Costa. When Sierra delivered a portion of cochineal or another commodity to the Mendes da Costas for sale in Great Britain, he might simultaneously repay a debt to another merchant by issuing a *libranza* drawn against his anticipated credit with the London commissions house from the sale of his dyestuff. This *libranza*, essentially a check, would then be presented to Mendes da Costa for payment. Mendes da Costa, in turn, had the option of accepting or rejecting it. If accepted and paid, Sierra's account was debited for the amount drawn.[11] Such credit was critical to allow Sierra to augment his business. Without such credit, he would have had to wait for the completion of one deal before he initiated another.

Commercial houses, of course, preferred to limit the credit drawn against them because they too operated with a finite supply of resources. The solidity of their businesses depended on their ability to pay their debts promptly, and any sense that illiquidity might make meeting obligations difficult could send rumors of the house's debility flying throughout the commercial world. As a result, commercial houses were cautious not to extend to merchants excessive lines of credit. Houses expressly advised their clients the amounts that they could draw. In March 1784, for example, Hananel and Jacob Mendes da Costa politely informed Sierra how much they would allow him to draw against the "six barrels of cochineal and four zurrones of indigo" that he had recently shipped to them. "We thank you for your willingness to draw much less than the value of your shipments, but surely you should not hesitate to draw up to ¾ of the value of the goods sent to us."[12] This line of credit allowed Sierra funds to buy additional commodities with which to transact. At the same time, Mendes da Costa felt secure that with the dyestuffs in its possession, acting as collateral in essence, there was little danger of Sierra defaulting.

Sierra also obtained credit to facilitate his purchase of manufactured commodities. One line of Sierra's business entailed the acquisition of textiles in European markets for sale throughout the Spanish empire. In the very same letter that Mendes da Costa granted Sierra the allowance to draw against his deposited goods, the house informed him that while "impossible to concede you a term of nine months for the clothing that you have ordered, we confirm that we will give you a two-month term for ⅓ and for the [remaining] ⅔ it will be necessary to charge you at the time you submit the order."[13] For Sierra and other merchants, business entailed a constant balancing act to maintain and even extend their access to credit.

Sierra depended heavily on additional sources of credit as well. One common transatlantic credit arrangement upon which merchants relied to supplement their own resources, although one that was declining in the late eighteenth century, was the sea loan, variations of which had existed in Europe for hundreds of years. Sea loans differed from typical mercantile loans because the lender also assumed responsibility for the riskiness of the sea voyage. In the typical sea loan, a long-distance merchant obtained capital from a creditor at an interest rate higher than the "market rate" of money. The high interest rate, however, included a risk premium, an additional charge that effectively shifted the risk of the voyage from the borrower to the lender. Once in possession of the loan, the borrower proceeded to organize his business venture as would any merchant. If, however, the venture were to fail as a consequence of the risks of the sea (piracy, shipwrecks, etc.), the borrower was not required to repay the loan because the lender had assumed responsibility for such risks. The appeal of a sea loan was that it reduced the riskiness of what was an exceptionally risky business by passing transportation risks to the lender. As was customary in such loans, the borrower was usually required to repay the loan shortly after arriving safely in port, since by then the risks of sea had expired.[14] Sea loans grew less common by the last quarter of the eighteenth century as merchants increasingly secured loans and maritime insurance separately.[15]

Before they largely disappeared, merchants turned to sea loans to acquire enormous capital investments. To finance his many business dealings in the years 1774, 1776, 1778, and 1782, Francisco de Sierra took sea loans totaling almost 480,000 pesos, borrowing nearly 285,000 pesos in 1774 alone. In 1776, the year of the final *flota* to Mexico, Cadiz merchants as a whole borrowed nearly 17 million pesos, entering deeply into debt to finance their acquisition and transportation of commodities. Many individuals secured small loans but some borrowed fortunes. M. Garcia borrowed 300,339 pesos; L. Asunsolo took out 343,485 pesos in sea loans; F. Estévanez was lent 248,654 pesos; M. Fernandez Rabago received just over 244,000; R. L. Laiglesia borrowed 357,132 pesos; A. Sáenz Santa Maria secured loans in the amount of 237,408 pesos; and Ustáriz y Compañía borrowed 295,622. Many others took on debts in excess of 100,000 pesos. In short, Cadiz merchants borrowed heavily to finance their overseas commercial ventures.[16]

While some merchants borrowed capital to purchase merchandise and finance their shipments, others obtained their commodities by becoming financiers, extending production loans to producers. In fact, the ability to secure export commodities was often contingent on the provision of credit; those merchants unable to finance production could not easily acquire such products.[17] Cochineal dye was obtained primarily through the provision of financing to producers. Operating through the *repartimientos* of the *alcaldes mayores* (district magistrates) of Oaxaca, the merchants of Mexico City acquired cochineal for export from indigenous Oaxacan producers. The *alcaldes mayores* advanced money to cochineal producers who repaid their debts at harvest time in finished dye. Had it not been for this production credit, output of this major export commodity would have been far lower.[18] Similarly, Mexican merchants financed the production of sugar, which was subsequently exported. Wealthy merchants from Mexico City advanced credit against the sugar harvests of Cuernavaca haciendas. By the turn of the nineteenth century, Mexico's sugar exports had become sizeable.[19] Merchant-planters in rural Veracruz loaned production funds to small-scale tobacco farmers. Even the Crown became creditor to tobacco producers through the Royal tobacco monopoly, the *estanco*, which loaned production funds to some of the larger tobacco growers of Veracruz.[20] Of course, the silver that was exported to pay for so much of the colony's imports was greatly dependent on the finances of the mercantile elites as well. Miners turned to *aviadores* (financiers), usually local merchants, to help finance their production. The *aviadores*, in turn, depended on the *almaceneros* of the Mexico City *consulado* for credit. It was due to their extension of credit to producers that the Mexico City merchants obtained much of the silver that they used to trade.[21] In other colonies, export merchants obtained different items through the extension of credit. In the Kingdom of Guatemala, for example, merchants secured silver and, especially, indigo by advancing credit to miners and planters to be repaid later in kind.[22]

The Mexico City merchant Juan Fernando Meoqui noted that during the era of flotas the cycle of credit in the colony began at the *feria de Jalapa*. The *almaceneros*, the wholesale merchants of Mexico who paid cash for large quantities of imports, immediately made medium-sized sales of merchandise on credit to merchants "*de tierra adentro,*" smaller merchants who operated in provincial towns.[23] The wholesalers also advanced small portions on credit to the northern miners and to haciendas throughout the colony, for which they were often repaid later in kind.[24] Retail shops in the cities and in the countryside secured imported commodities on credit from the *almaceneros* as well. Stein found that provincial storekeepers rarely invested much of their own capital but instead stocked their shelves with merchandise financed by well-to-do merchants who took a share of the profits.[25] The importance of credit for storekeepers in Michoacán, Mexico, was demonstrated by Silva Riquer.[26] For the viceroyalty of Río de la Plata, Socolow found similar practices in retail establishments.[27] Additional merchandise was distributed by the wholesalers to traveling salesmen, *viandantes*, who obtained "considerable merchandise on the strength of their word . . . . 'spending two years in traveling and the collection of sales made.'"[28] Kicza found that these peddlers often entered into year-long contracts with merchants who provided items on credit in exchange for a share of any profit generated. These itinerant merchants, in turn, ventured into rural areas selling their stock, undoubtedly extending credit themselves.[29]

Still, additional imported merchandise was dispensed to regional markets through the relations that the great merchants established with *alcaldes mayores*, Spanish district magistrates. These Spanish officials represented the Crown in indigenous areas of Spanish America but also entered into commercial partnerships with the *consulado* merchants, trading with the Indians on the latter's behalf. The *almaceneros* advanced the *alcaldes mayores* the funds and commodities that they needed to trade with the peasantry of their districts, splitting the profits at some predetermined ratio.[30] A typical example is provided by the 1782 case of Manuel Ramón de Goya, a prominent Mexico City merchant who established a partnership with the entering district magistrate of Zimatlán, Oaxaca, Ildefonso María Sánchez Solache. The agreement required that Goya furnish sixty to seventy thousand pesos' worth of cash and merchandise, which Solache was to distribute, on credit, to the indigenous population. The *alcalde mayor* invested none of his own resources into the company but shared in the profits as compensation for his labor.[31]

Credit was even critical at the most local level. To sell their merchandise, storekeepers and marketplace vendors regularly extended credit to consumers. According to R. Douglas Cope, credit was instrumental to the economy of Mexico City's *castas*. "Petty commerce could not function on a cash-and-carry basis; credit was the essential lubricant of the economic system, even at the simplest level, such as the purchase of bread, clothing and other necessities."[32] An identical reliance on credit was illustrated by Jane Mangan for the marketplace of colonial Potosí. Storekeepers and market women provided credit widely to their regular customers, without which many would have been unable to subsist.[33]

Credit greased the wheels of Atlantic world commerce, from the high-value endeavors of merchants in principal Atlantic ports to the sale of foodstuffs in the marketplaces of Potosí or Mexico City. The livelihood and success of a business person was closely associated with the ability both to obtain and dispense credit. Most merchants carried much of their wealth in the form of *dependencias activas*, accounts receivable. Referring to New Spain's capital, Kicza found that "a major part of the total value of commercial establishments of every size and character in the City consisted of *dependencias activas*, the collective debts of the many customers compelled to buy on credit."[34] Examining the surviving property inventories of the Guatemalan merchant Juan Fermín de Aycinena, Richmond Brown was especially struck by "the proportion of Aycinena's wealth represented as dependencies, or outstanding debts due him."[35] One draws the same conclusion from the records of Mexican *almacenero* Francisco Ignacio de Yraeta. Yraeta financed much of the merchandise that he sold, whether to other merchants, landowners, or miners. Undoubtedly exaggerating his plight, but reflecting his frustration by the need to always provide credit, Yraeta complained in 1778, "I have no money" because "it's necessary to advance funds to the hacenderos for their acquisitions, with not a little bit of risk."[36] The centrality of credit was by no means unique to the late colonial period. Hoberman's analysis of the inventories of twenty merchants of the seventeenth century revealed that 46 percent of their assets consisted of debts outstanding.[37]

Merchants who extended considerable amounts of credit were invariably recipients as well, borrowing funds from the church or other merchants. The same merchants' inventories that revealed large accounts receivable also showed substantial sums due to creditors, outstanding debts to other merchants. Thus the traders examined by Hoberman were also heavily indebted, owing amounts equal to 34 percent of total assets.[38] Between 1768 and 1796, Juan Fermín de Aycinena's debts ranged from 15 to 20 percent of his total assets. Aycinena was probably the wealthiest man in the Kingdom of Guatemala but still relied heavily on borrowed funds.[39]

Credit and Reputation

Access to credit, one factor that determined the extent of a merchant's trading empire, required that he maintain a good reputation.[40] According to Adelman, "reputation was not simply important; it was everything."[41] Business circles at the highest echelons were relatively small and impressions about a particular merchant's creditworthiness spread quickly. In 1773 trader Juan Antonio de Llano explained to Viceroy Antonio María de Bucareli of Mexico the importance of a merchant's reputation. The "principal fund" in commerce, he wrote, "consists of the reputation of its individuals without which it could not be sustained in any way; therefore this quality is highly esteemed among [merchants], as they know by experience that it alone without any other resource has enough power to consummate the most attractive contracts and unify the interests of merchants to a common goal in even the crudest ventures."[42]

Merchants thus sought to protect their reputations, to maintain good public images. When in 1803 Pedro Antonio de Aguirre and the brothers Joséf and Juan Bautista de Vea Murguía entered into a trade partnership with one another, they felt compelled to stress that payment of all their debts was a sacrosanct responsibility, since, as they affirmed in their company charter, "the greatest treasure of any commercial house consists of the good opinion and conduct of its associates."[43]

Reputation was closely associated with honor. In his didactic treatise on mercantile best practices written in 1818, purportedly, for the benefit of his son, a young and aspiring merchant, the Catalán trader Pedro Mártir Coll y Alsina advised always to be truthful and accurate in correspondence. Not only would this yield "utility," he counseled, "but also and importantly for the integrity and honor that the person [the author] will acquire; which is most esteemed in this world, and to which all Christians should aspire."[44]

In 1802 Cadiz *consulado* merchant Juan Vicente de Marticorena faced the possibility that he might need to approach the tribunal and request a moratorium on his debts, temporary relief from the pressures of his creditors. He wrote confidentially to a friend: "my sorrow and feelings for what is happening to me is the most painful thing that can occur to a man who wants to live and work as a Christian."[45] For Marticorena, the financial problems called into question his virtue and his status as an honorable Christian, which echoes the sentiments of Mártir Coll y Alsina.[46] His finances had been dire for at least five years prior, but he had somehow managed to survive with his good reputation more or less intact. This untarnished reputation was critical for Marticorena because it granted him access to lines of credit without which he would certainly have gone bankrupt. A low point was in July 1798 when Marticorena had the bad fortune of having a large number of his debts become due simultaneously, and he was neither able to pay them directly nor find a creditor against whom he could draw the funds. Marticorena assumed that his situation would explode, that news of his debts would travel "mouth to mouth which will ruin us, and those who until now view us with some consideration will pressure us more and more." Miraculously, Marticorena avoided the fate that befell his cousin and very own assistant, Pedro Fermín de Córdoba, who informed his superior in September 1798 that "they have placed an embargo on my personal effects in my own room."[47] Marticorena survived, but, ironically, his primary creditor, the Spanish commercial house of Viuda de Oviedo, Hermano e Hijos, failed to elude such misfortune, declaring bankruptcy, apparently in part because of the many letters of credit that the firm had allowed Marticorena to draw against it. For several years before its collapse, the director of Casa de Viuda de Oviedo, Hermano e Hijos had been attempting to collect from Marticorena some of his outstanding debts, on one occasion declaring "it is imperative that you search for and send us money so that we do not drown. . . . [T]o be frank in maintaining your credit and good reputation, you have pawned ours."[48]

Luckily for Marticorena, he avoided the revelation of his financial difficulties, which allowed him to continue scraping by with the hope of a better future. Marticorena kept his predicament closely concealed because as long as the mercantile community remained ignorant, he could continue his dealings, his reputation intact. Merchants' inclinations to conceal financial problems were emphasized by *consulado* member Antonio de Vicuña y Goenaga in 1787, a moment of great uncertainty in Spanish imperial trade. Merchants had lost great sums in the previous several years as demonstrated by the many bankruptcies, he commented, "and the total [loss] has not been disclosed since everyone hides in his heart what he has suffered without revealing it."[49] It was more than pride that inspired secrecy; more important was reputation.

For merchants who did go bankrupt, an obvious sign of decreased creditworthiness, some honor might nonetheless be salvaged if the insolvency was proven to be the result of events beyond the control of the subject— acts of God or simply unavoidable misfortune. Cadiz merchant Mariano Bernabe de Frías suffered a painful bankruptcy in 1786 but was absolved of any malfeasance by four tribunals and the Council of Indies. In a 1791 letter to the king, Bernabe de Frías undoubtedly took pride in proclaiming that despite his financial woes, "my honor [remains] uncorrupted."[50]

Another Cadiz merchant, Mateo Bernal, resisted the efforts of his creditors to embargo his assets for nonpayment of obligations. In a letter requesting that the king intercede on his behalf out of "paternal love," Bernal explained that he had combated his creditors' efforts because he believed that an embargo of his belongings would stain his honor and that this would "ruin his credit."[51] Of course, Bernal's creditworthiness was already suspect, but it is revealing that he couched his argument in terms of protecting his honor.

Reputation was so critical that merchants sometimes preferred to lose money than to be associated with a merchant or firm facing financial difficulties, a scenario that might cast doubts about their own financial condition. When Bernabe de Frías declared bankruptcy, Carlos Malagamba, to whom Bernabe de Frías owed funds, requested that the syndicate exclude him from the list of creditors. Apparently Malagamba's own finances were precarious, and he feared that the mere mention of his name in connection to a potentially uncollectible debt from Frías could cause panic among his own creditors who might then pressure him more severely or cut him off altogether. As Bernabe de Frías's attorney later noted about Malagamba, "it was less prejudicial for him to lose his share than to be mentioned in the bankruptcy given that his reputation was hanging in the balance in the plaza."[52] Reputations were fragile.

Malagamba was not alone in his conviction that it was better to forego certain profits than risk injuring a good reputation. In 1778, Ignacio Xavier Yanze wrote from Cadiz to his partner in Montevideo, Juan José

Puch, instructing him to temporarily withhold a shipment that he was scheduled to send to Yanze in Spain. In the eyes of Yanze, the business climate was too unpredictable due to the imminent introduction of free trade. While Yanze admitted that his decision would likely prevent them from profiting from a quick sale and might even require them to pay their creditors late, he argued that it was still better than taking unknown risks. From this strategy, Yanze predicted, "our greater creditworthiness will result, and credit comes before all else; I value it more than any profits that could result."[53]

In commercial networks of the Atlantic world, merchants' reputations were interconnected. In early 1785, the commercial empire of Cadiz merchant Francisco de Sierra teetered on the brink of failure as he proved increasingly unable to balance his accounts. Facing severe illiquidity, Sierra was forced to reject several letters of credit that his principal international creditors, the London house of Hananel and Jacob Mendes da Costa and Company and Amsterdam-based Echenique Sánchez and Company, tried to draw against him. Apparently, Sierra owed both houses considerable sums that would have been reduced upon his payment in Cadiz of the letters drawn against him. Sierra's rejection of these notes suggested to both of these commercial houses that his finances were sufficiently precarious that he neither had the money to pay nor positive balances with another commercial against which he could draw. But equally troubling to these English and Dutch houses was the potential impact on their own reputations if news circulated that their letters had been rejected, the possibility that Sierra had lost faith in them and had rejected their attempts to withdraw money from him that he neither owed them nor trusted that they would be able later to repay. To protect its standing, Mendes da Costa of London wrote a sharply worded missive to Sierra urging him to act honorably. The letter began by suggesting the possibility that Sierra's refusal to pay the note had been a misunderstanding or a clerical error since Mendes da Costa believed that Sierra "would not have committed such a dishonor." But, if such refusals persisted, Mendes da Costa threatened to reveal publicly Sierra's financial troubles: "You will see the damage that will necessarily be done to you if it were to be divulged that you did not meet your payments, and it will be necessary that this occur to justify our reputation in Cadiz, so that it does not enter the minds of our friends that our letters have been rejected because we are drawing on nothing."[54]

While the house of Mendes da Costa threatened to expose Sierra, the reality was a bit more complicated. On 8 March, after several additional letters had been rejected by Sierra, the London firm advised Sierra that "we are persuaded that if it were divulged, you would not be able to re-store your good reputation. Attentive to the friendship that we profess for you, we will guard your secret and continue to do so unless forced to publicize it in our own defense."[55] What seemed like a noble gesture on the part of the London firm actually had ulterior motives. Mendes da Costa preferred to keep the issue as secret as possible since its own reputa-tion could not help but be damaged by close association with a large, fi-nancially troubled merchant like Sierra. Furthermore, if Sierra were to go bankrupt, the hope of ever collecting his outstanding debts would have been greatly reduced. Protecting his reputation increased the likelihood that he would survive financially and that Mendes da Costa would ulti-mately collect its funds. Last, as would soon become clear, the London house might not have been so financially secure itself. Indeed, in April, only one month later, Mendes da Costa and Company wrote to Sierra that an embargo had been placed on the commercial house's trade by a local merchant. The proceeding, the letter claimed, was driven by politics and the jealousy that certain local firms directed towards the successes of Mendes da Costa. Unstated was the possibility that the actions directed at Mendes da Costa were inspired by the fact that the firm's principals were Portuguese Jews, making them more vulnerable to idle or even false gos-sip.[56] Presumably, this letter was sent to all of Mendes da Costa's clients with the hope of limiting the damage to its reputation. Indeed, just three days later a "junta of our creditors" met and deemed the firm in healthy enough financial condition to continue its operations.[57] Beneath the surface, how-ever, it seems possible that the crisis affecting the London firm had been precipitated or, at the very least, exacerbated by Sierra's financial woes.

Sierra continued throughout the month to refuse letters drawn against him by the Hananel and Jacob Mendes da Costa and Company, leading the latter to protest: "we do not see by what means you can justify your-self."[58] Months went by without word from Francisco de Sierra.[59] But the greatest shock reached Mendes da Costa and Company the following year. In June 1786 news arrived to London that Sierra's commercial operations had been halted. The reverberations of Sierra's predicament could not help but be felt in London. The house of Mendes da Costa wrote:

> It is impossible to express the mortification that the news of your em-
> bargo gave us as much due to the friendship that we profess for you as for
> the interest in which we find ourselves entangled. It is obvious that the
> loss is extremely painful for us and we never imagined that after such a
> sincere friendship you would have left unpaid such a considerable sum,

especially knowing that our misfortune and our embargo last year
originated from you having protested our letters.[60]

As the above relationship demonstrated, a merchant had to be cautious
with whom he associated or conducted business. One was judged by one's
friends and could not easily escape their financial difficulties. Surrounding
oneself with honorable community members and well-respected businessmen served to reinforce one's reputation. This is, at least, one reason why
merchants sought membership in the *consulado*. Affiliation with the guild
offered a merchant legitimacy, connection with an organization whose
members were the elite traders, almost like an accreditation agency.[61] The
consulado also served as an unofficial clearing house for information about
other merchants. Indeed, in 1789 senior guild officials petitioned the king
to establish a new *lonja*, a meeting place specifically designed for merchants
to exchange information.[62] Even without formal status, the chambers of
the *consulado* inevitably became a central location where business was conducted and rumors circulated. The perceived character of a merchant
might easily be soiled if the rumors were disparaging.

On New Year's Day, 1798, Pedro Fermín de Córdoba, the assistant to
Cadiz merchant Juan Vicente de Marticorena, alarmed his employer by
announcing that he had heard gossip that a list was circulating around the
consulado containing the names of the "many who are going to go bankrupt." Such a rumor caused Marticorena no small amount of consternation as he feared that his own name might appear given the financial
straits in which he found himself at the time.[63] If the list truly existed,
Marticorena was not identified, but rumors were again circulating eleven
months later during the week before Christmas. Fermín wrote to Marticorena that two traders, Sáenz Pardo and Ochoa de Sevilla, had declared
bankruptcy, and that "everyone is calling in his funds," adding, "they
have assured me of a list going around of those who are about to go bankrupt." Of immediate concern for Marticorena was the possibility that a
sizeable letter of credit that he had recently drawn against a firm might be
rejected due to murmurings about his financial state. Indeed, Fermín
noted delicately that "they might be talking a bit about your grace."[64]

A good reputation was always of importance to a merchant, but never
more than when his financial condition was insecure. For one, his positive
reputation could gain him the credit that he needed to weather short-term
financial instability. Even if a merchant were unable to garner additional
credit, good standing might at the very least buy him additional time to
make good on his obligations.[65] Reputation mattered; a merchant's ability

to access credit and manage his business dealings depended on the public perception that he was upstanding and honorable, an easily changeable condition.

Extending Credit, Incurring Risks

The sensitivity of merchants to reputation was well-founded. To operate his business smoothly, a merchant needed to provide credit to consumers and receive credit from other traders. It was thus imperative for merchants both to judge shrewdly the character of others—to determine whether they were sufficiently honorable and solvent to meet financial obligations and stay current on the payment of debts—and to maintain their reputations unblemished to guarantee themselves continued access to credit, the lifeblood of their commerce. These tasks were interrelated. A merchant's ability to pay his creditors and maintain his honor depended on his ability to collect his own debts. Again, the near failure of the London commercial house of Hananel and Jacob Mendes da Costa and Company, which was precipitated by its inability to collect from Francisco de Sierra, revealed the interconnectedness of accounts receivable and accounts payable.

No matter how carefully a merchant transacted his business, however, he inevitably extended some credit that was difficult or even impossible to recover. Avoiding bad debt altogether was not possible; over time, the extension of credit inevitably resulted in the loss of some portion of capital. Succeeding in the world of commerce depended on limiting the size of those bad debts. Even when loans proved collectible, they were often repaid late, especially in the case of long-distance trade in which myriad factors could force delays. The greater risk, however, was that debtors might default altogether, never repaying their obligations. Creditors recognized that some percentage of their loans would ultimately prove uncollectable. It was an unavoidable cost of doing business.

The management of one's business entailed maintaining an often precarious balance between credits and debts. The need to provide credit meant that a merchant benefited from having sufficient capital to permit him to trade even when he had large portions of his investments tied up in accounts receivable, outstanding debts. For this reason, merchants with deeper pockets enjoyed a comparative advantage over less well-capitalized traders. To succeed in business, Mexican merchant Francisco Ignacio de Yraeta explained to a business partner in 1778, "one needs three sums, one to have encumbered (*embromado*) here, one for the shipments to Cadiz, and one to attend to the business of the company."[66]

Clearly it would have been greatly in the interests of merchants to avoid the need to finance their sales, to reduce their exposure to the endemic risk of default. Not only would they have gained by lowering the losses from uncollectible debts, but they would also have avoided the significant costs arising from having their capital tied up for lengthy periods during which time they failed to earn interest. Most often sales were made interest-free, at least no rate was indicated, although buyers probably paid more to receive goods on credit than they would have had they paid cash.[67] The point, though, is that there were no penalties for repaying late; creditors' capital remained inaccessible in the interim.[68]

Refraining from extending credit was desirable but not practical. In the charter created upon the 1803 establishment of a Cadiz trading company titled Aguirre y Vea Murguía Hijos, the partners added several provisions that sounded like maxims of the merchant. The company should always seek to transact in "good faith." The partners should strive to get along harmoniously. And, the company should avoid making too many "credit advances" but should instead aim for "solidity." While the last seemed a prudent strategy, success in trade simply required the considerable extension of credit. Regardless, these partners clearly knew the risks of providing credit.[69]

Often times merchants operated with borrowed capital upon which they themselves had to pay interest. Such merchants had to service their debts even while they waited for other traders to make payment on non–interest accruing credit sales of merchandise. Avoiding such costs and risks by only dealing in cash would have been an appealing strategy, but it was not generally possible and seems to have grown increasingly more difficult in Spanish transatlantic trade after 1778.

Credit in Mexico During the Era of the Fleet Trade

Until the final fleet to Mexico in 1776, Spanish importers, the *flotistas*, did manage to sell a significant portion of their imports for cash, avoiding the need to provide risky financing. The arrival of the fleet marked the beginning of the trade fair held just outside Veracruz in the higher, healthier, and more protected village of Jalapa. In anticipation of the fair, hundreds descended upon Jalapa hopeful to benefit from the economic opportunities afforded by the flota's arrival. Muleteers came to transport merchandise to

Mexico City or to other corners of New Spain. Most important, Mexico's wealthiest *almaceneros* arrived with fortunes in hand, desirous to replenish their warehouses with the luxury items carried to Mexico by the flota.[70]

Long before the arrival of the convoy, the wealthy merchants of Mexico City began their preparations for the upcoming *feria*, converting as much of their wealth as possible into more liquid assets. Investments that under normal conditions would have been economically appealing were avoided in the months preceding the Jalapa fair because merchants did not want to tie up their funds in other ventures. This point was illustrated in late 1776 when the *alcalde mayor* of the Oaxacan district of Villa Alta issued several requests to his financiers that they supply him with the pesos he needed to finance the Indians' *repartimiento* production of cotton mantles, a normally lucrative venture. As the official regretfully noted, however, the funds "could not be found owing to the fleet," which had arrived in late July. Financing the *repartimiento de bienes* had to wait because all available assets had been mobilized for the Jalapa trade fair.[71] Brading noted a similar trend in Guanajuato where in 1761 the merchant Martín de Septién appeared to be stockpiling cash in anticipation of the following year's scheduled fleet.[72]

The amounts exchanged at the *feria* were enormous. Mexican *consulado* merchant Gaspar Martín Vicario reported in 1791 that the wealthiest Mexican merchants had typically invested from 200,000 to 600,000 pesos at the commercial fair, purchasing large portions of the cargo brought by the *flotistas*.[73] Garner estimated that during a typical fair in the second half of the eighteenth century, the *consulado* merchants as a whole purchased "up to 5 million pesos worth of merchandise at Jalapa," nearly one-third of the totals imported.[74] The *feria* at Portobello, which until it was terminated in 1739 supplied the markets of the viceroyalty of Peru, also attracted well-financed merchants in possession of large stores of cash, the best-funded merchants each introducing in excess of 500,000 pesos and as much as 877,600 pesos to each of the last Portobello fairs of the 1720s and 1730s.[75]

The *almaceneros* invested large sums into the purchase of imported luxury goods in the hope of profiting from their subsequent sale throughout the colony. Until the termination of the flotas, the wealthy merchants enjoyed a relatively favorable business environment. The merchants operated with the knowledge that the supply of luxury items was fairly stable and predictable; fresh supplies would not enter the market until the arrival of the following flota. Thus, the American traders enjoyed some degree of price stability. Armed with this knowledge, the *almaceneros* felt sufficiently secure to invest significant sums in the purchase of imported goods.

Brading suggested that the "monopoly" merchants of the American *consulados* exploited the financial exigencies of the *flotistas*, forcing the latter to sell their wares cheaply. Local merchants possessed the advantage since "time was on their side; they did not have to keep a ship in harbour, or pay for the costs of storage; and whereas the Spaniards had to sell, to avoid a loss, the natives did not have to buy." This allowed the Mexican merchants to "lay down the law in prices."[76] One should further point out that many of the importers arrived heavily indebted to financiers back in Spain, having financed their Atlantic world ventures by contracting sea loans that customarily required that the principal and interest be repaid to a designated receiver as soon as the risk of sea expired, that is upon safe arrival in port.[77] Thus, the importers faced some urgency to liquidate at least part of their cargo and settle their obligations, a necessity that very well might have worked to the benefit of their customers.

Of course, selling their cargo quickly for cash provided benefit to the importers as well, especially given the riskiness of extending loans. Selling *al contado*, for cash, freed them from the risk of lengthy delays or debtor default to which they likely would have been exposed had they sold on credit. Furthermore, they saved on commissions that would have had to have been paid to those agents empowered to collect the debts since the *flotistas* departed for Cadiz aboard the return voyage of the convoy. Unquestionably, the *flotistas* who sold for cash sold their merchandise at a price lower than they could have likely sold it on credit, but they benefited by mitigating their exposure to risk and other transaction costs. Furthermore, by selling quickly they could reinvest their principal in a "return" cargo. In short, they benefited by increasing the velocity of the circulation of their principal. What they lost by discounting to sell quickly, they recouped by reinvesting more promptly and by reducing their exposure to risky loans.[78] Indeed, Spanish *flotistas* in Mexico made this very point to Viceroy Bucareli in 1778. Import merchants, they claimed, aimed for "the quickest clearance of their stocks, and in this intelligence are founded their laws, ordinances, and their maritime contracts (sea loans). In the brief period of the trade fair they must cancel and conclude them, liquidate their bills, and make their necessary remittances for the return fleet. This is the letter and the spirit of their economic laws devised for the greater management of their overseas transactions."[79]

Furthermore, the well-financed Mexico *consulado* merchants tended to buy in bulk, which served to reduce the transaction costs borne by the sellers. Purchasing in volume and paying cash, the *almaceneros* naturally received favorable prices. While referring specifically to the *feria* of Acapulco, but equally relevant in transatlantic commerce, this point was made by Francisco Ignacio Yraeta in 1780, who noted "buying a lot, I will be able to get more equitable prices."[80] The importers could have sold their merchandise at higher prices, but only had they been willing to assume additional risks and sell on credit, incurring higher transaction costs on the greater number of transactions that would have been necessary.

Selling to the *almaceneros* did not free the *flotistas* entirely of the need to finance sales because by the late eighteenth century, at least, the quantities introduced in the fleets exceeded significantly the purchases of the wholesalers. Garner conjectures that in the 1760s and 1770s, "more than half of each fair's merchandise almost certainly was sold to non-*consulado* members," adding that much of the cargo was sold to "undercapitalized provincial and local merchants, who bought small lots on credit," which, he concludes, exposed the *flotistas* to increased "risk for financial failure."[81]

The *feria de Jalapa*, then, provided an opportunity to the importers to unload considerable portions of their merchandise in several large sales for which they were paid immediately in cash. A quick sale enabled them to reinvest their sums in merchandise to remit to Spain, especially critical during the era of flotas, since to miss the return fleet meant that funds could not be employed in transatlantic trade again until a subsequent sailing, perhaps many years hence.

Historians of Latin American are perhaps inclined to see the *feria* as a peculiarly Spanish institution, but trade fairs were far from unique to the Spanish colonial commercial system. Commercial fairs developed in key locations of medieval Europe to facilitate long-distance trade between distant regions. According to Meir Kohn, fairs emerged to centralize the process of conducting long-distance trade, to bring buyers and sellers together at a convenient location often at a significant moment, such as the arrival of a fleet. The fairs increased the efficiency of trade, permitting the exchange of large amounts of merchandise in a relatively short period. Furthermore, the fairs facilitated the acquisition of good information about prices. As such, commercial fairs worked to the benefit of both buyers and sellers. The physical and temporal concentration of a trade fair also reduced the cost of engaging in trade; the fairs lowered transaction costs.[82] One can see how these factors would have equally benefited merchants in Spanish imperial commerce.

With the termination of the fleets to Mexico (the last flota to Veracruz actually sailed from Cadiz in 1776), the *feria de Jalapa* ended. No longer was there need for a formal commercial fair now that ships arrived intermittently rather than en masse as had occurred during the previous centuries. Whereas during the era of trade fairs the *almaceneros* had descended to Veracruz in possession of fortunes to invest in the purchase of imported luxury goods, now the wealthy merchants had little reason to venture to the coast since the potential volume of business at any given time was small. Furthermore, the periodic arrival of ships produced increasingly unpredictable levels of supply, defeating the risk-reducing strategies that the *almaceneros* had customarily pursued. Unable to depend on the stability of prices, merchants found the new conditions to be less favorable. Certainly they saw little reason to stockpile large quantities of imported luxuries, knowing that more would arrive soon after. Instead, many of the Mexico City elites reinvested in other ventures. With the end of the fleets and the related trade fairs, the importing merchants lost the ability to easily sell large portions of their cargoes for cash.

The loss of large-scale cash-paying customers concerned the importers, who faced increasing difficulties unloading their wares. Indeed, the mere rumor of the flota's termination was felt almost immediately. In September 1778, a full month before the promulgation of *comercio libre*, seventy-seven "individuals of commerce," Jalapa agents of the Cadiz exporters, dispatched a letter to the Mexican Viceroy Bucareli outlining their dire predicament. The 1776 flota had returned to Spain eight months prior, but the importers still possessed considerable unsold stock:

> The fleet and the treasure it transports having arrived happily in Cadiz would on the one hand demonstrate the opulence and wealth of these provinces and its prodigious increase during the happy time of Your Excellency's government [but] at the same time will reveal to the commerce of Cadiz the damage to their trade. It is true that the vast majority of these treasures will have entered the Cadiz trading houses but these hardworking and honorable citizens amid all of these riches will at their desks examine the receipts from the sales that have produced them and will calculate in silence their losses, their bankruptcies, and their damages; they will lament the equal and greater losses that they threaten to suffer from the part of their goods unsold and leftover in this town.[83]

There was no denying that the flota had been overstocked, the agents admitted, but the situation was exacerbated by the fact that "buyers who were already somewhat hesitant" were scared away by the rumors of free trade and "the grave damages, funereal consequences, and great disorder" that always accompanied "individual register ships" (*registros sueltos*).[84] The uncertainty introduced by reform, they decried, had caused the wealthier

Mexican merchants to refrain from bulk purchases and had forced the importers instead to sell their goods on long term credit to subjects who while "industrious" and "honorable" possessed little capital, a scenario the importers described as "necessary but terrible"[85] and "very contrary to the essence and quality of wholesalers, and overseas traders."[86] Of course, *comercio libre* did not include Mexico as early as 1778, but, as argued above, the near-simultaneous suspension of the fleets coupled with the sharply increased granting of register ship licenses meant that Veracruz felt the brunt of the consequences regardless.

Merchants faced a new business environment after 1778. No longer were importing merchants able to sell their goods quickly and rapidly re-invest in a return cargo. In 1789, responding to his brother's frustrations at the slow process, Miguel Jacinto de Marticorena wrote from Veracruz to Cadiz reminding him that "commerce is no longer like it was before in which one sold an entire inventory together."[87] Unable to dispense of large lots profitably, merchants now had to choose between unloading merchandise on credit to less well-off traders or making cash sales of small quantities almost as if they were retailers.

Credit During the Era of Free Trade

Comercio libre opened transatlantic commerce to humbler merchants whose more limited control of resources made them more dependent on access to credit and less able to weather crises. In the colonies, the growing volume of trade that accompanied reform scared away many of the traditional merchants who were replaced by the less wealthy and more credit-needy. This was even the case in Mexico, to which *comercio libre* was not extended until 1789, due to the termination of the fleet and the major expansion of licensed register ships after 1778. In 1791 Mexican *consulado* merchant Juan Fernando Meoqui noted that the *Reglamento* of 1778 had driven wealthier merchants out of commerce, and they had been replaced by smaller trad-ers who were heavily leveraged to creditors.[88] In the same year Manuel García Herreros, another prominent Mexico City merchant, noted that during the 1780s Mexico creditors had faced growing levels of debtor de-lay and default, making financial markets increasingly unstable.[89]

Certainly merchants remained wary of the perils of selling on credit, but in the post-reform economy it was increasingly the case that the only way to unload merchandise was by financing sales. In a 1789 letter to Juan Vicente de Marticorena, Buenos Aires trader Juan Ignacio de Ezcurray bemoaned the commercial difficulties he faced owing to the market being "in the most unhappy state, and totally scarce in silver." Finding himself burdened with a large quantity of imported merchandise, he nonetheless managed to unload half, "although with the distress that the majority was on credit and at quite lengthy terms."[90] Clearly Ezcurray regretted his obligation to sell the items on credit. He had disposed of the merchandise but incurred the risks (and costs) of having to collect potentially difficult debts in the future. In any event, his capital remained inaccessible in the interim.

Juan Vicente's agent in Guatemala, Benito Lorenzo Lavaque, was hopeful, but perhaps not confident, that he would be able to find good buyers for merchandise that Marticorena had supplied him. Indeed, despite the depressed market, he reported in September 1789 that he had already sold some of the goods to a buyer on credit, adding that "because he was a secure subject I had no reservations in giving him the merchandise." Perhaps recognizing that this sale had been fortunate, Lavaque exclaimed: "Oh how I hope that for the remainder of what I possess that I will be presented with an individual of [similar] circumstances . . . so as to free myself from discomforts at the time of collection." As agent Lavaque knew well, it was much easier to convince buyers to take goods on credit than it was to later collect from them.[91]

Merchants benefited from turning over their stocks quickly and reinvesting their capital. Francisco García de Gazeta, Buenos Aires agent to Francisco de Sierra, intended to do just this in January 1786. Desirous of selling Sierra's goods rapidly and reinvesting in hides, García de Gazeta's plans were dashed by the limited opportunities to liquidate the cargo. Even worse, García perceived most of his potential customers to be poor credit risks. "All matters relating to sales or business are at present in an extremely fatal state in which one needs a year to sell on credit and then not even to upstanding people."[92] The news arriving to Sierra from Lima in the same year was no different. Factor Joaquín Sorauren complained in August that "sales are in total inaction. There is no one interested even in buying 1000 pesos [worth] in cash but only on terms of twelve to eighteen months," an option that he preferred to avoid.[93]

With considerable distress, in 1790 Juan Bautista de Marticorena wrote his brother from Guatemala about the inability to find buyers in Central America who could pay cash.

No matter how perfect the shipments are that come from there [Cadiz], it is a dream to think that the sales could be made here in cash, and the only advantage that one might get from such good planning is that one might succeed in placing the items with secure subjects and on reasonable terms . . . and so don't be surprised that I don't succeed in obtaining some cash because here the same occurs to everybody.[94]

Given the credit crunch that Juan Vicente was experiencing at the time, it is likely that Juan Bautista was responding to a request by his brother to sell quickly for cash. But as Juan Bautista explained, to sell merchandise, the provision of financing was nearly obligatory at that time, even for first-rate, high-quality merchandise. And Juan Bautista spoke from experience. He too was juggling his finances, as he explained to his brother several months later. A twenty-thousand peso debt that he had contracted came due, and to mobilize the funds Marticorena had to sell unfavorably a supply of indigo that he had intended to send to Spain. According to Juan Bautista, this exigency was unprecedented and an indication of the financial stresses of the time. "In other times obligations of this nature seemed to me to be apropos for an old shoe salesman, but nowadays, my dear brother, things have come to a situation in which a son cannot rely on his father, and even less a friend, for 100 pesos in a moment of need."[95]

Despite growing uneasiness with providing credit, merchants continued to do so. Writing to brother Juan Vicente in October 1791, Miguel Jacinto de Marticorena expressed surprise that some Veracruz traders were still financing sales to consumers and that the cost of borrowing had not risen in accordance with "present circumstances."

We anticipated that the highlanders who customarily descend each year around this time to make their purchases for the Feria de San Juan would not find anyone this year willing to finance them for even half a real unless they paid 40 percent above the cost of the items. But we are seeing occur the opposite because some of them are being financed at 28 percent and others at 30 percent [above cost] for foreign goods and at [only] 20 percent for Spanish [goods], and all at terms of fifteen months. And so you will see that except for a difference of 2 or 3 percent, sales are similar to the past years.

Many merchants, Marticorena included, had resisted selling on credit, fearful of making bad loans. They preferred to deal in cash but as a consequence had not sold much. Regardless, Miguel Jacinto defended his conservative approach, claiming that while only "small amounts . . . have been sold for cash, [they have been] better sold, perhaps."[96]

Providing credit was necessary, but it was also risky because collecting debts could prove difficult. As Francisco de Sierra's Buenos Aires factor anguished in 1786: "to garner a peso from sales it is necessary to offer advantageous prices and very favorable terms of sixteen months to two years [and even then] it won't be collected whether the subject is alive or dead." In other words, due dates came and went. Even the liquidation of a debtor's holdings at the time of his death did not guarantee that his creditors would be fully compensated.[97] As the Mexican merchant Francisco Ignacio de Yraeta put it bluntly in December 1787, "there are many buyers who pay late, badly or never in these times, in all parts."[98]

When merchants sold on credit, they incurred expenses that would not have existed had they made a cash sale instead. For one, creditors needed to monitor borrowers, to keep track of their whereabouts or their changing financial circumstances. More critical, creditors needed to collect debts, which required both effort and time, and sometimes proved impossible. Monitoring and collecting debts imposed transaction costs, and uncollected debts were a direct loss to a merchant's circulating capital. In the years following the promulgation of *comercio libre*, the need to provide credit and the related costs of monitoring and collecting debts grew significantly. In October 1804 Peruvian merchant Antonio Saenz de Tejada made this point to Francisco de Sierra, for whom he sometimes acted as agent:

> as I have told you and I repeat now I do not desire to manage deals that offer bankruptcy to their owners, despite the commission that they provide me which in calamitous times are truly earned because it costs a businessman, no matter how small he is, a lot of effort in [such times] to sell and collect, because one cannot sell anything for cash and so everything is financed for at least a year and most take another year or two and many thanks if one doesn't lose the debt.

As Saenz de Tejada observed, the provision of credit introduced a whole set of potentially aggravating tasks that both consumed time and incurred expenses, what economists call transaction costs. Worse still, debtors defaulted.[99] Merchants were somewhat compensated for these additional costs and risks because credit sales were normally made at a higher price than cash sales. By incorporating an implicit interest charge into the sale price, merchants shielded themselves from charges of usury. The downside of this nearly universal practice, however, was that if the buyer failed to pay on time, no interest accrued; the debtor neither paid any penalty nor did the creditor earn additional interest.[100]

Extending too many bad credits could land a merchant in difficulties. The *síndico* formed by the *consulado* to explore the 1809 bankruptcy of Cadiz merchant Pedro Martínez de la Junquera determined that much of his financial predicament arose from the large number of bad debts that he held in his portfolio. Martínez de la Junquera's assets totaled 2,506,488 *reales vellón*[101] (125,324 pesos), but well more than half, 1,497,556 *reales vellón* (74,877 pesos), consisted of "ancient debts" owed to him by individuals in Veracruz, Havana, and Lima, some of which he had inherited from his father and others which were complicated by the fact that the debtors themselves had suffered "bankruptcies of fatal result." The *consulado* concluded that none of these debts was likely to be collected for the benefit of Martínez de la Junquera's creditors.[102] He had perhaps bought low and sold high but too often on credit to marginally worthy customers.

A Cadiz Merchant's Post-Reform Commercial Empire of Debt

Juan Vicente Marticorena faced growing financial difficulties in the late 1780s stemming largely from the wide extension of dubious loans that he and his agents had made in the management of his trade. In 1788 Tomás de Balenzattegui, his agent in Buenos Aires, wrote to advise his boss of the "not very favorable progress" he was experiencing in collecting the outstanding debts on items he had sold on Marticorena's account. Marticorena was not alone, claimed Balenzattegui; all of the creditors were facing similar difficulties. But, he added, nothing could be done but to be patient since to employ "violent means," by which he presumably meant legal proceedings, would only exacerbate the situation.[103] Balenzattegui was correct on this final point. Not only did legal proceedings entail significant costs, but their outcome was often not particularly beneficial to creditors. Debtors frequently received lengthy moratoriums on their debts or ended up reaching a settlement that required them to pay only a fraction of their original obligations.[104]

Ironically, Juan Vicente himself contemplated the request of a moratorium in 1802 and even went so far as to meet with an attorney. Marticorena was increasingly pressed by his creditors to meet his obligations but simply did not have the funds accessible. His attorney explained that once he had been granted a moratorium "for a certain number of years you will not be bothered as can be evidenced by [the similar experiences of] many powerful and influential men." To obtain a moratorium required that the petitioner designate a special power of attorney accompanied by a sworn statement of credits and debits as well as a list of other property that would be used to pay obligations once the outstanding debts were collected. Once submitted, the tribunal would render a decision within fifteen days. Generally, if the petitioner could prove that he was solvent, he would be granted the moratorium, "and even if there are some who oppose the moratorium, it is always granted for a time."[105]

In any event, fourteen years after Balenzattegui advised against the employment of legal means to collect Marticorena's debts, the difficulties had apparently not fully abated. In 1802 he wrote that he had been trying since at least 1793 to collect from a variety of individuals who owed Marticorena funds totaling 1,395 pesos. In the ensuing decade, he had only collected 247 pesos and, with the exception of another 67 pesos that he expected to collect "soon," considered the remainder uncollectible "due to the death of some and the absolute indigence of the others."[106]

The news from Juan Vicente de Marticorena's cousin and agent in Mexico was no better. Juan Felipe de Laurnaga wrote in April 1798 that he was nearing completion of a "current account" summarizing Juan Vicente's dealings in the colony. The final draft, he anticipated, would indicate that Juan Vicente had a balance in his favor of roughly 4,064 pesos, of which 3,094 pesos were in the form of accounts receivable. Of the outstanding debts, Laurnaga considered a 731 peso debt owed by Mauricio Serrano to be lost. He judged another 183 peso debt collectible albeit "slowly." Laurnaga expected still another debt in the amount of 1,026 pesos to be repaid in three to four months. The final 1,054 pesos were to be repaid in several days. In the worst case scenario, he estimated, 900 to 1,000 of the outstanding 3,094 pesos would be lost, around 30 percent.[107]

But the situation facing Juan Vicente was the gravest in Lima, where his eldest brother, Juan Miguel, looked after his interests. On 16 April 1788 Juan Miguel wrote with the bad news that he was not collecting any of the debts that he was managing on Juan Vicente's behalf. "The collections are being complicated and delayed," he warned. "Time is passing without any progress and many of the due dates have long passed; I am faced with the pain of not being able to collect the 5500 pesos to which I referred in the account that I submitted."[108]

Two months later Juan Miguel submitted detailed accounts of additional dealings on behalf of Juan Vicente in a transaction involving "54 sacks, 3 burlap containers, and 30 half-cakes of wax,"[109] of which much of the former consisted of textiles. Juan Miguel experienced great difficulty selling the items and ultimately had to unload much of it on credit. In total, sales generated 148,231 pesos, but 46 percent (71,869 pesos) was outstanding, having been supplied on credit. A small amount, 8,877 pesos, Juan Miguel had bartered for cascarilla (Jesuit's Bark), the raw material used for the production of the anti-malarial drug quinine.[110]

Credit terms were generous to debtors, suggesting the difficulties that Juan Miguel had in unloading the merchandise. Don Clemente Arza, for example, had acquired a large supply of commodities in August 1787 without obligation to pay anything until January 1789. Many others received terms of twelve or fourteen months, and no due dates at all were stipulated for some of the sales, the buyers presumably given indefinitely to repay the loans.[111] Normally, merchants charged more if they provided goods on credit. In this case, however, Juan Miguel de Marticorena does not appear to have charged more to those to whom he sold on credit. His ledgers indicate that he sometimes sold a commodity to a cash-paying customer on one day and then the next day financed a sale to another customer at the same price or even less. Perhaps this suggests that not all consumers were fully informed, since it is hard to imagine why a buyer would relinquish scarce coin if he could receive the same commodity at the same price on credit. Of course, Marticorena might also have been differentiating between clients, granting superior terms for better credit risks or to his more regular customers. Regardless, these favorable terms suggest that Juan Miguel either faced a buyers' market or an assortment of poorly funded customers. Most likely, he encountered both.

Very little of the credit advanced had been collected when Juan Miguel remitted his accounts to his brother, although it is true that many of the loans had not yet expired. A man named José González had received on credit 3,086 pesos' worth of merchandise that he had purchased on behalf of three storekeepers. The deal required the storekeepers to pay weekly installments of 230 pesos, but they had not been paying regularly. Juan Miguel remained optimistic that these funds would prove collectible since the storekeepers had assets in their stores and, that failing, Juan Miguel could try to collect directly from González, although the latter had "recently declared himself in bankruptcy."[112]

Juan Miguel was less optimistic about his chances of collecting the entire debt owed by one Bruno Ximeli. In a ledger entry Marticorena noted: "I hope to collect the major portion in the future, but the rest will be difficult to get, due to the arrears that he has recently experienced." In a subsequent ledger notation, however, his opinion had deteriorated; he states, "there is some hope that he will be able to pay part of what he owes."[113]

Still another debtor, Toribio Silba, had not repaid any of his debt despite being "among the most creditworthy subjects." The case of Silba revealed the interconnectedness of the credit network. Apparently Silba's insolvency stemmed from his own difficulties collecting outstanding debts. According to Juan Miguel, Silba's debtors had preferred to default and face judicial settlements, perfectly cognizant that they would be granted moratoriums on their debts. Since Silba's debtors were not paying him, he was unable to pay his own creditors, Marticorena added. A couple of delayed payments or a bankruptcy might produce a domino effect that would be felt much more widely throughout the local economy.[114]

Another debtor to Juan Miguel de Marticorena, Manuel Ángel Santibáñez of Potosí, had not paid any of his obligation despite the fact that his debts were thirteen months past due. Juan Miguel was sufficiently concerned that he sent his assistant to Potosí to meet personally with Santibáñez since the latter had ignored several written inquiries. The clerk wrote back to Lima to explain that despite the passage of so much time, Santibáñez was still in possession of most of the merchandise that he had acquired originally from Marticorena. Apparently he had been unable to find any consumers. The letter is silent on whether or not Santibáñez had offered to sell the merchandise on credit or whether he was insisting on cash sales, but it seems possible that Santibáñez was cautiously seeking the latter and had thus sold nothing.[115]

Overall, the situation confronting Marticorena was alarming. According to one of his ledgers he had collected only 858 pesos of 23,610 worth of merchandise advanced, less than 4 percent. Another account revealed collections totaling 2,539 pesos out of 25,933 financed, under 10 percent. While he was not ready to write off any debts, one senses that Juan Miguel perceived the state of affairs as very critical.[116]

Undoubtedly Marticorena's difficulties stemmed partially from the enormous expansion of commerce in Lima at the time. Throughout America, the liberalization of trade after 1778 had resulted in the saturation of markets as merchants shipped excessive amounts of cargo. Peru might have suffered this fate more profoundly than anywhere. Estimates of the quantities imported into Peru after the restoration of peace in 1783 differ widely, but there is little doubt that the amounts greatly exceeded the colony's capacity to consume. Xabier Lamikiz found that "in 1786 more than 14,000,000 pesos in merchandise arrived via Cape Horn in a market that had previously tended to absorb only about a third as much."[117]

There were limits to what a creditor like Juan Miguel de Marticorena could do to collect outstanding debts. Creditors frequently sued in court to force debtors to fulfill their obligations. Indeed, Juan Miguel considered filing a suit against some of those who owed him money, but decided that this would be counterproductive. In reference to two of the larger debtors, Manuel Cevallos and José Vidal, José Miguel explained to his brother that to pressure them to pay would only drive them to bankruptcy, which would make collection of the debts even more unlikely. "One cannot hurry either of these debtors by any other means without serious contemplation [of the consequences] given the deplorable situation of commerce, because to do so, pressuring them with rigor, will only result in them declaring themselves bankrupt to relieve themselves at once with the extensions and discounts that will be granted to them." In Juan Miguel's opinion, it was wisest to show patience and hope that conditions improved sufficiently to allow debtors to pay. In the meantime, he reasoned, "there remains no other choice than to keep my eyes open as I am doing."[118]

Half a year after Juan Miguel sent these detailed statements, he again wrote to his brother Juan Vicente to update him on the financial situation. Conditions had not improved by September 1788, and Juan Miguel's already pessimistic assessment had declined considerably. One of the debtors had gone bankrupt in the interim and the proceedings had revealed that he possessed no assets other than a small boat valued at five to six thousand pesos, far less than his obligations. Juan Miguel bemoaned, "in such lamentable times as there have been in the last three years, perhaps I will have lost all or most of my capital as I have not had any dealings other than our unfortunate debts." Apparently Marticorena had lost faith in the creditworthiness of his fellow Limeños because he had decided not to finance any more sales despite the fact that he still possessed large supplies of imported items. And sales for cash were occurring only at steep markdowns. "There is still considerable existing stock . . . [but because] I did not want to sell the merchandise at the discounts that others have sold, I have suspended all sales until I see what results."[119]

By June 1789 Juan Miguel was desolate. He still possessed warehoused merchandise and many of the debts remained in arrears. Furthermore, Juan Vicente was clamoring to be paid and desperately seeking to liquidate some of his investments in Peru. But the news that Juan Miguel sent to Cadiz was dispirited: "of the financed items, nothing can be collected, and consequently neither can I sell the existing stocks that I have from this last [shipment] for cash as you desire because in such a case it would have to be at a 50 percent discount from cost, so that I do not know what to do."[120]

Unfortunately, we have no way of determining how much, if any, of these debts were ultimately collected. Shortly after this last correspondence, Juan Miguel and Juan Vicente had a falling out. Apparently, Juan Vicente accused his brother of incompetence or malfeasance because in

April 1790 Juan Miguel wrote Juan Vicente to express his dismay regarding his brother's accusations. Some time later, Juan Vicente initiated the process of stripping his brother in Lima of any authority over his business dealings. On 26 June 1793 Juan Vicente de Marticorena received a letter from Antonio Álvarez de Villar, who wrote from Lima to acknowledge receipt of the power of attorney that Juan Vicente had conferred upon him "to clarify the accounts." Álvarez further referred to a "breakdown" that Juan Miguel had experienced.[121] It seems difficult to believe Álvarez would have been too much more successful at collecting the debts; one must assume that many of these debts were forever lost.

Juan Vicente de Marticorena also suffered substantial losses in Guatemala where his credit extensions were vast. Juan Vicente's business dealings in Central America consisted largely of shipping European goods in consignment to his younger brother, Juan Bautista de Marticorena, who reinvested the revenues in indigo production to be remitted to Juan Vicente in Spain. The actual method by which Juan Bautista converted the imported goods into capital to be reinvested in indigo is unclear. Seemingly, some of the merchandise was advanced directly to the indigo producers, a practice that was apparently common in the indigo industry according to Robert S. Smith, who noted that "mercantile credit to growers, who pledged their crops as security . . . . [was] ordinarily made in clothing and other necessities."[122] Juan Vicente seems also to have owned an indigo plantation in Guatemala since one letter referred to his *inquilinos*, his tenants, who were unable to deliver the indigo as required, suggesting, perhaps, that through an intermediary Juan Vicente furnished them with credit to be repaid in dyestuff.[123]

Regardless of the process, the credit that Juan Vicente de Marticorena provided to indigo producers had resulted in substantial losses in Guatemala. In an 1803 letter addressed to Pedro Fermín de Córdoba, Juan Vicente's assistant in Cadiz, Miguel Jacinto de Marticorena, yet another Marticorena brother who had recently relocated to Guatemala from Veracruz, explained "that although it is true that Juan Vicente has in this Kingdom a fortune in credits, it is also the case that all are lost or uncollectible except for that of Gamboa which could be collected if God grants him a few years of life."[124]

As he had been for much of the previous two decades, Juan Vicente was struggling to stay solvent at the time due to the growing pressures to pay his own numerous and growing obligations. The greatest pressure was coming from the syndicate organized in the aftermath of the bankruptcy of the Casa de Viuda de Oviedo, Hermano e Hijos, a firm to which Juan

Vicente had been heavily indebted. The *consulado*-appointed receivers responded to a request from Juan Vicente for additional time by demanding that he produce a statement of his financial condition, presumably so that they could evaluate the likelihood that he would be able to meet his commitments. But the receivers were suspicious of Juan Vicente's report, suggesting that his accounting procedures were dubious and that his justification for needing additional time seemed "falsified." Marticorena claimed to possess more than 200,000 pesos in Peru and Guatemala, funds with which he would pay his debts. The syndicate, however, commented: "We cannot avoid thinking it odd that with more than 200,000 pesos in Guatemala and Peru you do not explain its condition whether it is in good or bad debts, merchandise or cash. If it is in the latter, [i.e.. cash] why has it not come to Spain and if it is in the former (i.e. merchandise) why do you not sell it?"[125] Marticorena's response revealed the quagmire into which his finances had deteriorated. As he explained, the situation was not as simple as it seemed since most of his wealth in America was in the form of debts owed to him for merchandise "sold on credit, [but] the debtors could not meet their respective obligations. . . . [W]hat is needed is time and prudent vigilance to take advantage of favorable opportunities and to not make matters worse by premature demands."[126] As the letter from Guatemala sent the month prior by his brother, Miguel Jacinto de Marticorena, indicated, however, the prospects of these debts being collected were poor.

Three years later, Juan Vicente's outstanding debts in Guatemala remained substantial. In order to placate yet another creditor, Juan Vicente attempted to draw a letter of credit against his brother Juan Bautista, a course of action that Juan Vicente had employed on several other occasions, to the growing annoyance of Juan Bautista. This time, however, Juan Bautista rejected the *libranza*, explaining that "this letter of credit is not valid, since the drafter does not have any liquid funds in my possession, but only some debts, some of which should be considered entirely lost and the rest hampered."[127] Not surprisingly, the relationship between the brothers was irreparably damaged by Juan Bautista's refusal to back his older brother's creditworthiness, although it had already been strained for years. Recalling the close connection between creditworthiness and honor, it is understandable how Juan Bautista's decision would have been viewed by Juan Vicente as betrayal. It must have been heart wrenching for Juan Bautista to take such a dramatic position, but it also undoubtedly reflects how dismal Juan Vicente's situation had become.

In Juan Bautista's defense, Juan Vicente had in recent years exploited his relationship with his wealthier and more politically connected younger sibling who had married into the Aycinena family, the wealthiest in Central America. In addition to repeatedly drawing nonexistent funds off of Juan Bautista,[128] Juan Vicente had continually failed to produce a long-requested accounting of his brother's dealings in Cadiz, dealings for which Juan Vicente had served as agent. Juan Bautista was especially incensed by a shipment of 152 *tercios* of indigo that he and fellow Guatemalan Pedro de Górriz had sent back in 1794 and for which he had never received a final reckoning despite numerous demands. His growing rage prompted him in 1800 to write a scathing letter to his cousin and Juan Vicente's aid, Pedro Fermín de Córdoba:

> I can say truthfully, that in the course of the many records and accounts
> of these [transactions] that I have asked from you over the past 14 years,
> never have you satisfied me not even with a blasted letter, a miserable
> performance that perhaps has never before been witnessed in all the
> marketplaces of the universe, and I don't mean just between merchants,
> but even between the most brutish drunkards of the most vial and
> uncouth country.[129]

Two years later, Juan Bautista severed commercial ties with his brother altogether, telling Juan Vicente that he would no longer provide him indigo on consignment "in light of the deplorable condition of your affairs and the danger that the creditors might take them from you forcefully." Perhaps to minimize the slight, Juan Bautista added that most of the dye belonged to his in-laws, the Aycinenas, and if this were not the case, his decision might have been otherwise.[130] Juan Vicente probably read the venomous letter sent by his brother to Fermín de Córdoba, his assistant, but it was only after the cessation of shipments consigned to him that he acted to appease Juan Bautista's frustrations, sending his aid in to Guatemala in 1804 to reconcile the accounts. Sadly, Fermín de Córdoba never arrived; the ship on which he sailed, Juan Vicente's schooner *Jesus, Maria, y Josef,* disappeared and was assumed to be one of "three merchant ships [that] were seized and their crews put to the sword by black pirates from the Island of Santo Domingo."[131] Despite the growing tension between the brothers, Juan Vicente seemingly held out hope that Juan Bautista would continue to accept his *libranzas* and help protect his reputation. He finally learned otherwise in 1806; blood was only so thick.

· · ·

Much of Juan Vicente Marticorena's difficulties stemmed from his inability to collect debts owed to him, and in this regard his experiences were far from unique. Indeed far wealthier and more powerful merchants also experienced high (and growing) levels of debtor default at the time. Upon his death in 1797, the executors of the estate of wealthy Mexican merchant Francisco Ignacio de Yraeta dissolved the trading partnership in which he was involved with his nephew and son-in-law, Gabriel de Yturbe e Yraeta.[132] At the moment of its dissolution, the partnership's outstanding debts totaled a whopping 405,278 pesos, much of it considered uncollectible by the executors. Twenty-two percent (88,045 pesos) of the debts were deemed *perdidas*, lost, and another 18.5 percent (74,831 pesos) were judged *dudosas*, doubtful. The partnership thus stood to lose up to 40 percent of its accounts receivable. This potential loss (162,876 pesos) represented around 20 percent of the company's net worth of 803,498 pesos.[133]

The merchants Blas Benito Ximénez and Juan de Eguino, whose finances became thorny as a result, in part, of the malfeasance of their factors in Peru, prepared a statement of their combined assets in 1776.[134] At the time, the two owed creditors 822,331 pesos; in turn, they possessed accounts receivable in the amount of 723,000 pesos, leaving them about 100,000 pesos in arrears. But, as in the above cases, a large portion of the funds owed them were "doubtful," 359,000 pesos or just under half. Quite obviously, the two men would not likely be able to pay their creditors in entirety either; a wave of uncollectible debts would ripple through the financial community.[135]

Indeed any significant default or bankruptcy was bound to have an impact well beyond the immediately relevant parties. A striking example was the 1802 bankruptcy of the Mexican Casa de Vertiz, which sent shockwaves throughout the empire. According to Rafael José Facio, the firm's losses mounted to more than two million pesos, a figure he later raised to 3.3 million, and entangled countless Mexican merchants, including many of his "acquaintances" whose losses reached 800,000 pesos.[136] Juan Phelipe de Laurnaga claimed to be one of those affected, having suffered "some loss in my interests." But the worst was yet to come, Laurnaga feared, as "many [more] entanglements and aggravations will involve me, which in the end might result in grave damage to me."[137] Bankruptcies or even just the final accounting upon a merchant's death had potentially profound and detrimental impacts on the entire mercantile community.

Juan Fermín de Aycinena, the wealthiest merchant in late colonial Guatemala, experienced shockingly high levels of debtor default, and they were growing markedly towards the end of his life. Inventories of his wealth were prepared in the years 1768, 1771, 1777, and 1796. In all of these years, his accounts receivable were substantial, but most remarkable was the high level of the debt that Aycinena expected to be uncollectible. The percentage of the outstanding debts owed to him that were considered either lost or doubtful in those years was 27 percent, 28 percent, 24 percent, and a whopping 53 percent respectively. In this last inventory, prepared upon Aycinena's 1796 death, the debts deemed dubious or lost totaled 36 percent of his estate's net worth of 2,196,029 pesos.[138] Importantly, bad debts had always been a characteristic of long-distance trade, but uncollectibles in Aycinena's last inventory dwarfed those of the earlier accounts. Aycinena's remarkably deteriorated financial conditions, of course, reflected his business in precisely the two decades since the promulgation of *comercio libre*. It should be noted, however, that by 1796 Spain had been at war against Revolutionary France for several years, and so it is likely that at least some of the increased defaults on Aycinena's accounts receivable reflected war-induced delays as well.

Ironically, the death of a trader probably hastened the day of reckoning for his debtors and creditors. The former could expect calls to make good on their debts; the latter could expect to discover how much of their accounts receivable would never be collected. Upon the settling of accounts following the death of his cousin, a merchant named Larrain, Juan Bautista de Marticorena was relieved to learn that Larrain did not owe him the 20,000 pesos he had feared but only 7000 pesos. Unfortunately, Juan Bautista had "no hope of collecting the indicated 7000 pesos."[139] Clearly, the death of a merchant caused ripples throughout financial circles.

• • •

Creditors had a limited arsenal of tools to collect difficult debts. Upon the expiration of the *plaza*, the loan term, a creditor could present the debtor with a demand for repayment, but the penalty to the debtor for delaying was not normally monetary as most loans to buyers were not interest bearing; any cost of the loan was bundled into a higher selling price. If indeed payment was not prompt, then the creditor was forced to consider other means to pressure for collection. Certainly the relationship of the two parties determined the patience of the creditor, a good or frequent customer receiving a longer grace period. At some point, however, lenders came to the conclusion that certain debtors were either dishonest or insolvent. As was observed above, a simple threat to expose the debtor's financial debility was sometimes enough incentive for the debtor to pay immediately. A bad reputation was lethal to a prominent merchant. Many debtors, however, were individuals of lesser means who were just not as susceptible to bad publicity; they simply struggled to make ends meet and balance their finances. If threats to expose the unpaid debts failed to motivate the debtor, the creditor could also seek recompense through legal proceedings, charging the transgressor in the tribunal of the pertinent *consulado*, for instance. But legal proceedings had many downsides. For one, it was expensive to bring a case to court and thus prohibitive for smaller sums. Second, the outcomes of such proceedings were not necessarily favorable to creditors. Juan Miguel de Marticorena's hesitancy to pursue this path reflected his knowledge that debtors were often granted lengthy moratoriums to repay. Still worse, courts often resolved debts by encouraging creditors to accept less than the full amount. This was the case, for instance, in the Cadiz bankruptcy proceedings of the merchant and insurer José Ysassi Montalvo. A reckoning of Ysassi's financial condition revealed that his liquidatable assets were only sufficient to cover 40 percent of his outstanding debts. Creditors were given little choice but to settle, having been informed that "the 40 percent offered can only take effect if it applies to all losses and transactions, since otherwise it is not possible to do it." They were given a take it or leave it ultimatum.[140] Last, when a merchant turned to a tribunal, it was tantamount to announcing to everyone in the community that he was encountering difficulties and might not collect the debt, which could be dangerous and harmful to his reputation, perhaps worse than losing the amount in question. Furthermore, the debtor sued in court was exposed as potentially insolvent, scaring away many of his customers and reducing the likelihood that he would be able to continue trading and pay off the debt. For example, when the Casa de Viuda de Oviedo, Hermano e Hijos declared its bankruptcy, the appointed receivers quietly pursued extrajudicially Juan Vicente de Marticorena to pay his outstanding debts. Lest they contemplate going public, Juan Vicente warned them "to publically formalize it would be prejudicial to me and to all [of us], jeopardizing the credit and making impossible my ability to continue commerce for the mutual benefit." Credit was the web that interconnected all traders. One weak segment could threaten the stability of the wider network.[141]

· · ·

Provision of credit was a critical component in facilitating commerce in the Spanish empire. But credit extension imposed severe risks, risks to which no merchant was immune. Merchants might have extended credit sparingly and judiciously, but none escaped the paradox of early modern commerce; to succeed in business required merchants to also be creditors, exposing themselves to the difficulty of collecting debts and the near certainty that some percentage would ultimately prove uncollectible. Even the wealthiest merchants such as Francisco Ignacio de Yraeta or Juan Fermín de Aycinena could not avoid the plague of extending bad loans. Perhaps the advantage that a wealthier merchant enjoyed over his less well capitalized colleagues was that he could withstand greater losses and endure lengthier delays. This was a point repeatedly stressed by the Mexico City *consulado* merchants in their denunciations of *comercio libre* back in 1791. But the curse of bad debts affected all traders and was a costly aspect of conducting business, one that seems to have become increasingly endemic in the aftermath of trade liberalization.

Chapter 6

Trade in War and Peace

The War on Prices

The era of free trade was abruptly interrupted by France's 7 March 1793 declaration of war against Spain. For much of the next two decades Spain was embroiled in the European hostilities, alternately at war with France or England. War had a profound impact on Atlantic world trade; it increased the riskiness of trade and reduced still further its predictability. Each merchant responded differently to these uncertain political circumstances. Some viewed the onset of violence as an opportunity to reap growing reward from international commerce. Others feared the added risk that war introduced and withdrew from or at least curtailed their business investments.

In general, war served to increase the price differential of traded goods between the market of origin and the market of consumption, between Europe and America. To begin with, growing price disparities reflected the reduction of trade that was inevitable whenever hostilities erupted, as the dangers of privateering increased and ports were blockaded by enemy navies. As fewer commodities arrived to market, their prices rose in reflection of their scarcity. Second, the price divergence resulted from the increased costs of getting goods to market during warfare, a reflection of elevated risk that sharply increased freight costs[1] and insurance premiums.

The decline in the flow of commodities between Europe and America naturally resulted in growing scarcity of imported items on both sides of the Atlantic. Colonial commodities grew dearer in Europe when war-induced scarcities resulted. Similarly, Spanish luxury goods became more expensive in America as stocks began to decline and the arrival of new shipments grew less likely, a phenomenon clearly described in 1800 in a report to the viceroy of New Granada by Colombian merchant and Cartagena guild member José Ignacio de Pombo:

> Commerce from the metropole to America in general, and particularly with the ports of this viceroyalty [was] reduced to an absolute standstill after the [outbreak] of this present war due to the superiority of the maritime forces of the enemy and their efforts, intelligence and vigilance, and due to the lack of protection for our commercial vessels; the entry of European and Peninsular goods ceased, of course; they rapidly rose in price everywhere, became scarce, and many absolutely unavailable, especially at the beginning of the war.[2]

The rising price of imported products, however, did not translate into an equivalent rising value for the same commodity in its market of origin. To the contrary. The same reduction in trade that led to scarcity of colonial goods in Spain generated growing stocks of the item in America. Colonial merchants found themselves with goods that they could not easily ship to Europe owing to the interruption of shipping. The result of these growing stocks was the reduction (or at least relative stagnation) in their price in America. At best, merchants' funds were merely tied up in goods that had to be warehoused until the cessation of danger. Even worse, merchant Pombo noted, some exporters found themselves with "fruits that now are detained without demand and without value, some of which rot while others shrink or deteriorate."[3] After complaining that the war had produced "scarcity of some [imported] goods and the high prices of all," requiring even "poor people and workers" to pay "prices three or four times what they had been," fellow Cartagenan Antonio de Narváez y la Torre recounted the war's equally devastating impact on locally produced commodities: "the value of our fruits has declined with the same rapidity and proportion, with incalculable damage due to the lack of exports."[4] In short, the war-induced price difference between Spain and America reflected both scarcity (price increase) in the consuming market and abundance (price decrease) in the producing market.

In 1799 the newly established *consulado* of Havana produced a report, summarized in Table 6.1, to demonstrate the war's effect on the prices of the island's principal trading commodities. As the table shows, the average price of imported goods had risen sharply (50 to 150 percent) during the period under analysis while the average price of its export goods had dropped by about one-third. This price divergence is precisely what one would expect from the interruption of trade caused by war. In fact, several factors might have understated the impact of war suggested by the data presented in this table. First, the Cuban *consulado* used the "peacetime" years of 1795–96 to compare with the war-torn year of 1799. In fact, during at least part of each of these "peacetime" years, Spain was actually engaged in hostilities with France (1795) and England (1796). Of course, the effects were being felt far more by 1799 as the British blockade of Cadiz had succeeded largely in isolating Spain from its colonies, clearly much worse in terms of the interruption of trade than the earlier years' hostilities. A second factor mitigating the impact of war on the prices displayed in Table 6.1 is that Havana was a principal beneficiary of the briefly permitted concession for neutral trade, which would have temporarily reduced the island's isolation. Until the concession was revoked, neutral ships were allowed to enter Havana, introducing supplies and extracting others.[5] Despite these qualifications, one clearly sees that the island's war-induced commercial isolation led to a price divergence: the price of imported goods rose and the price of exported goods fell.

The divergence of prices during wartime is also nicely demonstrated by the case of cochineal, the red dye that represented Mexico's second most

TABLE 6.1

Impact of War on the Prices of Havana's Internationally Traded Goods

Article	Avg. Price in Peacetime (1795–96)	Avg. Price in Wartime (1799)	Change in Price
IMPORTS			
Slaves	300 pesos	450 pesos	50%
Tambores & Guijos, Juegos	750 pesos	2000 pesos	167%
Paylas & Tachos	300 pesos	450 pesos	50%
Carnes de Vaca (Arroba)	10 reales	21 reales	110%
Cajas para Embraces	9 reales	20 reales	122%
Bueyes & Yuntas	90 pesos	140 pesos	56%
EXPORTS			
Azucar (arroba)	26 reales	18 reales	−31%
Miel de Purga, Barriles	11 reales	8 reales	−27%
Cueros al Pelo	15 reales	10 reales	−33%

SOURCE: Estado que presenta a un golpe de vista los perjuicios que causa la guerra a esta plaza a pesar del tráfico de neutrale, 20 September 1799, AGI, *Consulados*, legajo 340.

important export after silver. Cochineal was produced almost exclusively in the southern Mexican province of Oaxaca. Virtually all of the dye produced was shipped to Spain before being reexported to northern Europe. Thus, the interruption of trade resulting from war tended to make cochineal scarcer in Europe, inflating its price. In contrast, merchants in Mexico found themselves stuck with cochineal that they could not easily send to Spain. This caused the price to fall or, at the very least, rise less sharply than the meteoric rise in Europe. This phenomenon is visible in Figure 6.1, which charts the price of cochineal in Oaxaca, the province in which it was produced, and several northern European markets where the dye was widely consumed, for the years 1758 to 1821.[6] The years in which Spain was engaged in war are identified on the figure by the rectangular boxes a through f. As can be plainly seen, the differential between the price of cochineal in Europe and its price in Oaxaca tended to grow whenever Spain was at war. War tended to cause a major increase in the price of cochineal in Europe, a reflection of either real or expected scarcity, while in Mexico, the price of cochineal generally stagnated or fell during wartime. The resumption of peace caused cochineal prices in Europe and America to converge. The expected price convergence following the restoration of peace was also explained by Cartagenan merchant

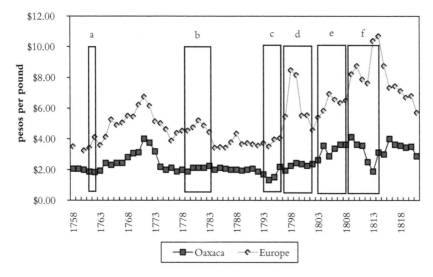

Figure 6.1. Cochineal Prices in Europe and Oaxaca: 1758–1821
SOURCE: Tooke, Newmarch, and Gregory, *A History of Prices*, 2: 400; Posthumus, Inquiry into the History, 1: 420–23.

Pombo: "there is no doubt that with peace the costs of insurance and freight will fall considerably and that goods of all types will be abundant in the ports of the Peninsula, an occurrence that will reduce their current price. [This is] due to the end of the inability to extract [goods] from America, which has led to their considerable increase."[7]

While the trend of price divergence is clear, the price of cochineal in Mexico was affected somewhat differently by the various wars. During the American Revolutionary War (rectangle b) the price of red dye in Mexico remained stable, although the price in Europe rose for the first several years of hostilities. During the 1793–97 First Coalition against Revolutionary France (rectangle c), the price of cochineal fell moderately in Mexico while the European value held steady, perhaps an indication of the continued surpluses in the latter. Rectangle d demarcates the years of the Second Coalition during which Spain was allied with France against Great Britain. The European price of cochineal, and thus the price divergence, reached very high levels for the first several years before descending sharply after the 1798 penetration of England's blockade of Cadiz to what was still a high price by historic standards. The greatest period of price disparity occurred after Napoleon Bonaparte's invasion and occupation of Spain (rectangle f). Dye prices rose to unprecedented levels in Europe while dropping precipitously in Mexico. Only with the war's end did European prices sustain a decline; prices on both sides of the Atlantic converged with the restoration of peace.

Prices are not determined exclusively by existing supply but also by anticipated changes to supply. During the earlier wars, the cochineal price in Mexico was stable or fell slightly while prices in Europe generally rose. This former probably reflected the expectations of the cochineal merchants in Mexico that the wars would be short-lived. Indeed, the Mexican merchant Rafael José Facio confirmed this in November 1797. Trade in Veracruz was anemic, he observed, due to the uncertainty of the war's longevity. The only exception, he added, was cochineal: "the Oaxacans continue propping up cochineal, hopeful for a rapid peace, [and] for that reason the current [price] in that city has not gone below 15 to 16 reales." Grana cochinilla was somewhat different than many other colonial commodities since it held up quite well for lengthy periods, although it did suffer some weight loss from desiccation. Thus, dye traders in Mexico might have preferred to wait out the war or hope for an opportunity to ship rather than to sell at bargain-basement prices. They could not possibly have anticipated how long the trade interruptions would endure. By the time Napoleon invaded Spain, merchants had certainly become war weary. In Mexico, the cochineal merchants feared the worst and sought to unload their wares at whatever price, thus the absolute drop in price there after around 1808.

Merchants' Strategies During Wartime

The outbreak of war elicited different strategies from different merchants. Some viewed the growing price disparities as an ideal opportunity to garner windfall profits, at least while shipping lanes remained open or until the additional trading costs of war, especially maritime insurance, forced them to reconsider their engagement. For example, on the day before Christmas 1796, Manuel de Arana, a merchant resident in Buenos Aires, instructed his partner in Cadiz, Antonio de Artechea, that "if the war against England is confirmed, you can ship me a nice consignment of goods . . . since in time of war, one usually earns greater profits as you well know."[8] While Arana viewed enthusiastically the potential profits brought about by the political turmoil, other merchants focused instead on the rising riskiness of commerce during war. On the very same day that Arana wrote to Artechea, another Buenos Aires merchant, José Ramón de Ugarteche, expressed the opposite viewpoint to Artechea, stating that due to the news of war with England he was withdrawing from trade until "things calm down" and that he had even disembarked a cargo of wool from a ship called the *Jasón*.[9] Nine months later Artechea was presented the same cautionary attitude from Francisco Valdovinos of Buenos Aires, who explained that "it is not my desire that my money is invested in merchandise while the war persists."[10]

War increased substantially the potential for profits since the difference in price between markets for commodities grew significantly. But rising profits were accompanied by the increasing riskiness of trade, driving many merchants to withdraw temporarily from commerce until the restoration of peace lowered risk. Furthermore, during wartime the costs of freight and insurance rose markedly, eroding profits. Interestingly, war probably reduced market uncertainty, the unpredictability that spikes in supply would suddenly lead to plummeting prices, since the partial interruption of trade caused by war provided greater guarantee that prices in the distant market would remain favorable. But international hostilities introduced a far more immediate risk, that merchantmen might be attacked by privateers, corsairs operating on behalf of Spain's enemies.

In 1794, the First Count of Maule, don Nicolás de La Cruz y Bahamonde, informed his brother in Chile, Juan Manuel de la Cruz, that many of his fellow Cadiz traders had grown nervous ever since France's invasion of Flanders and Holland, "removing their merchandise from the danger of the heat of war." None dared speculate but only sought to protect their wealth from the upheaval. In fact, French corsairs had already taken nearly as many Spanish prizes (ships) in this campaign, he speculated, as had the English in the entire War of American Independence. Regardless, the count observed that there were ample profits to be made, if only it were not for the risks. "Oh how I wish that you could send me from Lima four or six thousand loads of cacao; we would make money."[11]

War or even the expectation of war had the effect of throwing the local market into confusion. When war erupted, merchants in possession of a scarce or highly sought imported item had the opportunity to earn a sudden windfall, as prices spiked in expectation of continued scarcity. As a result, even mere rumors of impending war made merchants reluctant to sell their imported wares since they stood to benefit greatly if hostilities indeed interrupted shipping. In fact, vendors sometimes raised their prices as soon as rumors of war began to circulate although consumers were not always willing to pay the higher prices before the war was confirmed; the result could be stalemate and commercial stagnation.

On 31 July 1790 Miguel Jacinto de Marticorena of Veracruz informed his brother in Cadiz that rumors of imminent war between Spain and England were rampant in Mexico, presumably connected to the emerging conflict over Nootka Sound on Vancouver Island.[12] As a result, he reported, some commodities "have been sold with a bit more estimation than before the news." But more than anything, commerce was at a standstill since "as long as the war has not been declared the consumers will not want to exceed the prices that until now they have paid, and the vendors do not want to sell at these prices because they believe that they will never get lower than they are presently, and that in the event that war is confirmed, they might see some improvement." Miguel Jacinto added, with some delight, that their mutual acquaintance, the merchant Remigio Fernández, stood to earn *un dineral*, a fortune, if the rumors of war were confirmed because he was presently in possession of more than three thousand barrels of wine.[13]

The same occurred in Mexico in mid-1793 according to trader Juan Felipe Laurnaga, who noted that due to unconfirmed rumors that Spain had entered the war against France, trade was characterized by "a perfect calm." News of possible war had driven vendors to increase their prices, but their customers were not willing to pay the higher prices for fear that the reports were false. Laurnaga added that everyone was awaiting the arrival of a ship from Cadiz "to reveal once and for all whether or not war has been declared between France and us." The uncertain state of international affairs had immobilized trade.[14]

Any hostilities introduced added risks, but war with France concerned merchants less than engagement with the far superior British navy. Ironically, Laurnaga's correspondence in late 1796 echoed his remarks of three years earlier. In November Laurnaga wrote that commerce was at a standstill because merchants were uncertain whether Spain and England had gone to war. Laurnaga had probably already learned that Spain and France had signed the Treaty of San Ildefonso on 19 August 1796, a pact that made war with England a near certainty, but the news of Spain's 7 October 1796 declaration against England had clearly not yet reached Mexico. "While we desire impatiently the arrival of some boat from Europe that will take us out of this labyrinth of doubts in which we find ourselves, none appears, and so this commerce remains suspended and in a total calm."[15]

Just as rumors of war introduced uncertainty, wartime reports of potential peace treaties paralyzed vendors and consumers who respectively neither wanted to sell too cheaply nor pay too dearly. In the winter and spring of 1797–98, merchant Rafael José Facio of Veracruz commented to his partner Juan José de Puch about that port town's commercial inactivity "for fear that peace will be confirmed from one day to the next." The uncertainty stemmed from the ambiguity of news arriving from Europe. "The diversity of news about the reaching of peace treaties, the Congress of Lille, and recently the Royal Decree allowing neutral powers to introduce all classes of goods have caused damage in that everyone has begun [merely] sustaining themselves, buying no more than the absolute necessary. And all have resolved to do it so as not to expose themselves to experiencing losses."[16] Long-distance commerce benefited from predictability; international strife, however, introduced considerable uncertainty. Half a decade later Facio again advised Puch about the "inaction of this commerce," which he attributed to the "expectation of peace or war." Facio wrote in November 1803, the Peace of Amiens having been ruptured the previous May following the resumption of war between France and England. As Facio correctly recognized, Spain's neutrality was fragile:

> here there is great diversity of opinion but the majority thinks that the French and English will reconcile amicably and that it will not come to the point that we get involved with their discord. If that is the case, and we stay neutral, without the least risk that our ships will be seized, I urge

you to remit to me as quickly as possible my interests invested in goods. . . . [But] certainly if we were to have the misfortune that the scourge of war were to reach us, under no condition should you risk my resources, as I have told you in my previous [correspondence].[17]

The case of Remigio Fernández and the more than three thousand barrels of wine mentioned above actually points to one easily overlooked aspect of long-distance trade, the role of luck. While war was a frequent occurrence in Spain's early modern history, the second half of the eighteenth century was especially bellicose. The occurrence of war almost always affected merchants profoundly, although not always in the same manner. Two merchants of equal wealth, equal skill, and equal stomach for risk might experience drastically different results from the outbreak of war, depending on their individual circumstances at the moment of rupture. Fernández certainly would have profited handsomely from the good fortune of having found himself at the war's start in possession of so large a quantity of wine, a highly regarded (and price inelastic[18]) commodity, although in the particular case the 1790 war never erupted; the next war was still several years away. The profits that he might have realized had there actually been hostilities would have compensated him for some misfortune that he had experienced in some previous commercial lull. The point is that luck played an immeasurable role in the fortunes of long-distance traders.

At the same time that Fernández was sitting on his potential fortune in wine, another Mexican trader, Domingo Framil, had several hundred thousand pesos of imported merchandise warehoused in Veracruz. Perhaps Framil was disappointed that the war between Spain and England failed to erupt, because he was forced to unload his goods at very low prices. Miguel Jacinto de Marticorena reported on 6 December 1790 that news had arrived to Mexico that England and Spain had likely resolved their differences and that each nation's naval squadrons had returned to their respective home ports. Two weeks later Marticorena added that Framil had sold the entire lot worth three hundred thousand pesos at 4 percent above his cost, at least half of it on credit terms generous to the buyers. Had the war erupted, Framil's riches would have soared. Instead, he undoubtedly took a bath, bad luck indeed.[19]

Mexican merchant Rafael José Facio was fortunate to be holding imported items in 1798 in the early stages of the war against Great Britain, but he was unsure of his best course of action. In his April letter to partner Juan José de Puch, Facio explained that he had previously sold a portion of the merchandise at a hefty 60 percent markup, but that the continued news of war had led him to hoard the remaining stock in the hope of selling at even more favorable prices. This turned out to be a bad decision, Facio concluded, since prices had recently descended with the arrival of conflicting information about the war's status.[20] In fact, he might have been lucky and ultimately gambled well; peace was still years away.

In January 1797 Guatemalan merchant Pedro José de Górriz lamented to his trading partner in Spain about the misfortune of having his warehouses empty when war between Spain and England was declared "here" on 17 December 1796.[21] As was the case with most transatlantic merchants in Guatemala, Górriz was in the business of exchanging indigo for imported European goods. The war with England, the so-called First Naval War (1796–1802), severely interrupted shipping lanes to Central America, to a much greater extent than had occurred in the years immediately prior while Spain was engaged in war with France. "My losses have been very notable ever since the war with France was declared," lamented Górriz.[22] But the present hostilities had been far more debilitating still:

> I cannot adequately express to you the damages caused to my humble interests due to the fatal situation in which this war has ensnared me. In addition to finding myself without any merchandise with which I could make a half *real*, I see it impossible that I could buy [goods profitably] in these warehouses, given [the markups] of 60 to 70 percent that they ask for the textiles that they received on the last boats. Some greedier [merchants are demanding] up to 80 percent, and others even still do not intend to sell for the moment.[23]

Górriz begged his associate to send to him "a small lot to Veracruz on the first convoy that presents itself." Timing was everything in commerce, and Górriz had the bad luck of the war beginning at a poor moment in his commercial cycle. Had he only recently taken possession of a shipment from Spain, then he would have enjoyed a windfall. His only solace was that prices for locally grown indigo would "be cheap in the coming year if the war continues, which might perhaps remunerate all my losses."[24]

The end of war could also bankrupt a commercial venture. Many traders suspended business during war, but those who did not paid war-inflated insurance premiums and freight rates. These additional costs could easily be passed on to consumers as long as hostilities persisted; the end of the war, however, caused prices to immediately decline. Francisco de Sierra shipped a large lot of paper to Peru during the War of American Independence, incurring elevated insurance and freight costs. Unfortunately,

peace was declared before his commissions agent, the merchant Antonio
Saenz de Tejada, could sell the merchandise, meaning that Francisco de
Sierra had little prospect of recovering his investment no matter what
course of action Saenz de Tejada took.

> If it were necessary to sell the paper ream by ream it would take many
> years since months have passed without unloading even one. If one were
> to look for someone to buy the entire lot, there would be no one who
> would take it at twenty reales per ream because every day things get
> worse. So with this I didn't know what move to make because of the
> excessive loss that it offers due to its high cost from having been shipped
> from there in wartime and it having arrived here in peace.[25]

Merchants attempted to arrange their business dealings to avoid the
devastation caused by shifting political circumstances, although one can
imagine that the timing of war was impossible to predict and that Atlantic
world merchants furthermore lacked great flexibility to rapidly reallocate
their investments during even the most propitious times. In a letter to his
brother, Juan Bautista de Marticorena wrote of the dangers of getting
stuck with unsalable merchandise when fighting erupted. When Marticorena wrote in early May 1793, the war between Spain and France was
already several months old, but apparently an official declaration of war
had not yet reached Guatemala, only rumors. Juan Bautista expected his
brother's ships, *La Empresa* and *La Navarra*, to arrive shortly to the Hondu-
ran port of Omoa, but he considered it prudent to await their arrival before purchasing indigo for the return voyage.

> Until the arrival of your [ships] *La Empresa* and *La Navarra*, I await to see
> if I will buy 10 or 20 parcels (*tercios*) of dye on credit with the goal of
> making this small remittance to you, since although I could buy them
> [now,] I do not want to expose myself to a mess such as that which would
> occur if by chance the ships were not to come or there were an outbreak
> of war.[26]

Merchants were not always able to adopt such defensive postures, but as
long as Marticorena could hedge his bets, it seemed wise to do so.

By August Juan Bautista had reallocated his financial holdings after
learning of the war's outbreak. The news had caused a significant rise in
the prices in Guatemala for imported goods, a welcome relief after the
decade of surplus commodities and depressed prices. Marticorena and his
partner took advantage of the improved environment by selling a store
that they owned, along with its existing inventory. The sale netted them,

Juan Bautista estimated, 56 percent above the original cost of the commodities and fixtures, a nice return. Presumably, Juan Bautista imagined that the war would be brief and that selling everything at a war premium was wise. Several years later, however, European commodities were selling for much higher prices still, as Pedro de Górriz revealed above. In any event, Marticorena used his share of the proceeds on the sale of the store, twenty thousand pesos, to purchase indigo, hoping to make an equally satisfying profit by selling in the war-deprived markets of Europe.[27]

Juan Bautista de Marticorena's initial optimism that the war would help relieve the stagnant economy was quickly dashed. Indeed, the next several years proved financially troublesome. The interruption of trade due to the closing of shipping lanes slowed the circulation of his merchandise, making difficult his payment of a number of debts that came due. In January 1796, Juan Bautista informed his brother that he soon needed to repay a thirty-five thousand peso note and that an identical one would come due later in the year. To mobilize the necessary funds was not going to be simple. It was with biting sarcasm, and wishful thinking, that Juan Bautista added: "free of these quantities, I am resolved to never again go into debt."[28] But the worst was still to come.

When the war with Great Britain began, Juan Bautista de Marticorena's investments were not well positioned, and much of his capital became stranded abroad, according to another brother, Miguel Jacinto, who observed in 1798 that "the current war has caught Juan Bautista with most of his interests in Havana."[29] One can understand, then, Juan Bautista's exclamation later in the year that "this damned (*condenado*) war is breaking us into smithereens (*pedazos*), and if we do not see the end soon, I do not know what will become of us, or at least of me as I am greatly burdened by debts and with the only hope [being] a prompt peace."[30]

Sometimes merchants devised clever means to insulate themselves from the unpredictability of international affairs, the danger that war's outbreak could leave them vulnerable or regretting a recent deal. By mid-May 1793 news of Spain's engagement with France was apparently still not confirmed in Guatemala, and Juan Bautista de Marticorena wrote that some merchants were making conditional sales of European imports, the markup depending on the confirmation of Spain's combat status. "One or two sales of goods have taken place here at 30 percent [markup] in the event of peace and at 50 percent if war."[31] If the war status were confirmed, then the higher price would apply. A variable price such as this permitted commerce to proceed during a period in which the uncertainty of political affairs might otherwise have driven merchants to inaction.

While conflict was generally deleterious to mercantile interests, it did provide opportunities for speculators to stockpile commodities with the aim of later exporting locally produced goods whose prices were depressed by the disruption of trade. According to the viceroy of Río de la Plata, wealthy merchants of Buenos Aires, taking advantage of depressed prices, had warehoused large quantities of hides, generally impervious to decay, and other commodities during the War of American Independence. When peace was restored, he added, they profited handsomely.[32] To pursue such a strategy to any significant degree, however, probably required the possession of considerable wealth. Poorer traders' pockets were not sufficiently deep to tie up large sums in unmovable merchandise.

A strategy of stockpiling cheap commodities was only rational when merchants anticipated a brief end to the hostilities, since they otherwise risked tying up their funds for too long a period. In a letter to Juan José de Puch of Cadiz, Mexican trader Rafael José Facio pointed to the war-induced commodity price divergence, urging Puch to buy European goods in Cadiz at the existing low prices. As Facio explained:

> peace being confirmed, the fruits of this kingdom take on greater value
> for their ability to be exported, [and] the same occurs in that market with
> goods and merchandise, so that it seems to me worthwhile that before
> that moment arrives you take advantage of the time, proceeding to buy
> goods . . . with the objective of remitting them to me in the first register
> ships [once] peace is reached.[33]

If Facio and Puch pursued this course, they likely regretted their decision. Facio's advice was proffered in April 1798, but Spain's alliance with France in the war against England continued until the Peace of Amiens of 25 March 1802. While there were occasional opportunities to ship goods between Spain and Mexico in the interim, they were very risky and incurred very high costs in the form of war-inflated insurance and freight. Most merchants waited out the war despite claims to the contrary by the *consulado* of Mexico, which informed Viceroy Azanza that "residents of peninsular trading ports are motivated to trade despite the risks of war because the elevated profits that they anticipate will compensate them for the said risks." The Mexican merchants were likely exaggerating their counterparts' stomachs for risk, however, because they were attempting to dissuade the Crown from allowing the ships of neutral countries to visit Havana, a liberalization that would have hurt them financially.[34]

Merchants who bought cheaply during the war and quickly got their items to market after the restoration of peace benefited from the pent-up demand. The first several cargoes of a commodity whose supply was exhausted during the war fetched good prices once trade resumed; the trick, though, was to be among the first to arrive with scarce supplies. While the interruption of trade between Spain and northern Europe was not as severe as that which customarily affected transatlantic commerce, the end of war still provided golden opportunities to those who could most rapidly place scarce commodities in the market. Shortly after the January 1783 announcement of a truce in the American Revolutionary War between the bellicose European powers, the London merchant house of Hananel and Jacob Mendes da Costa learned of the departure from Cadiz of cochineal shipped by Francisco de Sierra. "We celebrate the departure of the ship 'Tres Hermanos,' and we hope that the seven barrels of cochineal will get here soon as dye is at 20/6 to 21/6 and the first shipments that arrive will be those that sell best since the dyers are undersupplied and in immediate need for the works that they have underway."[35] In the event, the shipment took over a month to arrive to England and by then, the cochineal price, while still buoyant, was beginning to show some signs of weakness. In mid-March the house of Mendes da Costa wrote to acknowledge the shipment's arrival but warned, "we anticipate [the price] to drop but it all depends on the quantities that come from there, and we would appreciate that you advise us for our guidance, if you can, when a quantity of this dye might be expected to arrive from Veracruz."[36] Fortunately for Sierra, his cochineal managed to sell quite profitably, fetching him just over 1,411 pounds sterling.[37] As Mendes da Costa of London predicted, however, the favorable cochineal prices did not last. While Francisco de Sierra's cochineal sold well in London in early May, by month's end, the windfall had concluded. Perhaps partially seeking to ingratiate themselves to Sierra, the London merchants reported, "we greatly appreciate having sold it, because today there are not any buyers of that dye, the news of the arrival to Havana of the ships from Veracruz having caused a total inaction in this sector. We anticipate that the price here will be established in accordance with the price there once the ships arrive to Europe."[38]

War shortages had pushed prices upward but the restoration of peace drove them back down to more normal levels. Those lucky enough to arrive to markets first benefitted greatly. One cannot help but wonder whether much of the commercial expansion that followed the American Revolutionary War resulted from inexperienced merchants overreacting to the war-inflated prices and the spectacular returns enjoyed during the first months of peace. Delgado Ribas indeed argues that Barcelona merchants wrongly interpreted high prices in 1783 to be the new norm under *comercio libre*. They responded accordingly, but self-destructively, by shipping excessive quantities to market.[39]

The lessons of the post-1783 commercial deluge were learned well by Miguel Jacinto de Marticorena. In 1798 he reminded his brother from Guatemala of both the benefits of acting swiftly to resupply the war-scarce market but also the perils of shipping too much, too late:

> in the event that peace is established, plan on making an expedition to Honduras. Be advised that its good or bad luck will depend uniquely on you being the first or at least one of the first who succeeds in arriving to the Gulf. . . . [I]n this way not only will you enjoy a clear and quick return [voyage] but also the advantage of selling with profit and security.

Marticorena was less sanguine about the long-term prospects of postbellum trade, predicting that the pent-up demand would be more than met by fresh supplies and that prices would subsequently tumble. As evidence, he pointed to the catastrophic oversupply that followed the War of American Independence: "with the experience of what happened in the years '85, '86 and '87 which were the ruin of this Kingdom, I am foreseeing the same occurring in the two or three following this peace."[40] The termination of hostilities permitted the first shipments of needed commodities to sell at elevated prices. But supplies quickly replenished, and those who missed the first wave were probably disappointed by the subsequent drop in prices. In the absence of inside information about the political climate, merchants needed good preparation and a bit of luck to get their wares to market immediately upon the war's conclusion.

Privateering

War introduced a variety of risks but none greater than privateering. Corsairs were always a threat to commercial vessels, but war escalated enormously the incidence of attacks as nations outfitted privateers to intercept the valuable merchantmen of their Atlantic world rivals. The strategic benefits of attacking one's enemy's trade was explained in 1805 by Field Marshall Antonio de Narváez y la Torre of New Granada. For "a nation whose power is founded on its riches and the trade which they afford, the real and most efficacious way to wage war against it is by waging it against this essential nerve center and backbone of its power and strength."[41] A similar sentiment is captured in the mid-eighteenth-century writings of English merchant Nicholas Magens, who argued: "The great object of a maritime nation should be, to take advantage of any rupture with another trading state, to destroy and distress their shipping, and commerce, and to cut off all resources for naval armaments."[42]

A distinction should be drawn between piracy and privateering; the former was illegal and its perpetrators might be punished by any of the European naval powers. Privateering, in contrast, was a sanctioned practice in which the government contracted shipowners to arm their vessels with the purpose of attacking enemy ships during wartime. Privateers were bound by recognized laws that determined how they could proceed and what constituted a legal prize, a legitimate seizure. Privateers sailing under the Spanish flag were required to obtain a *patente de corso*, a letter of marque, a license to operate as a privateer in service to the crown. To obtain such a permit, shipowners were expected to be honorable men and were required to provide a *fianza* (surety) guaranteeing their legitimate behavior. Acts of seizure by unlicensed ships were considered acts of piracy, and those responsible could be apprehended as criminals.[43]

According to historian Oscar Cruz Barney, Spain suffered from a severe shortage of sanctioned corsairs during the second half of the eighteenth century, leading the crown to gradually increase the potential rewards reaped by privateers. This resulted in an expanding number of Spanish privateers at the turn of the century, as shipowners responded to the growing economic incentives.[44] Given the important strategic role privateers played for a nation at war—denying the enemy easy access to the fruits of trade and, perhaps, needed war goods—the monarchy's desire to expand this fleet is understandable.

In mid-1779, the *consulado* became involved with the organization and funding of twenty ships to engage British merchantmen during the War of American Independence. On 9 August the guild sought the advice of the Junta de Marina regarding "the artillery and caliber that should be installed . . . to combat and defeat any enemy war frigate of 30 cannons or smaller . . . such as packet boats or sloops."[45]

One would imagine that merchants viewed privateers with considerable disdain, a formidable obstacle to their commercial interests. As suggested by their very name, however, privateers were privately owned and operated vessels, often financed by merchants themselves, who viewed investment in privateers as an entrepreneurial undertaking. A window into the economics of privateering in the Spanish world is afforded by the establishment in February 1805 of a "company," literally a partnership, to outfit and run a Spanish corsair. Eleven investors purchased a total of fifteen shares (see Table 6.2) in the company to equip a vessel called *El Buen*

Vasallo with the armament and provisions needed to operate for three months. Each of the fifteen shares sold for 10,000 *reales vellón* (500 pesos). Originally constructed in the town of Cartaya in the province of Huelva, *El Buen Vasallo*, according to the company charter, was to be armed with "a cannon of 24, two *obuses* (howitzers) of 12, two *pedreros* (small guns that threw scatter-shot), and additional munitions corresponding to a crew of 45 men."[46] The estimated cost to run the ship for three months was 150,000 *reales vellón*, the exact amount raised through the sale of the shares, but the partners were required to cover any additional expenses that might arise in accordance with their share of the company. Of course, the goal of the company was to profit by seizing English ships. The *armador*, the individual in charge of overseeing the organization of the project, was Juan Vicente de Marticorena, who with his three shares was also the largest shareholder. It was his responsibility to secure the *patente de corso* from the Crown as well as ensuring, to the best of his ability, that seizures were quickly judged *buenas presas*, legal prizes. At the end of the three months, the revenues generated by the sale of the ships and cargo, minus any expenses incurred by the *armador*, were to be distributed. After first deducting 2 percent "commission" to be paid to the ship's crew and its captain, Diego Sayago, who was also a shareholder, one-third of the remainder was allocated to the captain and crew and the other two-thirds was distributed pro rata to the shareholders.[47]

TABLE 6.2

Shareholders of the Corsair Ship El Buen Vasallo

Shares	Shareholder	Amount Invested
3	Juan Vicente de Marticorena for the marca ADM	30,000 rv
1	Juan Martín Larasa Micheo & Francisco Vicente de Yrañeta for the marca L	10,000 rv
1	Juan Martín Larasa Micheo & Francisco Vicente de Yrañeta for the marca M	10,000 rv
2	Francisco Mavito for the marca MV	20,000 rv
1	Francisco Moreno y Terrera	10,000 rv
1	Rafael María Chaparro	10,000 rv
1	Miguel de Mendiraval	10,000 rv
1	Antonio de Alsazua	10,000 rv
1	Juan de Puch	10,000 rv
1	Francisco Mavito for the marca FMH	10,000 rv
1	Diego Sayago	10,000 rv
1	Ignacio de Solotea	10,000 rv
	TOTAL	**150,000 rv**

SOURCE: AGI, *Consulados*, legajo 72, folios 244–48, 12 February 1805.

"In order to capture a boat of English dominion," Diego Sayago, captain of *El Buen Vasallo*, was instructed to pursue prizes around the Straits of Gibraltar and the Alboran Sea,[48] after first spending several weeks "between the bays of Espantel and Trafalgar," on the Atlantic coast of Spain, south of Cadiz. It was the captain's responsibility to ensure that his crew refrain from "pillage and disorder" upon the taking of a prize. Furthermore, enemy crews who surrendered and were taken prisoner were to be treated with "decency and humanity . . . in the same way that you would want to be treated if you were in their place."[49]

El Buen Vasallo's three-month voyage "against the enemies of the Crown" began in early April. In August, the shareholders were presented the opportunity to renew their interests in the venture for another three months. But *El Buen Vasallo* had not enjoyed much success thus far, its only achievement having been to assist another corsair in the taking of a boat called *Diana* which produced for *Buen Vasallo*'s backers a meager twenty-five thousand *reales vellón*, about one-sixth of their total initial investment.[50] Most of the shareholders elected to withdraw, but Juan Vicente de Marticorena and "three friends" reinvested in the corsair and remained active in the business of privateering for several years.[51]

After its poor beginnings, *El Buen Vasallo*'s fortunes began to turn considerably better. The new investors replaced the ship captain with "a valiant Catalán captain named Pablo Amorós."[52] In February 1806 *El Buen Vasallo* teamed up with a French corsair named *La Costa de Oro* to seize a small English craft off the coast of Marbella. The prize, along with its English crew, was brought into Marbella where it was declared legal and its cargo of 1409 silver pesos was divided.[53] The following month don Manuel de Quevedo, a Spanish navy lieutenant, declared legitimate the seizure by *El Buen Vasallo* of an English *místico*. When captured, the mystic was en route to Gibraltar with a cargo of oxen. Not only did the cargo prove valuable, but the vessel itself was subsequently outfitted by the investors into a second corsair.[54] In April, *El Buen Vasallo* seized a *falucho*[55] named *Virgen de Europa* traveling from Gibraltar to Tavira, Portugal, whose confiscated cargo consisted of forty loads of tobacco and some cotton.[56] Its greatest prize, however, occurred shortly thereafter when the crew of *El Buen Vasallo* took a 354-ton English brigantine loaded with six months' provisions destined for the English naval squadrons blockading Cadiz. The prize's value exceeded 700,000 *reales vellón* (35,000 pesos).[57]

While merchantmen rightfully feared privateers, the running of a corsair entailed numerous risks of its own, and eventually *El Buen Vasallo*'s string of luck was broken. On 29 May 1806 *El Buen Vasallo* engaged with a much larger twenty-two-gun *corbeta* (corvette),[58] sustaining damage and leading to the death of seven crew members and injury to another eleven, several of whom subsequently died. Captain Pablo Amorós was shot in the right shoulder but survived.[59] According to Juan Vicente de Marticorena, "it was a miracle that [*El Buen Vasallo*] escaped seizure."[60]

Captain Amorós and *El Buen Vasallo* resumed their privateering run several months later, joined by the English *místico* captured in March, which had been rechristened *La Fortuna* and outfitted and licensed to operate as an additional privateer. In September, *La Fortuna* helped seize *Venus*, a Danish ship originating in Belfast and traveling with papers deemed irregular.[61] *El Buen Vasallo* succeeded the following month in taking an English frigate named *La Veloz*. In informing Juan Vicente de Marticorena of the latter hoist, Roque Manuel de Artiaga, one of the other investors to the company, explained that he rushed home to read the ship's cargo registry to "María and Pepita," his wife and daughter, and "they went crazy with glee." Apparently, the good news also prompted a shopping spree.[62]

El Buen Vasallo's career as a corsair ended on 14 June 1807. Needing to return for personal business to his place of origin, the town of Echalar in Navarra, Juan Vicente de Marticorena had boarded the ship in Algeciras intending to stop briefly in Cadiz before continuing the journey to northern Spain. *El Buen Vasallo* was accompanied by the "precioso Jabeque[63] Esperanza*" that had been seized only "days before" and that Marticorena had loaded with merchandise to sell in the north. Upon leaving Algeciras, however, the ships were attacked by two enemy brigs near the cape of Trafalgar, resulting in a seven-hour battle during which Marticorena's vessels fired three hundred cannon shots. *El Buen Vasallo* and Esperanza attempted to flee up the River Barbate but were impeded by the brigs. Finally, the enemy ships dispatched six rowboats with one hundred men who pillaged the town and set fire to *El Buen Vasallo* and the *Esperanza*. As Marticorena lamented, "my bad luck wanted to come back to life."[64]

Mitigating the Risks of Privateering

While merchants might invest into the outfitting of a corsair, their primary contact or concern with the privateers came from the opposite perspective, as shippers seeking to avoid the loss of their cargo or vessels to these entrepreneurial predators. The dangers posed by corsairs escalated tremendously the riskiness of commerce during moments of international strife. In general, merchants withdrew from Atlantic world trade or at least dramatically reduced their levels of engagement during wartime.

Apart from divestment or the purchase of maritime insurance (discussed below), there was little a trader could do to reduce entirely the risks generated by privateering. Merchants did, however, employ strategies that lessened their risk or reduced their exposure. For one, transatlantic merchants attempted to limit the amount of merchandise that they shipped aboard any single boat, preferring to split their cargoes between two or more vessels, "to divide the risks of the sea."[65] By dividing their cargoes, they reduced their exposure to loss, although such division must have imposed certain costs. While the risks that bad weather might shipwreck a boat made this strategy rational at all times, it became even more imperative during wartime when the riskiness of trade expanded due to enemy corsairs.

The logic of dividing the cargo among several ships was explained to Viceroy Bucarelli in 1774 by a number of prominent Mexican merchants:

> We see many times two, three or more ships leaving the same port with the same destination and despite experiencing the same winds, one is lost and the rest are saved, concluding from this that it is rarer to lose two ships than one, and three than two, and thus it is riskier and more exposed to place all of one's capital aboard just one boat rather than to divide it between as many as possible.[66]

It was to reduce his risk of loss from shipwreck or other mishap that led Peruvian merchant Antonio de Querejazu to split his 1722 shipment of fifty thousand pesos between the ships *La Capitana* and *La Almiranta*.[67] In 1776, the Conde de Repáraz sought permission to divide his cargo of nineteen hundred *zurrones*[68] of cochineal among three ships, the frigate *Ventura*, the navío *San Nicolás*, and a third unnamed vessel. This was prudent, he argued, "in order to make the risk of sea less terrible."[69] Similarly, in March 1775 the *consulado* of Mexico issued a request to Viceroy Bucarelli that an additional ship be permitted to join the fleet and carry the excess stock of cochineal warehoused in Veracruz. The guild further recommended that each merchant's dyestuff be divided equally among several ships so as to reduce their exposure to risk.[70] When in October 1798, in the middle of the First Naval War, Guatemalan trader Pedro José de Górriz requested that Juan Vicente de Marticorena send him a shipment of merchandise from Cadiz, he stipulated that Marticorena should endeavor to "split the risk if two boats are present."[71] In the following year, Mexican merchant Rafael José Facio adopted a similar strategy with a large quantity of cochineal, shipping small portions of the dye aboard multiple merchantmen destined for Spain.[72] Fifteen years later, to reduce the risk posed by Spanish American insurgent corsairs, a Barcelona trading firm, Domingo Parés y Compañía, ordered its factors in Veracruz to remit cargoes of sugar and grain in multiple vessels.[73] Perhaps the most extreme example of dividing cargo dates from the 1757 flota to New Spain. Members of the Uztáriz family, one of the most prominent merchant clans of Cadiz, shipped merchandise aboard thirteen of the fourteen vessels en route to Mexico. This cumbersome division reduced the concentration of the family's commercial exposure.[74]

Another strategy employed to reduce risk of corsair attack was to ship aboard vessels flying the flags of neutral nations. In general, only a ship flying the flag of a nation at war with Spain was a legitimate prize for a Spanish privateer. Likewise, vessels traveling under the Spanish colors were legal targets of French or English corsairs whenever Spain fought with one or the other country.

This latter rule is well-illustrated by a somewhat comical affair dating from the start of the 1793 war with France. In May the Cadiz *consulado* addressed the Crown about a ship traveling from Lima called *Santiago Apostol alias Nuevo Aquiles*, which, along with its estimated cargo of 3.5 million pesos, was seized by French corsairs after a five-hour battle in which nine sailors were killed and thirty-six injured. Only several days later, the vessel was recaptured by two ships pertaining to England, Spain's ally against France. The guild merchants were concerned that England would try to keep the ship of its ally, Spain, arguing that it was a legitimate prize since it had become French property after the first seizure. Employing clever logic, the guild spokesmen argued that since neither Spain nor England recognized the legitimacy of the new French government, the seizure of the ship and its temporary possession by French corsairs could not be seen as having bestowed ownership on France given that an unrecognized government could not bestow ownership. To claim otherwise would be tantamount to recognizing the sovereignty of the Revolutionary French regime. In short, they argued, the original seizure by the French corsairs had to be interpreted as thievery and, consequently, the English were merely recovering stolen property; they were not seizing property that could be considered French, that is of the enemy, and thus a legal prize.[75] In the end, the guild prevailed and the *Nuevo Aquiles* was returned to Spain after first paying a reward of one-eighth of the value to the "recapturers."[76] Only ships of the declared enemy were fair game to corsairs.

Neutral ships were not, in theory, legal prizes. That said, what constituted neutrality could be contentious. For example, Spain initially remained neutral following the 1803 rupture of the brief Peace of Amiens and the resumption of war between France and England. Prior to the Treaty of Amiens, Spain and France had been allies against England, and so Spanish merchants were fearful that the English might refuse to recognize and respect their neutral status. In the event, the Cadiz *Consulado* expressed its relief in January 1804 that indeed England was demonstrating its recognition of Spanish neutrality "by means of the rigor and actions which they were proceeding in their tribunals to declare the illegitimacy of Spanish prizes."[77]

When Spain was at war, its merchants might ship aboard the vessels of third-party, neutral nations, hoping to escape predation by the corsairs of Spain's enemies. In theory this strategy could be effective, but in practice it afforded limited protection precisely because the neutrality of a ship could be challenged, especially when the neutral ships began trading in the goods of one of the belligerent nations. Privateers frequently boarded the ships of neutral nations and declared them legal prizes if their required papers were somehow deemed irregular or suspicious or if the cargoes they transported seemed to have originated from enemy nations. Merchant ships carried licenses, passports, cargo registries, navigation diaries, and lists of passengers, the legitimacy of any one of which might be challenged. Evidence that the cargoes belonged to nationals of the countries at war made seizure by enemy corsairs likely, although even lesser justifications were common.[78] So many neutral ships "have been pillage[d] by the English," one Cadiz commercial agent insisted in 1798, that "nowadays neutral ships are even riskier than those of our own."[79]

The security of neutral ships grew even less secure during the later years of the wars of the French Revolution. In Great Britain, Parliament engaged in considerable discussion that led to a number of acts that tended to narrow the scope of trade deemed legitimate for neutrals. Some in Great Britain desired far more stringent restrictions, such as Parliament member James Stephen, who penned a zealous pamphlet condemning Britain's tolerance towards neutral ships, especially those of the United States, which, he claimed, merely provided cover for the trade of England's enemies. According to Stephen, Britain's strategy had been to damage Napoleon's financial capacity to wage war by halting France's trade, but that this strategy had failed due to the trade of neutrals.

Our enemies . . . seem to have retreated from the ocean, and to have
abandoned the ports of their colonies; but it is a mere *ruse de guerre*—They
have, in effect, for the most part, only changed their flags, chartered
many vessels really neutral, and altered a little the former routes of their
trade. Their transmarine sources of revenue have not been for a moment
destroyed by our hostilities, and at present are scarcely impaired.[80]

Despite narrowing tolerance, neutral ships did provide some outlet to
Spanish shipping. In early 1781 Francisco de Sierra requested permission
to dispatch his sizeable stockpile of eighty thousand hides aboard Portuguese vessel in order to evade British corsairs.[81] During the height of the
First Naval War (1796–1802) with England, Barcelona merchant Joséf
Carbo hatched a plan to outfit a *pingue*, a small cargo boat, to transport
merchandise to Veracruz in company with a Genoese firm named Chi-
arele e hijo. The boat was to fly a Genoese flag and if intercepted by
corsairs, the captain was instructed to claim that all of the merchandise
belonged to the Genoese company, thereby reducing the dangers that
the *pingue* would be declared a legal prize. The conspirators hoped,
somehow, to return from Veracruz with a cargo consisting of Mexican
cochineal and Cuban sugar.[82] Apparently, Carbo had second thoughts about
his plan since two weeks later he announced that the contract with the
Genoese company had been canceled. According to Carbo, the English
privateers showed no respect whatsoever for the neutrality of ships but
intercepted them and declared them *buenas presas* (legal prizes) for even
the slightest irregularity of their papers. There had been several such cases
recently, he added, including a Maltese boat that had been taken to Gibraltar and declared a legal prize and another Genoese vessel seized while en
route to Barcelona.[83]

The strategy of employing neutral ships to circumvent enemy corsairs
temporarily became Crown policy when Madrid granted permission for
neutral vessels to stop in Spain's Peninsular and American ports between
November 1797 and April 1799 and again during the years 1805–8. Undoubtedly these ships sailed with greater security than did Spanish ships,
but it would be wholly inaccurate to conclude that they offered complete
protection from privateers. In 1798 the British naval blockade prevented
neutral ships from departing Cadiz, according to Spain's minister of finance, Francisco de Saavedra.[84] The same transpired in Mexico according
to Viceroy Miguel Joséf de Azanza, who noted in November 1798 that the
British navy was curtailing neutral vessels leading to the stranding of eight
thousand *zurrones* (sacks that held around two hundred pounds of cochi-

neal apiece) of cochineal in the warehouses of Veracruz.[85] In a mid-1800 missive to the viceroy of New Granada regarding the Crown's temporary adoption of neutral shipping, Columbian merchant José Ignacio de Pombo noted that "in retaliation for the depredations and piracy of France, the English had expanded in the present war to pursue and take control of the property of their enemies aboard neutral ships . . . declaring their cargoes legal prizes." Merchant Pombo concluded: "in this manner, one ran the same risk on neutral ships as national ones."[86] Clearly, neutrality offered only limited security.

The greatest beneficiary of the neutral shipping decree was the United States, which profited from the wars to penetrate Spain's monopoly of the Spanish Atlantic trade.[87] But American neutrality did not fully protect its fleet from the predations of corsairs either. As early as 1793, French privateers began attacking merchantmen flying the flag of the neutral United States, detaining for prolonged periods or seizing outright hundreds of American vessels and sparking in 1798 the so-called Quasi-War between the United States and France, an undeclared conflict waged exclusively at sea. Between June 1796 and June 1797 alone, the French seized an estimated 316 American vessels. Total losses sustained by U.S. shippers had reached twenty million dollars by 1800, and the conflict was far from completed. Following the rupture of the Peace of Amiens, neutral American ships in the Caribbean encountered assaults by both French and British forces who took 528 and 389 vessels respectively between 1803 and 1807.[88] While the use by Spanish merchants of the ships of neutral nations during wartime might have reduced risk relative to employing Spanish ships directly, it was no panacea; the neutrality of ships was barely recognized.

Even with the end of the Napoleonic wars, Spanish vessels remained targets of corsair ships, now sailed by American Creoles seeking independence from Spain. Certainly indicative of Spain's deteriorated position, during the wars of Latin American Independence, some Spanish merchants sought safety in the banner of their frequent enemy, England. "Insurgent corsairs," vessels outfitted by Latin American rebels, had become a formidable threat to Spanish shipping by 1816. To combat this risk, Spanish traders attempted to cloak their ownership of ships and cargo by sailing under the flag of Great Britain. Historian Michael Costeloe documents a case in which Spanish merchants proposed a deal to feign sale of their vessel to an English firm, which would then sail under the Union Jack with a predominantly British crew to either Havana or Montevideo. The use of British neutrality during this era, Costeloe concludes, "seems to have been fairly widespread among the Spanish merchants, both on the outward and the return journeys."[89] Perhaps it was British naval supremacy rather than neutrality that offered the real protection.

War was the enemy of Atlantic world merchants, even if some did manage to profit from its impact. When nations went to war, their merchants paid a high price by being forced to curb their commerce. Resorting to neutral ships was one way to protect against corsair attacks. Another was to operate through middlemen from neutral nations. Because Holland was at war with England during the American Revolutionary War, Dutch merchants employed the cloak of Belgian trading houses to continue trading. In September 1781, Amsterdam merchant Echenique y Sánchez encouraged Cadiz merchant Francisco de Sierra to send a shipment of goods but to direct it to Oostende merchants Messieurs Veuve de Jean Martín Smits & Fils "with a simulated letter and bill of lading as if it were effectively on their account, so that it can be shown [to British patrols], if needed. . . . For a 2 percent commission, this house is obliged to declare these goods neutral." In case such a ploy did not appeal to Sierra, Echenique y Sánchez also floated the possibility that Sierra could ship with the Portuguese to whom the English had "conceded the privilege of transporting any innocent good on behalf of anyone and even from one enemy port to another." According to the Dutch house, many prominent Spanish commercial houses were taking advantage of this latter loophole.[90]

Perhaps even more extraordinary, Belgian firms were also used to circumvent prohibitions on trade between warring nations' merchants. Despite the Spanish Crown's June 1779 ban on commerce with Great Britain, who "should be treated as the true enemies of the Spanish monarchy,"[91] Francisco de Sierra continued to trade with the London-based trading house of Fermín de Tastet and Company by shipping through the Belgian house of Donche and Vereruysse of Bruges. Fermín de Tastet and Company had arranged during the war to employ clandestinely the services of Donche and Vereruysse with many of their Spanish and other clients whose governments were at war with England.

> If during the war it were to suit you to make some expeditions to here, the Señores Donche y Vereruysse of Bruges are authorized to manage business for us, and we extend to you this capacity . . . and whatever goods arrive, our said friends will deliver them to us charging 2 percent, but you would not have to negotiate any of this with them but [simply] send them bills of lading as if the thing really belonged to them and leave the rest to us.[92]

The London firm of Hananel and Jacob Mendes da Costa also arranged to receive shipments from Sierra through an Oostende-based firm, Liebaert Baes Derdeyn and Company.[93] In fact, in December 1781 Sierra took advantage of the opportunity and shipped to the Mendes da Costas four "barrels" of *grana fina*, top quality cochineal dye, employing the middle-man services of Liebaert Baes Derdeyn and Company.[94]

In essence, these Atlantic world traders were colluding to avoid the predations of their respective governments' sanctioned privateers. It should be noted that Fermín de Tastet was himself a Spaniard, but it is not known whether this fact played a role in his firm's circumvention of English corsairs.

Fermín de Tastet and Company even advised Sierra that despite the war "we often provide insurance for friends abroad."[95] In fact, Sierra clearly trusted his fellow traders, securing coverage through this firm and others throughout the hostilities.[96] Of course, the irony is that by far the greatest risk to Spanish shipping during these war years was British privateers, and so this London-based commercial house was securing coverage for Spanish vessels in the event of losses sustained at the hands of British forces. Their commercial interests, however, superseded imperial politics.

Another effective means to avoid losses to privateers was for merchants to ship their valuable cargoes on warships. Ships outfitted to run as corsairs were typically small to medium-sized vessels selected more for their quickness and maneuverability than their sheer fire power. This choice was reasonable given the strategy of privateers to prey upon weaker, more vulnerable merchantmen rather than to engage in battle. Ideally, corsairs detained their targets without ever needing to fire anything more than a warning shot across the bow. Privateers tended to steer clear of well-armed enemy vessels, their success depending on limiting armed conflict.

During wartime, prudent merchants sought for their valuable cargo the added security of vessels armed for battle. "In the event war is declared," Juan Felipe Laurnaga wrote his cousin, Juan Vicente de Marticorena, in April 1793, "any goods that go from this kingdom to that will do so on warships of the King."[97] Indeed after war erupted that year, Viceroy Revillagigedo of Mexico revoked an earlier edict to reduce freight charges aboard ships of the Royal Armada. In explaining his action, the viceroy noted that he expected to witness rising demand for the limited cargo space on the warships, a demand that justified the higher freight rates. He knew that merchants would happily pay more for the security that the navy ships provided.[98]

Throughout the summer of 1798, Mexican trader Rafael José Facio
held back a large quantity of cochineal that he had purchased in the
spring, fearful of the riskiness that corsairs posed. In September Facio
announced that he would send the cargo to Spain "as soon as peace is
declared, or by chance a warship here is readied for there."[99] Of course,
peace was still years away, and unfortunately for Facio and his partner,
Juan José de Puch, Spanish warships were far too busily engaged in battle
to be widely redirected to mercantile pursuits. By October 1799 Facio was
still in possession of the cochineal, which was beginning to deteriorate, to
lose weight from shrinkage. In desperation, Facio suggested that for lack
of warships he might choose to "risk it all" and ship aboard a merchant
vessel.[100]

Facio was far from the only Mexican merchant desperate to export cochineal at the time. In December 1799 the Oaxacan *Diputación de Comercio*, the provincial chamber of commerce, asked the viceroy to allocate
space for the export of cochineal aboard warships that were presently being loaded with eight million pesos' worth of silver bullion. The situation
was dire, they explained, as the growing surplus of dye in Mexico had
discouraged additional investment into production. The viceroy granted
their request but warned that the ships needed to be ready to sail at a
moment's notice, making complicated the loading of the dye.[101] The
important point here is that the merchants considered only warships to
be adequately secure.

Finding themselves in a similar predicament in 1800, a number of
prominent Guatemalan *consulado* merchants petitioned Miguel Cayetano
Soler, Secretary of State, for Crown assistance in transporting to Spain a
large supply of indigo that had been stranded in Havana. Apparently, cargoes of indigo aboard two merchantmen, the brigantine *San Rafael* and
the frigate *Placentina*, had been disembarked in Havana earlier in the war
and placed in warehouses for safekeeping. The Central American merchants advised the minister of the hardships that this had caused them and
beseeched him to order several warships to carry the dyestuff the rest of
the way to Spain. Unfortunately for the traders, at least some, perhaps all,
of the indigo was still stranded in Havana when peace finally returned in
early 1802.[102]

No source is a better measure of the perceived riskiness of commercial
behavior than maritime insurance premiums. Insurance underwriters based
the premiums they charged on their estimations of the riskiness of economic activities. Logically, the riskier the venture, the higher the rate of

insurance demanded by insurers. Spanish insurance companies regularly offered more favorable rates to cargoes traveling aboard better armed ships, with warships considered the most secure. A policy written on 17 March 1796 for a voyage from Buenos Aires to either Cadiz or La Coruña, for example, stipulated a reduced rate if the cargo traveled aboard a warship.[103] Offering discounted rates for commodities placed aboard warships was a common practice among the insurance firms of Cadiz. Indeed the practice was not new; it was already established in the late seventeenth century.[104] A London insurance firm granted a discount of 1 percentage point to Spanish merchant Francisco de Sierra in February 1784 to place his goods aboard a warship for transport between Spanish American ports and Cadiz, and this was during peacetime no less.[105]

As Mexican trader Rafael José Facio and the Guatemalan *consulado* merchants found in the cases noted above, however, warships were most frequently unavailable during wartime, precisely when the risks posed by corsairs spiked. Peruvian trader Antonio Sáenz de Tejada went so far as to claim, with obvious exasperation, that during the American Revolutionary War the limited commercial space that existed on warships was being inappropriately monopolized by "the commander and other officials."[106] Even during peacetime, there was a shortage of cargo space available on warships, and merchantmen were often inadequately armed. Armament was expensive and bulky, and most shipowners preferred to utilize their limited space to transport commercial payloads. Many of the ships outfitted for war were returned to minimally armed merchant vessels upon restoration of peace.

The shortage of cargo space on warships prompted an extraordinary venture in September 1798, during the depths of the war with England. Wealthy Navarrese merchant Pio de Elizalde joined with a number of other traders, mostly Frenchmen, to outfit a well-armed brig called *Hippomenez* as "corsair and merchantman" to transport cargo round trip between northern Spain and Veracruz. The ship, Elizalde wrote, had been forged in copper, was 67 to 68 feet in length and would have a crew of 30 to 40 men. While the vessel had a capacity of 160 tons, the plan was to limit the cargo to 110 tons "with the goal of not hampering its mobility." The ship was scheduled for departure mid-Brumaire (a month in the new Napoleonic calendar corresponding to 22 October to 20 November), or as Elizalde added, "at the beginning of November in the old style." Shares in the venture cost 40,000 *reales vellón*, equivalent to 10,000 French Livres (5000 Spanish pesos). The whole venture stemmed from the inadequate availability of space on Spanish warships. Elizalde and his partners essentially outfitted their own warship to allow safer passage during the war.[107]

• • •

While the space available to private merchants directly aboard warships was minimal, merchantmen could still partially benefit from the security that warships provided by traveling in convoy with the armed vessels. One should not forget that the system of fleets organized in the sixteenth century was originally designed with the specific purpose of providing security to the valuable cargoes moving between Spain and its colonies. The annual sailings consisted of merchantmen escorted by warships of the Royal Armada, the latter ensuring the safe voyage of the former. With the calamitous exception of 1628 when the Dutch Vice Admiral, Piet Heyn, seized most of the Spanish fleet commanded by Juan de Benavides y Bazán,[108] the practice of warships escorting commercial vessels proved very effective. Even after the introduction of *comercio libre* and the final termination of the fleets, merchants and shipowners recognized the benefits and took advantage of traveling in convoy with one another and with warships when available.

Corsairs and pirates attacked weaker vessels whether alone or traveling in tandem with another vulnerable target. However, a convoy of ships, especially escorted by a warship, was too formidable an opponent for most corsairs. When the captain and crew of the Spanish corsair *Buen Vasallo* encountered several English merchantmen near the port of Tarifa in November 1806, they kept their distance because, as Captain Pablo Amorós explained, the English ships were "convoyed by warships, so that we have been unable to attack them."[109] In this case, the naval escort provided ample security to the commercial vessels; it was sufficient to dissuade *El Buen Vasallo* from attacking.

Quite rationally, merchants sought the protection provided by convoys, especially in wartime. Privateering inevitably curtailed commerce during hostilities, but the organization of armed convoys helped reduce risk to a more palatable level. In October 1779, in the middle of the American Revolutionary War, the *Consulado* reacted to the "slowness in which shipowners and shippers proceed in the preparation and loading of register ships licensed to Veracruz," by warning merchants that "they would be wasting an opportune occasion" if they failed to take advantage of the scheduled November departure of a convoy of four warships to Veracruz to escort vessels carrying mercury to the Mexican mines.[110] In October 1780, exactly one year later, cargo space aboard the three warships scheduled to depart for Havana and Spain in November was deemed inadequate to transport the "cochineal, indigo and fruits" warehoused in Veracruz and ready for shipment. It was decided instead that there should be readied the "necessary merchant ships that promised the greatest security and defense which, accompanying the three ships of war and without separating from them, will transport the fruits that do not fit on the King's three."[111] Merchantmen traveling in convoy with warships enjoyed considerable security and protection. The following year, in November 1781, the Cadiz *consulado* advised the king that it had convened a session to discuss "the traffic of these Kingdoms with America almost interrupted by the war and the means to reestablish their continuation in benefit to both [sides'] commerce."[112] The solution recommended by the guild was that the Crown provide an armed convoy to escort merchant vessels to the colonies. Apparently unwilling to await the formation of a Spanish naval escort, Francisco de Sierra was able to send his ship, *El Jasón*, with a French convoy that sailed from Provence in July.[113] The French forces, allied with Spain against Great Britain during the American War of Independence, provided the naval escort that the Spanish crown could not. This allowed Sierra's merchant vessel safer passage to America. In the peacetime year of 1784, the *consulado* even sought a Crown-financed convoy to protect ships sailing to Veracruz and Buenos Aires from a large force of "Moors," probably Barbary pirates, "capable of achieving the seizure of merchant ships, armed only in merchandise and with a defense inferior to the superior enemy forces."[114] In each of these cases, the elevated wartime risks drove merchants to seek the protection afforded by armed convoys. Worth noting, of course, is that the official convoyed flota to Mexico had been terminated only several years earlier, yet the need for one of its principal benefits had not disappeared.[115]

In the bellicose years to come, seeking the protection of convoys was a common strategy. "With the first convoy or in warships, send me all of my credit in ribbonry (*listonería*)," instructed Mexican merchant Joséf Ignacio Pavón y Muñoz in November 1799. He further stressed that the shipment should not be "in unaccompanied boats, because the losses that I have suffered have made me very fearful."[116] Buenos Aires merchant Manuel de Arana also possessed greater faith in the safety of convoys. In late 1796 he wrote his associate in Cadiz, Antonio de Artechea, requesting the prompt shipment of merchandise "if the war against England is confirmed." But, he added, "it must be in some convoy coming to Montevideo."[117] In early 1797 Guatemalan merchant Pedro José de Górriz urged his partner to ship him "a small lot" via Veracruz "on the first convoy that presents itself."[118] Pavón of Mexico, Arana of Buenos Aires and Górriz of Guatemala all considered unescorted vessels to be too risky; for each, the convoy (even in absence of proper warships) represented the safest vehicle to navigate dangerous Atlantic world routes.

In 1797, the newly created *consulado* of Havana suggested, self-servingly, that supplying armed convoys was part of the Crown's duty as a good sovereign and that its failure to do so would legitimize the Cubans' seeking provisions elsewhere. "If the goodness of Your Majesty does not consider worthy to protect adequately the commerce of nationals with powerful escorts to convoy merchant vessels, [then] there is left no other possibility than to grant this plaza the recourse to which it has been accustomed in previous wars with England, to obtain supplies wherever they can be found."[119]

In response to the commercial crisis that emerged during the independence movements in the colonies, in December 1817 the Cadiz *consulado* similarly urged the Crown to extend assistance to mercantile interests by increasing its naval presence and providing escorts. "The principal help that Your Majesty can lend for the good of commerce and the foment of the Royal and merchant Marine is to arm a squadron of ten war frigates and ten brigs or schooners to cleanse the sea of corsairs and to provide convoys which are necessary for the mercantile boats."[120] Five months later the *consulado* lamented the continued "lack of protection for the merchant marine" against the increasingly troublesome "corsarios insurgentes."[121] By this late date, however, "Spain's naval capacity was so weak that despite many promises and much pressure from the Ministers of the Navy, there was very little protection afforded the merchant marine by the central government."[122]

A case from several years earlier provides a more quantifiable sense of how merchants perceived the protection afforded by escorted convoys. On 28 August 1793, Juan Bautista de Marticorena gave instructions to his brother, Juan Vicente, on how to approach the issue of insuring merchandise on a voyage between Spain and Central America. Fearing that insurance premiums had reached as high as 16 to 20 percent due to the war with France, Juan Bautista favored foregoing coverage altogether, since to pay such high rates "would be like working for the insurers." While he might have been willing to take a greater risk, Juan Bautista was no daredevil; he felt compelled to add that he assumed his brother "understood that the boat in which the merchandise comes should be in convoy to Havana, since if traveling alone it seems to me it would be negligent not to insure, depending on luck [in a situation] where the risk never ceases."[123] In this particular case, underwriters clearly believed that there was a significant probability of capture by the enemy, and so they demanded the high premium of 16 to 20 percent. One cannot be sure what percentage of ships the insurance companies anticipated would be seized, but 5 to 10 percent seems plausible given the elevated rates. Given such riskiness, many traders would have seen Juan Bautista's preference to forego coverage as needlessly reckless. But Marticorena was an experienced trader and must have considered the convoy to have been a tolerable substitute, comfortably reducing the risk.[124]

The same conclusion is suggested from a different case dating to the War of American Independence. On 9 May 1780, Juan Miguel de Marticorena wrote his brother urging him to approach their fellow Navarrese, the Cadiz *consulado* merchant Juan José de Lacoizqueta, to inquire about the possibility of investing with Lacoizqueta in the underwriting of insurance to America. According to Juan Miguel de Marticorena, Lacoizqueta was presently extending coverage on boats and merchandise soon to depart in convoy. Underwriting convoyed ships, Juan Miguel believed, presented an appealing business venture at the time because rates were very elevated and the risks, he believed, were minimal. "There is no doubt that they will be free in regard to risks from enemies, due as much to the formidable escort that accompanies them as to the situation of the English here in America who are taken up in defending themselves against the French."[125] While Juan Miguel probably overly minimized the riskiness, Lacoizqueta clearly agreed that the venture was appealing and secure, rebuffing Juan Vicente de Marticorena's proposal to invest in the deal. Apparently Lacoizqueta had no desire to include new investors, considering that it was "money already earned, due to the security that the convoy brings."[126]

· · ·

War introduced a host of new risks to Atlantic world trade. Ironically, war probably reduced market risk in most circumstances since along with war customarily came scarcities of imports, but this was of little benefit to merchants if they could not easily get their merchandise to transatlantic destinations in the first place. Indeed, the interruption of commerce due to war stranded cargoes and contributed to commercial losses of those traders whose invested capital thus ceased to circulate. With hostilities came privateers who eagerly seized the valuable cargoes of their enemies. During the frequent European political crises into which Spain became embroiled, French or British corsairs wreaked havoc on Iberian Atlantic world commerce.

Merchants engaged in transatlantic commerce could not avoid the riskiness that war introduced, but they did find ways to lessen the risks. Traders divided their cargoes over as many ships as possible, attempted to evade privateers by shipping in vessels flying neutral banners, or sought the greater safety of warships and convoys. None of these strategies was effective in making trade absolutely safe during times of war. Furthermore, the opportunities to divide cargo, employ neutrals, or use convoys were limited. Spain's Atlantic world commerce was simply too extensive for these risk-reducing strategies to be adequate alone. While sometimes costly, purchasing marine insurance provided merchants with another strategy to deal with at least some of the risks, most importantly those stemming from war.

Chapter 7

Underwriting Risk: The Structure and Organization of Insurance Partnerships in Late Eighteenth-Century Cadiz

Economists draw an important distinction between risk and uncertainty. Risk, unlike uncertainty, has the ability to be measured; observers can calculate the probability of a risk taking place. The multitude of "risks" examined in the previous chapters fall largely in the category of uncertainties. The characteristics of long-distance business ventures, for example, are too idiosyncratic to be quantified for the purpose of risk pooling. Each commercial transaction encompasses too many subjective decisions and unique characteristics to allow insurance adjusters to predictably measure outcomes based on probability.[1]

In contrast, certain risks are more capable of being serialized due to their more regularized qualities. Each time such a risk is undertaken, the likely array of perils and the probability of a certain bad outcome are similar. Such a risk can be measured and its expected probability calculated. Once known, it can be transferred to another party who will accept a premium in exchange for bearing this predictable risk. The risk-taker assumes that over the long run the occurrence of bad outcomes in his large pool of risks will equal the expected probability of the event. The premium is thus set at a rate that ensures a return to the risk pooler and allows the entrepreneur to engage in his trade without worrying as much about this danger. In essence, the risk has been eliminated; the insurer will always enjoy a return, assuming the probability calculation was accurate, and the trader no longer has to consider the loss that might have been sustained by such a risk. The premium paid has become a fixed (and pre-dictable) business expense.[2] The remainder of this book examines the measurable risks endured by Spanish merchants as well as the Cadiz-based insurance industry, the very institution assembled to eliminate them.

Sea Loans

There were two primary financial instruments employed by long-distance merchants to spread risk, to pass some of the great riskiness of transporta-tion to another party: sea loans, also known as bottomry loans, and mari-time insurance. Sea loans[3] provided to merchants or shipowners engaged in ocean commerce both funds on credit to help finance their commercial ventures and insurance against the dangers of the voyage. The lender, usually another merchant, gave funds to the borrower with the stipulation that if the financed item, whether ship or cargo, were to be lost during the course of the voyage, the lender would absorb the entire financial loss; the borrower would owe nothing, neither principal nor interest. If the ship arrived safely, in contrast, the borrower would repay the principal with interest at a previously determined rate that reflected both the use value of the money and a risk premium. Sea loans, thus, permitted the borrowing merchant to pass the risks of the voyage onto the lender; the loan recipient could engage in oceanic commerce without being exposed to the full host of risks. The lender assumed the sea risks but earned interest in excess of what he would have earned had he only made a simple loan. In effect, he also collected a risk premium.[4]

One might wonder why a lender would willingly risk his funds during the sea voyage and then forego the potential profit of selling the com-modities in the distant market. Put differently, since the lender was only paid if the goods arrived safely, why would he not choose to bring them to market himself, or through a factor, and then sell the items for a profit? The answer lies in the market risk of oceanic trade, the risk that goods might not sell profitably in the distant market, perhaps due to market satu-ration. By making a sea loan rather than investing his funds directly in oceanic trade, the lender limited his own exposure to the voyage alone; he earned a premium for enduring the sea risks (which were themselves somewhat predictable) but did not expose himself to commercial risks. Sea loans, thus, divided the total of all risks between the lender and the borrower. The former incurred the risk of the voyage and the latter as-sumed the market risk. It was a financial instrument that served to reduce the risk to which traders were exposed.

The authoritative study of sea loans in the Spanish empire was written by Antonio-Miguel Bernal. According to his findings, sea loans in Cadiz became increasingly less utilized over the second half of the eighteenth century. Bernal divided the years 1760 to 1825 into three periods, 1760–78, 1779–96, and 1797–1825. During the first period, Bernal identified an average of 1,176.4 *escrituras* (loan contracts) per year. By 1779–96, the annual average number of sea loans written in Cadiz had declined to 590.9. During the final period, sea loans had virtually vanished, averaging fewer than 30 per annum. Clearly, sea loans fell out of use during this half century.

Bernal proposes several theories to help explain the decline of sea loans. For one, he suggests that the near disappearance of such loan contracts after 1797 was a reflection of the general malaise of Spanish trade due first to the wars of the French Revolution and Napoleon and then to the loss of the colonies. The drop in commerce reduced demand for credit. The middle period, 1778–96, provides a bit more of a puzzle for Bernal. He presents the hypothesis that "between 1778 and 1797, the system of financing commerce and the origin of the capital underwent an important change in the Cadiz marketplace; increasingly, foreign participation was less, and private capital investments of the Cadiz community greater."[5]

A closer look at the data suggests an additional explanation. Figure 7.1 plots the number of sea loans recorded by Bernal for each of the individual years 1760–1810. Despite a notable, and predictable, plunge during the

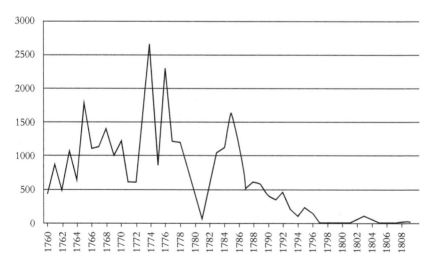

Figure 7.1. Number of Sea Loans Per Year: 1760–1810
SOURCE: Bernal, *Financión de la Carrera de Indias,* 387–88.

worst years of the American Revolutionary War, the number of sea loans remained fairly buoyant until the mid-1780s, the really significant drop occurring in the years 1784 to 1794, after which such loans became negligible. As the next section will demonstrate, the decline of sea loans occurred at the same time as the Cadiz insurance industry began to flourish. Seemingly, during the 1780s, insurance and financing became disaggregated. Merchants began securing their financing and insurance independently. Sea loans became increasingly uncommon because merchants instead chose to buy maritime insurance and obtain their credit elsewhere.

In one important way, the insurance industry was a marked improvement over the traditional system of sea loans. Sea loans were extended from one individual to another, and so unlike insurance companies, which were composed of numerous shareholders, the risk was not widely dispersed. The lender essentially assumed all of the risks associated with the uncertainties of transportation, although it is possible that creditors sometimes took out insurance policies with third parties to insure their sea loans. With maritime insurance, in contrast, large amounts of risk were pooled; insurers eliminated the risk altogether, at least in theory, by underwriting a portfolio large enough to ensure that actual losses were sustained at the level statistically expected based on calculated probabilities.[6]

Insurance

In the late eighteenth century, sea loans were being increasingly replaced with marine insurance. When merchants secured maritime insurance, in contrast to the sea loan, they acquired their financing elsewhere; investment capital and insurance against the risks of sea were obtained independently. Marine insurance in the eighteenth century functioned very similarly to modern coverage. Merchants paid premiums to insurers who guaranteed that in the event of a loss, the merchants would be indemnified as stipulated by the policy. By purchasing insurance, merchants reduced their personal exposure to losses from such factors as shipwrecks, fire, bad weather, or piracy. Insurance transferred these risks from the individual merchant to a larger entity, the insurance company, whose large volume of business allowed it to prepare for and absorb such losses. A commercial loss that would have been catastrophic for the individual merchant was, in theory, easily absorbed by the collection of shareholders who comprised the insurance company; they expected some bad outcomes and worked them into the premiums they charged. Had merchants not been able to transfer these risks, they would not have been able to engage as widely in oceanic commerce. Certain ventures would simply have been too risky for all but the biggest gamblers with the deepest purses. Much like the sea loan, then, insurance was an economic practice that made possible economic activities that would have been otherwise too risky for individual traders to undertake.

Spanish maritime insurance has been the subject of several short academic studies, but none has looked closely at the day-to-day operations of the industry.[7] This absence of focused scholarship is surprising given the wealth of surviving archival records for the Spanish maritime insurance industry in the second half of the eighteenth century. For the most part, this chapter and the next are based on two types of sources. First, a significant amount of information was extracted from the charters of eighty-four insurance companies established in Cadiz between 1790 and 1814. These charters provide a wealth of detail about the insurance industry during this time, ranging from the capital structure of each company to the responsibilities of the directors and the shareholders. They further offer a window into the mercantile community's perceptions of which activities entailed the greatest risks.[8] Second, nearly eight hundred insurance policies were located and used to construct a detailed database of actual risks underwritten in Cadiz between August 1759 and August 1818. Policies normally indicated the identity of both the insurer and the insured, the items covered, their value, their origin and destination, the name of the carrying vessel, and the insurance premium charged, always expressed as a percentage of the insured value. This last piece of information is all-important because it enables the historian to measure quantitatively the levels of perceived risk (expected probabilities) of a wide number of variables. In contrast, surviving sea loan contracts rarely stipulated the loan rate, making analysis of these instruments far less illuminating. Furthermore, with sea loans, even when rates were indicated, one cannot determine the proportion attributable to the risk premium versus the interest on the funds. The premium rate for an insurance policy, in contrast, covered risk exclusively.

Insurance policies were almost always preprinted forms containing boilerplate language, but they also provided blank space for specific conditions to be added to the policy, conditions designed to more narrowly and specifically outline the risks covered. These addendums, while more idiosyncratic, provide fascinating qualitative details regarding commerce and insurance.[9]

Expansion of the Cadiz Insurance Industry in the Late
Eighteenth Century

In the last fifteen years of the eighteenth century, the Cadiz-based maritime insurance industry experienced dramatic growth as numerous companies entered the business of underwriting risk. There is doubtfully any single explanation for why the industry took off when it did, but a number of factors certainly contributed. First, the growing uncertainty affecting Spanish Atlantic world commerce post–*comercio libre* might have encouraged wealthy Cadiz merchants to withdraw from direct involvement in colonial trade and specialize in the underwriting of measurable risk instead. This book has argued throughout that the increasingly competitive conditions of the American trade system that emerged after 1778, and especially after the end of the American Revolutionary War, multiplied dramatically what was already a very risky business. Before *comercio libre*, supply was more predictable, the uncertainty of trade and the dangers of overly supplied markets more muted, making profits more dependable. Free trade reduced the appeal of long-distance trade by raising dramatically the degree of competition and thus the severity of market risk; at least some old-time merchants no longer viewed oceanic commerce with the same security and chose to withdraw in favor of more predictable ventures. Underwriting the riskiness of oceanic voyages likely seemed a good candidate. Importantly, the rising uncertainty of long-distance trade brought about by free trade did not affect the typical risks covered by insurance underwriters. Rising uncertainty arose from the dismantling of institutions that served to reduce the volatility of supply; insurance, in contrast, covered only the risks of getting the goods to market, the voyage. And these risks were not directly affected by the 1778 reforms.

Underwriting insurance on long-distance commerce was an obvious industry for veteran merchants to enter. Long engaged in transatlantic commerce, insurance was a business that was familiar. Moreover, the profitability of underwriting risk seemed more guaranteed given the measurable probability of the events customarily insured; at least the performance of the insurance business was not directly affected by the increasingly volatile, freer markets, assuming that the insured were able to pay their premiums. Insurance companies received in premiums a piece of the profitability of oceanic trade without incurring any of the business risks, risks that were growing due to saturated markets and the corresponding drop in commodity prices.

The growth of the insurance industry in Cadiz was perhaps given a boost by politics in Great Britain. In 1793 Parliament enacted a law prohibiting British underwriters from covering the risks of enemy vessels. While such a law might seem unnecessary, for most of the century London firms had continued to provide coverage to merchants of Spain or France even when Britain was at war with those nations, a policy that had the paradoxical effect of reimbursing the enemy for the successes of the British Navy. British policymakers further justified the new policy, expressing concern that London insurers might be tempted to reveal military secrets to the shipowners who they covered to reduce their likelihood of seizure. For a brief period in 1748, late in the War of the Austrian Succession (1740–48), Parliament had prohibited the extension of insurance to England's enemies, but the ban lapsed at war's end. The Act of 1793, however, continued in effect throughout the French Revolutionary Wars.[10] While the spurt in Cadiz-based insurance companies predated this law, some of the firms formed after 1793 might have been encouraged by the British ban to open operations in Cadiz. Of course, Spain remained allied with England until 1796, and most of the firms were formed in 1796 and the four years immediately preceding.

As noted, the expansion of the insurance industry in the 1780s occurred on the heels of the decline of sea loans, a concurrence that is most certainly connected given these two financial instruments' overlapping function. Again, sea loans provided insurance against the risks of sea and commercial financing. Its replacement with marine insurance meant that merchants who had customarily relied on sea loans, obtaining their insurance and credit together, had now to secure their credit separately. Not all Spanish merchants engaged in the Indies trade had previously depended on sea loans; some had instead secured marine insurance in the markets of Amsterdam, London, or elsewhere. Obviously, the ability to obtain coverage directly in Cadiz was more convenient.

Many of the financiers who had been deeply involved in the business of extending sea loans shifted into the insurance underwriting business. Entering this new industry made great sense for these financiers given the parallel functions of these financial instruments. Table 7.1 provides a hint to the degree to which individuals shifted from sea loans to maritime insurance. Of the eighty-five creditors identified by Bernal as most important[11] in the extension of sea loans during the years 1760–1824, twenty-one (column one) appeared as shareholders in insurance firms established in the 1790s. These were only the individuals whose names matched sufficiently to provide a good degree of confidence that they were the same. Another handful of surnames appearing in both sets were certainly family members but were not included. For example, the creditor (sea lender)

TABLE 7.1

Partial Overlap of Sea Loan Financiers and
Insurance Shareholders

Most Frequent Sea Loan Financiers (1760–1824)	Shareholders in Insurance Firms
Alcalde, J. I.	Alcalde, Juan Ignacio
Alvarez Campana, J.	Alvarez Campana, José Ignacio
Behic, D.	Behic, Domingo
Butler, A.	Butler, Augustín
Casalduero, A.	Casalduero, Andres
Fernández Ravago	Fernández de Ravago, Francisco
Izquierdo y Cia., M.	Izquierdo e Hijos, Miguel
Lasqueti, J.	Lasqueti, Josef María
Leceta, J. F.	Leceta, Juan Francisco
Martínez Junquera, M.	Martínez Junquera, Pedro Tomás
Martínez Texada	Martínez Texada
Mosti, A. J.	Mosti, Antonio Joséf
Noble, P. J.	Noble, Patricio Joséf
O'Druyer, A.	O'Druyer, Antonio
Pérez Gallego, J. A.	Pérez Gallego, Joséf
Rodríguez Carasa	Rodríguez de Carasa, Joséf
Sáenz de Tejada, M.	Sáenz de Tejada, Juan Manuel
Terry, D. T.	Terry, Domingo Tomás
Tomatti, A.	Tomaty, Antonio
Villanueva, J.	Villanueva, Joaquín de
Iriarte, F.	Yriarte, Francisco de

SOURCES: Column 1, Bernal, *Financiación de la Carrera de Indias*, 459–60, table 6.52; Column 2, AGI, *Consulados*, legajo 78.

M. Landáburu (Matias Landáburu) was the father of insurance shareholder Juan de Dios Landáburu but is not included in Table 7.1.[12] In addition, the overlap would unquestionably increase greatly if one were to move beyond Bernal's list of eighty-five. Finally, the shareholders of only half of the eighty-three insurance firms were cross-checked, a large but incomplete sample, limiting the results still further. Even with these limitations, there is no question whatsoever that many financiers moved from sea loans to the underwriting of risk.

The location of Cadiz was ideal for the development of the insurance market. Despite the 1778 opening of other peninsular ports to the Indies trade, Cadiz maintained its overwhelming dominance as Spain's leading international port.[13] In addition, the large and wealthy mercantile community located there could easily and credibly enter this trade. These were experienced merchants with sufficient financial resources to instill faith and confidence in potential policyholders. Smaller, less well-to-do traders had increasingly invested in Atlantic world trade, but they were not well suited for the insurance industry. Only the most deeply pocketed merchants could be trusted to insure long-distance trade. The *consulado* merchants, then, had a comparative advantage in underwriting commerce. And they pursued insurance underwriting because their previous commercial advantages diminished due to the 1778 reforms.

While the aforementioned eighty-four insurance charters dating from 1790 to 1814 suggests the rapid growth of the Cadiz insurance market, the industry's late-century emergence clearly precedes 1790. In August 1780, for example, the *consulado* was urging the increased standardization of the process of indemnifying losses fearful that deviations from a norm might "produce considerable discomfort or setback to the public cause of commerce and the good reputation of Spanish insurance companies, and that this important sector, which is backed by more than 9 million pesos, would be damaged to such a point that foreigners would return to this business that they had abandoned upon the establishment of the Spanish companies."[14]

Six years later, Don Juan de Mora y Morales, a Licenciado at the *consulado,* published a boastful tribute to this flourishing financial sector. In praising this emerging industry Mora y Morales stressed that it not only saved local merchants considerable inconvenience by allowing them to obtain coverage in Spain, but also helped the nation preserve sizeable sums that had previously been sent to insurers in the markets of northern Europe. The successes of the insurance companies, he claimed, had earned Cadiz the respect of foreign merchants "because to the present time there has never been an occurrence or catastrophe which has forced any [company] to suspend its payments or fail to cover its obligations." This achievement, Mora y Morales expounded, had not come easily. Insurance company directors had to be vigilant to a wide variety of factors such as the relative riskiness of the seasons, the condition of transoceanic vessels, the specific dangers of each American and European port, the different types of merchandise and the damage to which each might be subject, as well as the often secretive activities of other nations' courts that might provide indication of some "discord or rupture."[15]

The merits of Mora y Morales's congratulatory essay aside, the expansion of this financial sector was indeed rapid. Between December 1790 and May 1803, there were at least eighty-three insurance companies founded in the city of Cadiz.[16] These "companies," partnerships more accurately, were established with the goal of profiting from the underwriting of risk, to collect in premiums more than they paid out in losses. Table 7.2 shows the years in which these companies were established. After several slow years, the establishment of insurance companies exploded in 1792 and the growth continued through 1796. The year 1794 marked the peak with the founding of sixteen insurance underwriting firms. Interestingly, the years of greatest formation straddled the outbreak of the war with France; peace still existed in 1792, but by 1796 Spain was deeply embroiled in the hostilities. The proliferation of companies began before the sharp increase in risk due to war, but the peak occurred during the early years of political instability. Insurance premiums rose with the outbreak of hostilities, which naturally explains the continued entry of new firms despite the growing likelihood of indemnifiable losses. At least two firms that formed in mid-1793 explicitly stated their intention to operate "for the time that the present war lasts between this Monarch and the French nation."[17] In 1797, however, the creation of new companies suddenly halted. Only two companies were started in 1797, and no new underwriters emerged in 1798, 1799, or 1800. The cessation of new companies during these three years almost certainly reflects investors' reassessment of the riskiness of the insurance business. Spain was now engaged in the First Naval War with England (1796–1802), the supreme naval power of the era, and insurance-related losses soared.

The insurance companies of Cadiz were formed for fixed periods of time after which the partnerships normally dissolved. For example, a company chartered on 1 July 1794 under the protection of La Santísima Virgen María de Regla planned to operate for a period of six years before ceasing operations.[18] Of the eighty-three companies established during this period, thirty-two stipulated that they would underwrite insurance for a period of five years and another forty-five determined to remain in business for six years. In most cases the partnerships proposed to dissolve after the specified period, but in several cases the partners left open the possibility that they would continue to operate if deemed desirable.[19]

Utilizing their years of duration, Figure 7.2 shows the number of companies known to be underwriting insurance in Cadiz in each of the years

TABLE 7.2

Number of Insurance Companies Established Each Year from 1790 to 1803

1790	1791	1792	1793	1794	1795	1796	1797	1798	1799	1800	1801	1802	1803
1	7	12	14	16	12	12	2	0	0	0	2	6	1

SOURCE: Derived from AGI, *Consulados*, legajo 78.

1790 to 1808. The steep slope of the figure reflects the flurry of companies established during the first several years of the 1790s. The equally steep decline after 1797 reveals that the creation of new insurance companies failed to keep pace with the closure of existing firms. It should be noted that Figure 7.2 depicts only the firms recorded in the examined documents and does not display any companies that were formed prior to 1790. In fact, there absolutely were underwriters in Cadiz before 1790, as is obvious given that the celebratory discourse of the *consulado*'s Licenciado Mora y Morales was presented in 1786. The firms memorialized by Mora y Morales were not captured by the data displayed in the figure. If the data were more complete, the upward slope of the figure would be less steep. Regardless, Figure 7.2 clearly suggests the increasing attractiveness of this business in the years preceding 1797.

The entry of so many new firms speaks for itself, but contemporaries also commented on the sector's rapid growth. In early 1798 the *consulado* addressed a letter to Francisco de Saavedra, minister of finance, seeking his input on the difficulties that then faced the insurance industry. The *consulado* emphasized the importance of this sector for the economy, re-

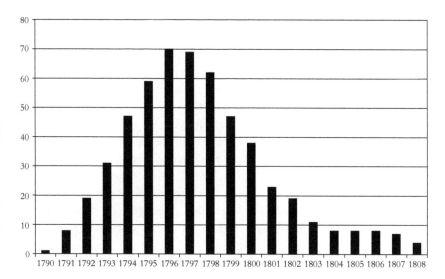

Figure 7.2. Minimum Number of Insurance Firms Operating in Cadiz: 1790–1808

SOURCE: Derived from Noticia extractada de los Directores de Compañas de Seguros establecidos en esta plaza y registradas en esta contaduria del *consulado* del tiempo en que empezó a correr el termino de ellas y del en que deben concluir, segun escripturas, AGI *Consulados*, legajo 78.

minding Saavedra that not too long before most of the insurance business had been conducted in other European markets leading to the export of an estimated 1.5 million pesos per year in premiums, a real drain on Spain's capital.[20] Without question, the last decades of the eighteenth century witnessed a flourishing of this Cadiz-based industry.

Structure of the Cadiz Insurance Industry in the Late Eighteenth Century

The insurance companies of Cadiz were actually partnerships in which individual investors subscribed to shares of ten thousand pesos apiece. Shareholders did not actually put up any funds; instead, they merely guaranteed responsibility for the coverage of losses up to their share amount. When, for instance, a company was formed in 1792 under the directorship of Nicolás María de Alva, the charter stated: "in accordance with practice, the fund will not be deposited, it being sufficient the obligation which each [shareholder] has assumed by signing the contract (escritura), making themselves responsible for the payment of that which corresponds to their shares."[21] A subscriber acquiring two ten-thousand-peso shares, then, accepted the obligation to pay up to twenty thousand pesos in any losses sustained. Of course, his decision to invest reflected his faith that he would instead be sharing in the company's profits, not paying out losses. Most shareholders were also merchants and, as experienced traders themselves, they had a direct understanding of the risks involved and undoubtedly believed the business model was well structured to absorb risks, a good way to make a few pesos without directly tying up any of their principal.

Ideally, claims were to be paid out of the revenues from insurance premiums, but it was possible for these funds to be inadequate, especially at the start of operations before many premiums had yet been collected. Most commonly, insurance company directors responded to shortfalls by demanding that shareholders deposit funds, their portion of outstanding debts, but a firm established in 1803 incorporated a different policy, advising shareholders that "if fortune is adverse in the early moments of this partnership to a degree that premiums charged during that time do not succeed in covering losses sustained to that point, the directors are allowed to take money at interest on the company's account, doing so in consultation with [company] advisers . . . avoiding in this way the need to bother shareholders to immediately make deposits [of funds]."[22]

Such a policy certainly reflected the belief that incoming premiums would allow the rapid repayment of such loans, but short-term borrowing might have also reflected cash-flow problems faced by individual merchant-shareholders during these disruptive war years. The difficulty of producing capital on the spot might not have reflected any real financial debility, just lack of liquidity. But company directors had to nonetheless monitor the financial condition of shareholders since even one's bankruptcy could affect the firm's ability to meet its obligations. This issue was addressed in several of the companies' charters. A firm founded in Seville in September 1797 introduced a clause stating:

> it is the condition that if one or more of the shareholders during the term of this company come to be in bankruptcy, arrears, or similar circumstances, [then] on the same day that the directors and counselors learn this, they will cancel their share or shares and will reduce any future amounts underwritten proportional to that member's [holdings.] And if it results that the past and pending operations to that date produce profits, these will remain for the benefit of the other partners, and if by the same reckoning losses are sustained, the remaining partners will cover them, prorated among themselves, the honor of the company [depending] on the fulfillment of what is due for its solvency.[23]

The Cadiz mercantile community was small, and knowledge of individuals' financial predicaments traveled quickly. It was thus critical that directors act quickly to protect their firms' reputations by distancing themselves from insolvent partners. In the case above, the remaining partners were left covering the ousted partners' debts, a necessary burden, as another company charter stressed, "to sustain the honor and credit of this society."[24]

In contrast, some firms were limited liability partnerships such as one formed in 1793 for which Juan Vicente de Marticorena served as counselor and whose charter specified that "shareholders are not responsible for one another."[25] A company founded in 1803 declared that "no shareholder was responsible for any other . . . but [only] for the interest that he has taken, paying and satisfying the proportions that correspond to the share or shares that pertain to each party."[26] Presumably, the insured could only recover their losses proportional to the number of solvent partners. One would imagine that this clause would have reduced the appeal of such a company to policyholders, but there is no indication that merchants took this into account or even knew about such clauses.

The question of the degree of liability between partners did provoke some controversy. Late in 1798 the Cadiz *consulado* was forced to seek the counsel of Minister Miguel Cayetano Soler on this very issue. According to the guild's officers, a number of the city's insurance firms included shareholders who had gone bankrupt, but their charters were ambiguous as to whether the surviving partners were liable for the failed partners' debts.[27] Minister Cayetano Soler was apparently silent because four months later the *consulado* wrote to remind him of its inquiry.[28]

Juan Manuel de Arzubialde, director of one of the Cadiz firms, faced this very issue the following year. On 16 February 1799, Arzubialde called a shareholders' meeting to discuss how to deal with the financial difficulties of some of the partners. As Director Arzubialde explained to shareholder Juan Vicente de Marticorena, who was absent from the meeting, he had floated the idea that solvent partners should also pay the debts of those who were insolvent "because without this reciprocal responsibility, an insurance company cannot exist." His proposal did not go over well, however, and "everyone grew angry and stormed out." In a subsequent reunion, which Marticorena also failed to attend, Arzubialde prudently shelved the notion.[29]

The lengthiest discussion regarding the degree of liability of partners in an insurance company actually arose upon the establishment of an insurance partnership in Havana, Cuba.[30] On 24 January 1795, a large firm consisting of 160 shares of five thousand pesos apiece was founded in Havana. Having been asked to read and comment on a draft of the company's charter, several merchants expressed concern about a clause that limited the liability of partners for one another's debts. According to the merchants, policyholders needed to feel absolutely secure that their losses would be indemnified even if financial crisis were to impair some of the shareholders. The officers of the partnership, however, rejected this criticism, responding that it was unreasonable to expect shareholders to assume liability for their partners' losses. While protection of the company's reputation would ensure that the partners would cover small shortfalls, they claimed, no partner would agree to cover large ones as this could spell their financial ruin. Such limited liability should not dissuade customers, the officers argued, given that in the past it had been necessary for a merchant to approach many different underwriters, each of whom would underwrite a small portion of the larger risk. If any one of them went bankrupt, the insured had no expectation that his debt would be covered by a different underwriter. An insurance partnership was really just a collection of individual underwriters who served the mercantile community by allowing the merchant to make a single contract rather than negotiate independently with each of the underwriters. As in the past, however, the liability of one partner did not transfer to another. Apparently this argument convinced the critics and the issue was dropped.[31]

Most shareholders were merchants themselves. As a consequence, in addition to underwriting the risk of others, they were also major consumers of insurance. There were apparently no restrictions against a merchant insuring his cargo or ship with the very company in which he was a shareholder. In 1794 Juan Vicente de Marticorena secured insurance coverage to both Honduras and Veracruz with a firm directed by Manuel Joséf de Armas. At the time, Marticorena held a share in the company. Of course, this meant that Marticorena was self-insuring a small portion of his risk, a portion equal to his share of the company.[32] But Marticorena perhaps preferred to use the services of his own company because he felt more informed about the solvency of the partners and had an inside track to collect a claim quickly if the need should arise. Maybe his partnership in the company assisted him in securing coverage in the first place. An additional possible benefit of insuring with one's own firm is suggested by a company resurrected in 1801 after a several-year war-induced suspension of operations. Reacting to its bad experiences during the war, the company, founded under the protection of Nuestra Señora del Rosario y San Antonio de Padua, introduced a new regulation requiring that all premiums be paid in cash at the moment the risk was initiated rather than, as was custom, upon the termination of risks. The only exception to the new policy, the charter stipulated, applied to "socios," company partners, who could continue to secure coverage in the customary fashion. While it is not evident that such a policy became widespread in Cadiz, if it had, partnership in a firm would have provided an additional benefit, the ability to secure coverage without the need to pay the premium up front.[33]

Established in February 1802, just a month prior to the signing of the Treaty of Amiens and the temporary cessation of conflict, a firm directed by Juan Miguel de Urrutia stipulated its intention of underwriting coverage exclusively for its twenty-two partners. Structured more as a mutual association than as an actual insurance company, this firm allowed its partners to pool their risks without the added burden of taking on additional clients over whom they had less control and knowledge.[34]

· · ·

The Cadiz companies ranged in size; the average of the 83 companies consisted of shares totaling 331,226 pesos committed. Approximately one-third of the companies were composed of shares totaling fewer than 300,000 pesos. Sixty percent of the companies had total share values ranging from 300,000 to 400,000 pesos. Only one company had shareholders subscribing for more than 500,000 pesos (see online Appendix B). On 1 May 1792 a company was founded under the directorship of Juan Bonneval for which 52 shares of 10,000 pesos apiece were acquired, a total subscription of 520,000 pesos.[35]

Figure 7.3 illustrates the total capital committed[36] to the Cadiz insurance industry in each year from 1790 to 1808, again excluding companies already in existence prior to the start of this period. This amount represents the theoretical total loss to which the industry was committed in any individual year. At its peak, in the years 1796 and 1797, the companies as a whole had more than 23.5 million pesos committed by their partners. This approximate figure is corroborated by a 1796 *Consulado* letter that estimated the Cadiz insurance companies to be backed by 24 million pesos at the time.[37] By 1808, the final year examined, the amount committed had plummeted beneath one million pesos.

While the growing industry was viewed with satisfaction and pride by the local mercantile community, it was not large by international standards. Indeed, a comparison with the much older and more fully established London insurance market reveals that the Spanish underwriting business was very small. Estimates for the year 1810 alone placed the total value of risk underwritten in London at 146 million pounds sterling, equal to almost 680 million pesos, or nearly thirty times the values committed in Cadiz.[38]

Importantly, these amounts committed do not necessarily reveal anything about the insurance coverage actually extended. In the latter years of the 1790s, for example, capital commitments were very high, but many

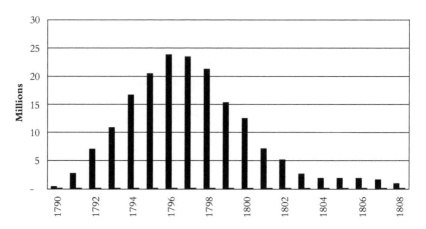

Figure 7.3. Minimum Total Capital Committed to Cadiz Insurance Companies: 1790–1808
SOURCE: AGI, *Consulados*, legajo 78.

of the companies curtailed or even halted their actual underwriting of risk. In other words, the actual risks assumed might have been well below the capital committed to the companies.

By the same token, the capital committed was by no means the upper limit that the Cadiz insurance industry could underwrite, the industry's total underwriting capacity. The total insurance coverage extended by a company might exceed substantially its total capital committed. This did not imply malfeasance on the part of the company directors since most of the risks covered by a company did not result in claims. The capital committed needed only be sufficient to cover all losses sustained by the company's clients. It was the responsibility of the individuals who ran the insurance companies to judge the firm's degree of exposure and make sure that risks were adequately spread over a diversity of ships and cargo so that there was little probability that claims would exceed the capital committed to the firm by its shareholders.

A company directed by *consulado* member Juan Esteban Tellechea, for example, insured in the year 1795 cargo and ships valued at 949,576 pesos. The company, however, had only 30 shareholders at 10,000 pesos per share, a total of 300,000 pesos committed to cover losses. Thus, the company had insured in 1795 more than three times its capital committed, and it is almost certain that the company had additional risks from the previous year, which had not yet terminated. Barring an almost unimaginable catastrophe, however, Tellechea's company had adequate capital committed to cover all losses that might reasonably be anticipated to occur. The probability that a third of the policyholders would sustain total losses must have been exceptionally low. Obviously, under normal circumstances, most voyages occurred without any incidence of loss. This, after all, was the nature of maritime insurance; the insurers covered many risks comforted by the knowledge that only a few would require indemnification and the rest would provide more than ample revenues to do so.[39]

Upon the establishment of an insurance company, one to three individuals were designated as directors of the firm (see online Appendix B). In most cases the directors were also shareholders. Of thirty-eight firms examined, thirty-two employed a director who was also a shareholder; in the other six cases the director shared a surname with another shareholder suggesting a likely family connection.[40] That a shareholder usually served as director is not surprising; other shareholders undoubtedly felt more secure in the knowledge that the director shared with them an economic interest in making sound decisions, especially since the director was also paid a commission on the value of insurance underwritten. The director was in charge of the day-to-day operations of the company, determining which ships or cargo to underwrite, how much coverage to extend per ship, what premium rate to charge, and a host of other matters. The director also maintained the company's books and was responsible for collecting premiums, paying losses, and managing any legal disputes.

For their services, directors were customarily paid a commission of a half-percent (0.5 percent) of the total risk insured, a compensation that could be quite sizeable.[41] While compensating the directors in this way motivated them to seek business, one imagines that they might have also been tempted to underwrite risky policies that earned them handsome commissions. Obviously, this conflict of interest was mitigated if they were also shareholders, since their potential loss from signing riskier voyages would have exceeded their half percent commission. But nonpartner directors had no direct financial incentive to avoid underwriting riskier schemes. While not reducing this potential conflict of interest directly, a firm directed by don Francisco de Paula and don Joseph Maria Beyens stipulated that it would only award the half-percent commission "on the risks that expire safely," that is without any indemnification.[42] An insurance partnership formed in 1802, under the protection of la Santísima Trinidad and María Santísima en su Concepción en Grácia, devised an alternative compensation model for its directors, the brothers José Antonio and Francisco José Carazo. The company charter stipulated that the directors would not be paid any commissions but would instead receive 20 percent of the partnership's distributed profits. It further clarified that if the company were profitless, the directors would have no right to demand any compensation whatsoever. While 20 percent might seem like a huge compensation package, most of the Cadiz companies had recently fared very poorly, several having gone bankrupt during the recent wars with Great Britain.[43] In both of these cases, the directors might still be tempted to take bigger risks, but at least they were not rewarded when these turned out badly. The greatest disincentive to underwriting overly risky ventures was probably the knowledge that one would be removed from the directorship and have one's reputation for competency badly tarnished.

Company directors were often members of the Cadiz merchant guild. A cross-check of the directors with the member list of the *consulado* revealed that thirty-seven of eighty-three companies were directed by a guild member (see online Appendix B). Many of the additional companies were directed by individuals sharing a surname with a *consulado* member. This significant overlap is not surprising. Insurance was a branch over which the *consulado* had jurisdiction. According to the Law of the Indies, the *consulado* of Seville was required to oversee the industry, an obligation that passed to Cadiz after 1717. Insurance-related disputes were to be addressed within the guild's chambers.[44] Choosing a director with status in the guild was thus logical and must have occasionally served the interests of the insurance underwriters. But one need not search for sinister evidence of influence peddling to explain the overlap; the Cadiz *consulado* members were the leading commercial figures in the Spanish empire. They were the major exporters of European wares to America and, consequently, were major consumers of maritime insurance. The directors were undoubtedly chosen primarily for their profound knowledge of oceanic commerce and its concomitant risks. Given this requisite expertise, it is no surprise that the pool of qualified directors was significantly drawn from *consulado* membership.

All of the newly chartered companies sought divine assistance in their dealings, placing themselves "under the protection" of Jesus, Maria, or a favored patron saint, perhaps understandable given the nature of insurance. The companies were in the business of providing protection against what were often "acts of God." As a result, seeking divine protection might have been seen as a prudent step. A firm called Compañía Española de Seguros was established in November 1791 under the directorship of don Antonio Lasqueti and placed itself under the protection of Nuestra Madre y Señora de las Angustias y San Antonio de Padua. This company went one step further; it proposed celebrating semi-annual masses in honor of "our protectors . . . with the goal of imploring their protection as well as the Almighty's." The partners further agreed to give one hundred pesos annually to poor children. In an industry so vulnerable to misfortune, anything the partners could do to procure added protection was worthwhile.[45]

In general, the directors were entrusted with deciding which risks to underwrite, taking into consideration a wide variety of circumstances. The company charters, however, provided guidelines that the directors were expected to obey. Some charters spelled these out with great detail, while the shareholders of others seemed content to defer to the director's "prudent discretion [regarding] the circumstances of the ships, seasons, and other [factors]."[46] These guidelines, analyzed in the following sections, illustrate some of the risks perceived by the experts to be most common as well as ways in which they sought to reduce their dangers.

RISK CONCENTRATION

One understandable concern of the shareholders was that the companies avoid concentrating too much exposure in one place, to avoid placing too many eggs in one basket. To better control their exposure, the Spanish insurance companies sought to spread widely the risks that they underwrote. Charters thus limited the amounts their underwriters could cover on any single ship, since, obviously, if one company were to underwrite an entire vessel plus all of its cargo and the ship were to sink, then the company would incur too great a loss. It was prudent to limit exposure on any single ship to an amount the company could comfortably absorb. Obviously, the probability of losing multiple ships was much lower than that of losing just one.

The 1791 charter establishing a company to be directed by Augustín de Valverde Hijos y Compañía under the protection of Nuestra Señora de la Salud set a limit on coverage of one thousand pesos per share on merchandise placed aboard vessels destined for Veracruz, Cartagena, Buenos Aires, Lima, or Honduras. For ships sailing to the Caribbean Islands (Islas de Barlovento), Caracas, and New England the limit was set at the reduced rate of five hundred pesos per share. This particular company consisted of thirty shares, and so, by this prescription, it thus permitted a maximum coverage per ship of thirty thousand pesos for a voyage from Cadiz to Veracruz. Maximum coverage for the return voyage was set at one thousand pesos per share from any Spanish American port except Honduras and Cartagena, from which the limit was halved.[47] The charter did not provide specific explanation for why these ports were treated differently. Likely, the lower limits permitted for the Caribbean ports and Caracas reflected the belief that ships destined for these locations were more exposed to accident or piracy.

Just as companies sought to limit too much exposure on one ship, they also attempted to limit excessive exposure in a single convoy. After setting its limits per vessel per share, a company founded on New Year's Eve, 1790, under the directorship of Joséf de Urda stipulated that the maximum allowed coverage per ship would be lowered whenever three or more ships upon which the firm had insured property were traveling together. For example, the company stipulated a maximum of one thousand pesos per share per ship but only five hundred pesos when three or more ships were sailing together. In the latter case, the firm's total exposure might be greater (3 ships at 500 each = 1500 pesos per share), but less than it would have been had the lower limit for multiple ships not been stipulated.[48] At first glance this might seem contradictory given the definite perception that convoyed ships were safer, but the goal of this stipulation was to limit the concentration of exposure. In fact, the firms often charged a lower premium to convoyed risks. Also, while convoys reduced the risk of piracy and privateering, they concentrated the dangers of weather-related accidents. Reduced exposure was important if convoyed ships encountered a powerful storm. Finally, perhaps the firm saw in this arrangement the added advantage of encouraging merchants to divide larger cargoes over a number of ships, an additional spreading of the risk.

Most risks (i.e., a cargo or a ship) were underwritten by multiple companies, a small percentage of the total risk being covered by each. For instance, when on 6 November 1789 Juan Joséf de Puch and Remigio Fernández insured fifty-two *zurrones* of *grana fina* (sacks of high grade cochineal weighing approximately two hundred pounds each) and a load of silver bullion valued together at a hundred thousand pesos for a voyage aboard several frigates from Veracruz to Cadiz, the policy contained eighteen separate lines of insurance.[49] Likewise the mercantile firm titled Señores Martínez y Gadeyne Hermanos insured their two ships, *San Francisco de Paula* and *Virgen del Carmen alias la Gallega*, for 33,142 pesos for their January 1802 trip from Cadiz to Veracruz. To secure this coverage required twenty-three different underwriters.[50]

The great number of firms underwriting these two policies reflected the desire of each to avoid too much exposure on any single voyage. A company would earn the same in premiums by insuring a cargo of one hundred thousand pesos as it would by insuring ten cargoes valued at ten thousand pesos each, but in the former case the risk of catastrophe would be far greater. By spreading its risks over many ships and many cargoes, the insurance company took fewer gambles and prudently reduced the likelihood of catastrophic losses.

SHIP TYPE

The company charters also distinguished between ship types, willingly taking on greater exposure if the ship was deemed more militarily secure. So, for example, a company established on 12 April 1791 under the directorship of Manuel José de Armas stipulated that it would underwrite coverage to or from Veracruz, Havana, Cuba, Puerto Rico, Caracas, Campeche, the Barlovento Islands, and the Canaries not to exceed one thousand pesos per company share (in this case thirty shares) if the vessel were a *navío de guerra*, a large warship. The maximum coverage per share was lowered to eight hundred pesos if the ship were a *fragata de guerra*, a war frigate, a vessel smaller and less well-armed than a warship. The company would only underwrite for six hundred pesos per share on warships of *menor porte*, smaller vessels such as *urcas*, *paquebots*, and *bergantínes*. The schedule continued to express reduced maximum coverage down to the mere one hundred pesos per share that the company would cover on a smaller than 150 ton merchantman, an unarmed vessel designed exclusively to carry freight.[51] As the example suggests, commerce conducted aboard well-armed warships was perceived to be much less risky than trade in small, unarmed merchant vessels. Most companies outlined similar schedules.

COMMODITIES INSURED

The charters also sometimes differentiated between distinct classes of merchandise. Several documents, for example, instructed directors to allow greater coverage per share on precious metals than other items. A firm under the protection of Nuestra Señora de Balbanera y el Señor San Miguel directed by Carassa Hermanos Bernal y Compañía permitted coverage on warships of 1500 pesos per share for precious metals but only 1000 pesos per share on "goods and fruits."[52] Other charters stipulated lower premium rates for gold and silver, offering a one-half percent point reduction relative to premiums for other goods.[53] The willingness to endure greater exposure on silver and gold reflected their relative freedom from simple damages (averías simples) such as those caused by the ship taking on water or experiencing a small fire. Because noniron metals were undamaged by dampness, they sustained fewer losses and were thus less risky to insurers.

For the same reason, some of the charters instructed directors to charge one percentage point more than other merchandise (1.5 percentage points more than silver and gold) for underwriting the coverage of the casco y quilla, the ship's hull and keel.[54] Over the course of the voyage, the ship was more likely than other items to sustain some indemnifiable damage, the result of a mishap entering a port or a skirmish with an enemy. The higher premium rate was justified by the greater likelihood of a collectible loss being sustained. One firm, perhaps considering the ship to be simply too risky to insure, forbade its director altogether from underwriting such coverage.[55]

Insurance was sometimes procured on human cargo, slaves purchased on the coast of Africa to be sold in America. A company formed in 1791 and directed by Antonio Lasqueti limited coverage on slaves to a maximum of 200 pesos per company share equal, in this case, to 8000 pesos per vessel.[56] The Compañía de Seguros Marca JPH, in contrast, banned its director from insuring African slaves at all, although no rationale for this prohibition was provided.[57] Yet another firm, this one under the directorship of Manuel Ximénez Pérez Padre e Hijo y Compañía, specified in its charter that it intended to extend coverage "on the lives" of the slaves but added that "the company [would] not [be] responsible for the value of those who died violently," this clause presumably included to avoid paying for those who died at the hands of the shipowners or by suicide. This exclusion, perhaps, responded to the likely temptation of slave traders to jettison slaves too ill to sell in order to collect insurance on them instead.[58]

Only a few actual insurance policies were discovered that underwrote the slave trade. In July 1817, Cadiz merchant Antonio de Artechea bought policies for the voyage on his ships *La Piedad* and *El Nuevo Pajaro* from Bilbao to the African coast slave markets of Guinea and south. The policy covered the transport of the slaves to the Spanish colonies for sale. Coverage on the slaves, who were valued at 75 pesos each, specifically excluded death from natural causes or disease as well as death from lack of water or spoilage of provisions. It did, however, insure against fatalities from fire, shipwreck, or violence connected to an uprising. *La Piedad* acquired 322 slaves, of whom 311 survived and were sold in Santiago de Cuba. Whether or not the 11 individuals who perished resulted in indemnification to the policyholder was not indicated. The crew of the other vessel, *El Nuevo Pajaro*, purchased 361 slaves on the coast of Africa, but encountered great difficulties in its transatlantic voyage as the ship captain and many of the slaves fell gravely ill en route. Landing first in Puerto Rico, the captain disembarked and 12 slaves were sold. *El Nuevo Pajaro* then proceeded without its captain to Havana where the surviving population of 250 slaves were unloaded. In total, 99 slaves had died during the middle passage, 96 from disease, an exempted cause of death. Only three of the slaves were covered by the policy having perished "from violent death" after throwing themselves into the ocean. The two ships' slaves had been valued at 75 pesos apiece for a total coverage in excess of 51,000 pesos. On *El Nuevo Pajaro*, merchant Artechea was assessed a premium of 22 percent and presumably the same for *La Piedad*. His total premium, thus, exceeded 11,000 pesos, a hefty fee given that most of his losses were not indemnified.[59]

While probably more in the realm of life insurance than marine insurance, coverage was obtained on the life of Pedro Fermín Moreau de Lisson, who sailed in 1778 to Mexico to take his post as Alcalde Mayor of the district of Tlapa in the province of Puebla (modern Guerrero). Purchased by Francisco de Sierra, the policy valued Fermín's life at 1600 pesos for a term of one year including the voyage on the *Concepción de Terri*. For this policy, Sierra paid a premium of 12.25 percent or 196 pesos. The policy did not explain the relationship of the two men, but possibly Sierra had provided Fermín with some of the expenses that he would need to assume his post, funds that would be lost if Fermín were to die during the voyage or shortly after arriving in Mexico.[60]

AVERÍAS

Spanish maritime insurance distinguished between different types of losses or damage, *averías*,[61] that might be sustained over the course of a voyage, and most of the charters addressed how their directors should deal with each. There were three types of *averías*—*averías ordinarias, averías simples*,[62] and *averías gruesas*.[63] *Averías ordinarias* consisted of "minor expenses incurred by the captains or masters of any ship, either in the voyage or in the ports where they arrive as a result of storm or . . . the unloading."[64] There was some variation in the treatment that the charters stipulated for *averías ordinarias*. Many of the charters refused altogether to insure against these minor losses. Director Pedro Smits was instructed by his company's charter to "exclude in the risks to America all *averías* except the *gruesa*."[65] A firm directed by the Carazo Hermanos demanded the identical exemption.[66] This exclusion was also often an amended clause on individual policies.

The distinction between *avería simple* (particular average) and *avería gruesa* (general average) was most crucial and indeed continues to be recognized in modern international maritime insurance laws. An *avería simple* was damage or loss sustained at sea that was to be borne exclusively by the owner of the lost property, who presumably held a policy to protect himself. Examples of such losses generally included ships and cargo seized by corsairs, vessels and merchandise lost to shipwrecks or storms, or items damaged by fire or flooding. If the owners had insurance, they turned personally to their underwriters for indemnification. Sometimes the conditions under which losses at sea were suffered required that all investors share in the loss proportional to the value of their cargo. Such losses were called *averías gruesas*. A classic example of an *avería gruesa* resulted when ship captains voluntarily sacrificed some portion of the cargo in order to save the remainder. If, for example, a vessel were caught on a sandbar, the crew might jettison cargo with the hope of lightening the load and freeing the ship. Similarly, if seized by pirates, a ship captain might win freedom by paying the captors a ransom, perhaps a portion of the cargo. Such losses were deemed *averías gruesas* and, consequently, spread proportionally among all the owners of the registered cargo.[67]

Some of the charters, undoubtedly hoping both to limit costs and reduce the propensity for small, frivolous claims, ordered their directors to only indemnify losses that exceeded some percentage of a cargo's value.[68] For instance, a company directed by Tomás Martínez de Junquera stipulated in its 1794 charter that it would only indemnify *averías* that exceeded 10 percent of the insured cargo's value and even then only the excess, the amount exceeding 10 percent.[69] In effect, this proposal operated as a deductible; the company avoided the cost and hassle of small, petty claims, which were probably very common given the moist conditions of the ship's hold. A deductible undoubtedly elicited more responsible behavior on the part of merchants as well. Because they absorbed minor losses from water damage, they had an even greater incentive to more carefully package their commodities. This, in turn, likely reduced larger *averías* that might have been incurred by the company.

• • •

The last fifteen years or so of the eighteenth century witnessed the rapid expansion of the Cadiz maritime insurance industry. Evidence for the long decade after 1790 reveals that nearly one hundred partnerships were established in Cadiz to underwrite risk to destinations throughout the Atlantic world and beyond. The flourishing of the insurance industry was applauded by observers who viewed the previous practice of purchasing coverage abroad as a major drain of the Spanish mercantile community's valuable resources. Many of the great merchants who had been deeply engaged in long-distance trade obtained shares in the firms, eager to profit from this emerging financial sector. One can imagine that despite having lost their exclusive commercial privileges, these large merchants might have taken some consolation in their new opportunities to underwrite risk. While the profitability of Atlantic trade after 1783 was reduced, profits from insurance should, in theory, have been guaranteed given the accepted probabilities of the risks underwritten. Furthermore, the potential for insurance profits rose sharply after 1793, as the outbreak of war caused risk, and consequently premiums, to climb sharply. War coincided with the proliferation of insurance firms that undoubtedly formed to benefit from the rising premium rates. The acquisition of a share in an insurance firm must have seemed a good investment in the early 1790s. By decade's end, however, the insurance industry was in shatters as the riskiness of Atlantic world commerce had reached unparalleled heights.

• • •

The analysis in this chapter has been largely based on the charters filed with the *consulado* upon the founding of each firm. The information in these charters revealed a great deal about how the firms were structured and what measures they envisioned taking to reduce or limit their exposure.

The chapter that follows is based on analysis of nearly eight hundred policies actually underwritten by Cadiz insurers. While the charters provided guidelines, the policies themselves outline precisely how different risks were actually addressed. As the violence of war elevated the risks of sea, the insurance directors became increasingly inventive in the ways that they conditioned their coverage. Regardless, they clearly miscalculated the probability of ships being seized by corsairs. In fact, losses skyrocketed during the war, forcing firms to indemnify too many of their policyholders. Indeed, many went bankrupt.

Chapter 8

Insuring Against Risk: Analysis of Insurance Policies and the Perception of Risk in Atlantic World Trade

To succeed in long-distance trade required patience, nerve, luck, and sound commercial sense. Good judgment was critical, as has been repeatedly stressed in this book, to manage effectively the endemic risk and uncertainty. To understand early modern commerce requires attention to these strategies of risk-management. Indeed, many mercantile practices and behaviors make sense only in consideration of these perils.

Among merchants' numerous risk-reducing strategies, marine insurance was prominent. By purchasing insurance, merchants could actually eliminate much of the risk they faced, passing it onto underwriters whose volume of business allowed them to turn these risks into relatively guaranteed profits. In theory, if not always in practice, all parties won. Insuring themselves against the risks of sea, traders limited their own risk exclusively to the uncertainties of business, the possibility that prices in distant markets would be too low to cover outlays, let alone provide a return on investment. In essence, maritime insurance divided the transaction into two segments, the voyage and the marketing. Underwriters bore the risks of the former and the traders endured the latter.

Picking up where the previous left off, this chapter examines the micro-level business of marine insurance. Whereas the analysis in Chapter 7 was based on the company charters that outlined the perceived best practices of operating an insurance partnership, this chapter utilizes the actual policies discovered and thus moves from the theoretical to the actual experiences of underwriting risk on Spanish imperial trade. The company charters dated from the relatively brief and tumultuous period 1790 to 1814. The insurance policies used in this chapter, in contrast, allow a much longer view of the evolution in risk, beginning in 1759 and continuing until 1815 and the eve of independence.

• • •

Merchants or shipowners seeking maritime insurance coverage first approached an insurance broker, called a *corredor*, who operated out of the *consulado*, which was required to oversee the business of underwriting. The role of the *corredor* was to match the individual with insurance firms and then to supervise the issuing of the policy. Policies were written on preprinted forms that began with a lengthy preamble of boilerplate language. Blank spaces allowed the broker to fill in the name of the policyholder, the proposed route, and the name of the ship and ship captain. The broker then secured coverage from insurers, who affixed their signatures at the bottom of the policy, hence the term "to underwrite." In addition to their signatures, insurers stipulated the rate of premium and any additional policy conditions, such as the exemption of certain types of coverage.

Insurance for cargo was usually extended *tierra a tierra*, from its placement on the ship to its unloading at its destination. Coverage on the vessels themselves continued for some specified time in harbor, typically twenty-four to forty-eight hours following arrival, but sometimes for as long as thirty or forty days. Conditions such as these were specially negotiated from policy to policy.

Payment of premiums was not normally due upon the signing of the contract. Instead, premiums were collected only after the cessation of the insured risk. Given the very hefty premiums charged under certain circumstances, most notably war, this arrangement was probably necessary, as policyholders would have often needed to sell at least a portion of their wares to generate the funds. The typical policy stipulated that insurance premiums were due on outbound voyages, from Spain to Spanish America, six months after the date the policy was issued. Return voyages normally required that premiums be paid *al vencimiento de riesgos*, upon the termination of risks, literally when the ship arrived and the cargo was removed safely. Given that the firms were located in Cadiz, these policies were understandable. The safe arrival of a ship in America could not be immediately known, thus the generous six-month term. Of course, even half a year was inadequate in most cases for the ship to sail to America and news of its safe arrival to return to Spain. Regardless, six months was the nearly universal term stipulated on policies for the payment of outbound premiums.

Collection of premiums as scheduled was not always easily accomplished; of course, debts of any type were notoriously difficult to collect within the Spanish empire. Evidence suggests that premium collection grew more troublesome during the most difficult years of war at the turn of the nineteenth century. Several firms established in these years introduced guidelines aimed at improving their rate of collection. As noted above, a company revived in 1801 demanded that all premiums be collected up front, upon the initiation of the covered risk.[1] Another partnership stipulated that only those policyholders who had good credit should be relieved of the obligation of paying immediately because "there are many insured, punctual in collecting but negligent in paying."[2]

As with any contract, it was imperative that the language accurately and precisely reflected both parties' understanding of the conditions. In the case of insurance policies, there was considerable potential for fraud or misunderstanding, and it was the responsibility of the *corredor* to mitigate this possibility. In 1782, the Crown issued a lengthy and detailed ordinance outlining the functions and duties of a *corredor*, duties that had previously been outlined in the 1737 *Ordenanza de Bilbao*. Article 32 addressed specifically his obligations in his capacity as insurance broker:

> Due to disagreements occurring between insurers and insured with greater frequency than the nature of such a contract should allow, originating undoubtedly from ambiguity of the terms when the insurance policies are opened: I declare that [policies] in which a Broker has not become involved and affixed his signature are null and void; I expressly command [the Brokers] to review the said policies in detail and with such attention to the pacts reached that no interpretation nor other understanding than the intended meaning is possible.[3]

The *corredor* was responsible for reviewing the policy and confirming that the language was clear and unambiguous. Once approved, the broker affixed his seal and the policy became a binding contract. Without the *corredor*'s seal of approval, an insurance policy was not legally enforceable. For his services, the *corredor* received compensation in the amount of 0.25 percent of the insured value.[4]

Interestingly, policies were not always secured before a ship set sail. This was especially the case for ships and their cargo returning to Spain from the colonies. Cadiz merchants began securing coverage for return cargo the moment their agents in America alerted them of the value and makeup of cargoes soon to be dispatched. The correspondence, however, might reach Cadiz after the vessel with insurable goods had departed America. As long as there had been no calamitous news of shipwreck or pirate attack, however, this was no obstacle to securing coverage, assuming there were willing insurers. It was not out of the realm of possibility, however, for an insurer unknowingly to underwrite coverage on property that had already been lost. Of course, it was fraudulent for a merchant to insure property that he knew had already sustained loss. According to the seventeenth-century mercantile historian Joseph de Veitia Linaje, whether fraudulent or not, a policy contracted on a ship already lost was null if the insurer could have received by land news of the loss prior to the policy's underwriting.[5]

Juan Vicente de Marticorena found himself in this situation in 1797. Receiving news that his brother was about to dispatch to Cadiz a cargo of 34 *zurrones* (sacks) of Guatemalan indigo divided between a vessel called *La Natalia* and either the *San Rafael* or *La Havana*, Marticorena scrambled successfully to find the necessary 18,120 pesos' worth of coverage, 12,000 on *La Natalia* and the balance on the other ships. Some time later, Marticorena learned from his brother that, in fact, all of the dye had been placed on *La Natalia*, requiring that he void the policy on either the *San Rafael* or *La Havana* and take out a second one for *La Natalia*. This task, however, proved difficult. First, a number of the insurance firms contacted had already insured their limit on *La Natalia* and were unwilling to take on additional risks on a single sailing. Second, and more problematic, *La Natalia*'s arrival was already overdue. Apparently it had set sail in early November 1796 from Omoa, Central America, and had never arrived to Havana as scheduled. Although there was not yet concrete evidence that anything bad had occurred to *La Natalia* and there was some conjecture, perhaps just wishful thinking, that the ship had bypassed Cuba and simply sailed straight to Spain, there was, quite naturally, growing concern. Marticorena was advised that the only coverage still available was at the "exorbitant premium of 70%, rebating 20% for safe arrival."[6] By now, Marticorena was in a predicament. Buying insurance, he stood to lose half of the value if the cargo in question arrived undamaged, and a full 70 percent if the ship and its load failed to arrive at all. The alternative was to gamble entirely and forego insurance, the option that Marticorena ultimately selected. All of this transpired in January; news finally reached the Cadiz *consulado* in early February that English corsairs had indeed seized *La Natalia*.[7] More than a month after Juan Vicente had been instructed to secure proof that the insured portion of the indigo had in fact been aboard *La Natalia*,[8] his brother in Guatemala, Juan Bautista de Marticorena, had still not learned the ship's fate and continued to hold out hope, writing, "even among those who are least confident, there is some hope that it arrived safely to the Canaries."[9]

In what was perhaps a very similar case, although the underlying details are lacking, Cadiz trader Antonio de Artechea secured coverage on some hides that were shipped in his name from Montevideo aboard the *San Joséf alias La Hermosa Andrea*. The policy was dated 19 March 1805 but the *La Hermosa Andrea*, it was later learned, had been seized on 3 March. Artechea appears to have insured only a tiny portion, 2000 pesos, of the cargo valued at 31,874 pesos. The policy, like Marticorena's just discussed, demanded a 70 percent premium if the ship were to be lost to be reduced to 50 percent arriving safely to Cadiz. If, however, the ship departed Montevideo and then sought refuge in any American port, then the premium would be lowered to just 10 percent.[10] In this case, the policy was issued after the ship set sail, indeed after it had already been apprehended. Of course, news of its seizure had not yet arrived to Cadiz allowing Artechea to obtain coverage. It is possible that the boat was overdue to arrive, explaining Artechea's willingness to pay and the insurers' demand for such a high premium. The clause reducing the rate to 10 percent if the ship returned to America might have been designed to assuage Artechea's concerns that he might be insuring a risk that he never really incurred.

Assessment of Risk and Premium Rates

The rates of premium charged in the insurance industry reflected perceived levels of risk. As the apparent riskiness of a voyage increased, so too did the rate demanded by the insurance companies. The profitability of an insurance partnership was obviously the difference between premiums collected and losses indemnified.[11] Always expressed as a percentage of the value of the insured item, insurance premium rates provide a statistical measure of the perceived riskiness of regularly encountered events at sea.

A variety of factors influenced insurance premium rates charged in the plaza of Cadiz, some of which were noted in Chapter 7. It is doubtful that insurance actuaries employed especially sophisticated statistical analysis to arrive at the rates; modern actuarial science emerged only in the twentieth century. Instead, rates reflected the collective experiences of insurance directors who assessed the probability of each potential risk in light of past events. Whether the directors' ultimate assessments were well-founded is not always clear, but what is certain is that the rates reflected their perception of the riskiness of each event underwritten. The sections below examine the diversity of factors that were considered by the insurance companies in assessing risk in oceanic commerce.

SEASON AND WEATHER

One of the greatest dangers for oceanic travel was bad weather. Unexpected storms were a major cause of shipwrecks and resulted in heavy losses for oceanic traders. Consequently, insurers charged higher insurance premiums for vessels likely to be exposed to difficult weather conditions. Of course, forecasting inclement weather was not easily accomplished, but weather did change seasonally and insurers did adjust their premiums accordingly.

At least some of the companies operating in Cadiz offered coverage to vessels sailing to northern European ports where weather conditions deteriorated significantly during the winter. Insurers accounted for the added risk of winter sailing by charging higher rates during these months. The 1794 company charter of the firm directed by Tomás Martínez de Junquera, for example, specified different insurance rate schedules for the summer and winter seasons. The charter advised insuring voyages between Cadiz and Hamburg at the rate of 7 percent but proposed a 2 percentage point decrease during the less dangerous months of April through the end of August. Likewise, the firm scheduled 6 percent premiums to Holland with the same two-point reduction during the summer. These rates reflected the expectation of more perilous weather conditions during the months September through March.[12] Seven years later, a firm directed by Antonio Vallarino also proposed charging higher insurance premiums to northern European destinations during the winter.[13] The practice of seasonally adjusting insurance premiums to northern ports was widely practiced by insurers in other European markets; it was not a Spanish innovation.[14]

Other companies chose instead to reduce their exposure during the winter season as a means of reducing the risks of northern voyages. The 1791 charter establishing a company to be directed by Manuel Joséph de Armas specified that coverage per company share on ships sailing to northern European destinations should be reduced during the winter months, indicated as 30 September to 1 April. So, for example, the company proposed limiting coverage to 250 pesos per share on warships sailing to European ports during the nonwinter months but lowering this to

66 percent of this level (roughly 165 pesos per share) for vessels sailing during the winter.[15]

More risk-averse firms chose to avoid coverage altogether to northern Europe during the winter. The partnership directed by Ventura Imaña under the protection of María Santísima del Carmen and el Glorioso Arcángel San Miguel chose to underwrite coverage for northern ports during most of the year, but opted to abstain from *comercio del norte* between October and March.[16]

Season did not seem to have figured as largely into the assessment of insurance premium rates for trade to the colonies. While travel is clearly less disrupted by winter weather in most of Spanish America than in the North Sea, ships sailing to the Caribbean faced a potentially even greater risk during the hurricane season, which occurs annually from, roughly, June to November, peaking in August through October. While insurance premium rates were regularly adjusted to reflect seasonal risks to the north Atlantic, few such policies were uncovered for voyages between Spain and America despite the risk of tropical storms during the summer months.

The risk of Atlantic hurricanes could be largely mitigated, however, by simply avoiding travel during the most dangerous months. Modern climatological data reveal that between 1886 and 1991, 96 percent of "intense hurricane activity" took place between August and October, with a full 57 percent occurring in September.[17] Spaniards certainly understood this tendency. The commander of the 1768 flota to New Spain, Francisco Javier Everado Tilly, the Marqués de Casa Tilly, suggested to his superiors that ships not be allowed "to travel outside of benign weather." In defense of his position, Tilly pointed to the 17,505,000 pesos allegedly lost to shipwrecks in the previous 45 years, and this, he added, excluded the ill-fated flota of 1715 commanded by Juan Esteban de Ubilla.[18] The security of traveling in "the month of April, the most propitious and gentle time to return to that kingdom" inspired shipowner Tomás Ruiz de Apodaca to advise his wife in 1759 to forego altogether obtaining insurance on their 30,000-peso ship "unless with the arrival of our [new] King the state of peace of our court is altered, with some of the Crowns of France or England."[19] Ruiz de Apodaca, like any experienced sailor, chose to sail prior to the dangerous hurricane season.

Remaining in port during the most violent months was the surest way of avoiding a shipwreck. In fact, in the early colonial period an annual sailing schedule emerged that was designed to avoid the Caribbean from August through October. By Royal Cédula of 20 January 1582, the convoy to Havana and Veracruz was to depart Cadiz by May, which under normal conditions placed it in the Caribbean in July, just before the high hurricane season began. The flota wintered in Veracruz before beginning its return voyage to Havana in February, and then on to Spain in late March.[20] This was, at least, the intended schedule.

While ideally planned to avoid the stormy months, delays commonly resulted in alterations to the schedule, and the fleet often arrived into the Gulf of Mexico at peak hurricane season. De la Fuente found that from 1586 to 1610 fleets departed Havana for Spain overwhelmingly in July and August, vacating the Caribbean before September and October, by far the worst hurricane months.[21] During the eighteenth century, however, eight of the thirteen flotas arrived in America during the worst months— August, September, and October. Return voyages to Spain, in contrast, generally escaped the peak hurricane season by departing between May and July.[22]

Despite the obvious danger of encountering a catastrophic tropical storm, Cadiz-based insurers did not normally increase premiums for voyages set to take place in the less favorable weather season. This failure seems surprising given the regularity of this practice for sailings to northern European ports as well as the otherwise acute attention of underwriters to all identifiable dangers.

ROUTES

While merchants secured insurance coverage in the plaza of Cadiz for voyages to all parts of the world, the overwhelming majority of surviving policies were written for trips to and from Spanish America. Table 8.1 highlights the major routes of surviving policies for the years 1759 to 1818 and indicates the number of policies and share of the total for each route. As is indicated, the voyage between Cadiz and Veracruz was the most frequently insured, comprising 30 percent of the total policies discovered. Insurance policies secured for the trip from Cadiz to Río de la Plata (defined here as both Buenos Aires and Montevideo) were second most frequent, representing 14 percent of the total located.[23]

All of the most frequently insured destinations highlighted in Table 8.1 were located in the Spanish empire. Policies were also written to insure ships and cargo journeying to and from destinations outside the empire. On 6 October 1790 merchants identified as Magon Lefer Hermanos y Compañía secured coverage in Cadiz for their cargo and a portion of the their vessel called *La Libertad* for a voyage from Marseille to India, the "Oriente," China, and back to Europe. The value of the insured cargo

TABLE 8.1

Frequently Insured Routes in Cadiz Market: 1759–1818

Voyage (either direction)	No. of Policies	Percentage of Total
Barcelona – Veracruz	24	3%
Cadiz – Río de la Plata	112	14%
Cadiz – Lima	80	10%
Cadiz – Cartagena	20	3%
Cadiz – La Guaira	13	2%
Cadiz – Central Am.	58	7%
Cadiz – Havana	45	6%
Cadiz – Veracruz	233	30%
Santander – Havana	13	2%
Santander – La Guaira	11	1%
TOTAL	**609**	

SOURCE: Online Appendix C.

and ship totaled 10,000 pesos and was assessed an insurance premium of 28 percent, equal to 2,800 pesos.[24] On 16 January 1793 a company called Godet Segalas y Compañía took out coverage on "goods" returning from Asia aboard the French vessel *La Felicidad*. The voyage from India and the Orient was headed to Toulon, France, and was assessed 14.75 percent on its 5,000 pesos' worth of cargo.[25] Cadiz insurers also underwrote slave ships that traveled along the coast of Africa in pursuit of human cargo. On 29 August 1818 *consulado* merchant Antonio de Artechea acquired coverage for his ship, *El Nuevo Pajaro*, its provisions, and other goods for a journey from Santander to Cuba by way of the African coast. On his insured value of 37,000 pesos, Artechea was assessed a hefty 24 percent premium or 8,880 pesos.[26] While Cadiz-based insurance companies engaged in ventures outside of the empire, their primary business unquestionably and unsurprisingly involved transatlantic routes within the empire.

Naturally, insurance premium rates varied depending on the destination of a ship. One would imagine that distance would affect the premiums since the longer the voyage, the greater the risk that some mishap might occur. According to Frank Spooner, distance was one of the principal two determinants in assessing insurance rates in the Amsterdam market in 1769, season being the other. As he argues, greater distance reduced the movement of information, which, in turn, escalated riskiness. In addition, the ability of a ship's government to offer protection declined with distance from home. Spooner further points to the greater difficulty of provisioning the ship or acquiring needed repairs on longer voyages. Each of these risk factors was directly related to distance, and, thus, longer voyages paid higher premiums.[27]

Evidence from the Spanish insurance market does not support any correlation between rates and distance traveled. Longer voyages did incur slightly higher rates, but other factors seem to have played more critical roles. Spooner's data revealed an extraordinarily high correlation between premium rate and distance traveled in the Amsterdam insurance market in 1769 (r = 0.94).[28] Computation of the correlation coefficient (r) for the entire collected set of Spanish American insurance data exposed no correlation whatsoever (r = 0.14) between distance and premium rate. The total absence of any apparent statistical correlation might reflect the fact that many of the years under consideration were years during which Spain was at war and insurance rates spiked astronomically, tending to mask correlation. To try to reduce the distortion caused by war, a second regression was performed that examined the years 1783 to 1792, a rare decade of uninterrupted peace for Spain. This data set revealed only moderate correlation between distance and premium (r = 0.40), suggesting that distance was one but not the major factor considered by insurers in assessing risk. Certainly, the Spanish data was considerably less correlated than the data set employed by Spooner.[29]

Table 8.2 displays the aggregate data somewhat differently. The average and median premium rates for selected major routes for the decade 1783 to 1792 were computed and are presented along with the corresponding maritime distance. As this simplified data clearly illustrates, underwriters charged more, on average, for the lengthy voyage to Lima than they did for the less than half as far journey to Havana. This observation is consis-

TABLE 8.2

Comparison of Insurance Premiums and Distance in Nautical Miles for Various Spanish American Routes: 1783–92

One Way Voyage Between (either direction)	Number of Voyages	Sailing Distance in Miles	Median Insurance Premium	Average Insurance Premium
Cadiz & Havana	25	3979	1.50%	1.64%
Cadiz & Honduras	40	4438	2.00%	2.26%
Cadiz & Veracruz	102	4769	1.50%	1.75%
Cadiz & Río de la Plata	15	5238	2.00%	2.20%
Barcelona & VC	26	5334	1.96%	2.00%
Cadiz & Lima	28	9020	2.80%	2.63%

SOURCES: Online Appendix C. Nautical distances calculated from sea voyage calculator at http://www.e-ships.net/dist.htm.

tent with a theory suggesting a direct correlation between premiums and distance; the longer voyage incurred a higher rate. The remaining data is far more ambiguous, however. The route from Cadiz to Honduras, for example, incurred higher rates than its distance would justify. Slightly shorter than the voyage to Veracruz, it nonetheless incurred significantly higher premiums. In fact, rates to Honduras were comparable to those to Río de la Plata (Buenos Aires or Montevideo) despite the latter destinations being nearly 20 percent farther.

One likely reason that the premiums charged on the policies examined by Spooner were much more highly correlated to distance than the policies underwritten by the insurers at Cadiz is that Spooner's ports were primarily distributed along a single linear route. For example, while voyaging from Amsterdam to Smyrna (Turkey) a ship passed many of the other destinations commonly insured in Amsterdam such as London, Rouen, Lisbon, Cadiz, and Leghorn (Livorno). One would expect the perceived risk to be less (and thus the premium rate) if the ship were to end its voyage at one of these closer, en route ports.[30] In contrast, the routes covered by the Cadiz insurers were more dispersed, emanating from southern Spain in a spokelike fashion; the sea lanes to Veracruz and Buenos Aires were distinct. Furthermore, the variation in distances was not as great in the Spanish empire. Aside from Lima, most of the distances underwritten were in the 4,000 to 5,000 mile range, a relatively small difference. There was much greater variation in the distances between those ports that Spooner investigated.[31]

Furthermore, not all stretches of a voyage are equally dangerous, and so distance alone does not reflect relative riskiness. As Spooner indicates, his strong correlation applied only in the summer months. During the winter season some routes incurred much higher rates than their distance would seem to indicate, an obvious reflection of different risks figuring more largely. Winter rates to Archangel (Russia), for example, were more than double those to Smyrna despite the latter being located 50 percent farther from Amsterdam, an obvious indication that the route to Archangel was especially perilous in the winter.

Most of the routes to America entailed sailing on the open sea, which afforded fewer dangers since ship captains could often see potential enemies long before they neared. To reduce their exposure to attacks, Spanish ships on the open sea used secret means to communicate to avoid being attacked by enemies falsely flying Spanish flags. In 1760, for example, the convoyed merchant ships *El Rosario de Murguía* and *Nuestra Señora del Rosario y San Francisco Xavier* employed a complex series of signs and countersigns,

TABLE: 8.3

Sign and Countersign of El Rosario de Murguía *and* Nuestra Señora
del Rosario y San Francisco Xavier*: 1760*

Day	Sunday	Monday	Tuesday	Wednesday	Thursday	Friday	Saturday
Santo	Santiago	San Dionisio	San Genaro	Santo Thorivio	San Bernabé	San Ysidrio	San Raphael
Contraseña	Galicia	Leon	Navarra	Pamplona	Asturias	Murcia	Valencia

SOURCE: AGI, *Consulados*, legajo 772, exp 4, Havana, 12 October 1760.

displayed in Table 8.3, to allow daily confirmation of each other's identity.

The open sea posed few risks; instead the greatest perils were close to land. Corsairs most frequently sought cover near coasts from which they could quickly attack unsuspecting targets. Navigational hazards such as sandbars, outcroppings, or difficult harbors were not factors in the middle of the Atlantic. In short, the greatest dangers of the transatlantic route occurred on either end, near to Iberian or American shores. The distance in between was not as critical.

Some policies left undetermined the precise route of an insured vessel. On 3 January 1803, José de Riquena and Martín de Abraga took out insurance on a very large shipment of calf hides (*cueros de novillos*) valued at 167,185 pesos that was to travel aboard two frigates named *La Esperanza* and *Luisa*. The merchants were apparently unsure, however, where best they could dispose of their cargo because the policy was left very open-ended. Departing from Montevideo, the boats were to travel to "Europe" where they would then proceed to a number of possible destinations. Presumably the frigates intended to call first at a peninsular port—at least Spanish commercial laws required this. The final port, however, was to be determined later. The policy provided a detailed schedule of premium rates to possible final destinations in Cadiz, Portugal, Galicia, Cantabria, the coast of France to Rouen, and anything north of Calais. The policy excluded coverage to either the Baltic or the Mediterranean without providing any rationale. In the end, frigate *Luisa* stopped at Santoña, just east of Santander in Cantabria, while *La Esperanza* completed its journey in Hamburg. The premium rates were 3.5 and 5.75 percent respectively.[32]

A policy such as the one secured by these Montevideo merchants was called "indefinido" because its specific route was indefinite. Generally, insurers preferred not to extend such open-ended coverage since such voyages were naturally less predictable. The introduction of any greater uncertainty entailed increased perceived risk. Many of the Cadiz insurance companies avoided *indefinidos* altogether. A firm founded in 1791 under the protection of La Santísima Trinidad and Nuestra Señora del Rosario prohibited its director, Ruperto López García, from extending indefinite coverage, claiming that such policies invited fraud.[33] Tomás Martínez de Junquera's firm also banned the coverage of indefinite voyages.[34]

Firms that did not entirely reject "indefinidos" might impose special restrictions on these open-ended policies. A firm called La Compañía de Seguros Marca JPH allowed its director to underwrite *indefinidos* but on the condition that such policies expired at the end of one calendar year. This reduced the ability of the insured from conducting business unendingly under the protection of the single policy. La Compañía de Seguros Marca JPH further specified that "these indefinite insurance policies will always include the condition that they will neither cover war nor its consequences."[35] This latter stipulation erased perhaps the greatest threat of an indefinite voyage, that over the lengthy voyage political conditions might change and peace might give way to war. In any event, the longer a policy provided coverage, the greater the likelihood of a loss being sustained.

War and Insurance Rates

Without any question, the political situation affected insurance premiums more than any other factor. With the outbreak of war came the immediate danger of privateering, enemy ships at the service of their crowns attacking Spanish commercial vessels. While most other risks encountered by merchant ships might strike at anytime, privateering, the greatest danger of all, occurred exclusively during wartime.

The idea behind insurance is that the risk takers can guarantee themselves a profit by pooling policies sufficient that the actual number of bad outcomes equals the expected number based on the probability of such a risk-event taking place. The risk is eliminated because the policyholder no longer bears it, and the insurer knows with considerable confidence how many of the risks will require indemnification. The premiums are set at a rate that guarantees collecting more than must be paid out; profits are secure.

Despite this, the heightened risks of war scared many firms into suspending operations; maybe the estimation of probabilities became too difficult, making war more in the realm of an unmeasurable uncertainty than a measurable risk and leading more cautious firms to refuse to underwrite it. It must have simply seemed too much of a gamble, too likely to result in large, frequent, and unpredictable indemnifications. In any event, a number of the insurance firms in Cadiz refused to underwrite coverage during wartime. A company established on the final day of 1790 indicated its unwillingness altogether to endure war risks. The charter of this company, directed by Joséf de Urda under the protection of Jesus, Mary, and Joseph, stipulated that the underwriting of policies should cease immediately upon the news or even the threat of war.[36] Several months later a partnership formed under the directorship of Augustín de Valverde Hijos y Compañía stated in its charter that its intention was to insure only during times of peace, and so in the event of war or its likelihood, the director was instructed to suspend operations until the shareholders could convene and decide how to proceed.[37] The identical policy was adopted by two firms established in November 1791, one directed by Ruperto López García and the other by Antonio Lasqueti.[38]

Several companies that did not initially avoid war risks changed their policies as political conditions deteriorated. A partnership directed by Tomás Martínez de Junquera was established on 20 February 1794, a full year after the formation of the First Coalition against France and the official entry of Spain into the war. Indeed the firm might have formed precisely to profit from the rising marine insurance premiums. But on 30 June 1797, Junquera's firm abruptly halted its underwriting. By then Spain had changed sides, had declared war against Great Britain, and now faced British Admiral Horatio Nelson's emerging blockade off the coast of Cadiz. The partnership did not dissolve, perhaps under the hope that hostilities would end promptly. Finally, on 9 March 1798 the shareholders voted to disband altogether pointing to "the near total inaction which the commerce of this plaza is experiencing as a result of the war with England." On 11 February 1802, as hostilities diminished in the month prior to the Treaty of Amiens, the partners decided to reestablish the company, but they were still wary of covering war. The revised charter instructed: "we order the director not to sign any policy whatsoever on ships coming from or going to America and Asia without exempting risks of war and hostilities and related events."[39] Originally established during wartime, the shareholders had nonetheless come to conclude that war was too great a risk to endure.

The experiences of Director Martínez de Junquera's firm were not unusual. A partnership founded in late 1794 under the protection of Our Lady of Rosario and San Antonio de Padua and directed by Antonio Vallarino pursued a nearly identical course. Director Vallarino's firm halted business during the wars but revived its operations in November 1801.

The 1801 charter, however, stipulated word-for-word the same language as that of the firm directed by Martínez de Junquera forbidding the director from covering war.[40] Apparently, this language had become boilerplate for some of the firms.

Wartime premiums could be extremely high, and so shareholders of a company formed on 8 March 1802 feared that their directors might be enticed by the delusion of easy profit. According to the firm's charter: "since recent experience has made us see the excessive losses that the insurance companies have suffered . . . we prohibit the directors," the brothers Juan Antonio and Francisco José Carazo, "from insuring risks of war, hostilities and related events no matter how advantageous the proposed premiums."[41]

Wartime rates were much higher than peacetime rates, and the insurer able to stomach the risk had the potential of profiting handsomely. A company founded in April 1791 under the protection of La Sacra Familia boldly proclaimed in its charter that "it does not make sense to suspend this business in time of war because underwriting during it indemnifies many of the losses which are inevitable at the start of the conflict." The firm did not discount altogether the perils of insuring war-related risks, stipulating that during wartime, amounts underwritten in any single policy should be reduced to one-third of the level permitted during peacetime. In addition, the total of all risks underwritten by the company during wartime was to be limited to half the level allowed in peacetime.[42]

A company established under the protection of El Patriarca San Joséf and San Augustín employed this same argument in March 1797. "Experience demonstrates," the charter claimed, "that in this state and circumstance [of war], it makes no sense to suspend the business of these companies because by underwriting in said time many of the losses that customarily occur at the beginning of hostilities and in the continuation of the same war are recouped due to the higher premiums."[43]

Apparently, some businessmen were attracted to the insurance business because of the high rates of war. At least two firms opened their doors in mid-1793 in the early months of the war with France to take advantage of the elevated premiums. Their charters specifically noted their intention to engage in underwriting "for as long as the present war between this monarchy and the French nation lasts."[44]

It is not clear how many of the Cadiz-based insurance partnerships suspended operations altogether during the lengthy wars at the turn of the nineteenth century, but obviously a number did. Even those firms that chose to endure the risk and continue to accept policies responded to the rising dangers of oceanic commerce by lowering the limits per share that they would underwrite.

The supply of insurance, then, must have grown increasingly scarce during wartime as some companies withdrew from the business and others scaled back their operations. According to Spooner, "the rise in war-risks increased the demand for insurance" in the Amsterdam market of the late eighteenth century, a finding echoed by Kingston for the British market.[45] It is not clear whether this occurred in the Spanish empire. War was unquestionably the greatest danger faced by Spanish merchants and shipowners, but their universal response was not merely to purchase protection in the form of maritime insurance. During the late-century wars many merchants elected to withdraw temporarily from commerce, assessing the risk to be too great and too costly with or without insurance. A few traders, in their efforts to avoid paying the high premiums, threw all caution to the wind and shipped with either limited or no insurance, although this gamble must have been unorthodox and had the potential of resulting in their financial ruin. The point is that in contrast to Amsterdam and Great Britain, the *absolute* demand for insurance probably fell in the Spanish empire, a reflection of greatly reduced trade volumes, even while the riskiness of commerce skyrocketed. Perhaps the more important question is whether there was an actual shortage of protection available for purchase due to the scaling back of the insurers, whether the supply of insurance fell more rapidly than the demand. To be sure, the supply of inexpensive insurance disappeared.

Insurance losses were especially severe at the start of a conflict, as several of the charters indicated. It was normal, when war erupted, for ships to be caught at sea, unaware of the deteriorated political situation. Spain declared war against England in June 1779, for example, but news of the war only reached Mexico in August. During the intervening months ships stationed in Veracruz proceeded unaware of the acute dangers.[46] Of probably limited value was a Royal memorandum sent to the colonies' viceroys back in March that had warned of the possibility of war and ordered them to prevent ships from leaving their ports: "Despite the fact that peace now exists with England without any new development, it is imperative always to live with care and suspicions that the English will commit without warning some attack as they usually do, particularly against the ships that navigate from these to those dominions."[47] By the time the message had reached most of the American ports, the war had already begun and ships en route were already in danger.

Underwriters, similarly, extended coverage prior to hostilities, never anticipating the heightened risks that loomed. In early February 1797, the Cadiz *consulado* addressed this very issue indirectly in a letter it sent to the Minister of Finance, Pedro Varela. The guild lamented the recent loss of two ships, including the aforementioned indigo-laden *La Natalia*, which had been seized by British corsairs as they neared the Iberian Peninsula. These ships were but the tip of the iceberg, according to the *consulado*, as property losses to British privateers since the start of hostilities had already reached five to six million pesos, an enormous sum given that barely half a year had passed since the war's start.[48] Ships already at sea when war was declared were easy targets for enemy corsairs; outfitted with less armament than was prudent during wartime, they had little chance to defend themselves from attack. Furthermore, during peacetime, vessels often sailed alone, a condition that was generally avoided during wartime. For all of these reasons, the months immediately following the outbreak of hostilities left many ships especially vulnerable to privateers.

Shortly after Spain's 1793 entry into the war against Revolutionary France, a ship called *Santiago Apostol alias Nueva Aquiles* was seized by French corsairs as it traveled from Lima. The capture, which sparked considerable consternation in Cadiz, prompted the *consulado* to dispatch a letter to Spanish Minister Diego de Gardoqui, advising him of the broader financial implications. According to the guild, *Nueva Aquiles* was but one of numerous ships that had departed American ports before the onset of conflict and were sailing to Cadiz uninformed of the new military dangers. Virtually every notable merchant in Cadiz, the *consulado* suggested, would experience an immediate financial setback from privateering either as an investor in a ship or a shareholder in an insurance company.[49]

In December 1796 Buenos Aires merchant José Ramón de Ugarteche expressed his concern about a number of ships that had departed for Spain shortly before the news of war with Great Britain had reached Río de la Plata. Ugarteche estimated that thirty ships carrying seven to eight million pesos' worth of cargo had set sail without knowledge of the war, making them vulnerable to capture by enemy corsairs.[50]

Spanish merchantmen were again caught unaware following the rupture of the tenuous Peace of Amiens. While seemingly futile, the *consulado* sent a letter to Spain's vice consul in Lagos, Portugal, asking the official to instruct all fishermen to warn any Spanish merchant ships that they might encounter at sea of the resumption of war with England. The *consulado* even offered a reward of 200 pesos to any fisherman who brought proof of a ship captain having been so advised. A 2,000 peso reward was offered if the warning led to the safe arrival of the trading vessel to either a Spanish or Portuguese port. While it seems dubious that this method would have saved very many ships, it certainly illustrates the dangers resulting immediately after the eruption of war.[51] In fact, in early 1805 the guild rewarded 200 pesos to captain Juan Fernández and the crew of a fishing boat called *Virgen de los Remedios* for having warned the *polacra La Sacra Familia* as it approached Spain from Havana.[52]

Before news of this same military campaign had reached the viceroyalty of New Granada, British ships began seizing vessels near the port of Cartagena. In his report to the viceroy, Field Marshall Antonio de Narváez y la Torre complained that the British corsairs "that have infested these seas" had begun commandeering Spanish ships even before the declaration of war, although it should be noted that the official date on which hostilities initiated was always debated.[53]

Losses sustained from privateering in the first months of war must have been especially onerous for the insurance companies. Presumably most merchants were financially protected, having purchased insurance coverage that included the risks of warfare. During peacetime, insurance was fairly inexpensive, so traders had little incentive to forego protection. The financial brunt of the first several months of conflict, then, primarily fell onto the insurers because they were forced to indemnify a large number of policyholders whose property had been captured by the enemy. After the initial phase of war, insurers could, and did, adjust their practices, withdrawing from business altogether or increasing their rates to reflect more accurately the elevated riskiness of commerce.

Assuming good fortune, staying in business during war permitted an insurance firm to recoup the losses it sustained at the war's outbreak by charging high wartime premiums. And premiums during wartime were indeed elevated. In April 1780, in the midst of Spain's engagement in the War of American Independence, for example, merchant Francisco de Sierra contracted at 22 percent to ship 500 barrels of aguardiente valued at 7,536 pesos to Veracruz aboard the frigate *La Sacra Familia alias La Angélica*. On the very same day Sierra insured at the same rate another 500 barrels aboard the navío *La Caridad*, also destined for Mexico.[54] Later in the month, the Royal Company of San Fernando de Sevilla insured its vessel to Montevideo for 60,000 pesos paying a 23 percent premium.[55] A week later, Juan Martínez de Iriarte insured his frigate, *Nuestra Señora del Rosario y San Francisco de Assís alias la Felicidad*, for 15,000 pesos at the even higher rate of 28 percent.[56] If these voyages were completed without any losses, the insurers collected nice returns, returns that would have helped offset the losses sustained when the war began and insured vessels were captured.

One would imagine that such high premium rates proved profitable for the insurers, but evidence suggests otherwise. Despite charging rates ranging from 23 to 28 percent, the underwriting of policies nearly halted in the one and a half years to follow. Between the end of May 1780 and January 1782, only two insurance policies were located and both indicated that insurance rates had climbed very sharply from the already high rates of spring 1780. In December 1780 Francisco de Sierra took out insurance at 40.25 percent on 6,000 pesos of cargo to be shipped from Cadiz to Lima aboard the frigate *El Jesús*.[57] The following June Sierra shipped goods valued at 50,000 pesos to Veracruz aboard his frigate *El Jasón* again paying an insurance premium of 40.25 percent.[58] It should be noted, however, that at this time Sierra was acquiring most of his insurance coverage from commercial houses in northern Europe, not Cadiz. The rates he paid there seem to have been cheaper, and it is not clear why he chose to pay these particularly elevated rates in Cadiz. Presumably he had failed to get coverage from Amsterdam, London, or anywhere else.[59]

The underwriting of policies resumed in 1782, although rates remained elevated. Juan Vicente de Marticorena entered into contracts for four separate policies in June to ship goods from Cadiz to both Lima and Veracruz. For three of the policies he paid rates of about 30 percent and paid 25.25 percent for the fourth.[60]

During the early stages of the wars of the French Revolution and Napoleon, insurance rates were low in comparison to the elevated rates of the American Revolutionary War. This trend held until shifting alliances changed Spain's enemy from France to Great Britain. While at war with France, most of the transatlantic routes could be covered in Cadiz for 5 to 8 percent, although a few of the policies charged considerably higher rates, most notably to La Guaira, where several policies were written at 12 to 25 percent.[61]

Spain's alliance with France and the outbreak in 1796 of the First Naval War against Great Britain caused the perceived risks of trade to rise enormously and the costs of insurance to increase accordingly. Rates began climbing sharply even before Spain declared war against Great Britain as insurers recognized that the July 1795 treaty between France and Spain meant that the latter's declaration against England was inevitable and imminent. Indeed, hostilities between Spain and Great Britain began in October 1796, and almost immediately premium rates increased to unprecedented levels. In early 1797 Buenos Aires merchant Francisco Valdovinos, learning of the existing unconditional[62] rates of 30 to 40 percent, instructed his partner in Cadiz, Antonio de Artechea, to withdraw their money from commerce and invest instead in bonds. Valdovinos was of the opinion that "no business to America can endure this burden."[63] In the event, the superior English navy virtually halted commerce in and out of Cadiz and very few policies were actually written over the next several years. The few that were contracted demanded premiums ranging from 30 to even 60 percent.[64] These astronomical rates do not seem to have been aberrations. In a 1798 issue of *Correo Mercantil de España y sus Indias*, a commercial newspaper published in Madrid, maritime insurance rates for 14 March quoted for the plaza of La Coruña were 40 to 50 percent to Montevideo and 50 percent to Havana, the only American destinations noted.[65]

Following the brief reprieve provided by the Peace of Amiens, rates again surged to very elevated levels. Antonio de Artechea insured two cargoes in March 1805 at the rate of 50 percent. On 11 March 1805, Artechea and Pedro Olavarría procured coverage to transport tallow (*sebo*) from Montevideo to Vigo and Bilbao on the frigate *La Vizcaya*. The value insured was 11,000 pesos, which resulted in a premium of 5,500 pesos.[66] Eight days later, on 19 March, Artechea and Martín de Alzaga secured protection for a shipment of hides valued at 31,874 pesos aboard the vessel *San Joséf alias La Hermosa Andrea*. Their 50 percent premium, thus, cost them 15,937 pesos. In the event, Artechea and partners were fortunate that they had secured coverage since both ships were captured and the merchants had to seek indemnification from the underwriters.[67] Shortly after Artechea and his partners procured these policies, the underwriting of policies again seems to have largely halted; at least, few policies were discovered in the archives. The last policy of 1805 was dated 7 December; nearly three years passed before the next policy discovered was underwritten on 11 October 1808.[68]

The near absence of policies located for the one and a half year period from May 1780 to January 1782 and then again for the nearly three years from December 1805 to October 1808 is undoubtedly an indication of the severe decline in commerce during these years of war. Indeed, in his study of Spanish international trade John Fisher found a "paucity of data" for the years 1779–81.[69] But the lack of data might also suggest that the insurers were finding the rates of 23 to 28 percent in the early years and 50 percent in the later period too low to justify taking on such elevated risk. It would seem that with rates this high handsome profits would have been guaranteed for the insurance firms, but the fact that many partnerships chose nonetheless to disband suggests otherwise. Evidence presented below demonstrates convincingly that most firms lost money during the post-1793 era, despite such elevated premium rates. Clearly the firms perceived the risks of war to be excessively high, more in the realm of gambling than anything predictable by actuarial science. Undoubtedly, many merchants also balked at paying these excessive rates, choosing to wait out the war. In short, the insurance market could not sufficiently absorb the overwhelming risk that the wars entailed. Both insurers and merchants curtailed their operations.

• • •

Again, losses were especially acute at the start of war, leading some insurers to devise strategies to attempt to minimize the tremendous losses normally sustained before they could adjust their rates or underwriting practices. About 5 percent of the nearly eight hundred policies located included clauses that automatically provided for a rate increase in the event that war were to erupt during the term of the coverage. The earliest policies found containing this clause were secured by Tomás de Apodaca, owner of a boat (*navío*) called *Nuestra Señora del Rosario y Santo Domingo alias El Halcón*, who purchased coverage in August 1759 for a voyage from Cadiz to Veracruz. On his *navío* and its equipment Apodaca took out two policies, one for 30,000 pesos and the second for 6,000 pesos. On the larger policy, which specifically covered the ship's armament and *avío* (costs of provisioning), the shipowner was assessed a rate of 6.75 percent but under the condition that the rate would increase to 26.75 percent if war were to erupt in the interim, a 20 percentage point war supplement. The smaller policy, covering the vessel exclusively, also charged 6.75 percent but demanded a 24 percentage point increase for a total of 30.75 percent in the event of hostilities. At the time that Tomás de Apodaca procured his coverage, France and Great Britain had been at war for more than three years of the Seven Years' War. Spain had managed to stay neutral, but Spanish insurers prudently recognized the potential for Madrid to become suddenly embroiled without much warning. Quite rationally, then, they demanded a premium surplus if they were to cover the shipowner for war risks. In fact, Tomás de Apodaca had the fortune of avoiding the steeper rates as Spain stayed out of the war until January 1761. Shipowner Apodaca paid only 6.75 percent.[70]

In December 1776, under similarly precarious peacetime circumstances, *consulado* merchant Francisco de Sierra purchased 25,000 pesos' worth of coverage for cargo to be shipped from Buenos Aires to Cadiz.

226 INSURING AGAINST RISK

The policy stipulated that Sierra pay a premium of 3.5 percent but that a 20 point "aumento," a surplus, be assessed if at the time of his sailing, Spain were at war with any "Christian" country other than Portugal. In the event that Spain battled its Iberian neighbor, the assessed surplus would have been only 10 percentage points. Since war did not erupt at this time, Sierra presumably paid the lower rate, 3.5 percent.[71] Several years later, just as Spain entered the War of American Independence in June 1779, Sierra again secured insurance in Cadiz, this time with several partners and for goods valued at 24,000 pesos to be shipped from Veracruz to Cadiz. Had it not been for the war, Sierra and partners would have paid the stipulated peacetime rate of 3 percent, but because of Spain's military engagement a 20 percentage point *aumento* applied, raising the premium to 23 percent. In the end, the partners decided to cancel their policy, perhaps judging the premium to be too high or imagining the hostilities would be short-lived.[72]

In February 1796, between the establishment of peace with France and the start of war with Great Britain, three merchants, Antonio de Artechea, Sebastián de Arana, and Mariano de Arana, secured coverage for a shipment of 53,500 pesos' worth of goods from Cadiz to Buenos Aires. The rate was an inexpensive 1.75 percent, but under the condition that the premium would increase to 16 percent if war broke out within fifteen days from the sailing of the ship.[73] A final example dates from 19 July 1803 when traders Antonio de Artechea and Clemente de Santa Cruz contracted 24,000 pesos of insurance for their cargo and boat, *San Joséf alias La Hermosa Andrea*, at the rate of 5 percent with an increase of 45 percentage points for a total of 50 percent if war were confirmed.[74]

These variable rates helped compensate the insurance firms from the inevitable losses that they sustained at the start of a conflict. Given the great losses customarily sustained at a war's start, it seems likely that any fear of war would have curtailed the writing of policies without the addition of conditional higher premiums. Of course, the question arises why such conditions were not universally inserted into marine insurance policies, a clause regularly contained in a policy. It would certainly have been in the interest of the insurers and better reflected their perceptions of war's riskiness. Policies written during wartime, after all, regularly charged elevated rates, and so providing for rates to rise automatically if war began would have always made sense. That policies did not regularly have such clauses suggests, perhaps, that there was enough competition in the Cadiz market that merchants could turn to alternative insurers and obtain coverage under "normal" circumstances without such conditions. During moments when rumors were circulating about increasingly volatile international relations, however, the willingness of insurers to underwrite policies unconditionally understandably evaporated. At such a moment, merchants faced a choice: accept the variable rates; proceed without insurance; or wait until the military situation became clearer.

During times of growing military uncertainty, then, the insurers responded by writing policies that attempted to diminish the costs of uncertainty in the near future. Had the firms not devised such variable rates, then commerce might very well have reached a stalemate; insurers would have been unwilling to insure cargo at peacetime rates and merchants would have neither been willing to insure their cargoes at wartime rates nor risk their capital by shipping uninsured. Trade would have been paralyzed until the political situation became clearer. Variable rates allowed commerce to continue despite the international ambiguity. Sometimes the lower rates applied and at others the higher rates kicked in.

While variable rates seem pretty straightforward, they introduced potential controversy. In signing the policy, both insurer and insured agreed to the conditions, but the policy still left open some degree of interpretation. Most problematic was establishing on what date the condition of wartime or peacetime should come into effect, when hostilities actually began or concluded. This was the issue in a dispute that erupted between merchant Manuel Sáenz de Tejada and several Cadiz insurance partnerships at the beginning of Spain's involvement in the American Revolutionary War. The firms had underwritten coverage for a boat called *La Portobeleña*, which had recently voyaged from Cadiz to Honduras. *La Portobeleña* arrived without incident in Central America, but the companies demanded that the policyholder pay the conditional war *aumento* stipulated by their policy because the vessel had arrived about a week following the declaration of hostilities. Sáenz de Tejada argued that that *La Portobeleña* was not liable since the short period between the war declaration and the ship's arrival had not been sufficient to create any real dangers, which in fact they had not faced. Not only had the English privateers not had time enough to target Spanish vessels, he insisted, but England had not even had time to announce broadly the state of conflict. Sáenz was certainly correct that had a British vessel encountered *La Portobeleña* during this disputed week, it could not possibly have known that Spain and England were at war and that this Honduras-bound vessel was a legal prize.[75]

After the eruption of war with Great Britain in 1796, a number of insurance companies requested that the *consulado* meet to determine the

war's starting date so that the firms would know whether they could collect the *sobrepremio*, the higher rate, on policies that they had written conditionally. Faced with this question, the *consulado* held a lengthy, high-
level meeting in April 1797 to determine what date to utilize, but there
were apparently substantial differences of opinion among the meeting's
attendees. Two members of the committee cast votes for August 24, the
day, they claimed, on which the British blockade truly began. A single
representative voted for September 22, which was the midpoint between
the embargo of Spanish boats in London (September 16) and the departure of the Spanish naval squadron commanded by Juan de Lángara (September 28). Another chose the date on which the king signed the papers
ordering Lángara's squadron to depart. Four committee members voted
for September 15, the date that the English captured a mail ship named *La
Princesa* as it returned from Buenos Aires, a bellicose act. Finally, one
voted for October 3, the date on which Lángara seized the first English
ship. After much debate, the *consulado* recommended to Minister Varela 24
August 1796 as the date marking the start of the war for insurance purposes.[76] Ships at sea on or after that date would be subjected to "wartime"
conditions. Ignoring the likelihood that the committee had members who
were interested parties, merchants who were either investors in affected
vessels or shareholders in insurance companies, the debate reveals the possibility of controversy with the variable rate policies. Despite the *consulado*'s proposal, by late May the ministry had still not decided upon this
critical date once and for all. In the meantime, the firms were uncertain
how to proceed.[77] Despite their potential for ambiguity, such conditional
policies reduced the considerable commercial paralysis that would otherwise have been inevitable during times of military uncertainty.

In at least one case several insurance firms attempted to use this ambiguity to avoid indemnification to one of their policyholders. Truthfully,
the extreme weakness of their case suggests the possibility that their real
motivation was to postpone the day of reckoning, delay the payment of
an incontrovertible debt. In November 1798, the *consulado* received a petition from several of the city's underwriters to be released from the obligation to indemnify the owners of a ship called *La Experiencia* that was
seized by British privateers off the coast of Mahon, Menorca, while en
route to Smyrna, Turkey. The insurers argued that they should be relieved
of paying this 87,680-peso loss because when they had undersigned the
policy "the latest declaration of war against England was concealed from
them." The merchant guild rejected the petition on a number of solid
grounds. First, the policy stipulated a 20 percent *aumento* in the case of

war, a clause that demonstrated that the insurers recognized at the very least the possibility of hostilities. Second, the insurers had collected without any complaint the hefty premium of 12,100 pesos. Last, the *consulado* argued that spread over thirty-four shareholders, the loss was not too catastrophic. The guild added, more generally, that the insurance policy was "such a solemn contract," and despite the tremendous losses sustained by the industry during the war, enforcement of all its aspects was imperative.[78] Despite the *consulado*'s clear recommendation against the petition, a Royal Order was ultimately issued to grant the insurers an eight-month grace period.[79]

In addition to determining the official start date of the war, the *consulado* seems also to have been sometimes involved with the determination of the size of the *aumento*, the markup that went into effect at the outbreak of hostilities. A policy written for Francisco Fernández de Ravago on 9 June 1777 for an expedition of the frigate *San Miguel* from Cadiz to Veracruz stipulated that if war were to erupt during the course of the coverage, a surplus premium would be applied in an amount to be decided by the *consulado*.[80]

Variable rates were employed when there was some degree of ambiguity or uncertainty about Spain's military status. In the depths of war, when the dangers were clear and present, such conditional rates were not normally stipulated. Instead, rates were simply elevated, reflecting the unquestioned riskiness of oceanic commerce. The last conditional rate discovered prior to Spain's entry into the War of American Independence was 2 June 1779, for example, the very month Spain declared war against Britain. After this date, rates started rising immediately, from 3 percent to Montevideo before the war, for instance, to 13.25 percent and then to 23 percent by April of the following year.[81] Insurers and Spanish merchants alike had definitely concluded that the war was not going to end anytime soon. The next variable rates were not located until November 1782, shortly before hostilities subsided and regular peacetime rates returned. Presumably, conditional rates were again needed to allow commerce to proceed. Merchants would have been hesitant to take out policies stipulating war rates if they believed peace was imminent. Variable rates proffered a functional compromise.

• • •

While variable-rate policies helped reduce what could have been crippling uncertainty, some merchants undoubtedly refrained from taking out such policies because even the possibility of having to pay wartime rates was unacceptable. Insurance rates were quite affordable during peacetime, but wartime rates repelled many traders. As noted, rates during the War of American Independence averaged around 23 percent and peaked at 50.25 percent.[82] At such premiums, many merchants chose simply to wait out the war or even ship without insurance hoping for a rapid end to the conflict and the restoration of peacetime rates. This was the strategy adopted by Guatemalan merchant Juan Bautista de Marticorena, who advised his brother in 1793 that "if the insurance [premiums] are running around 16 to 20 percent because of the war" he should refrain from purchasing insurance "since to the contrary would be like working for the insurers."[83] Marticorena's cavalier position, however, was probably unusual. In stark contrast, a young Francisco de Sierra declared in 1773, "I always proceed with the precaution of insurance."[84]

One might wonder why merchants would ever pay rates as high as 50 percent to insure their property, but they did. On 5 September 1779, Francisco de Sierra contracted to insure 2,300 pesos' worth of "goods" for the rate of 50.25 percent. Sierra was shipping his items aboard the *Sally*, a "Goleta Americana," destined for Marblehead, "near Boston." This presumably American-owned schooner sailed directly into the war several months before Spain had become directly involved in the conflict.[85] On 19 July 1803 merchants Antonio de Artechea and Clemente de Santa Cruz bought 24,000 pesos of coverage to be applied equally to cargo and vessel for a voyage from Veracruz to Cadiz. Because of the war, the traders paid a premium of 50 percent or 12,000 pesos.[86] To secure insurance during wartime, merchants had to pay dearly. That they contracted coverage despite premiums that consumed half of the property's value suggests that they considered the protection afforded to be necessary.

That many traders considered insurance obligatory, however, does not fully explain the economic rationale for buying it at such astronomical rates. Clearly, in paying 50 percent of the value of a commodity, merchants must have anticipated a windfall if their goods arrived safely to market. For example, in the first case given above, one imagines that if Francisco de Sierra's shipment succeeded in evading privateers and arriving safely to Marblehead, then he would have sold his "goods" at many times what would have been their value in peacetime. In the unfortunate event that the goods were seized, which given the elevated rate must have been quite likely, Sierra would have been reimbursed for his cargo minus the premium. To illustrate numerically, had Sierra's cargo arrived to Boston and sold for three times its value in Spain, a hypothetical windfall return, he would have grossed 6,900 pesos, a net profit of 3,444.75 pesos after paying insurance (ignoring all other costs). In contrast, had the Sally been intercepted and the goods confiscated, Sierra stood to lose 1,155.75 pesos, 50.25 percent of his 2,300 peso merchandise.[87] Obviously, had Sierra's cargo arrived, he would have been handsomely rewarded. By insuring his cargo, Sierra passed 50 percent of the risk of sea onto the insurers, whom, in essence, became his equal partners for the risk of the voyage.

Given the high premium rates, one can fully understand why many merchants chose to wait out the war. But the point here is that the merchant willing to take a risk was not acting irrationally in paying the elevated premium. If the ship arrived safely, then the cost of the premium was more than compensated by the profits reaped, profits that were far greater than one could hope to earn during peacetime. If the ship were lost, the merchant at least recovered a portion of his investment. These were highly speculative and risky ventures to be sure. As the Mexico City merchant guild argued in 1798, "residents of peninsular trading ports are motivated to trade despite the risks of war because they expect elevated profits to compensate them for the said risks."[88] A report the following year claimed that shortages on certain imported goods in Mexico could generate for an importer profits of "100 to 150 percent."[89]

Paying such exorbitant rates, then, might have made sense when a merchant expected to sell his goods at greatly inflated wartime prices. Of course, this expectation could easily be false. Merchants could pay high premiums only to learn that expected shortages did not exist in distant markets or, perhaps, that consumers were unwilling to pay high prices in the hopes that the war would end soon. There was no guarantee that wartime scarcities would induce consumers to pay prices high enough to cover such expenses.

High premiums could only be passed onto consumers during wartime. The sudden end of conflict would mean that those who had paid such high premiums would likely never recover their costs due to commodity prices dropping to reflect the end of expected scarcities. This point was made by the *consulado* of Guatemala in the late 1790s after Crown officials ordered a shipment of Guatemalan indigo to be warehoused in Havana as protection against the war. On behalf of the indigo's owners, the *consulado* wrote to Spanish Royal Finance Minister Miguel Cayetano Soler hoping to win the dyestuff's release as well as placement on a warship. As the *consulado* argued, "with the intention of navigating during wartime many have insured at 40 or so percent; if they (their shipments) arrive in this [war] time, they will very easily be able to endure this elevated premium due to the [high] estimation at which [indigo is] selling, but if it results that peace

is made during the voyage, the owners will have suffered so many losses
having paid such exorbitant premiums." Competing dyestuff unburdened
with wartime expenses would have easily undersold their shipments. "After
all, how can those who have insured at 40 or more percent sell at the same
price?" Even more egregious, if it is true, the Guatemalan indigo traders
claimed that it was a group of insurers, the same who had charged them
such high premiums, who were behind the edict to warehouse the dyestuff until the war's end.[90]

Wartime premiums helped spread what was clearly enormous risk. But
a merchant buying such coverage still had to have a healthy appetite for
risk and sufficient capital to absorb a likely loss. It was a gamble that many
traders undoubtedly refused to take. From the perspective of the insurers,
while collecting 50 percent on a premium might have seemed very tempt-
ing and profitable, as has been shown, many companies preferred to suspend
operations rather than underwrite such risks. To break even, a company
charging 50 percent premiums needed just over half of the total risks it
underwrote to arrive safely to port, a seemingly good bet. That they withdrew anyway suggests the uncertainty that such rates were sufficient, that
a 50 percent safe arrival rate was assured. Interestingly, merchants might
have needed a lower rate of successful arrival than the insurance companies did to make worthwhile the payment of such elevated rates. At least
this would be the case if they truly earned windfall returns of 100 percent
or more by arriving with scarce commodities during wartime.

Sometimes merchants took out policies that covered for all risks except
the most expensive one, the risk of war. The rationale of such an approach,
of course, was that it provided basic coverage without the extremely costly
wartime premiums. On 13 July 1782, Juan Vicente de Marticorena and
Laureano Ortiz de Paz procured insurance on a shipment of goods from
Cadiz to Lima aboard the navío Nuestra Señora de Guadalupe alias La Mexicana. The policy insured the cargo for 9,000 pesos and demanded a premium of 5.25 percent but stipulated that the coverage did not extend to
war losses.[91] This policy was taken out toward the end of the War of
American Independence at a moment when steep wartime premiums
were still being charged. Two weeks later, the same two merchants purchased another insurance policy for 15,000 pesos to be shipped on the
very same ship. The latter policy did include coverage for war losses but
charged 20.25 percent, nearly four times the former policy.[92] Ignoring the
rationale that Marticorena and Ortiz de Paz had for insuring in these two
different manners, one sees the tradeoff between the two policies. The

first saved 15 percentage points but left the cargo unprotected in the event of seizure by privateers.

Insurers also, sometimes, chose to offer basic coverage that excluded losses from war, a practice that seems to have grown more common in the first years of the nineteenth century; at least many of the cases discovered date from the brief peace following the Treaty of Amiens, a time when insurers must have still been reeling from the enormous losses indemnified during the just-ended conflict. Seven weeks after the 25 March 1802 treaty was signed, Antonio de Artechea took out four policies on a single day in partnership with several other traders. In total, the policies provided for 139,200 pesos of coverage on cargoes to be shipped from Cadiz to Buenos Aires aboard the frigate *Carlota de Bilbao*. Each of the policies stipulated a premium of 3.75 percent but with the condition that "it will not respond to war."[93]

In June 1777 shipowner Francisco Fernández de Ravago adopted the middle ground, taking out war coverage for only part of his frigate, the *San Miguel*, valued at 43,000 pesos. In total, nine insurers underwrote the policy, several covering war risks and the balance excluding them.[94]

Another alternative possibility led to the unusual policy procured by Antonio de Artechea and Ysidrio de Gorrondona in August 1803. The policy was written at a time of military uncertainty after the French-English rupture of the Treaty of Amiens but before Spain itself reentered the war. Aretechea and Gorrondona secured coverage for their 31,875-peso cargo of cocoa and hides shipped aboard the brigantine *Tres Amigos* from La Guaira to Santander. In the previous month Artechea had insured a vessel and cargo at the rate of 5 percent under the condition that the premium would increase to 50 percent if war were to erupt. On the cocoa and hides, in contrast, merchants Artechea and Gorrondona paid 15 percent but without any conditional increases. The policy does not offer any explanation for this high peacetime premium, yet it seems plausible that the merchants saw it as a compromise rate, preferable to the possibility of a 50 percent premium. Likewise, the insurers may have seen the guaranteed 15 percent as a fair premium given the very real chance that Spain would not enter the war before the ship's safe arrival to Spain. This served as yet another solution to the uncertainty of international affairs, a means to overcome the potentially crippling stagnation that such ambiguity might have introduced.[95] In the next few months, several policies were written at higher than normal peacetime rates yet without the staggeringly elevated war premiums often attached conditionally.

It was to avoid the "high premiums that the insurers solicit" that Pio de Elizalde and his mostly French partners outfitted a heavily armed ship to sail between northern Spain and Veracruz in summer 1798, during the war against Great Britain. While the cost of the ship, its crew and its fortifications were substantial, Elizalde viewed this as preferable to the "35 percent payable in cash that they have asked me for in Hamburg." Elizalde was further ambivalent about the security of the firms due to the heavy losses many had sustained since the war's inception. "The impossibility of securing insurance in certain plazas and the excessive premiums that are being asked for in others as well as the lack of confidence they inspire in the event of loss requires that this expedition be made without coverage, confident in the superior mobility that this ship is believed to have."[96]

Moral Hazard and Coinsurance

One of the age-old dilemmas facing underwriters is the concept known as moral hazard, the danger that the acquisition of coverage will alter the behavior of the policyholder, especially leading him to take greater risks, comfortable in the knowledge that his property is insured. One can easily imagine a scenario in which a shipowner chooses not to outfit his vessel with expensive armament because he knows that if he is captured by corsairs, the insurers will indemnify him. In essence, the shipowner might conclude that it is a bad investment to spend the money on armament merely to lessen the likelihood that the insurance company will have to pay a loss. Even more insidious, insurance might encourage reckless (or even fraudulent) behavior since it might be desirable for the policyholder to incur a loss. If, for example, a ship were nearing the end of its useful life, the owner might benefit from scuttling it and using the insurance indemnification as a down payment on a new vessel. Indeed, this latter problem was sufficiently real that the 1737 *Ordenanza de Bilbao*, perhaps the most authoritative compendium of Spanish mercantile laws, expressly forbade shipowners from insuring more than 80 percent of the value of their vessels "because insuring a greater amount than one's interest in a ship can result in grave damages." Violation of this upper limit resulted in the nullification of the policy, although in practice establishing the fair value of a ship might have been open to manipulation. Regardless, by forcing the shipowner to assume the risk of one-fifth of the value of the vessel, the law reduced the existing moral hazard.[97]

One of the primary ways in which insurers reduce the risk of moral hazard, the danger that policyholders will act irresponsibly, is by forcing them to share in the cost of any losses.[98] For one, having outfitted their vessels for costly transatlantic voyages, shipowners often insured both their ships and the freight charges that they were expected to collect upon the voyage's termination. But having insured their "profits," (the freight charges) they no longer needed to complete the trip to realize the gain. While deliberately abandoning their ships might have been an extreme act, taking unneeded risks to quicken the venture might have made great sense. As a result of this "moral hazard," shipowners were normally only allowed to insure two-thirds of the "fletes, útiles y aprovechamientos."[99] Explaining the insurers' dilemma to the king in 1780, the *consulado* noted that shipowners who "were insured, would show little or no care to avoid imminent risk."[100]

To reduce the conflicting interests of moral hazard, some insurance policies began incorporating what was essentially coinsurance, a requirement that the policyholder absorb a portion of any losses sustained. In the first such policy discovered, dated 16 January 1782, Francisco de Sierra and doña María Ygnacia Ordizgoyti procured insurance on goods valued at 42,000 pesos to be shipped aboard the frigate *Nuestra Señora de las Mercedes alias la Medea* from Cadiz to Veracruz with a stop in Havana. As this policy was written during the War of American Independence, the premium was set at 20.25 percent, clearly reflecting the added risk of privateers. But the policy contained an additional clause, one that became increasingly common in the decades to follow. The stipulated premium was 20.25 percent; however, if the ship failed to arrive safely to port, the rate would be raised to 25.25 percent, a 5 percentage point increase. In essence, Sierra and his partner stood to lose an additional 5 percentage points if their cargo was lost. The insurers forced them to share a portion of losses sustained beyond the regular premium. In doing so, the underwriters provided an incentive to the insured to behave less recklessly, thus reducing the risks associated with moral hazard.[101]

By the end of 1782, the policyholders' penalty for being captured, that is coinsurance, had risen to 10 percentage points above the safe-arrival premium. On 26 November 1782 Francisco de Sierra secured coverage on one thousand *barriles* of aguardiente that he shipped to Veracruz aboard the saetia (a galley-style ship) *La Virgen del Carmen*. The policy provided 5,000 pesos of coverage and stipulated a rate of 25.25 percent to be raised to 35.25 percent if the ship failed to arrive. Adding yet another angle to the policy, a clause lowered the rate to 5.25 percent if peace were to be reached prior to departure. The various possibilities of this complex policy are illustrated in Table 8.4.

TABLE 8.4

Summary of Possible Premiums for Merchant Sierra's Policy
Covering 5,000 Pesos' Worth of Aguardiente,
Dated 26 November 1782

Condition	Rate	Premium (pesos)
If ship arrives safely during wartime	25.25%	1,262.5
If ship fails to arrive during wartime	35.25%	1,762.5
If peacetime	5.25%	262.5

SOURCE: AGI, Consulados, legajo 499, exp. 5.

The application of a higher rate for vessels that were captured ceased
with the end of the American Revolutionary War, but reappeared after
Spain and France declared war in 1793. In 1793 and 1794, the rate of coinsurance was quite low, when it was used at all, ranging from 3 to 5 percentage points. When Antonio de Artechea, Francisco Martínez de Hoz,
and José Martínez de Hoz secured coverage on 16 September 1794 from
Montevideo to Cadiz, their policy called for an increase from the premium rate of 6 percent to the rate of 9 percent in the event of capture, a 3
percentage point differential.[102]

As the war progressed, and the total volume of losses amassed, insurers
began demanding a higher coinsurance. The higher coinsurance reduced
the insurers' losses but also encouraged policyholders to take additional
risk-reducing precautions. In November 1795 Antonio de Artechea and
Vicente Antonio Murrieta agreed to a 20 percentage point increased premium in the event of nonarrival.[103] The only policy discovered for 1799
was written for merchant Joséf Gil de Sagredo and his heirs and provided
12,677 pesos of coverage for the vessel El Águila scheduled to sail to Veracruz from Cadiz. The premium rate was set at 40 percent if the ship arrived safely, to be increased to 60 percent in the event of seizure, a 20
percentage point coinsurance.[104]

The absolute highest rates discovered on any policy were contracted
by Antonio de Artechea and his partners in March 1805. On 11 March
1805 Antonio de Artechea and Pedro Olavarría secured coverage for a
shipment of tallow from Montevideo to Vigo and Bilbao, paying a premium of 50 percent with the added condition that the rate would be
increased to 70 percent if it were lost. A week later Antonio de Artechea
and Martín de Alzaga took out coverage on hides being transported from

Montevideo to Cadiz. The policy carried the same rates of 50 percent for safe arrival and 70 percent if lost.[105]

Insurers continued to demand higher levels of coinsurance, perhaps reflecting their assessment that insured merchants had been inclined to take unwarranted risks, comforted by the knowledge that any losses would be indemnified by the insurance companies. By the end of the era under consideration, policies sometimes stipulated rate increases in the event of total loss in the amount of 30 to 35 percentage points. On 15 May 1818, Antonio de Artechea insured a frigate called *La Piedad* for 30,000 pesos for a voyage from Cuba to Santander. The premium of 12 percent was to be increased to 45 percent if *La Piedad* were captured or lost, a 33 percentage point increase.[106]

In total fifty-three cases were found that provided for coinsurance effected through an increased premium in the event of loss. On average, the prescribed increase was 15.2 percentage points, but the general trend was decidedly upward. When these types of policies first appeared in 1782, insurers were content to pass 5 to 10 percent of the losses onto the policyholder, but this percentage increased dramatically in the first decades of the nineteenth century. On the eve of Spanish-American independence, the rate of coinsurance had reached 30 to 35 percent.

There seems little question that the main purpose of coinsurance was to force the policyholder to share more of the risk, but this strategy had an additional benefit to the insurers since it addressed the risks of moral hazard. By absorbing a portion of any losses sustained, the insured had additional incentive to proceed cautiously, to avoid unnecessary risk. Had they been protected by insurance policies that passed all losses onto the insurance companies, shipowners might have taken calculated risks such as trying to sneak into well-blockaded ports or embarking on a journey inadequately outfitted with bulky and expensive armament. Coinsurance provided an additional material incentive to merchants to engage in less risky behavior; it reduced risks associated with moral hazard. Obviously merchants always benefited by avoiding capture since any hope of enjoying profits depended on safe arrival to port. The use of coinsurance raised the costs of being captured and encouraged them to take greater precautions.

A numerical example helps illustrate the effect of coinsurance. On 12 September 1817 Antonio de Artechea took out coverage on a cargo of cacao and silver to be shipped from Lima to Cadiz. Valued at 22,500 pesos, Artechea was charged a 10 percent premium conditional on the cargo arriving safely. But in the event of loss, the premium would be raised to 40 percent. This 30 percentage point increase was sufficiently injurious that

Artechea would have avoided taking big risks. If there had been no coinsurance and the cargo were seized by corsairs, Artechea would have stood
to lose only the 10 percent premium, 2,250 pesos, since he would have
been reimbursed for the rest of the cargo. But this premium had to be paid
regardless, and so the vessel had little to lose if it arrived, for example, to a
blockaded Cadiz and chose to make a risky dash to the safety of port. If it
succeeded, the cargo might sell for a handsome profit. If it were captured,
Artechea would be indemnified, minus his 10 percent premium. The 30
percent coinsurance changed this risk assessment. If the ship were seized,
Artechea would have had to pay 40 percent, 9,000 pesos. Clearly, the costs
of storming a blockaded port were much higher by reason of the coinsurance even while the premium for safe arrival stayed unchanged.[107]

Of course, in this particular case, the insured, Artechea, was not at the
helm of the ship; his interest was merely as owner of a portion of the
cargo. As a result, one must wonder about the effectiveness of coinsurance
in eliciting risk-averse behavior in such a case since it was the ship captain
making the critical decisions, not the policyholder. While Artechea's policy accorded him real material enticements not to act recklessly, the shipowner might have been responding to a very different set of incentives.
The point is that Artechea might have had the burden of paying the coinsurance and yet had little control over the riskiness of the captain's decisions. The insurers succeeded in passing the costs onto Artechea, forcing
him to share more risk, but Artechea had only limited ability to respond
in a rational manner by reducing the riskiness of his behavior. Perhaps
Artechea's only recourse was to be extra vigilant in selecting a good captain navigating a seaworthy, well-fortified vessel. Indeed, the standard
contract between a merchant and shipowner (a voyage charter) stipulated
on which ship the cargo would be placed as well as its tonnage, armament,
and the size of its crew.[108] Had he made this decision prudently, the insurers would have also benefited.

Convoys

It was in the interest of the insurance companies that the merchants for
whom they wrote insurance proceed carefully, taking every possible precaution to avoid incurring an indemnifiable loss. Coinsurance was one
way that policies were constructed to provide material incentives to policyholders to behave responsibly. Another mechanism employed by the
insurance underwriters to reduce the riskiness of the policies that they
underwrote was to provide discounts to merchants who shipped their

goods in convoy with others, especially in convoys escorted by warships of the Royal Armada.

The centuries' old system of flotas and galleons originally emerged in the sixteenth century to protect against the pirate attacks that had grown increasingly common as Spain's enemies learned of the great riches being transported from America to Spain. Until the eighteenth century, the majority of trade between the Peninsula and its premier colonies in Peru and Mexico was conducted by means of convoys. The final end of regulated trade was advanced by Bourbon modernizers who argued that it would accomplish a number of goals, among them to promote commercial growth, to increase government revenues, and to strip the empire's wealthy merchants of their "monopoly" on trade, the latter of which was an instrumental part of the Crown's attempts to reassert its authority over powerful interests at home and in the colonies.[109]

The end of flotas and galleons, however, also resulted in the rising riskiness of trade. Often forgotten in the lengthy debates over the fleet system was its original intent, to provide greater security for transatlantic voyages. Freelance piracy had largely been curtailed by the late eighteenth century, but commercial losses to government-sanctioned privateers remained an extraordinary risk during wartime.[110] And since predicting the outbreak of war was exceedingly difficult, convoyed travel was always advantageous.

Throughout the decades for which insurance policies survive, underwriters provided substantial incentives to merchants and shipowners to take advantage of the security afforded by armed convoys. A typical merchantman sailing alone was an easy target for a fast, skilled, maneuverable enemy corsair. Multiple ships traveling in unison, however, could defend themselves more effectively, and their collective firepower was often a deterrent to privateers in the first place. In search of prizes along the coast near Tarifa in 1806, Pablo Amorós, captain of the Spanish corsair highlighted in Chapter 6, encountered a British commercial convoy escorted by warships. Wisely, Amorós elected to keep his distance. As he explained to Juan Vicente de Marticorena, one of his financiers, "although some English [vessels] have passed by, they were convoyed by warships, so we have been unable to attack them."[111]

Experienced merchants understood that traveling in convoy afforded valuable protection. Indeed, many traders refused to dispatch their commodities on ships that traveled independently. Typical was a letter dated 29 November 1799 in which Mexican trader Joséf Ignacio Pavón y Muñoz ordered his partner in Cadiz, Juan José Puch, not to ship him anything unless it traveled on a "convoy of warships."[112]

The Cadiz-based insurance industry also recognized the added security that convoys provided and regularly underwrote policies that encouraged merchants to take advantage of them. The first such policy discovered was dated 7 August 1779, during the War of American Independence. Trader Francisco de Sierra procured coverage on goods valued at 10,000 pesos to be shipped from Cadiz to Montevideo aboard the frigate *La Sacra Familia alias La Angélica*. The premium was set at 12.25 percent but a discount was offered to 10.25 percent if the commodities traveled in convoy to the Canary Islands, the most perilous portion of this journey.[113] Throughout the following spring merchants secured insurance from Cadiz to various Spanish American ports at the wartime rates of 22 or 23 percent. All of the policies stipulated that the rate would be reduced to 17 percent if the ship traveled in convoy. In April 1780, for example, shipowner Fernando de Reyna insured some cargo along with his frigate named the *Nuestra Señora de Guadalupe alias La Mexicana* for 69,655 pesos at the rate of 23 percent. Destined for Veracruz, the policy stipulated that the premium would be lowered to 17 percent if Reyna accompanied the convoy sailing under Commander Joséf Solano.[114] Francisco Fernández de Rasago took out 16,226 pesos of insurance for his brigantine named *La Amistad*, which was also given a rate reduction if it traveled in Solano's convoy. Apparently Fernández de Rasago was allowed to separate from the other ships once in the Gulf of Mexico since his policy indicated New Orleans as his final destination.[115]

In June 1781, as hostilities worsened, Francisco de Sierra took out 50,000 pesos of coverage on his frigate *El Jasón* for a voyage to Veracruz. In this case, Sierra was not granted any discount; rather the policy was conditional on the frigate sailing with, interestingly, a "French convoy." Even with the security that this escort provided, Sierra paid the considerable premium of 40.25 percent.[116] This rate seems steep given that only three months later, the London firm of Fermín de Tastet and Company quoted Sierra a rate of only 20 percent to Buenos Aires if he traveled in convoy, a 10 percentage point discount from the unescorted rate of 30 percent.[117]

Some policies of this type could be quite complicated, incorporating a variety of different clauses and conditions. Merchants Juan Joséf de Puch and Francisco de Lemonauria secured two policies in July and August 1793 to transport a variety of goods, including gold, silver, cotton, indigo, and cacao, aboard the brig *San Severo* from Puerto Cabello and La Guaira, both in Nueva Granada, to Santander, Spain. Each policy provided 30,000 pesos of coverage and stipulated a rate of 20 percent to be reduced to 15 percent if the vessel arrived safely (coinsurance). However, if the San

Severo were to voyage the entire way in convoy with warships, then the premium would only be 8 percent. Finally, if the brig left in convoy but was separated en route, then the premium would be 20 percent if captured and 10 percent arriving safely. In short, if the vessels sailed alone and arrived safely, they paid 15 percent, but in convoy the rate was only 8 percent. This policy illustrates very clearly the perception that convoys were a significant deterrent to privateering and thus greatly reduced risk. The convoyed rate provided nearly a 50 percent reduction over the regular rate, a substantial savings. In fact, an addendum to the policy noted that the *San Severo* did travel in convoy to Puerto Rico and then on to La Coruña where it briefly made port to evade potential confrontation with enemy corsairs. Ultimately, the brig arrived safely at Santander.[118]

Similar-sized discounts were procured by merchants Antonio de Artechea, Vicente Antonio Murrieta, and Mariano de Arana, who purchased two policies on 23 July 1793 to ship packages from Cadiz to Buenos Aires aboard the frigate *Nuestra Señora de Pía*. The policies specified premiums of 8 percent if sailing unaccompanied, reduced to 4 percent in convoy. An additional policy clause stated that if the convoy were led by a ship called *San Pedro de Alcántara*, then the rate would be lowered even further to 3.5 percent, presumably a reflection of *San Pedro de Alcántara's* superior defenses.[119]

By the 1790s, 50 percent discounts on insurance premiums seem to have been the norm for traveling in convoy. This was still the rate of discount in April 1809 when Antonio de Artechea and Joaquín de Arana procured coverage for cargo valued at 24,000 pesos to be shipped from Cadiz to Río de la Plata aboard the frigate *La Reina de los Ángeles*. The policy stipulated a rate of 10 percent but offered a discount to 5 percent if the ship traveled in convoy with another frigate, *La Carlota de Bilbao*. Apparently the merchants considered the convoy and its discount worth the inconvenience. A note attached to the policy indicated that *La Reina de los Ángeles* had indeed arrived safely accompanied by both *Carlota de Bilbao* and additional warships belonging to either Spain or Great Britain.[120]

The perception that escorts afforded greater security was neither new in the eighteenth century nor a view held exclusively by Spanish insurers. Martin Ravina found that in the last decade of the seventeenth century, resident foreigners in Cadiz who were underwriting risk offered two percentage point discounts to convoyed vessels.[121] In the eighteenth century London policies regularly charged lower rates to convoyed ships.[122] Philadelphia insurance underwriters also provided discounted premiums to merchants who shipped their cargoes in convoys. A ship sailing in 1762 was charged a premium of 20 percent on its voyage from Virginia to

London, to be reduced to 12 percent if it arrived in convoy. Coverage in the Philadelphia market was sometimes only available on ships sailing with escorts.[123] Dutch insurers discounted convoyed risks as well. In 1769 vessels sailing from Holland to Suriname alone paid 8 percent premiums but only 4 percent if escorted. In February 1778 unescorted ships from London to the Caribbean were paying triple the convoyed rate.[124] Indeed, argues Spooner, "the role of convoys was a well-accepted routine: for the West Indian consignments; for the winter fleets sent to Spain and Portugal; for the returning East Indiamen; and above all, for the trade to the Mediterranean." The preference for convoys by Dutch merchants was actually growing in the late 1770s.[125]

Insurance firms provided steep discounts to their customers who shipped their commodities in convoyed vessels because their greater safety reduced anticipated losses. Merchants undoubtedly responded to such financial incentives by seeking opportunities to place their cargoes aboard ships traveling in unison. All parties benefitted.

As with most aspects of marine insurance, underwriters had only limited ability to enforce all of the conditions stipulated in a policy. Insurance agents could observe that a ship departed and arrived in convoy but what happened in between was usually outside of their ability to monitor. While traveling in convoy afforded protections to shipowners, they also benefitted from getting their ships to port before their counterparts. Wherever employed, ships broke from the convoys as they approached port and raced to be among the first to unload their wares.[126] More pernicious, ships might take advantage of discounted premiums by setting sail with the convoy only to stray once at sea. In 1782 Francisco Paula Carballeda, captain of Francisco de Sierra's vessel *El Jason*, wrote to his boss to inform him that they had made port at Guárico (Cap-Haïtien) after noticing "an enemy frigate and various corsairs" seemingly in pursuit. Captain Carballeda added that he had taken extra caution because he was supposed to be traveling in convoy but was not, and so "in the event that we suffered a mishap which was verifiable, perhaps they would not pay the insurance or there would be a dispute about it."[127] In other words, the ship captain had violated the terms of his policy and feared that the underwriters would find out.

Prior to the termination of the fleet system to Mexico and Peru in 1778 and 1739 respectively, most commodities traveled in convoy. As restrictions were lifted and the fleet ultimately disbanded, the opportunities to ship goods in vessels escorted by warships were reduced. As discussed at length in earlier chapters, the outcry of support for the fleet system on the part of the *consulado* merchants was primarily motivated by fears that the end of the fleet system would greatly increase market risk, the danger of oversupply of transoceanic markets. Several years into the new trading system, these same traders started expressing a new concern. The merchants began petitioning the Spanish Crown to organize escorted convoys to and from America, pointing to the greater security of convoys.

On 19 April 1793, a month into the war with France, *consulado* officers Zuloaga, Micheo, and Ramos sent an official correspondence to Finance Minister Diego de Gardoqui requesting on behalf of international merchants that the Crown provide armed convoys to escort merchant ships to America. The guild suggested two convoys per year, one in mid-April to mid-May and a second in November. They further proposed that both travel to Veracruz, dropping off en route those ships destined for other ports, identifying specifically Cartagena, Honduras, the Barloventos (Caribbean), Caracas, and Campeche. The November convoy, they proposed, could also escort as far as the Canary Islands ships destined for the South Seas and Buenos Aires, after which the sea dangers were much reduced. Vessels desiring to take advantage of the convoy for the return trip, the officers suggested, could congregate in Havana and await the escort. Among the benefits that such a convoy would provide, claimed the *consulado*, was to economize on "insurance premiums which have the circumstance of having in wartime the greatest influence on negotiations and business."[128] Several weeks later the guild sent a second letter to the minister assuring him that news of a convoy would be well received by both insurers and policyholders.[129] Over the next several years, the *consulado* made numerous additional requests to the Crown for the organization of convoys escorted by naval squadrons.[130]

For most of the previous decade, the *consulado* merchants had sought the resurrection of the flota system, pointing especially to the riskiness of trade that resulted from the unfettered flow of commodities across the Atlantic. The resurgence of petitions for convoys after 1793 was designed to counter a different source of riskiness, the growth of privateering related to the resumption of international hostilities. These missives show the centrality of the convoy system as an institutional response to the tremendous riskiness of oceanic trade. While the traditional fleet had served to reduce market risk, any convoy offered protection to ships against enemy corsairs.

The *consulado*'s April 1793 appeal for naval escort was not a cloaked attempt to resurrect the traditional fleet, which had been dismantled by the Bourbon reformers. According to its proposal, participation in the resurrected convoys was not to be obligatory; merchants and shipowners were free to travel unescorted if they so desired. The convoy, then, did not propose to reinstate regulated trade; it only sought to defend against corsair attacks. Ship captains were free to voyage alone, to forgo the protection of an escort; however, traveling alone, they would pay considerably higher insurance premiums.

Nearly a quarter century later, several years after the end of the Napoleonic wars, Spanish merchants were once again clamoring for state protection in the form of armed convoys. As the Spanish American wars of independence intensified in the aftermath of the Spanish monarchy's 1814 restoration, commercial vessels increasingly found themselves targeted by "corsairs of the insurgent provinces," Spanish American patriots seeking the independence of the colonies. Asked by the Finance Ministry in 1819 to comment on the growth of this "piracy," the Cadiz *consulado* insisted that the most effective remedy would be to outfit armed convoys to escort the mercantile vessels. Rejecting critics' concerns that the "necessary convoys" were too costly, the *consulado* retorted that a 2 to 4 percent tax on the value of commerce would more than cover the costs of the convoy and would lower the costs of insurance by an even greater percentage. The authors concluded by urging the Crown to introduce regular convoys every three to four months to the "Septentrional" (northern) colonies and every six to eight months to the "South Seas."[131] The glory days of the regulated flotas and galleons had long passed, yet the *consulado* merchants still recognized and sought the protection that armed convoys had always afforded commercial vessels. These were not would-be monopolists; they were rational merchants seeking to reduce risk to tolerable levels.

Calculation of Rates

Insurance company directors responded to a variety of factors in establishing premium rates on Atlantic world voyages. Modern day actuaries employ highly complex statistical models to help them assess risk and establish corresponding rates. In the eighteenth century, however, the science of statistics was not yet well developed. Instead, the rates were determined more subjectively by underwriters, who drew upon experience and collective wisdom to determine the probabilities of risk events. Despite the lack of statistical models to calculate the assessment of risk, the premium rates charged by the Cadiz-based firms show considerable consistency, at least during peacetime.

In an attempt to determine which risk factors had an impact on premium rates, a multiple regression[132] was performed employing a number of independent variables. Rather than analyze the entire set of insurance data, a subset was selected with the goal being to reduce the impact of war, the greatest risk factor of all. Specifically, multiple regressions were performed on the data for the decade running from the end of the War of American Independence to the start of the wars of the French Revolution, roughly from spring 1783 to early 1793. This decade was selected for analysis because rates could be assumed to have been largely uninfluenced by the fear of war. These years of peace are thus ideal to measure the factors that contributed to insurance premiums under normal (peacetime) conditions.

The independent variables examined were: (1) distance traveled in thousands of miles; (2) insured value of cargo or vessel in thousands of pesos; (3) type of item insured (precious metal, nonmetal good, vessel, combination, or miscellaneous); and (4) year in which insurance was contracted. In other words, the regression measured the quantitative impact of these factors on the premium rates actually charged during the decade of roughly 1783–92.

The regression performed resulted in a multiple correlation coefficient (r) equal to 0.618 ($r^2 = 38.2$ percent), indicating that over 38 percent of the variation in rates was explained by these four variables. This suggests that these independent variables are indeed influencing the insurance premium charged, an important conclusion because it reveals that the underwriters were considering these factors and acting with considerable consistency in determining the premiums that they demanded, despite the fact that they lacked the tools to employ sophisticated actuarial models.[133] Basing their decisions largely on past experiences, they nonetheless acted predictably.

Multivariate regressions also indicate the quantitative contribution of each independent variable in explaining the dependent variable (the b–coefficient). In other words they reveal the contribution of each tested risk factor in determining the insurance premium rate. Given a set of independent variables, the aforementioned four factors, the model makes a prediction of the expected value of the dependent variable, the insurance rate. Likewise, one can assess the quantitative impact on premium rates charged of each of the independent variables utilized. Indeed, the multiple regression performed on the insurance premium data for the peacetime decade 1783 to 1792 yielded a number of interesting and statistically significant results.

The regressions indicate that premium rates were indeed influenced by the item insured, for example. The items insured were classified into five separate categories,[134] and the predicted impact (the b-coefficient) on premium rates was measured for each. The most interesting results came from the largest three categories – ships, precious metals, and other (nonprecious metal) commodities. The ship itself was the most costly item to insure, holding all other variables constant, while precious metals were the least expensive. To insure the vessel, the model indicates that insurers charged 0.78 percentage points more (t = −5.173)[135] than they did for other (nonprecious metal) commodities, and 1.19 percentage points more (t = −6.626) than for precious metals.

The higher rate charged to insure the ship reveals that underwriters perceived the ship more likely to incur damage and result in claims than the cargoes themselves. Certainly this seems logical since there were many possible hazards that could have affected the vessel but not necessarily the cargo. Entering port, for example, exposed the vessel to a variety of dangers; it might be thrown against a rock or damaged on an unseen sandbar, neither of which would necessarily cause harm to the cargo as well. Even an encounter with the enemy might leave the ship scarred and the freight unscathed. The ship's greater exposure to hazards explains the higher premiums demanded by underwriters.

Qualitative evidence supports the model's statistical conclusion that ships paid approximately a percentage point more than other goods. The July 1794 charter for the partnership established under the protection of the Santísima Virgen María de Regla, for instance, instructed director Tomás Martínez de Junquera to charge an additional percentage point on policies covering the "hull and keel." Pointing to the risk that resulted from a boat's entry or exit of a port, the same charter called for a one percentage point increase for every additional port visited by a vessel.[136]

The regression also indicates that underwriters charged 0.407 percentage points less (1.187 − 0.780) for silver and gold than other commodities, all additional factors held constant. Archival evidence reveals that insurance companies indeed discounted the premium on precious metals, a practice justified by their greater durability. The 1794 charter of a partnership directed by Antonio Vallarino stipulated that *plata y oro* (silver and gold) should be charged a half percentage point less than other commodities.[137] Nearly a decade later Director Juan Miguel de Urrutia's firm provided for an identical discount on silver.[138] Indeed the general practice in Cadiz seems to have been to grant a one-half percentage point discount to silver and gold. When in August 1784 brothers Juan Vicente and Juan Bautista de Marticorena joined merchant Antonio Esteban de Garbalena to insure indigo and silver valued at 28,000 pesos to be shipped from Honduras to Cadiz, they were charged 4 percent for the dyestuff but only 3.5 percent for the *plata*.[139] Five years later partners Juan Joséf de Puch and Remigio Fernández shipped from Veracruz to Cadiz silver and fifty-two zurrones of grana cochineal valued together at 100,000 pesos. Despite the already low premium of 2 percent on the cochineal, they were granted a 0.5 percentage point discount on the silver.[140] This qualitative evidence lends strength to the credibility of the model that predicts that precious metals paid 0.407 percentage points less than other commodities.

The model also measured the impact of distance traveled by sea on premiums. All other factors held constant, every thousand ocean miles voyaged increased the premium rate by 0.184 percentage points ($t = 7.953$). So, for example, in comparing a voyage from Cadiz to Lima (9,020 miles) with the trip to Buenos Aires (5,191 miles), one would expect the former premium to run approximately 0.70 percentage points higher [$(9020 - 5191)*0.184 = 0.705$].

Last, the effect of the passage of time was measured and revealed that insurance rates generally dropped over the course of the decade examined. The model predicts that holding all attributes of an insurance transaction constant, the predicted rate would have fallen 0.12 percentage points per year. Thus, at the start of the decade a merchant paid 1.19 percentage points more than he did at the end of the decade to underwrite an identical risk ($t = -7.027$). This trend is shown graphically in Figure 8.1, which depicts premiums charged on nonmetal goods between Cadiz and Veracruz (either direction) for the entire peacetime decade under scrutiny. Despite several aberrations, the general slope, highlighted by the trend line, is a downward slope resulting in a typical premium of approximately 1 percentage point lower by decade's end.

The decline in insurance premiums during this decade was noted by contemporaries as well. A 1788 report on commerce produced by the *consulado* of Seville applauded the reduction in rates in the decade since the 1778 promulgation of *comercio libre*. This decline, the guild suggested, had resulted from the expansion of underwriters as well as the overall growth of trade. Facing greater competition, the insurance firms had lowered their rates, but, the *consulado* added, they were still profiting due to the greater volume of business.[141] In 1793, prominent Veracruz merchant and *consulado* member Tomás Murphy reported a sharp drop in insurance rates between Mexico and Spain over the same decade. According to Murphy, the proliferation of insurers had caused a drop in premiums from "6 to 8 percent,

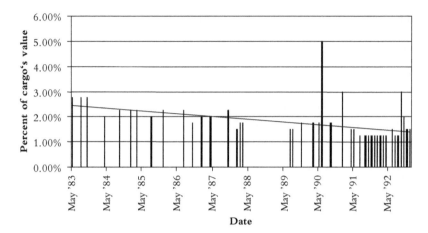

Figure 8.1.   Premiums on Nonmetal Goods to and from Cadiz and
Veracruz: 1783–92
SOURCE: Online Appendix C.

where they were, to 1.25 to 1.5 percent." While Murphy greatly overstated
the extent of the decline, he was certainly correct that rates had dropped.[142]

A final independent variable evaluated, the total insured value, revealed
no statistically significant relationship to the premium rate charged
(t = .051). The amount insured did not seem to have had any effect on the
rates charged by underwriters. This is not surprising; for one, there is no
logical reason that rates would fluctuate with value, except in the case of a
very low-valued policy in which the firms might lose in transaction costs
much of the premium charged. Second, larger cargoes tended to be underwritten by multiple insurers, and so a high insured value did not necessarily imply a concentrated risk, rendering the measure somewhat mean-
ingless. In any event, the regression revealed no relationship.

Evolution of Insurance Rates, 1759–1818

For several of the routes, a sufficiently large number of policies were located
to permit discussion of the long-term evolution of insurance rates. Table 8.1
presented above showed the frequency for which located policies were underwritten for the major transatlantic Spanish American routes. Not all of
these routes permit interesting analysis of the evolution of risk since the
policies are either too few or inadequately dispersed over time. The most
complete sets exist for the routes (both directions) between Cadiz and Vera-

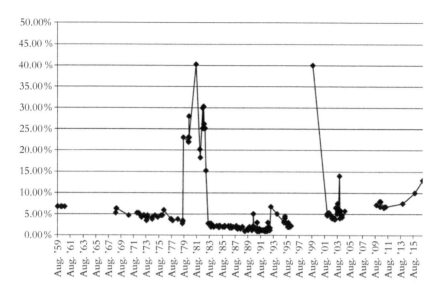

Figure 8.2.   Effective Insurance Rates Between Cadiz and Veracruz:
1759–1818
SOURCE: Online Appendix C.

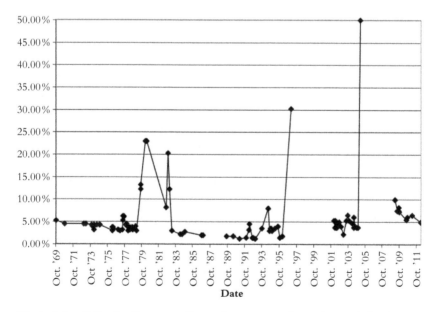

Figure 8.3.   Effective Insurance Rates Between Cadiz and Rio de la Plata:
1769–1815
SOURCE: Online Appendix C.

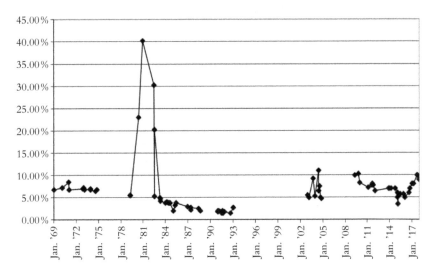

Figure 8.4. Effective Insurance Rates Between Cadiz and Lima: 1769–1817
SOURCE: Online Appendix C.

cruz; Cadiz and Río de la Plata; and Cadiz and Lima. Figures 8.2 through 8.4 display the data for "effective" insurance rates for these three routes.[143]

Significantly, but not surprisingly, all three figures suggest similar trends in the evolution of the perceived risk. In each case, insurance premiums experienced a secular decline in rates from the beginning of the period under analysis, 1759 for Cadiz–Veracruz and 1769 for the other routes, until about 1793. After 1793, insurance rates rose steadily, ultimately exceeding the rates existing in the mid-eighteenth century. Each of the figures illustrate the sharp rise of effective rates during the War of the American Revolution. The figures pertaining to the Cadiz–Veracruz and Cadiz–Río de la Plata routes also exhibit elevated spikes during the wars of the French Revolution and Napoleon. The absence of a spike for the Cadiz–Lima route for this latter crisis merely reflects the fact that no war insurance policies were discovered, not that this route was immune to the dangers of hostilities, which it obviously was not.

Figures 8.5 and 8.6 move beyond these individual routes to illustrate the aggregate effective insurance rates for the eleven most common Spanish Atlantic world routes.[144] The same data is plotted on both figures, but Figure 8.6 employs a logarithmic scale, which more clearly displays *relative* change over time.[145] As in the case of the individual routes, one can see the consistent decline in rates during the first thirty-five years under examination. The outbreak of war in 1793 initiated a steady upward climb of

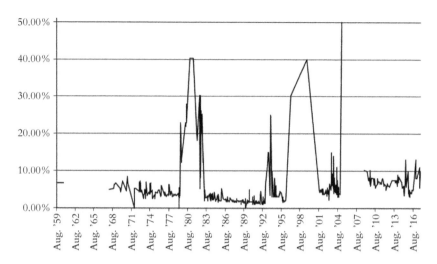

Figure 8.5. Effective Rates of All Major Routes: 1759–1818
SOURCE: Online Appendix C.

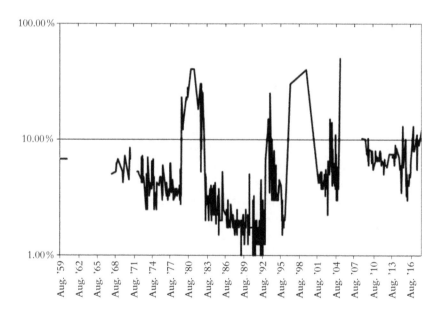

Figure 8.6. Effective Rates of All Major Routes Displayed Logarithmically: 1759–1818
SOURCE: Online Appendix C.

effective insurance rates that lasted to the end of the period. Even after the Napoleonic wars had concluded, rates remained high relative to the earlier era. These two long-term trends are especially evident in the logarithmic Figure 8.6.

The various effects of war on the riskiness of trade were discussed extensively in Chapter 6 and elsewhere. Indeed Figures 8.5 and 8.6 demonstrate without any ambiguity the tremendous impact of hostilities. Also interesting are the general trends of peacetime rates. Again, the figures very clearly demonstrate a long-term decline in insurance rates from the early years under investigation until around 1793. The explanation for this secular decline is probably multifaceted. Several scholars have recorded the general drop in insurance rates charged in other European markets for Atlantic world routes over the course of the eighteenth century, decline they attribute to the general improvement in navigation and the reduction of piracy.[146] With the exception of wartime spikes, freight rates in the Atlantic world also dropped over the course of the eighteenth century, a reflection, partially, of falling insurance costs. Freight rates were especially low during the peaceful decade 1783 to 1792, precisely when Cadiz insurance rates attained their lowest levels.[147] The declining insurance rates evident in the Cadiz data can also be attributed to the maturation and growing competition of that port's insurance industry. As shown in Chapter 7, the last several years of this era of decline witnessed the proliferation of insurers. Sheer competition naturally drove rates downward.[148]

The decline in rates during the decade 1783–92 occurred at the same time as the demand for coverage rose. *Comercio libre* led to rising quantities of goods being sent to distant markets and thus increased the demand for insurance. Conveniently, the entry of new firms increased the supply of coverage in Cadiz even more rapidly.

As was argued in Chapter 4, the growing quantities of trade goods also increased the riskiness of international trade. More traders entered commerce after 1778 and commodities began flooding markets, especially after the restoration of peace in 1783. The growing market risk, the uncertainty of trade caused by the entry of more and more merchants, however, did not necessarily affect insurance rates because marine insurance did not cover the business end of the transaction. Once the goods arrived in market, the coverage ceased, even though the riskiest portion of the venture had only just begun. This explains why no evidence of growing market risk is displayed in the figures.

Informed by past experiences, insurance rates reflected the perceived probabilities of certain events taking place. While in theory rates were established "scientifically," in practice they were ultimately subject to the changing emotions of humans. What is striking about the period (see Figures 8.5 and 8.6) after 1793 is that even during moments of peace, the insurance rates remained elevated relative to the period preceding the outbreak of the wars. For example, during the brief interlude of peace following the signing of the Treaty of Amiens (25 March 1802 to 16 May 1803),[149] rates between Mexico and Veracruz, the most fully documented route, averaged 3.5 times greater than they had been back in 1792. Peace had been restored, but the markets still quivered.[150] Perhaps the Atlantic financial world recognized the fragility of peace; indeed war between France and Great Britain resumed after only fourteen months, and Spain's subsequent reentry must have seemed just a matter of time to most observant parties, even if one merchant's claim was sincere that in Mexico "the majority thinks that the French and English will reconcile amicably and that it will not come to the point that we get involved with their discord."[151] Furthermore, it is certain that the preceding decade of war-related losses had frightened directors and damaged the finances of insurance firms, making underwriters skittish. Perhaps too the new experiences had led the actuaries to reassess the probabilities of bad outcomes. In any event, the higher peacetime rates charged during the Peace of Amiens allowed the companies to recover some of the hefty losses sustained during the previous decade of hemorrhaging. Regardless, they reveal the subjectivity of risk analysis at the time.

Even after the June 1815 defeat of Napoleon at Waterloo, insurance rates remained high. While surviving policies end just three years later, the data displayed in Figures 8.5 and 8.6 suggest that rates were on the upswing after Napoleon's final defeat. One would expect the defeat of Napoleon to have calmed markets and reduced risk, but by 1815 Spanish commerce was under attack from a whole new enemy. During Napoleon's occupation of Spain, American Creoles had for the most part claimed loyalty to the abdicated Spanish monarch, Ferdinand VII. Napoleon's defeat and Ferdinand VII's restoration, however, forced the Americans' hands. Most of the colonies now moved more formally for separation from Spain and their rebellions had an observable impact on risk. Spanish mercantile ships that continued to bring their wares to colonial ports were harassed by what the Spanish minister of finance termed the "corsairs of the insurgent provinces." Insurance losses continued to mount.[152]

The effects on insurance rates of war-induced anxiety can be best observed for the Cadiz to Lima route. During 1791, the penultimate year before the outbreak of war, insurance rates charged between Cadiz and

Lima reached an all-time low, averaging just 1.78 percent. No policies were discovered dating from the war, but underwriting resumed during the brief Peace of Amiens. During the fourteen months of peace preceding the resurgence of Franco-Anglo hostilities, rates for this journey averaged 5.17 percent, around triple the prewar rate. In the years after Napoleon's final defeat at Waterloo, rates were even higher, averaging 7.45 percent through the end of 1817. In this final year for which data survives, the average rate was an elevated 9 percent. In fact, the effective rate was arguably much higher since in most of these latter policies insurers imposed substantial rates of coinsurance (25 to 31 percentage point increases), reducing dramatically the indemnification in the event of loss.[153] The end of the Napoleonic Wars, then, did not result in a major reduction in the perception of riskiness.

* * *

Oceanic trade entailed countless dangers and so the ability to reduce or eliminate any was critically important to merchants' business prospects. Marine insurance was an age-old tool used by traders to reduce the riskiness of long-distance voyages and thus increase their likelihood of making profits rather than losing their fortunes. Insurance in Cadiz lessened the financial perils of hurricanes, shipwrecks, navigational accidents, fires, flooding, and war, among others. Protection against the latter became especially critical in the final decades of Spanish imperial rule due to the nearly endless warfare that entangled Spain. Britain's superior navy paralyzed Spanish shipping, and had it not been for insurance coverage, few merchants would have dared take the risk of engaging in oceanic trade. Even with its availability, commerce dropped precipitously.

Examining insurance policies provides a window into the minds of the Spanish mercantile community, allowing the historian to quantify these traders' perceptions of the riskiness of certain elements of long-distance trade. Premium rates show numerically how merchants of the era viewed the myriad dangers that these voyages encompassed. Willingness to pay rates of 50 percent or more indicates the potential profitability of trade during war but also suggests that commerce during such moments resembled gambling as much as business. Premium rates also illustrate the community's perceptions of the relative effectiveness of the measures employed to reduce the riskiness of long-distance shipping. For example, the considerable rebates provided by insurers to ships traveling in convoy reveals both the effectiveness and rationality behind this practice.

Marine insurance allowed merchants to engage in risky commercial ventures because it transferred the risk to underwriters whose sole business was to pool risks. The underwriting of many individual policies covering many distinct events guaranteed, at least in theory, that the partnerships would earn profits. As the following chapter indicates, however, in practice this did not happen. At least a number of the firms' directors grossly underestimated the probability of losses to privateers. Premiums, as astronomical as they were, proved inadequate to meet the many indemnifications required. The young Cadiz financial industry teetered on the edge of catastrophe.

Chapter 9

War and Commercial Crisis: The Profitability of the Cadiz Insurance Industry in the 1790s

The purpose of maritime insurance is to transfer risk from the individual trader to the collection of partners who comprise the insurance company. In theory, a loss that would financially ruin a merchant is easily absorbed by a company that has built the cost of indemnifying losses into its expected revenues from insurance premiums. In the case of the typically sized Cadiz firm, an insurance indemnification was spread over forty partners or so, not devastating for any single one. Furthermore, a merchant's single risk was most often divided into smaller risks underwritten by multiple firms, which served to spread the risk still more widely. Insurance companies employed still additional strategies to avoid excessive concentration of risk exposure, disallowing too much coverage on any single vessel, for example. The overall portfolio of an insurance company, then, represented many small risks spread out over many independent risk events. The law of large numbers suggested that a company's portfolio would prove profitable over the long run since the probability of uneventful voyages far outweighed the likelihood of losses. If the actuaries estimated correctly the probability of events and then underwrote a large-enough volume, then the profitability of the firm should be guaranteed.

This chapter sheds light on the profitability of insurance underwriting in Cadiz. While the underwriting business should have generated predictable and reliable profits, it seems that the firms did not generally fare well in the years after the outbreak of war, the years for which the best company records survive. Revenues proved insufficient to indemnify covered losses; directors miscalculated the probability of Spanish vessels being seized; and the general financial disquiet that swept over Spain exacerbated problems within the insurance business. In the end, the underwriting business in Cadiz floundered. The ensuing crisis was probably made worse by structural problems in the organization of the insurance firms.

• • •

The business of insurance aims to employ the most reliable data accessible to predict the probability of risk events under all foreseeable scenarios. Armed with this information, actuaries assign premium rates sufficient to guarantee the profitability of the underwriting, that the premiums collected will be more than ample to indemnify the losses sustained by policyholders. By pooling a large number of policies, the firm can feel secure that actual losses should approximate predicted losses. After payment of overhead, any surplus revenues represent the profits of the partnership.

Directors underestimated the probability of losses during the wars of the French Revolution and Napoleon. This conclusion is based on surviving evidence that suggests companies generally lost money and even went bankrupt during the decades of war. The archival evidence utilized in this chapter comes largely from financial documents deposited in the *consulado* in connection with bankruptcy proceedings carried out against several of the firms in Cadiz. These records allow a glimpse at the negative income statements of these companies and provide a fuller picture of the financial troubles.

Of course, these sources are a poor sample of the totality of firms since they come primarily from firms that went bankrupt. While this bias is undeniable, other evidence suggests that the income statements of most firms were negative after 1793, that the companies discussed here were not exceptional. Miguel Antonio Bernal documents a steep decline in insurance firms operating out of Cadiz during these wars. His sources indicate that there were eighty-seven Cadiz insurance companies in 1800 but only twenty-two by 1805, a trend that he attributes to their rising bankruptcy.[1] Similarly, the merchant Nicolás de la Cruz y Bahamonde, the Conde de Maule, claimed in his memoirs that between 1793, the year war erupted with France, and the end of 1798, at which time Spain was engaged in hostilities with England, "the fifty-four insurance companies established in this plaza were all more or less ruined by losses, which totaled 15 million pesos."[2] In 1800, the *consulado* of Cadiz claimed that losses sustained by the insurance companies during the war had reached sixty million pesos, a staggering figure if accurate.[3] The conclusions of Bernal and the claims of Cruz y Bahamonde suggest that the bankrupt companies examined below are in fact quite typical of the experiences of most of the Cadiz firms.

A letter sent by Pedro Fermín de Córdoba to his employer Juan Vicente de Marticorena suggests that the former had lost faith in the industry as early as March 1799. Marticorena had left Cadiz to address some personal finances in Madrid, and perhaps to escape the growing pressures he was facing to pay his many debts, but was nonetheless engaged in the outfitting of a vessel called *Menorca*, which, somehow, had allegedly received a passport of safe passage from England. Skeptical, Fermín de Córdoba urged his boss to take out insurance anyway, arguing that neither the British nor the French could be counted on to respect such concessions. But, importantly, Fermín de Córdoba insisted, "it is imperative to try to insure the hull in one of the foreign marketplaces, because here it cannot be considered because there are not more than two companies that can be counted on to pay . . . because the rest that underwrite are in bankruptcy." Marticorena already knew perfectly well that the insurance partnerships were hemorrhaging funds; he himself was a shareholder in more than a dozen of them. Perversely, he was also deeply in arrears in paying his share of company losses, the primary reason why many of the Cadiz companies could not be relied to pay promptly. Perhaps his poor payment record was another reason that Fermín de Córdoba viewed more prudent the acquisition of coverage abroad.[4]

Income and Losses

The archival sources shedding light on the profitability of the insurance industry are more widely available for the period after the outbreak of war in 1793. For the period prior to 1793, income statement records were located for only two insurance companies. The first firm is perhaps atypical because it seems to be a Cadiz-based office of a French establishment. The director, don Juan Payan, corresponded regularly with Marseilles and kept his books in *livres tournois*, the money of account in which French trade was conducted.[5] But the firm was viewed as a Cadiz firm, referred to in the documents as "the Cadiz company under the direction of don Juan Payan." In any event, these records, which illustrate the company's dealings from 27 February 1783 to 31 October 1784, certainly reflect underwriting on business in and out of that port. The period covered begins shortly after the Americans and British signed the preliminary articles of peace bringing an end to the American Revolutionary War and continues for the next twenty months of peace, a time in which Spanish Atlantic trade volumes boomed. The company turned a nice profit during these months as displayed in Table 9.1. In this particular case, the total value of risks underwritten was not indicated, limiting the ability to assess the firm's profitability. Regardless, that it profited at all distinguishes Payan's firm from the other companies for which data was discovered.[6]

The most detailed set of company records for the prewar era, running from April 1790 through January 1793, belonged to a company directed by Juan Pedro Jaureguiberry. Director Jaureguiberry's firm's underwriting business was divided fairly equally between maritime risk within Europe and between Europe and America, but also entailed limited coverage to Asian destinations. Table 9.2 displays a summary of the company's overall performance for this nearly three-year period.[7]

During these years, which conveniently concluded just as the war began, the company underwrote coverage on property valued at 3,284,684 pesos, charging premiums totaling 67,436 pesos for an average rate of just over 2 percent. The firm's indemnifications and other expenses of 88,542 pesos, however, exceeded premiums by a notable margin. After the directors

TABLE 9.1

Income Statement of the Firm Directed by
Juan Payan in French Livres Tournois

Total Expenses	Total Revenues	Profits
£447,155	£529,348	£82,193

SOURCE: AGI, *Consulados*, legajo 428 (unpaginated).

TABLE 9.2

Net Profits of Insurance Company Directed by Juan Pedro Jaureguiberry
for the Period April 1790 Through January 1793 (in Pesos)

Year	Total Underwritten	Total Premiums	Total Losses & Other Expenses	Commission	Profits
1790	649,465	14,931	12,624		
1791	1,314,752	27,047	19,598		
1792	1,267,656	23,339	56,320		
1793	52,810	2118			
TOTALS	**3,284,684**	**67,436**	**88,542**	**8034**	**[29,577]**

SOURCE: AGI, *Consulados*, libro 444B.

had collected their commission, which amounted to about 0.25 percent of the insurance underwritten,[8] the company's losses totaled 29,577 pesos.[9] As was universally prescribed in the charters of the insurance companies, the firm's director proceeded to distribute the debt burden, the losses, in accordance with the partners' relative shares. Seventeen of the nineteen partners were assessed charges of 1,363 pesos each and two were ordered to remit 2,727 pesos, the latter amounts reflecting two shares apiece.[10]

Although this particular firm lost money during this era of peace, it was probably not typical of the industry at this time. The experiences of Payan's firm discussed above must have been more common. Certainly the rapid entry of new firms into the Cadiz market during the 1790s suggests that the underwriting business was perceived to be profitable. In contrast, the income statements dating from the years of war after 1793 reveal financial losses, a reflection of the broader crisis affecting the Cadiz underwriting business; this changing fortune, of course, was unanticipated by the many merchants who signed up for shares in the first several years of hostilities.

• • •

For the period after 1793, surviving records are more abundant. Table 9.3 summarizes the performance of a company known as Marca M, directed by Juan Esteban Tellechea, for the period December 1793 through the end of 1796, an era of Spanish war against France, and then after October 1796, versus England. The greater riskiness of this company's underwriting allowed its director to charge higher premiums than had Jaureguiberry's firm, although still quite low on average.

Director Thellechea of Marca M underwrote 2,400,631 pesos of coverage, about 75 percent of the amount that Jaureguiberry's firm had underwritten, and charged premiums totaling 104,847 pesos for an average rate of

TABLE 9.3

Net Profits of Insurance Company Called Marca M: 1794–96 (in Pesos)

Year	Total Underwritten	Total Premiums	Total Losses & Other Expenses	Commission	Profits
1794	663,257	N/A	N/A	N/A	N/A
1795	949,576	N/A	N/A	N/A	N/A
1796	787,797	N/A	N/A	N/A	N/A
TOTALS	2,400,631	104,847	135,345	10,343	[40,841]

SOURCE: AGI, *Consulados*, legajo 522, exp. 8, folio 850.

4.37 percent, more than double that charged by Jaureguiberry. Despite the higher rate, Thellechea's company fared poorly, losing 40,841 pesos in the three years under examination due to their obligation to indemnify insurance claims that exceeded 135,000 pesos.[11] Table 9.4 lists twenty-five vessels on which Marca M paid claims during these three years, either on the ship itself or a portion of its cargo. Eighteen of the ships were taken by corsairs, six shipwrecked, and one simply described as *perdido* (lost). The firm paid additional claims to individuals for unspecified reasons. To cover the firm's losses, Thellechea assessed each of the thirty shareholders 1,361 pesos.[12]

Another firm, La Compañía de Seguros de Europa, was first directed by the Conde de Repáraz directly and later by his trading house, Uztáriz Bernoya y Compañía, between 11 June 1793 and the end of May 1796. Like Marca M, La Compañía de Seguros de Europa's portfolio generated losses. During the 35.5 months under examination, the company underwrote

TABLE 9.4

Claims Paid by Marca M Insurance Partnership: 1794–96

Name of Insured Vessel	Cause of Loss	Indemnification (pesos)
Fragata Concepcion de Montevideo	Seized	3,200
Fragata la Riojana	Seized	3,000
Fragata la Benavente	Shipwrecked	14,300
Bergantín la Begoña	Seized	4,500
Polacra la Concordia	Seized	4,000
Bergantín de Areñon	Lost	1,128
Fragata la Perla de Veracruz a la Guaira	Seized	3,000
Bergantín San Francisco de Paula	Seized	569
Fragata La Aurora	Seized	4,000
Bergantín San Pedro de la Havana para Montevideo	Shipwrecked	3,000
Fragata la Sacra Familia	Seized	5,134
Bergantín Dichoso, y la Feliz	Seized	3,397
Fragata la Industria	Shipwrecked	1,698
Bergatin la Ursola	Seized	3,000
Fragata Tridente en el Fayal	Shipwrecked	5,161
Bergantín la Natalia	Seized	2,321
Fragata Amable Sofia	Seized	2,000
Fragata la Margarita de Montevideo	Shipwrecked	1,921
Bergantín Bolero	Seized	500
Bergantín la Industria	Seized	3,000
Fragata Bascongada	Seized	20,000
Bergantín San Feliz	Seized	2,000
Bergatin el Corario en el Fayal	Shipwrecked	3,144
Fragata Magdalena	Seized	11,307
Fragata la Preciosa	Seized	3,000

SOURCE: AGI, *Consulados*, legajo 522, exp. 8.

TABLE 9.5

Income Statement of La Compañía de Seguros de Europa:
11 June 1793 to 31 May 1796 (in Pesos)

Period	Total Underwritten	Total Premiums	Total Losses & Other Expenses	Commission	Profits
1–Jun–93 to 30–Jan–94	49,246	1862	497	198	1166
1–Feb–94 to 6–Feb–96	777,808	27,308	45,660	2891	[21,243]
10–Feb–96 to 31–May–96	50,977	1428	0	129	1298
TOTALS	**878,031**	**30,598**	**46,157**	**3218**	**[18,779]**

SOURCE: AGI, *Consulados*, legajo 522, exp. 8, folio 857, June 16, 1796.

just 878,031 pesos of coverage at an average rate of 5.3 percent.[13] The company incurred losses of 18,779 pesos as summarized in Table 9.5.

There seems little doubt that the wars of the last decades of Spain's colonial empire were bad for the insurance industry, and most company partners probably ended up losing money on these ventures. As explained in Chapter 7, merchants did not deposit any funds into companies upon acquiring partnership shares; they only guaranteed that they would contribute in the event that the company sustained losses and needed to indemnify policyholders in excess of what it collected in premiums. The opportunity to generate income without tying up any capital must have been very appealing to Cadiz merchants whose direct investments in oceanic deals often took years to recoup. A merchant deemed creditworthy could simply affix his name to a company charter and await the anticipated distribution of profits. The law of large numbers suggested that the companies would profit since most ships voyaged without incident. Given the opportunity to generate income without any actual outlay, many Cadiz merchants were naturally attracted to the newly established firms.

• • •

The experiences of merchant Juan Vicente de Marticorena provide a more micro-level examination of the crisis facing the underwriting business during this era. Like many of his fellow Cadiz traders at the time, Marticorena took advantage of the new opportunities afforded by the establishment of multiple insurance firms, acquiring shares in at least fifteen separate firms, most of which sustained losses. In an 1801 petition to the king, Marticorena lamented the financial setbacks that he had suffered since the outbreak of the wars, a substantial part of them, he explained, stemming from his insurance holdings.[14] Indeed, lists that Marticorena had prepared

TABLE 9.6

*Snapshot of Juan Vicente de Marticorena's Losses as
Shareholder in Various Insurance Companies*

Firm (Identified by Director)	Marticiorena's Debt (Pesos)
Armas	1300
Alzueta	3712
Fontanes	3000
López	1500
Muralla	2353
Necochea	1400
Perez Villaverde	5500
Tellechea	750
Urda	1300
Uztáriz y Bernoya	2500
Ximénez Perez	4770
Juareguiberry	1300
Gelos	2000
Buena Fe*	1300
Totals	**32,685**

SOURCE: AGI, *Consulados*, legajo 437, folio 696.
*For some reason Marticorena did not identify this company
by its director. It is probably the firm directed by Mateo Gomez
de Leys.

several years earlier documented his outstanding share of the losses sustained by the companies in which he had invested, amounts that he had still not paid. As displayed in Table 9.6, Marticorena owed funds to fourteen partnerships in the late 1790s. Given that shareholders were only required to make contributions when losses exceeded premiums, it can be concluded that fourteen of the fifteen insurance firms in which Marticorena had become vested were indeed sustaining losses, an indication of the crisis facing the industry. These amounts do not include the total losses sustained by Marticorena as an underwriter but only his debts still outstanding. During the previous several years Marticorena had made several remittances, payments to meet earlier demands that partners cover losses.[15]

At the moment of the list's preparation, Marticorena owed 32,685 pesos, his portion of the partnerships' losses. Almost certainly, these debts increased as the war losses sustained by the companies continued to mount.[16]

• • •

Marticorena's dismal experiences reflect the crisis facing Cadiz's financial sector as a result of the ongoing war. The broader extent of the industry's problems becomes more fully apparent from an alarming letter dispatched on 9 February 1798 by the *consulado* of Cadiz to the minister of finance, Francisco de Saavedra. *Consulado* members Ardurrena, Murguía, and Aretio made reference to a letter the guild had received several weeks earlier from Andrés Mathews, director of one of Cadiz's insurance firms. Mathews had apparently asked the *consulado* to grant his firm an *espera*, a temporary moratorium on its debts. Among the factors that drove Mathews to seek the guild's intercession was the "very disagreeable results" experienced by his firm owing to the "multiplicity of seizures that the enemies have carried out," which, he estimated, had, in total, cost Spanish mercantile interests in excess of twenty million pesos. Mathews's firm sustained an especially big hit; in the preceding eight months, Director Mathews had been forced three times to solicit funds from shareholders to meet the firm's underwriting obligations. In total, he had demanded 10,000 pesos from each of the company's forty shareholders, 400,000 pesos in all. But this was not even half of the insurance claims against the company. In addition to the 400,000 pesos to be contributed by the shareholders, Mathews had also been forced to pay out all of the company's accrued revenues from premiums paid, another 511,603 pesos. In total, then, this one firm had already sustained claims in excess of 900,000 pesos, a staggering sum.[17]

Certainly not exaggerating, the *consulado* argued that "the present situation facing the commerce of this plaza is among the most critical ever experienced in any era" and threatened to result in "the absolute extermination of the insurance companies." The guild further warned that such a grave outcome would be costly to Spanish interests as it would force merchants to pay higher rates in foreign insurance markets and would cause the outflow of scarce capital in the form of premiums. The officers expressed their support for Mathews's requested *espera* and suggested the possibility that the minister might show consideration for "the deplorable state of the multitude of honorable vassals who compose the directors and shareholders of the insurance companies of this plaza." Specifically, the *consulado* proposed that all insurance companies might be granted moratoria on their debts until "six or eight months from the declaration of the next peace in order to give time for funds detained in America to return."[18]

Four days later the *consulado* dealt with yet another insurance firm director whose company faced bankruptcy. The guild reported that company director Joséf Muralla had petitioned for "royal protection" from the many policyholders demanding indemnification of their losses. Apparently, Muralla was concerned that the policyholders would sue him directly given that his firm could not cover their losses due to a number of its shareholders facing personal illiquidity or even insolvency. The commercial crisis, the *consulado* claimed, had made many of the firms vulnerable to bankruptcy as their shareholders proved unable to meet their obligations.[19]

Later in the same month, on 27 February 1798, the *consulado* found itself addressing a third director's request for a moratorium, relief from the pressures being exerted against his firm by clients demanding indemnification. According to Director Gabriel Hernández, his company's financial troubles stemmed from the present inability of its partners to access their funds in America, an illiquidity that only peace could resolve. He thus requested that the moratorium stay in effect for a full year following the war's end, time sufficient for remittances of wealth from the colonies to occur.[20]

As the crisis continued to unfold, the *consulado*'s position shifted, growing less tolerant of the firms' difficulties. In February 1798 the *consulado* had floated the possibility of extending a moratorium to all the insurance companies for "six to eight months from the declaration of the next peace,"[21] but by July the guild's compassion had been tempered by more "mature reflection." The rising number of requests for moratoria was the subject of a 24 July 1798 official dispatch from *consulado* officers Pedro Martínez Murguía, Melchor Aretio, and Tomás Izquierdo to Minister Miguel Cayetano Soler. While not denying that the insurance companies' financial difficulties were genuine and caused largely by war-induced commercial disruptions, the officers nonetheless expressed reservations about providing widespread relief. First and foremost, the officers warned that such an act "will produce, in the opinion of this *consulado*, a scandal in all of Europe, and a general distrust in [Spain's] national and international commerce." Furthermore, not all companies faced equally dire financial predicaments, and it would be unfair to "confuse those directors who have proceeded with fine and rational conduct with those who have not [and thus] . . . must solicit moratoria." In addition, the officers added, a general moratorium would unfairly penalize policyholders by denying them prompt indemnification in accordance with their insurance contracts.[22]

Instead, the *consulado* proposed a multiple-point plan to help resolve the growing quagmire. The *consulado* recommended that a brief payment reprieve be granted to any company whose creditors (policyholders) threatened legal proceedings for nonpayment of claims. During this hiatus, directors would prepare detailed accounts of their firms' financial conditions, and with this report in hand, both parties and an appointed *consulado* representative would then attempt to craft a workable payment schedule. The officers also advised that the directors be denied their commissions in the interim. The circumstances were additionally muddied, according to the guild officials, by the fact that many of the creditors demanding indemnification happened also to be shareholders in one or more of the insurance firms.[23] Such individuals faced demands to contribute their shares of their company's debts, yet proved unable to collect promptly their own insurance losses.

Insurance losses were, ideally, indemnified with revenues collected from previous premiums. When a partnership's funds proved inadequate, as they often did during this period, the director demanded that shareholders deposit funds. So, perhaps the most alarming detail of the entire report was the acknowledgement that in many of the insurance companies there were "frequently four or five bankrupt shareholders."[24] In early 1799, Pedro Fermín de Córdoba, assistant to Juan Vicente de Marticorena in Cadiz, explained to his boss who was away in Madrid that judicial proceedings had become nearly a daily occurrence as "Directors or their creditors testify against all of the shareholders who have not paid."[25] Juan Vicente was hardly a disinterested party. He still owed considerable amounts to the insurance firms in which he was a partner. Indeed, the previous July he had narrowly escaped judicial action on the part of the firm directed by Ximénez Perez Padre y Hijo. Nearly a year earlier, October 1797, Juan Vicente had received a demand to deposit 4,640 pesos, his share of losses sustained in underwriting. Apparently, Marticorena evaded payment for several months and then tried to pay with a *pagaré*, a promissory note, prompting the firm to retort with the obvious point that the creditors wanted to be paid in cash.[26] By July 1798, Marticorena had still not met his obligations[27] and the firm's position had deteriorated still further, having landed in the *consulado* tribunal to face the demands of its creditors. Marticorena's assistant warned his boss that "the trustees with sword in hand are going to go after all of the shareholders."[28]

At the same time, Marticorena was delinquent in his share of debts to the insurance firm directed by Juan Francisco de Alzueta. Seemingly the director was facing enormous pressures from the firm's creditors, but he was helpless without the outstanding funds of shareholders like Marticorena. On 3 July 1798 Alzueta wrote Juan Vicente virtually begging him to make good on his obligations and warning him of the dire consequences of his continued delinquency. Collection of shareholders' obligations,

Alzueta explained, was critical for "the continuation of the company's credit, the reputations of its shareholders, and my own, which until now thanks to God I have known how to preserve without experiencing the vexations that many of my cohorts are at the hands of their creditors via judicial means, whose proceedings your grace knows very well from experience have transcended to individual members of the companies." Given Marticorena's dire financial condition at the time, it is doubtful that Alzueta's veiled threat elicited the desired response.[29]

Admittedly, these were extraordinary times; the war had significantly disrupted commercial flows, leading to the illiquidity of many in Cadiz, so much so that one observer commented that "Cadiz has come to be in such a deplorable condition, and so devoid of confidence, that fathers don't even trust their sons."[30] But one cannot help but wonder whether the structure of the insurance industry was not partially at fault for the financial exigencies. In the rush to create insurance partnerships in the 1790s, it is possible that too little concern was placed on the exposure of shareholders. Many merchants signed up for multiple shares in numerous companies, making their potential exposure exceedingly elevated. As repeatedly stressed, merchants were attracted to this investment opportunity because it required no upfront commitment of capital. They simply signed onto a partnership with the expectation of receiving a regular distribution of profits. Of course, in their rush to earn easy returns, they simultaneously exposed themselves to considerable risk, perhaps more than they could endure during these difficult times. While companies aimed to avoid excessive concentration of the risks that they underwrote, there was only so much opportunity for diversification in a trade that entailed similar routes to a limited number of ports on a finite number of vessels. And, all of the companies adopted similar strategies and operated in the same market. While a shareholder's risk exposure might be tolerable in Company A, it was doubled if his share in Company B underwrote comparable risks. Given the relatively small number of ships and insurance firms, such duplication must have been inevitable and frequent. And, as has been indicated, merchants like Marticorena had interests in more than a dozen different firms.

· · ·

Oversight of the insurance industry was one of the Crown-mandated functions of the merchant guild, a responsibility that in these years the *consulado* seemingly performed inadequately, to the detriment of Cadiz's commercial stability. Although over the course of 1798 the guild grew less tolerant of the problems faced by the industry, by then the crisis was too well-advanced to be remedied. The companies were only as solvent as their partners and when many of the latter went bankrupt, the city's financial markets teetered. The many traders who had prudently purchased insurance to reduce their risk became imperiled as well.

Risk within the Cadiz insurance market, it seems, was excessively concentrated in too few hands. One gets a sense of this potentially disastrous structure by examining the shareholder lists of the insurance partnerships. Of the eight-four companies for which the list of shareholders survive, a random sample of forty, nearly half, was collated to examine the duplication of shareholders across the companies. Table 9.7 illustrates each of the individuals who signed for at least seven shares. The most frequent of all signees was Miguel de Iribarren, who affixed his signature to thirty-one separate shares. Admittedly, it is possible that Iribarren was not solely responsible for these shares. For example, in 1795 he acquired four shares in a company directed by Pedro de Smidts and Sebastián and

TABLE 9.7

Individuals Possessing Seven or More Partnership Shares

Shareholder	# shares	Pesos Committed
Miguel de Iribarren	31	335,000
Guillermo Fanto	16	160,000
Joséf Lizarra	14	140,000
Mateo Gomez de Leys	13	130,000
Fermín Elizalde	11	110,000
Benito de la Piedra	12	107,500
Joséf Nolasco	10	102,500
Pedro de Urraco	10	100,000
Gabriel Hernández	10	100,000
Rafael Montis	9	92,500
Joaquín Perez de Carasa	9	90,000
Pedro Antonio Fontanes	9	90,000
Rafael Vicario de Yñigo	8	80,000
Joséf Xavier de Goenaga	8	80,000
Pedro Smidts	7	75,000
Joséf de Urda	7	70,000
Juan Francisco de Vea Murguía	7	70,000
Francisco de Yriarte	7	70,000
Salvador Marchena y Ramos	7	70,000

SOURCE: Noticia extractada de los Directores de Compañías de Seguros, AGI, *Consulados*, legajo 78, docs. 1, 32, 34–58, 72–74, 76–79, 80–84, 92.

Joséf María Lasqueti, but he did so in the name of commercial houses identified by their emblems, Marca AA; F; M; and L.[31] Thus, his personal exposure was unlikely equivalent to the thirty-one shares he obtained. In addition, not all of the shares overlapped in time, so that in several cases firms disbanded before additional shares were acquired. Despite these caveats, Table 9.7 strongly suggests the degree to which individual merchants became highly exposed due to their acquisition of multiple shares.

By far the largest shareholder was Miguel de Iribarren whose thirty-one shares in the forty firms examined were nearly double the sixteen acquired by Guillermo Fanto, the second most frequent signee. In signing up for thirty-one shares, Iribarren committed himself to the potential for losses totaling 335,000 pesos in these forty firms alone. And very likely Iribarren and the others listed held additional shares in the firms not among this sample of forty examined. Consequently, Table 9.7 understates their actual exposure. Indeed, historian Martínez del Cerro González, whose book focuses on Basque and Navarrese merchants exclusively, counted a total of fifty-five shares to which Iribarren had subscribed among all eighty-four firms.[32] Similarly, as noted above, Juan Vicente de Marticorena held shares in at least fifteen companies, but does not appear at all in Table 9.7. Either most of his shares were coincidentally in companies distinct from the sample of forty examined, or his identity was not directly obvious in the lists of shareholders since sometimes trading company names were provided instead. For example, several shares were purchased by "Marca JVM," almost certainly short for Juan Vicente de Marticorena. Thus, the table should not be viewed as a completely definitive list, but merely as an indication of the concentration of shareholders in the business.

The lists of insurance partners were deposited in the *consulado*, but there is little indication that the guild considered dangerous the practice of individual merchants signing onto so many firms. Even after the requests for moratoria on debts began amassing in 1798, there is no evidence that this concern was raised. In a world in which the greatest merchants regularly invested 500,000 pesos or more into transatlantic trade, perhaps these partners' financial exposures did not seem so alarming. Rather than consider the possibility that the problem was systemic, the *consulado* instead logically expressed its belief that the crisis was due to the fact that "many of the directors have proceeded with little or no caution in the underwriting of insurance and the impact of their lack of reflection has affected all commerce."[33]

The *consulado* seems to have failed in its responsibility to oversee the stability of the insurance industry in Cadiz. Too much risk was concentrated in too few hands, and when the catastrophic wars of the late eighteenth century produced unprecedented and unanticipated losses, the Cadiz financial sector proved vulnerable. Directors who had estimated the probabilities of risk events and had assigned the corresponding premiums had erred. Merchants who had subscribed to underwrite risk were unable to cover the associated debts. Many were like Juan Vicente de Marticorena, whose insurance losses occurred at the same time as the war ravaged his personal commercial dealings.

Ironically, in August 1796, several years before the depths of the crisis, the Crown, apprehensive about certain perceived structural weaknesses in the insurance industry, ordered the *consulado* to introduce reforms. Quite prophetically, the Crown expressed concern that none of the shareholders had actually deposited any funds into the companies; it ordered this shortcoming remedied. The officers of the *consulado*, penning a response, argued that the insurance industry and the local economy would collapse if shareholders were required to deposit the full value of their shares. At the time, the guild noted, there were sixty firms operating in Cadiz, each with approximately forty shares of 10,000 pesos apiece. If required to be deposited in the firms, this would remove twenty-four million pesos from circulation, the authors calculated, an unfathomable burden to commerce. In any event, such a requirement would spell the end of insurance in Cadiz, as no merchant would invest so much into an industry whose expected returns were so minimal. During "happy times," the guild estimated, a shareholder could only expect to earn over the course of the entire five-year existence of a firm 400 to 500 pesos per 10,000-peso share.[34] Requiring that shareholders deposit funds would drive the industry back abroad where no such requirements existed. The *consulado* thus recommended the suspension of the Royal Order, and, in the end, there is no evidence that any reforms were ever implemented. It was only several years later that the Crown's concerns proved warranted as many of the firms proved unable to indemnify the losses of their policyholders. Had the Royal Order been implemented, at the very least requiring shareholders to deposit some percentage of the values underwritten, the collapse of the insurance industry might have been partially avoided.

• • •

A growing number of Spanish merchants entered Cadiz's fledgling insurance industry in the 1780s and 1790s, acquiring shares merely for guaranteeing their financial support in the event of losses. At a time when the business portion of international trade had grown increasingly risky, underwriting the risks of sea must have appealed to prudent traders. Under normal circumstances, the hazards of the ocean voyage were fairly regular and consistent, allowing their probability to be effectively measured. Dozens of insurance firms opened for operations in these years, beginning to underwrite marine coverage for the booming transatlantic trade expanded by *comercio libre*. The growing business of insurance was lauded by the commercial community, which took pride and satisfaction that this financial sector had emerged in southern Spain and that Spanish traders no longer needed to obtain their policies in northern Europe.

The early enthusiasm for the underwriting business was unquestionably bolstered by the peaceful international diplomatic climate of the late 1780s. Barring an unexpected hurricane, the risks of the sea voyage were very manageable. The rates for coverage were low, but the "investors" had invested nothing but their promises. The income that the shareholders were distributed periodically must have seemed like easy money. No wonder traders flocked to the industry, signing up for multiple and even dozens of shares.

The warfare that erupted in Europe after 1793 was unprecedented in its scope. For nearly a quarter century, Spain was embroiled in conflict alternately with either France or Great Britain. The cost to transportation was immense as the navies of France and, even more profoundly, Great Britain ravished Spain's commerce with its colonies. What had seemed a low-risk commitment in the peaceful years preceding the wars suddenly became high-risk speculation. The predictability of sea voyages declined radically; premium rates skyrocketed in some cases to 50 percent and higher yet produced revenues inadequate to cover the losses anyway. Small but easy profits became large and mounting losses. Cadiz's insurance industry collapsed under the burden. In some regard, it merely experienced the same general malaise that affected the rest of Spain's international economy.

The widespread failures affecting the Cadiz firms are probably not too surprising in retrospect. For one, the sheer size of indemnifiable losses during the war years was extraordinary. Again, in 1800 the *consulado* estimated insured commercial losses to have totaled sixty million pesos since the start of hostilities seven years earlier.[35] For sake of comparison, the annual average value of Spain's imports in the decade preceding 1793 was just under seventeen million pesos. So the sixty million pesos that was estimated to have been lost was equivalent to three and a half years worth of Spain's imports. The strain on Cadiz's financial community was, obviously, devastating.

Not only were the losses sustained by the insurers enormous but they fell too heavily on a small number of individuals. The Cadiz community that stepped forward to obtain shares in the insurance companies was rather limited. A few individuals took on unreasonably large amounts of risk. When the wars erupted and the riskiness of transportation skyrocketed, these shareholders became far too financially exposed. Added to this was the fact that most of the insurers also had investments in the hobbled international trade. Funds were stranded in America or tied up in commodities that could not easily reach their final markets. Of course, some shareholders had pockets deep enough to cover honorably their obligations. Others, such as Juan Vicente de Marticorena, struggled to pay their insurance debts. The worst off went bankrupt.

The fortunes of the insurance firms followed those of their shareholders. Despite efforts to avoid excessive concentration of risks, the opportunities to diversify risk portfolios were limited. Directors spread their underwriting over as many ships and as many cargoes as possible. They furthermore varied the destinations that they covered, hoping that by diversifying the sea routes they would reduce the likelihood of major losses. In the end, however, the directors had too few alternatives. Spain's trade focused overwhelmingly on its colonies, a small number of destinations supplied by a small number of vessels sailing largely from Cadiz. The opportunities to diversify were not great, and when the British blockaded Cadiz, as they did successfully during several of the war years, the tremendous vulnerability of Spanish trade became all too clear. Both the insurers and the insured paid a high price.

Added to the merchants' woes were the growing fiscal demands of the Crown. Taxes on trade had always been substantial, but wartime led the Crown to seek emergency funds. Already battered by commercial and insurance losses, the *consulados* of the empire received a Crown order in mid-1800 for a "donation" of 300 million *reales vellón* (15 million pesos), of which 40 million (2 million pesos) corresponded to Cadiz. The four *consulado* deputies appointed to pen a response to the king claimed "to paint a painful but realistic picture of this plaza," advising the king of the "the situation of many merchants who were rich at the beginning of the war, and now find themselves poor" due to the 60 million pesos lost to the community. So dire had circumstances become that "even the most powerful households must cash in bonds in order to eat because they have no money." The fifteen years of commercial experimentation after 1778 followed by warfare since 1793 had left Cadiz's financial community devastated.[36]

Chapter 10

Conclusion: Staying Afloat

Staying afloat in early modern commerce required merchants to gauge the riskiness of every commercial activity and organize their endeavors to maximize the potential for profits while minimizing their exposure to risks. Indeed, risk management was as critical to the successful businessman as identification of lucrative opportunities. In long-distance, early modern trade, one could certainly grow rich if one did not first go bankrupt.

No matter how conservatively a merchant organized his dealings, however, he could not escape the reality that long-distance trade entailed enormous uncertainty. A seemingly endless list of perils might derail a venture well-designed from the start. Risk threatens business dealings of entrepreneurs even in the twenty-first century; in the early modern era, it was many times greater. For modern historians to truly comprehend the mercantile practices of these early modern, long-distance traders requires that they elevate risk management to the center of analysis. What seems like odd or even uncompetitive behavior to the modern eye might make great sense as a defensive measure against endemic and systemic risk and uncertainty.

The large merchants who dominated long-distance trade in the Spanish empire for the better part of three centuries have been traditionally depicted by historians as a privileged group that used its political and financial clout to protect its interests while engaging in uncompetitive

274

economic practices, largely to the detriment of Spain and its colonies. This image suggested specifically that the colonial commercial system was irrationally organized, choked Spain's economic progress, and generated unwarranted monopoly rents, all for the benefit of the privileged traders of the merchant guilds.

None of these conclusions are wholly incorrect, but they largely fail to appreciate the unpredictable environment in which these traders engaged. Without having adequately reflected on the role of risk in oceanic commerce, historians have tended to paint an overly one-dimensional portrait of the large merchants and their commercial practices. Long-distance traders responded to conditions of poor information, tremendous uncertainty, and endemic risk by adopting defensive strategies and embracing risk-reducing institutions. Avoiding risk, however, neither meant that the Spanish merchants lacked entrepreneurial spirit nor that they were somehow the precapitalist rentiers that historians sometimes imply. To the contrary, no merchant could long operate in the highly risky Atlantic world trade without constantly anticipating and taking active measures to avoid catastrophe. Being successful in early modern, long-distance trade required that merchants act defensively to prevent economic misfortune. Fortunes came gradually to patient and shrewd traders, but financial ruin could happen overnight.

Spanish merchants operated under conditions very similar to their counterparts in the other empires of the Atlantic world. The perils and dangers faced by British, Dutch, French, Portuguese, and other merchants were similar to those that plagued Spanish traders. Economic historians of early modern Europe, especially those focused on Britain and the Netherlands, have contemplated more fully the role of risk and uncertainty in shaping the economic behavior of merchants. In contrast to historians of the Spanish empire, these scholars have shown how traders created institutions or adapted existing ones to deal with the ever-present dangers and uncertainties that they encountered.

Spanish merchants had many strategies at their disposal to deal with risk. Chapters 7 through 9 explored the insurance industry that flourished in late-eighteenth-century Cadiz. Wealthy residents of this Andalusian port, mostly merchants themselves, subscribed to shares of underwriting partnerships in order to profit by selling insurance that assumed the risks of sea faced by merchants engaged in Atlantic world commerce. In exchange for a premium, insurance transferred a portion of trade's riskiness from the policyholder to the partnership. Had they not been able to transfer this risk, merchants would not have engaged as widely as they did in commercial activities. But even these precautions ultimately proved inadequate. When for a quarter century war engulfed Europe as a result of the French Revolution, many of the Spanish merchants and other financiers engaged in insurance and long-distance trade were destroyed. The Cadiz mercantile community had underestimated the levels of risk brought on by the fighting. In the end, their pockets were too shallow to absorb the losses.

Merchants pursued many other tactics to mitigate risk in less bellicose times as well. They divided their cargoes among many ships; they opted to ship, when possible, aboard war vessels rather than less-well-protected merchantmen; they attempted to dispatch their cargos in convoys instead of lone vessels; they sought to sell their wares to individuals who paid cash so as to avoid the risks associated with extending credit. In short, Atlantic world merchants operated constantly with an eye to limit their exposure to risk and uncertainty. Wise merchants even rejected business dealings that they deemed too risky, no matter how great the potential for profits.

As the first half of this book stressed, one of the greatest risks of long-distance trade in the early modern era was market risk, the danger that the demand for products could drop sharply as a result of the oversupply of the market. Merchants throughout the Atlantic world tried to inform themselves as best as possible of the existing commercial conditions of distant markets. But obtaining reliable and timely information was extremely difficult even for the largest merchants whose trusted agents and correspondents resided in every corner of the globe. The consequence of deficient information was that early modern traders most often operated in an environment characterized by a high degree of uncertainty. Markets shifted suddenly and merchants found depressed the demand for a commodity into which they had invested large sums to acquire and distribute to distant markets. Market risk plagued all long-distance traders, threatening to spoil ventures that took many months or even years to carry out. The great distances and long delays of trade made quick adjustment to conditions virtually impossible.

Businessmen throughout the early modern world took measures to reduce the market risk resulting from poor information and slow transportation. Historians of other Atlantic world empires have shown convincingly how merchants erected trade institutions to help minimize the obstacles presented by information deficiencies and sluggish transportation. Most notably, significant portions of long-distance trade were undertaken by large chartered trading companies whose market share allowed them to better control for the dangers of market inundation among other risks. The long-term successes of the Dutch East India Company and the

English East India Company, for example, stemmed significantly from their abilities to mitigate risk and uncertainty.

Monopoly companies were the exception within the Spanish empire, operating to only a few minor colonial ports. The major routes were instead plied by private merchants. Lacking the formal, institutional protections that the chartered companies of other Atlantic world empires afforded their investors, long-distance traders in the Spanish empire were more exposed to the perils of market risk. As Chapter 3 argued, however, the mercantilist structures of the Spanish commercial system did provide some insulation from the risks of the market, although this was never its original intent. Commercial regulation served to limit the amount of competition faced by large merchants and thus reduce the volatility of supply to distant markets. Historians have argued that monopoly practices allowed merchants to earn excessive profits, a thesis largely rejected here. Spanish imperial merchants faced considerable competition from one another, preventing them from earning monopoly profits under most circumstances; but the limits placed on the numbers of merchants and ships participating in Spanish imperial trade meant that total supply was constrained to quantities that the distant markets could reasonably absorb. The peculiar characteristics of the Spanish trade system clearly deviated dramatically from "pure competition," but this was an understandable expedient in light of the enormous unpredictability of such commerce. Spanish trade regulations made the uncertainty of long-distance exchange tolerable.

The gradual reform of imperial trade regulations during the reign of Charles III allowed imperial trade to expand substantially. But *comercio libre* stripped the Spanish merchants of the informal protections that had partially safeguarded them from the risks of market volatility and undoubtedly contributed to the explosion of bankruptcies that followed. During the decade that preceded the outbreak of war in 1793, dozens of Spanish merchants engaged in Atlantic world commerce went bankrupt, largely the consequence of the onslaught of trade that commercial reform encouraged. Unregulated commerce yielded unfettered market risk. Some of the large merchants anticipated the increasingly risky business environment and withdrew from direct trade. Many, for example, reoriented their activities to providing insurance instead. While market risk expanded in the increasingly competitive post-1778 environment, the riskiness of Atlantic world transportation, the commercial "middle passage," was largely unaffected by liberalizing reforms. Insurance covered all of the risks leading up to the point of arrival to markets. Merchants' redirection of their entrepreneurship from trade to insurance thus made some sense.

Many traditional merchants continued to participate in long-distance commerce and were joined by smaller, less experienced, and less well-capitalized traders who took advantage of the increasingly generous distribution of licenses to partake in imperial trade, often from ports only recently opened. The consequences were mounting competition for a limited market, rising crises of oversupply, and unprecedented numbers of bankruptcies.

While some within the commercial community experienced deep difficulties and even bankruptcy, *comercio libre* did bring about potentially promising changes for Spain. Its implementation in 1778 unleashed a torrent of competition, causing trade to expand, government revenues to increase, and consumer prices to tumble. Rising competition drove out less efficient and less talented merchants, leaving in business the leaner and more capable. Unfortunately, this experiment with commercial liberalism was harshly interrupted by the wars of the French Revolution and Napoleon. Had violence not prematurely interrupted the new trade regime, it is possible that Spain's empire would have emerged more dynamic. In the event, however, the era of free trade was too brief; conditions had not greatly improved by the war's eruption in 1793. Perhaps free trade could have ultimately strengthened Spain's economy, but in reality the economy never had a chance to stabilize.

Jeremy Adelman has recently conjectured that the political independence of the Spanish American colonies should be seen less as the result of Creole patriots separating themselves from mother Spain and more as a consequence of the total breakdown of the empire. "Social revolutions were not the cause of imperial breakups, but their consequences."[1] In many ways, the evidence and arguments presented in this book support Adelman's thesis. The outbreak of independence movements sparked by Napoleon's 1808 invasion and occupation of Spain continued a process that was already well underway, the unraveling of the ties between Spain and its colonies. By 1808, the Spanish empire was already greatly weakened by the erosion of commercial and other ties, which escalated with the outbreak of war in 1793. Creole elites who viewed independence as an opportunity to win greater freedom of trade (and certainly there were many noneconomic goals of the patriots as well) were not rebelling solely against Spain's mercantilist policies, but were also reacting to the decades of upheaval, the enormity of risks that had crippled transatlantic trade. Continued subservience to an enfeebled Spain implied for the colonies continued connection with a European monarchy incapable of providing the security needed to conduct trade safely, to help mitigate the riskiness of commerce. Spain's incessant involvement in European warfare had rendered imperial commerce intolerably risky, and the Spanish monarchy could no longer provide ample protection, one of the prime tasks of a sovereign state.[2]

In 1816, as rebels throughout Spanish America resisted post-Napoleon Spain's attempts to reestablish control, merchants of the Cadiz *consulado* were asked by the ministry of finance to comment about the possibility of reintroducing and enforcing the "Laws of the Indies," specifically the possibility of reestablishing Spain's exclusive access to colonial markets, which had been largely lost due to neutral and enemy ships entering Spanish American ports during the wars. Apparently the ministry had been confronted by certain unidentified groups with a list of obstacles that prevented Spain from reasserting its exclusivity to trade within the empire, and it sought the *consulado*'s opinion. Not surprisingly, the *consulado* minimized the impediments, arguing emphatically in favor of reestablishing Spain's commercial monopoly. The *consulado*'s transparent rationale aside, the perceived obstacles to regaining dominance do provide a window into at least some of the economic grievances that drove the Spanish American independence movements. In general, the list presented by the ministry of finance pointed to the failure of the Spanish government to provide the colonies with security from risk. For one, it claimed, Spain lacked an adequate merchant marine that could securely extract the colonies' exports or provide them with their needed imports. Spain's defenses were so weak, the skeptics claimed, that "any insurgent ship can blockade the ports of the Peninsula, and thus [Spain cannot] defend the lengthy coasts of America or uphold its sovereignty if some [foreign] power were to get involved in the dispute." The list further maintained that critics believed that "the shortage of ships . . . has been the cause of the revolution."[3] Presumably these detractors were partially echoing the claims of Spanish American rebels. While any single explanation of the aspirations for independence is absurdly monocausal, all of the points expressed in the *consulado*'s report identify a common theme. The decades of war had destroyed Spain's ability to provide adequate protection for its colonies. Unable to provide an environment conducive to safe trade, the Spanish Crown no longer served a purpose for the richest and most powerful inhabitants of Spanish America, its commercial elites. While its economic empire teetered on the edge of collapse, its political empire imploded.

Within half a decade of the ministry of finance's investigation, the movements of independence had succeeded. Spanish rule was replaced throughout Spanish America by alliances with Great Britain, the most powerful naval and commercial nation of the nineteenth century. The *Pax Britanica* ushered in an improved environment for international exchange, one in which many age-old risks were mitigated by British naval hegemony. While the newly formed Spanish American republics experienced the near-total disintegration of national stability in the early decades following their independence from Spain, Latin America would become deeply integrated into the booming world economy during the second half of the century. Much as the export market had driven the colonial economies, international trade became the most dynamic sector of most of these nations in this Liberal age inspired by comparative advantage. The rapid economic growth that continued until the Great Depression, however, occurred under more highly propitious conditions. The Spanish empire in the second half of the eighteenth century was plagued by the constant warfare and related privateering that had contributed to the multitude of risks affecting international trade. By the nineteenth century, these political hazards had largely diminished. Furthermore, technological advances in shipping, most notably the wide scale adoption of steam-powered ships, increased the speed and predictability of transatlantic voyages. Less dangerous sea lanes and more efficient transportation reduced both risk and uncertainty, creating a business climate that allowed trade to flourish and merchants to more easily stay afloat.

REFERENCE MATTER

NOTES

Chapter 1

1. One notable exception is the recent book by Xabier Lamikiz. See Xabier Lamikiz, *Trade and Trust in the Eighteenth-Century Atlantic World: Spanish Merchants and Their Overseas Networks*, ed. the Royal Historical Society (Rochester, NY: Boydell and Brewer, 2010).

2. Frank Hyneman Knight, *Risk, Uncertainty and Profit*, Hart, Schaffner & Marx Prize Essays 31 (Boston: Houghton Mifflin, 1921), 197–98.

3. Peter Musgrave, "The Economics of Uncertainty: The Structural Revolution in the Spice Trade, 1480–1640," in *Spices in the Indian Ocean World*, ed. M. N. Pearson, *An Expanding World: The European Impact on World History 1450-1800,* Vol. 11. (Brookfield, VT: Variorum, 1996), 338.

4. Frank Hyneman Knight received a doctorate in economics at Cornell University in 1916. For nearly forty years, he taught at the University of Chicago where he was one of the founders of the "Chicago School" of economics.

5. Knight, *Risk, Uncertainty and Profit*, 19–20, 233.

6. The law of large numbers suggests that as the sample size increases, the difference between actual and expected outcomes will approach zero. The actual will come close to equaling the probability of some event. This allows insurers to cover risks that individuals cannot bear. One uninsured shipwreck will destroy a shipowner. But the insurer knows that if it insures a large number of vessels, the percentage lost will equal (approximately) the probability of any single ship becoming shipwrecked. So, knowing from experience that roughly one in fifty ships will be wrecked, an insurer can feel secure that if it insures five hundred vessels, the law of large numbers

284 Notes to Chapter 1

suggests that only about ten will be lost. With this knowledge an insurer can price premiums to guarantee profits, assuming the probability estimates were correct and that no conditions change that increase the probability of a ship being lost.

7. Knight, *Risk, Uncertainty and Profit*, 213.
8. Ibid., 231, 241–42
9. Ibid., 259–60.
10. Ibid., 265.
11. Douglass Cecil North, *Institutions, Institutional Change, and Economic Performance*, Political Economy of Institutions and Decisions (Cambridge: Cambridge University Press, 1990), 118. North's scholarship has had a revolutionary impact on the field of economic history in the past quarter century. This role is discussed in Avner Greif, "Microtheory and Recent Developments in the Study of Economic Institutions Through Economic History," in *Advances in Economics and Econometrics: Theory and Applications: Seventh World Congress*, ed. David M. Kreps and Kenneth Frank Wallis, Econometric Society Monographs 26–28. (Cambridge: Cambridge University Press, 1997). For an excellent and accessible discussion of the so-called New Institutional Economics, see Oliver E. Williamson, *The Economic Institutions of Capitalism: Firms, Markets, Relational Contracting* (New York: Free Press, 1985), ch. 1.
12. North, *Institutions*, 6.
13. Knight, *Risk, Uncertainty and Profit*, 252.
14. D. A. Brading, "Bourbon Spain and Its American Empire," in *The Cambridge History of Latin America*, ed. Leslie Bethell (Cambridge: Cambridge University Press, 1984), 1:413–14.
15. Traditionally Spanish merchants had taken out sea loans, *préstamos a la gruesa ventura*. In addition to the actual funds loaned, these instruments provided insurance against the risks of sea. Essentially, the lender assumed all risks until the borrower arrived to the destination. Once safely arrived, the lender's risks terminated and the borrower's began. See Antonio-Miguel Bernal, *La Financiación de la Carrera de Indias (1492–1824): Dinero y Crédito en el Comercio Colonial Español Con América* (Sevilla: Fundación el Monte, 1992).
16. Jack P. Greene and Philip D. Morgan, *Atlantic History: A Critical Appraisal* (Oxford: Oxford University Press, 2009), 3.
17. Alison Games, "Atlantic History: Definitions, Challenges, and Opportunities," *American Historical Review* 111, no. 3 (2006): 755.
18. Greene and Morgan, *Atlantic History*, 9.

19. Crosby's classic and well-known work is Alfred W. Crosby, *The Columbian Exchange: Biological and Cultural Consequences of 1492* (Westport, CT: Greenwood, 1972); Crosby expanded his work in *Ecological Imperialism: The Biological Expansion of Europe, 900–1900*, Studies in Environment and History (Cambridge: Cambridge University Press, 1986). Another classic work on the impact of disease is William Hardy McNeill, *Plagues and Peoples* (Garden City, NY: Anchor/Doubleday, 1976). More recently the impact of the transatlantic transference of disease has been examined in the popular study by Jared M. Diamond, *Guns, Germs and Steel: The Fates of Human Societies* (London: Jonathan Cape, 1997).

20. Appointed in 1948 to be the first director of the United Nation's Economic Commission on Latin America (ECLAC), Argentine Raul Prebisch and his British colleague, Hans Singer, developed the economic theory underpinning dependency theory. Known as the Singer-Prebisch thesis, it argues that the prices of primary products tended to decline relative to the prices of manufactured goods (known as the terms of trade). This meant that over time Latin American exports could purchase an increasingly smaller basket of manufactured imports. So, Latin America benefitted less from engaging in trade than did the developed nations. Indeed, dependency theorists argued that Latin America's engagement in international trade tended to underdevelop the region. Prebisch's prescription to this structural problem was Import Substituting Industrialization. These ideas were developed in Raúl Prebisch, *The Economic Development of Latin America and Its Principal Problems* (New York: United Nations, 1962). Another of the pioneering economists and a colleague of Prebisch at ECLA was the Brazilian Celso Furtado. See Celso Furtado and Ricardo W. de Aguiar, *Development and Underdevelopment* (Berkeley: University of California Press, 1964). For a recent biography on Prebisch, see Edgar J. Dosman, *The Life and Times of Raúl Prebisch, 1901–1986* (Montreal: McGill-Queen's University Press, 2008).

21. There is an extensive bibliography on dependency theory and Latin America. An early and influential classic was Andre Gunder Frank, *Capitalism and Underdevelopment in Latin America: Historical Studies of Chile and Brazil* (New York: Monthly Review Press, 1967). Frank wrote numerous subsequent works in which he continued to revise and further develop his theories of underdevelopment. Another landmark work on dependency in Latin America is Fernando Henrique Cardoso and Enzo Faletto, *Dependency and Development in Latin America* (Berkeley: University of California Press, 1979). Connected to dependency theory is the World Systems school

associated with Immanuel Wallerstein. See Immanuel Maurice Wallerstein, *The Modern World-System*, 3 vols., Studies in Social Discontinuity
(New York: Academic Press, 1974). The classic interpretation of colonial
Spanish America through the lens of dependency remains Stanley J. Stein
and Barbara H. Stein, *The Colonial Heritage of Latin America: Essays on Economic Dependence in Perspective* (New York: Oxford University Press, 1970).

22. The historiography of the slave trade and slavery is, of course, enormous and rather fruitless to attempt to summarize here, but several good
starting points include: Philip D. Curtin, *The Atlantic Slave Trade: A Census* (Madison: University of Wisconsin Press, 1969); J. E. Inikori and Stanley L. Engerman, *The Atlantic Slave Trade: Effects on Economies, Societies, and
Peoples in Africa, the Americas, and Europe* (Durham, NC: Duke University
Press, 1992); David Eltis, James Walvin, and Svend E. Green-Pedersen,
*The Abolition of the Atlantic Slave Trade: Origins and Effects in Europe, Africa,
and the Americas* (Madison: University of Wisconsin Press, 1981); Herbert
S. Klein and Ben Vinson, *African Slavery in Latin America and the Caribbean*,
2nd ed. (Oxford: Oxford University Press, 2007); David Brion Davis, *The
Problem of Slavery in the Age of Revolution, 1770–1823* (Ithaca, NY: Cornell
University Press, 1975); David Brion Davis, *Inhuman Bondage: The Rise
and Fall of Slavery in the New World* (New York: Oxford University Press,
2008); and David Eltis, *The Rise of African Slavery in the Americas* (Cambridge: Cambridge University Press, 2000).

23. Ironically, Bernard Bailyn, probably the most prominent scholar
actively promoting Atlantic history, was not immediately enamored with
Braudel's work, one of its lone critics. See Bernard Bailyn, "Braudel's
Geohistory—A Reconsideration," *Journal of Economic History* 11, no. 3 (1951).

24. Games, "Atlantic History," 749, 741.

25. A great place to begin is Bernard Bailyn, *Atlantic History: Concept
and Contours* (Cambridge, MA: Harvard University Press, 2005). In 1995,
Bailyn initiated at Harvard University the International Seminar on the
History of the Atlantic World, an annual conference that has helped spawn
many new works in the field. Indeed, the seminar website (http://www
.fas.harvard.edu/~atlantic/) is the best resource on works produced in
Atlantic world history. Also see the varied essays in Greene and Morgan,
Atlantic History, and Jorge Cañizares-Esguerra and Erik R. Seeman, *The
Atlantic in Global History, 1500–2000* (Upper Saddle River, NJ: Pearson
Prentice Hall, 2007). Excellent introductions are also provided by the texts
of Douglas R. Egerton, Alison Games, Jane G. Landers, Kris Lane, and
Donald R. Wright, *The Atlantic World: A History, 1400–1888* (Wheeling, IL:
Harlan Davidson, 2007); and Thomas Benjamin, *The Atlantic World: Euro-*

peans, Africans, Indians and Their Shared History, 1400–1900 (New York: Cambridge University Press, 2009). On the British Atlantic world see the essays in the *American Historical Review* forum titled "The New British History in Atlantic Perspective," as well as David Armitage and M. J. Braddick, *The British Atlantic World, 1500–1800* (New York: Palgrave Macmillan, 2002). A recent, excellent summary of the literature is provided by Games, "Atlantic History."

26. A handful of Latin Americanists have answered the call to broaden their work into an Atlantic history context. On political, social, and economic issues, see, for example, Jeremy Adelman, *Republic of Capital: Buenos Aires and the Legal Transformation of the Atlantic World* (Stanford, CA: Stanford University Press, 1999); Jeremy Adelman, *Sovereignty and Revolution in the Iberian Atlantic* (Princeton, NJ: Princeton University Press, 2006); Franklin W. Knight and Peggy K. Liss, *Atlantic Port Cities: Economy, Culture, and Society in the Atlantic World 1650–1850* (Knoxville: University of Tennessee Press, 1991); Peggy K. Liss, *Atlantic Empires: The Network of Trade and Revolution, 1713–1826*, Johns Hopkins Studies in Atlantic History and Culture (Baltimore: Johns Hopkins University Press, 1983); Gabriel Paquette, *Enlightenment, Governance, and Reform in Spain and Its Empire, 1759–1808* (New York: Palgrave Macmillan, 2008); Camilla Townsend, *Tales of Two Cities: Race and Economic Culture in Early Republican North and South America: Guayaquil, Ecuador, and Baltimore, Maryland* (Austin: University of Texas Press, 2000); and John Huxtable Elliott, *Empires of the Atlantic World: Britain and Spain in America, 1492–1830* (New Haven, CT: Yale University Press, 2006). For a more cultural, intellectual, and history of science approach see Daniela Bleichmar, Paula De Vos, Kristin Huffine, and Kevin Sheehan, eds., *Science in the Spanish and Portuguese Empires, 1500–1800* (Stanford, CA: Stanford University Press, 2009); Jorge Cañizares-Esguerra, *How to Write the History of the New World: Histories, Epistemologies, and Identities in the Eighteenth-Century Atlantic World*, Cultural Sitings (Stanford, CA: Stanford University Press, 2001); Jorge Cañizares-Esguerra, *Puritan Conquistadors: Iberianizing the Atlantic, 1550–1700* (Stanford, CA: Stanford University Press, 2006); and *American Historical Review* 112, no. 3 (2007), and 112, no. 5 (2007), feature articles and debates on Spanish Atlantic history. For an overview of the literature, see Kenneth J. Andrien, "The Spanish Atlantic System," in *Atlantic History: A Critical Appraisal*, ed. Jack P. Greene and Philip D. Morgan (Oxford: Oxford University Press, 2009), 55–80.

27. For Cuba see Franklin W. Knight, *Slave Society in Cuba During the Nineteenth Century* (Madison: University of Wisconsin Press, 1977). On

Brazil consult the classic work by Stuart B. Schwartz, *Sugar Plantations in the Formation of Brazilian Society: Bahia, 1550–1835*, Cambridge Latin American Studies 52 (Cambridge: Cambridge University Press, 1985).

28. Jeremy Baskes, *Indians, Merchants, and Markets: A Reinterpretation of the Repartimiento and Spanish-Indian Economic Relations in Colonial Oaxaca, 1750–1821* (Stanford, CA: Stanford University Press, 2000).

29. Kris Lane, "Gone Platinum: Contraband and Chemistry in Eighteenth-Century Colombia," *Colonial Latin American Review* 20, no. 1 (2011): 61–79.

30. There are many excellent works on the silver trade. See, for example, P. J. Bakewell, *Silver Mining and Society in Colonial Mexico: Zacatecas, 1546–1700*, Cambridge Latin American Studies 15 (1971; repr., Cambridge: Cambridge University Press, 2002); P. J. Bakewell, *Miners of the Red Mountain: Indian Labor in Potosí, 1545–1650* (Albuquerque: University of New Mexico Press, 1984); D. A. Brading and Harry E. Cross, "Colonial Silver Mining: Mexico and Peru," *Hispanic American Historical Review* 52, no. 4 (1972): 545–79.

Chapter 2

1. Frank Hyneman Knight, *Risk, Uncertainty and Profit*, Hart, Schaffner & Marx Prize Essays 31 (Boston: Houghton Mifflin, 1921), 260.

2. Most studies of long-distance trade recognize this endemic problem, one that is well highlighted in John J. McCusker, "The Demise of Distance: The Business Press and the Origins of the Information Revolution in the Early Modern World," *American Historical Review* 110, no. 2 (2005): 295–321. The differing legal structures and economic institutions that merchants of diverse regions encountered shaped their unique attempts to mitigate such information asymmetries. Bernard Bailyn has argued that in seventeenth-century commerce in the British empire, "demand fluctuated almost incalculably. . . . Reliable factors and correspondents were, therefore, of paramount importance, for the success of large enterprises rested on their judgment." See Bernard Bailyn, "Communications and Trade: The Atlantic in the Seventeenth Century," *Journal of Economic History* 13, no. 4 (1953): 380. In their classic work on shipping, *Sea Lanes in Wartime: The American Experience, 1775–1942* (New York: Norton, 1942), Robert Greenhalgh Albion and Jennie Barnes Pope point to the constant dangers faced by early American merchants who were forced to operate with only limited information about supply and demand. The result was that they often sent cargoes to heavily glutted markets. This problem is also described in Cathy Matson, "Introduction: The Ambiguities of Risk

in the Early Republic," *Business History Review* 78, no. 4 (2004): 595–606. According to Kalevi Ahonen, *From Sugar Triangle to Cotton Triangle: Trade and Shipping Between America and Baltic Russia, 1783–1860* (Jyvaskyla: University of Jyvaskyla, 2005), merchants engaged in the sugar trade to St. Petersburg employed individuals in the West Indies to record the volumes of sugar shipped to Baltic ports so that they could make more informed decisions whether or not to send additional boatloads. Philip Lawson, *The East India Company: A History* (London: Longman, 1993), 21–22, shows that one of the main benefits of the English East India Company was its internal committee structure entrusted with the collection and dissemination of relevant commercial information. The Company also erected its own imperial mail system to move news more efficiently. Similarly, the VOC, the Dutch East India Company, converted Batavia (modern day Jakarta) into a business hub where economic information could be distributed to the company's ships. See Niels Steensgaard, "Dutch East India Company as an Institutional Innovation," in *Trade in the Pre-Modern Era, 1400–1700*, ed. Douglas A. Irwin (Cheltenham, UK: Elgar Reference Collection, 1996), 446. On the VOC's collection of information also see Peter Musgrave, "The Economics of Uncertainty: The Structural Revolution in the Spice Trade, 1480–1640," in *Spices in the Indian Ocean World*, ed. M. N. Pearson, An Expanding World (Brookfield, VT: Variorum, 1996), 347.

3. McCusker, "Demise of Distance," 299.

4. Stanley J. Stein and Barbara H. Stein, *Apogee of Empire: Spain and New Spain in the Age of Charles III, 1759–1789* (Baltimore: Johns Hopkins University Press, 2003), 192.

5. Xabier Lamikiz, "Patrones de Comercio y Flujo de Información Comercial Entre España y América Durante el Siglo XVIII," *Revista de Historia Económica/Journal of Iberian and Latin American Economic History* 25, no. 2 (2007): 232–37.

6. Jeremy Adelman, *Sovereignty and Revolution in the Iberian Atlantic* (Princeton, NJ: Princeton University Press, 2006), 78.

7. Regarding the establishment of commercial networks in Spanish America, especially through marriage, see Ruth Pike, *Aristocrats and Traders; Sevillian Society in the Sixteenth Century* (Ithaca, NY: Cornell University Press, 1972), 107–10; John E. Kicza, *Colonial Entrepreneurs, Families and Business in Bourbon Mexico City* (Albuquerque: University of New Mexico Press, 1983), 60; Louisa Schell Hoberman, *Mexico's Merchant Elite, 1590– 1660: Silver, State, and Society* (Durham, NC: Duke University Press, 1991), 64–68; D. A. Brading, *Miners and Merchants in Bourbon Mexico, 1763–1810* (Cambridge: Cambridge University Press, 1971), 112–13; Jesús Turiso

Sebastián, *Comerciantes Españoles en la Lima Borbónica: Anatomía de Una Élite de Poder, 1701–1761,* Serie Historia y Sociedad (Valladolid: Universidad de Valladolid, 2002), 119–20; and Adelman, *Sovereignty and Revolution,* 44–46. For an in-depth discussion of this practice as a specific attempt to reduce risk, see Peter Mathias, "Risk, Credit, and Kinship in Early Modern Enterprise," in *The Early Modern Atlantic Economy,* ed. John J. and Kenneth Morgan McCusker (Cambridge: Cambridge University Press, 2000), 15–35.

8. Bailyn, "Communications and Trade," 380–82.

9. The extensive correspondence of Juan Vicente de Marticorena is deposited as Cartas a Juan Vicente de Marticorena y a Pedro Fermín de Córdoba, desde la península, Europa y América, AGI, *Consulados,* legajos 432–39. Several works have utilized portions of this correspondence.

10. Julián Bautista Ruiz Rivera, *El Consulado de Cádiz: Matrícula de Comerciantes, 1730–1823* (Cádiz: Diputación Provincial de Cádiz, 1988), 181. For Juan Miguel de Marticorena's license to travel to Peru, see AGI, Contratación, 5521, N. 191, 24 December 1776.

11. AGI, Contratación, 5525, N. 9, R. 1, 1 January 1782.

12. On merchant Juan Bautista de Marticorena's marriage into the Aycinena family see Richmond F. Brown, *Juan Fermín de Aycinena: Central American Colonial Entrepreneur, 1729–1796* (Norman: University of Oklahoma Press, 1997), 70–71. Also see Victoria Eugenia Martinez del Cerro González, *Una Comunidad de Comerciantes: Navarros y Vascos en Cádiz (Segunda Mitad de Siglo XVIII)* (Sevilla: Consejo Económico y Social de Andalucía, 2006), 228. He is also mentioned briefly in several of the articles in Jordana Dym and Christophe Belaubre, *Politics, Economy, and Society in Bourbon Central America, 1759–1821* (Boulder: University Press of Colorado, 2007).

13. AGI, Contratación, 5531, N.3, R.19, 25 October 1787.

14. Correspondence addressed to Marticorena between 1762 and 1809 appears in AGI, *Consulados,* legajos 432–39.

15. See Cartas a Francisco Sierra desde España, Europa, y América, AGI, *Consulados,* legajos 420–28.

16. All of the above-mentioned letters are located in AGI, *Consulados,* legajos 421, 426–27.

17. Ibid.

18. The only real clue to Sierra's capacity to communicate in French was his practice of noting on the letters the dates on which he received and responded to letters. He generally wrote these dates in French when the letter was composed in French. Of course, it is certainly possible that Sierra employed the services of a translator.

19. Cartas a Francisco de Sierra desde España, Europa, y América, London, 17 January 1786, AGI, *Consulados*, legajo 428 (unpaginated). The London prices are stated in shillings/pence. There were twenty shillings to the pound sterling and twelve pence to the shilling.

20. Joséph Zengolio to Monsieur Francisco de Sierra, Genoa, 19 July 1784, AGI, *Consulados*, legajo 427 (unpaginated).

21. Libro de cartas del dueño del navío el Jasón a particulares, desde Veracruz, Cadiz, Buenos Aires, etc., Francisco de Sierra to Francisco Bulini, February 1776, AGI, *Consulados*, libro 157, folios 82–82v.

22. For Holland, see N. W. Posthumus, *Inquiry into the History of Prices in Holland* (Leiden: Brill, 1946); and for Great Britain see Thomas Tooke, William Newmarch, and T. E. Gregory, *A History of Prices and of the State of the Circulation from 1792 to 1856* (New York: Adelphi, 1928).

23. Echenique y Sánchez a Francisco de Sierra, Amsterdam, 1 November 1781, AGI, *Consulados*, legajo 421 (unpaginated).

24. Fermín Tastet y Compañia to Francisco de Sierra, London, 9 November 1781, AGI, *Consulados*, legajo 421 (unpaginated); Fermín Tastet y Compañia to Francisco de Sierra, London, 30 November 1781, AGI, *Consulados*, legajo 421 (unpaginated).

25. Miguel Jacinto de Marticorena a Juan Vicente de Marticorena, Veracruz, 26 January 1789, AGI, *Consulados*, legajo 433, folio 220.

26. Diego Maria Gallardo, *Almanak Mercantil Ó Guia de Comerciantes para el Año de 1802* (Madrid: Vega y Compañía, 1802), 258, 191. This book can be consulted online at: http://books.google.com/books?id=hxvw_ s8hqakC&printsec=frontcover&source=gbs_ge_summary_r&hl=en #v=onepage&q&f=false.

27. Lamikiz, "Patrones de Comercio," 241–44, provides an excellent summary of the evolution of the colonial mail system. While he observes that transatlantic mail delivery improved dramatically after 1739, he nonetheless concludes that the poor flow of information remained an obstacle to merchant decision making.

28. Gallardo, *Almanak Mercantil*, 258.

29. Carta Reservadas, El Conde Revillagigedo hace un difuso informe sobre averiguar si hay decadencia en el comercio de aquellos reynos y en caso de haberla, hallar las causas de ella y sus remedios, 31 August 1793, AGI, México, 1554, folios 14–17, 22. A copy of this is deposited at BNM, Manuscritos, ms1398, folios 324–402. A very similar version appears as Instrucciones de gobierno que dejaron a su succesor el virrey Conde de Revillagigedo, AGI, México, 1238.

30. Only a random sample of the letters was tabulated from the many hundreds of surviving letters addressed to Sierra. The data from which Tables 2.3a and 2.3b are constructed appears online (see table of contents) in Appendix A. All of the data was extracted from Cartas a Francisco de Sierra, AGI, *Consulados*, legajos 420–28.

31. A standard deviation of 10 days, for example, is much more significant if the average duration is 20 days than if the average is 100 days. In other words, if a person expects (based on the average) to receive a letter in 10 days and it ends up taking 20 days, the delay will be perceived to be much greater than if it was expected to take 100 days but actually took 110 to arrive. In both cases the standard deviation might be 10 days, but the impact (risk) is much greater in the former case. The coefficient of variation reflects this. Coefficient of variation equals standard deviation divided by mean.

32. For an especially clear discussion of the risks associated with heavy dependence on agents, see Nuala Zahedieh, "Credit, Risk and Reputation in Late Seventeenth-Century Colonial Trade," in *Merchant Organization and Maritime Trade in the North Atlantic, 1660–1815*, ed. Olaf Uwe Janzen, Research in Maritime History, Vol. 15. (St. John's, Newfoundland: International Maritime Economic History Association, 1998), 59–61.

33. The economics literature dealing with the issue of information asymmetry and the principal-agent problem is extensive. Indeed, the 2001 Nobel Prize in Economic Science was awarded to three economists, George A. Akerlof, A. Michael Spence, and Joseph E. Stiglitz, whose pioneering work addressed these very issues. Interesting work in history has explored the principal-agent problem as well. Perhaps the most notable recent contributions are those of economic historian Avner Greif. Greif, "Reputations and Coalitions in Medieval Trade: Evidence on the Maghribi Traders," *Journal of Economic History* 49, no. 4 (1989): 857–82, argues that traders in the Maghreb devised practices of mutual benefit in which they collectively agreed to identify and ostracize cheaters, whether agents or fellow traders. The cost of being dishonest, permanent banishment from commerce, encouraged good behavior on the part of economic actors. Greif has also examined a similar problem during the Genoese medieval Commercial Revolution. To increase the performance of representatives in faraway settlements, office holding dynasties, *podesterias*, developed a mixture of high salaries coupled with financial penalties that encouraged cooperation and good management. See Avner Greif, "On the Political Foundations of the Late Medieval Commercial Revolution: Genoa During the Twelfth and Thirteenth Centuries," *Journal of Economic History* 54, no. 2 (1994): 271–87. Other noteworthy historical studies that have addressed

the principal-agent problem include: Ann M. Carlos, "Principal-Agent Problems in Early Trading Companies: A Tale of Two Firms," *American Economic Review* 82, no. 2 (1992): 140–45; Ann M. Carlos and Stephen Nicholas, "Agency Problems in Early Chartered Companies: The Case of the Hudson's Bay Company," *Journal of Economic History* 50, no. 4 (1990): 853–75; Santhi Hejeebu, "Contract Enforcement in the English East India Company," *Journal of Economic History* 65, no. 2 (2005): 496–523; David Sunderland, "Principals and Agents: The Activities of the Crown Agents for the Colonies, 1880–1914," *Economic History Review* 52, no. 2 (1999): 284–306; Nuala Zahedieh, *The Capital and the Colonies: London and the Atlantic Economy, 1660–1700* (New York: Cambridge University Press, 2010), 106–12.

34. Xabier Lamikiz, *Trade and Trust in the Eighteenth-Century Atlantic World: Spanish Merchants and Their Overseas Networks*, ed. the Royal Historical Society (Rochester, NY: Boydell and Brewer, 2010), 33–40.

35. Ibid., 57–61.

36. Ibid., 126–33.

37. Domingo de Yriarte a Francisco de Sierra, Vienna, 7 March 1781, AGI, *Consulados*, legajo 421, (unpaginated).

38. Lamikiz, *Trade and Trust*, 107.

39. Xabier Lamikiz, "Un 'Cuento Ruidoso': Confidencialidad, Reputación, y Confianza en el Comercio del Siglo XVIII," *Obradoiro de Historia Moderna* 16 (2007): 113–42, discusses a case in which Cadiz merchant Juan de Eguino discovered that his Lima agent was cheating him. Despite Eguino's advanced age, he traveled to Peru to confront him. Also see Lamikiz, *Trade and Trust*, 153–61.

40. Juan Bautista de Marticorena a Juan Vicente de Marticorena, Nueva Guatemala, 2 April 1793, AGI, *Consulados*, legajo 434, folio 999.

41. This is clearly evident from the several decades of correspondence to Cadiz *consulado* merchant Juan Vicente de Marticorena. Throughout, he and his correspondents discuss diplomatic matters and changing political winds. See AGI, *Consulados*, legajos 432–39.

42. On the so-called Nootka crisis see William R. Manning, *The Nootka Sound Controversy* (Washington, DC: American Historical Association, 1904).

43. AGI, *Consulados*, legajo 433, folios 871, 1011, 1032.

44. Pedro José de Górriz a Juan Vicente de Marticorena, Nueva Guatemala, 3 December 1796, AGI, *Consulados*, legajo 436, folio 636.

45. José Ramon de Ugarteche a Antonio de Arrechea, 24 December 1796, AGI, *Consulados*, legajo 440.

46. Rafael José Facio a Juan José de Puch, 30 April 1798, AGI, *Consulados*, legajo 429.

47. Correspondencia general del consulado, 7 February 1797, AGI, *Consulados*, libro 96, folio 223, noted that in the first months of the war with England, Spanish merchants had lost five to six million pesos to privateers.

48. Juntas de Gobierno celebradas, 15 April 1797, AGI, *Consulados*, libro 20, folios 46–47v.

49. Juntas de Gobierno celebradas, 20 October 1797, AGI, *Consulados*, libro 20, folio 62.

50. Correspondencia general del *consulado*, AGI, *Consulados*, libro 100, folios 65–66.

51. Hananel Jacob Mendes da Costa a Francisco de Sierra, London, 17 January 1783, AGI, *Consulados*, legajo 424 (unpaginated).

52. Hananel Jacob Mendes da Costa a Francisco de Sierra, London, 24 January 1783, AGI, *Consulados*, legajo 424 (unpaginated).

53. Bailyn, "Communications and Trade," 382.

54. José Ramon de Ugarteche a Antonio de Arrechea, 8 April 1797, AGI, *Consulados*, legajo 440.

55. Los Comerciantes de la ciudad de Barcelona al Rey, 28 September 1773, AGI, Indiferente General, 2410.

56. Antonio García-Baquero González, *El Libre Comercio a Examen Gaditano: Crítica y Opinión en el Cádiz Mercantil de Fines del Siglo XVIII* (Cádiz: Universidad de Cádiz Servicio de publicaciones, 1998), Informe de Don Matías de la Vega, 22 November 1787, Document 8, 139–47. For original see Dictámenes de los componentes de la junta general de comercio para mejorar el tráfico y comercio con Indias, AGI, *Consulados*, legajo 73, folios 32–41.

57. See, for example, one sent from Veracruz to Juan Vicente de Marticorena, 1 August 1798, AGI, *Consulados*, legajo 437, folio 450.

58. Diego Sáenz de Texada a Francisco de Sierra, 27 April 1782, AGI, *Consulados*, legajo 424 (unpaginated).

59. Correspondencia y documentos de don Juan José Puch (1777–1819), Rafael José Facio a Juan José de Puch, 17 April 1798, AGI, *Consulados*, legajo 429.

60. Ibid., 30 April 1798.

61. See "Carta para Señor don José Fernández Gil a Guatemala," México, 10 November 1779, in Maria Cristina Torales Pacheco, ed. *La Compañia de Comercio de Francisco Ignacio de Yraeta (1767–1797)* (México: Instituto Mexicano de Comercio Exterior con la colaboraciâon de la Universidad Iberoamericana, 1985), 2:234.

62. See "Carta para los señores directores de la Real Compañía de Filipinas," México, 17 June 1789, in Torales Pacheco, *Compañia de Comercio*, 2:262.

63. Cartas a Francisco Sierra desde España, Europa y América, 1785–88, Echenique Sánchez a Francisco de Sierra, Amsterdam, 30 January 1783, AGI, *Consulados*, legajo 424 (unpaginated).

64. See, for example, Cartas a Francisco Sierra desde España, Europa y América, 1785–88, Echenique Sánchez a Francisco de Sierra, Amsterdam, 13 March 1783, AGI, *Consulados*, legajo 424 (unpaginated).

65. Hananel Jacob Mendes da Costa a Francisco de Sierra, London, 14 March 1783, AGI, *Consulados*, legajo 424 (unpaginated).

66. Cartas a Francisco Sierra desde España, Europa y América, 1785–88, Antonio Sáenz de Texada a Francisco de Sierra, Lima, 5 October 1784, AGI, *Consulados*, legajo 426 (unpaginated).

67. Turiso Sebastián, *Comerciantes Españoles*, 122.

68. Take for example the diversity of goods that Peruvian merchant Juan Miguel de Marticorena listed among his imported items. These included cera, Durois, estamenas fraylescas, panos, Buches, Tripes, Bayetas, Rompecoches, capas, sombreros, aravias, lienzos, olanes, velillos, clarines, tehillas, prusianillas, panuelos, ruanes, medias, estopillas, sarasas, angarillas, chupasy chalecos, listoneria, tercianelas, texidos, calzetas, quimones, buratos, Filipichines, Franelas, Sargas, perdurables, chamelotes, camellones, cristales, bretanas, manteleria, velillos, clarines, cintas, listados, bramanes, platillas, carolinas, melanias, ras, rasos, gorros, etc. See Juan Miguel de Marticorena a Juan Vicente de Marticorena, Lima, 20 June 1788, AGI, *Consulados*, legajo 433, folios 109–17.

69. Adelman, *Sovereignty and Revolution*, 78.

70. Hoberman, *Mexico's Merchant Elite*, 60.

71. The Second Count Revillagigedo pointed in 1793 to the shallow consumption in Mexico's market. Revillagigedo estimated that New Spain's population was around 3.5 million but it imported on average only about thirteen to fourteen million pesos, a per capita import consumption of just four pesos, far too low he believed. See AGI, MéxicoCarta Reservadas #627, El Conde Revillagigedo hace un difuso informe sobre averiguar si hay decadencia en el comercio de aquellos reynos y en caso de haberla, hallar las causas de ella y sus remedios, 31 August 1793, AGI, México, 1554. A copy can be consulted at BNM, Manuscritos, ms1398, folios 324–402, 31 August 1793. Revillagigedo makes nearly identical arguments in AGI, México Instrucciones de gobierno que dejaron a su succesor el virrey Conde de Revillagigedo, AGI, México, 1238.

72. AGI, Indiferente General, 2416 (unpaginated), 18 October 1779.

73. John R. Fisher, *The Economic Aspects of Spanish Imperialism in America, 1492–1810* (Liverpool: Liverpool University Press, 1997), 45.

74. See Roland D. Hussey, "Antecedents of the Spanish Monopolistic Overseas Trading Companies (1624–1728)," *Hispanic American Historical Review* 9, no. 1 (1929): 7.

75. With frequency, the Spanish *consulados* petitioned the Crown to delay the flota to permit the sale of existing supplies in colonial markets. The connection between supply and the flota is discussed below. See Clarence Henry Haring, *Trade and Navigation between Spain and the Indies in the Time of the Hapsburgs* (Cambridge: Cambridge University Press, 1918), 214. See also Murdo MacLeod, "Spain and America: The Atlantic Trade, 1492–1720," in *The Cambridge History of Latin America*, ed. Leslie Bethell (Cambridge: Cambridge University Press, 1984), 356. According to Lutgardo García Fuentes, in the second half of the seventeenth century the Spanish *consulados* complained constantly about overly supplied American markets, especially in Peru. See Lutgardo García Fuentes, *El Comercio Español Con América, 1650–1700*, Publicaciones de la Excma. Diputación Provincial de Sevilla. Sección Historia, ser. 1a, no. 16 (Sevilla: Escuela de Estudios Hispano-Americanos Consejo Superior de Investigaciones Científicas, 1980), 73; Testimonio de la representación hecha por la diputación del comercio de España sobre que por el excelentísimo Señor Virrey de este reyno se informe á S.M. los perjuicios que se infieren á ámbos comercios verificadose la llegada de flota á Veracruz el próximo año de 1764, AGI, México, 2503.

76. Carta de Tomás Ruiz de Apodaca, 6 April 1760, AGI, *Consulados*, legajo 405, folios 15–16.

77. AGI, *Consulados*, legajo 68, folios 933–34, 6 April 1771.

78. Nicolás de la Cruz y Bahamonde, *De Cádiz y Su Comercio: Tomo Xiii del Viaje de España, Francia e Italia*, ed. Manuel Ravina Martín (Cádiz: Servicio de Publicaciones, Universidad de Cádiz, 1997), 282.

79. Ruiz Rivera, *Consulado de Cádiz*, 143.

80. Sobre la quiebra de don Mariano Bernabe de Frías del comercio de Cadiz, 1787–91, AGI, Indiferente General, 2316.

81. AGI, Indiferente General, 2314, 15 September 1788.

82. Expedientes de los cinco gremios mayores de Madrid y sus negociaciones, AGI, Indiferente General, 1623, folios 417–18.

Chapter 3

1. Economists of the New Institutional Economics (NIE) argue that the main purpose of economic institutions in capitalist economies is to

economize on transaction costs, to reduce the costs and risks associated with business transactions. Merchants, thus, seek ways to organize their activities to be more cost efficient and make trade more predictable and less risky. The literature on New Institutional Economics has grown increasingly rich in the past two decades. The classic starting point for NIE remains the work of Nobel Laureate Douglass North. See Douglass Cecil North, *Institutions, Institutional Change, and Economic Performance*, Political Economy of Institutions and Decisions (Cambridge: Cambridge University Press, 1990), ch. 1. An excellent theoretical overview is contained in Oliver E. Williamson, *The Economic Institutions of Capitalism: Firms, Markets, Relational Contracting* (New York: Free Press, 1985), ch. 1.

2. On these general arguments, see Kenneth Joseph Arrow, *Limits of Organization*, Fels Lectures on Public Policy Analysis (New York: Norton, 1974).

3. Mark A. Burkholder and Lyman L. Johnson, *Colonial Latin America*, 6th ed. (New York: Oxford University Press, 2008),170, 202.

4. Clarence Henry Haring, *Trade and Navigation Between Spain and the Indies in the Time of the Hapsburgs* (Cambridge: Cambridge University Press, 1918), 91. Interestingly, Haring's own work is tremendously reliant on the seventeenth-century work by Veitia Linage, *Norte de la Contratación de las Indias Occidentales* (Buenos Aires: Comisión argentina de fomento interamericano, 1945).

5. Oligopoly is a condition in which several suppliers are able to collude to dictate the price of commodities. In theory, but not often in practice, they can influence market terms as effectively as monopolists.

6. Monopoly is an economic condition in which there exists a single source of supply, a sole producer of some commodity, for example. In no way did the fleet system meet these conditions; oligopoly, a condition in which there are few operators, is more appropriate, although I consider oligopoly to be equally incorrect in describing colonial trade.

7. Haring suggests that in the first half of the colonial era, officials on both sides of the Atlantic fixed minimum values below which traders were not permitted to engage in transatlantic commerce. Haring concluded that this served "to confine trade to the wealthier Andalusian firms." Haring, *Trade and Navigation*, 136. If this restriction did, in fact, exist, it was not consistently applied. Hoberman leaves no doubt that by the seventeenth century, midsize traders were important participants at least in transatlantic commerce. See Louisa Schell Hoberman, *Mexico's Merchant Elite, 1590–1660: Silver, State, and Society* (Durham, NC: Duke University Press, 1991), 35–40.

8. Robert S. Smith, *The Spanish Guild Merchant: A History of the Consulado, 1250–1700* (New York: Octagon Books, 1972), 34–44.

9. John E. Kicza, *Colonial Entrepreneurs, Families and Business in Bourbon Mexico City* (Albuquerque: University of New Mexico Press, 1983), 51.

10. Peter Mathias, "Strategies for Reducing Risk by Entrepreneurs in the Early Modern Period," in *Entrepreneurs and Enterpreneurship in Early Modern Times: Merchants and Industrialists within the Orbit of the Dutch Staple Market*, ed. Clé Lesger and L. Noordegraaf (Den Haag: Stichting Hollandse Historische Reeks, 1995), 7.

11. Enriqueta Vila Vilar argues for the seventeenth century that it was "the wealthiest who could best withstand the protracted terms that transatlantic commerce entailed to the detriment of the weaker ones." Enriqueta Vila Vilar, "El Poder del Consulado Sevillano y los Hombres del Comercio en el Siglo XVII: Una Aproximación," in *Relaciones de Poder y Comercio Colonial: Nuevas Perspectivas*, ed. Enriqueta Vila Vilar, Allan J. Kuethe, and Carlos Alvarez Nogal (Madrid: Consejo Superior de Investigaciones Científicas, 1999), 26.

12. See "Carta para Señor don José Fernández Gil a Guatemala," México, 2 December 1778, in Maria Cristina Torales Pacheco, ed., *La Compañia de Comercio de Francisco Ignacio de Yraeta (1767–1797)* (México: Instituto Mexicano de Comercio Exterior con la colaboraciâon de la Universidad Iberoamericana, 1985), 2:221–22.

13. Jesús Turiso Sebastián, *Comerciantes Españoles en la Lima Borbónica: Anatomía de Una Élite de Poder, 1701–1761*, Serie Historia y Sociedad (Valladolid: Universidad de Valladolid, 2002), 121.

14. Susan Migden Socolow, *The Merchants of Buenos Aires, 1778–1810: Family and Commerce*, Cambridge Latin American Studies 30 (Cambridge: Cambridge University Press, 1978), 67.

15. Manuel Rodriguez de la Vega y Martin de Sarratea al Virrey Marques de Loreto, Buenos Aires, 21 July 1789, AGI, Indiferente General, 2435.

16. Cartas a Dn. Antonio de Artechea desde distintos puntos de España y America, 1786–99, Vicente Antonio del Murrieta to Antonio de Artechea, Buenos Aires, 18 December 1794, AGI, *Consulados*, legajo 440.

17. As Stein and Stein so eloquently put it, "vested interests had long ago staked out claims, cemented alliances, and ensured profits by access to privilege." Stanley J. Stein and Barbara H. Stein, *Apogee of Empire: Spain and New Spain in the Age of Charles III, 1759–1789* (Baltimore: Johns Hopkins University Press, 2003), 43.

18. The process as described by Haring for the sixteenth century is not too fundamentally different than that explained by Stein and Stein for the

eighteenth. See Haring, *Trade and Navigation*, 59–63, esp. 60n2; Stein and Stein, *Apogee of Empire*, 120–23.

19. Perhaps the best example of such collusion is the OPEC cartel. On rare occasion OPEC members have agreed to limit supply sufficiently to drive up prices. But more often than not, these schemes have failed as one or another member increased output to take advantage of higher prices. That OPEC's eleven member nations cannot regularly hold together as a cartel is indicative of the difficulties of oligopolistic collusion. In any event, modern-day governments usually erect antitrust laws to prohibit such anticompetitive behavior.

20. D. A. Brading, *Miners and Merchants in Bourbon Mexico, 1763–1810* (Cambridge: Cambridge University Press, 1971), 96.

21. Julián Bautista Ruiz Rivera, *El Consulado de Cádiz: Matrícula de Comerciantes, 1730–1823* (Cádiz: Diputación Provincial de Cádiz, 1988), 44–45, 133–216.

22. Xabier Lamikiz, *Trade and Trust in the Eighteenth-Century Atlantic World: Spanish Merchants and Their Overseas Networks*, ed. the Royal Historical Society (Rochester, NY: Boydell and Brewer, 2010), 117.

23. Hoberman, *Mexico's Merchant Elite*, 20–21.

24. Kicza, *Colonial Entrepreneurs*, 51. Membership in the new *consulado* in the much smaller market of Guatemala was around eighty at the end of the eighteenth century. Ralph Lee Woodward, *Class Privilege and Economic Development: The Consulado de Comercio of Guatemala, 1793–1871* (Chapel Hill: University of North Carolina Press, 1966), 7n2.

25. Hoberman classified medium-sized investors as those shipping between 1500 and 7000 pesos. If anything, she was conservative in this regard, 7000 being a fairly small investment. Hoberman, *Mexico's Merchant Elite*, 36, table 1.

26. Ibid., 35–38, tables 1–2.

27. Ibid., 36.

28. Economists recognize what is sometimes called the "cartel cheating problem," that cartels (oligopolies) create enormous incentives for their members to "cheat" by selling to customers at a price slightly below the cartel price. If no collusion were to exist, the market price would fall to equilibrium, well below the price sustained artificially by oligopolists holding back supply. Cartel cheaters benefit doubly, by selling their quota at the inflated price plus marketing more on the side. Because of the "cartel cheating problem," effective cartels must introduce some mechanism of monitoring their members and punishing transgressors.

29. Richard Garner generously provided me with a spreadsheet containing the data that he had compiled from the original document, AGI, *Consulados*, legajo 801, Xalapa, 1761. He and Stefanou discuss this document and data in Richard L. Garner and Spiro E. Stefanou, *Economic Growth and Change in Bourbon Mexico* (Gainesville: University Press of Florida, 1993), 166–70.

30. Garner and Stefanou, *Economic Growth and Change*, 171.

31. Ibid., 169.

32. The data were generously provided to me by Richard Garner, who compiled them originally from AGI, *Consulados*, legajo 801, Xalapa, 1761.

33. Bottomry loans are so named in English because typically they were taken by ship owners who literally provided the keel or ship's bottom as collateral against the loans. The most complete study of sea loans (also known as *préstamos a la gruesa ventura* or *escrituras de riesgo marítimo*) in the Spanish empire is Antonio-Miguel Bernal, *La Financiación de la Carrera de Indias (1492–1824): Dinero y Crédito en el Comercio Colonial Español Con América* (Sevilla: Fundación el Monte, 1992). Also see Oscar Cruz Barney, *El Riesgo en el Comercio de Hispano-Indiano: Préstamos y Seguros Maritimos Durante los Siglos XVI a XIX* (Mexico City: UNAM, 1998); Florence Edler de Roover, "Early Examples of Marine Insurance," *Journal of Economic History* 5, no. 2 (1945): 172–200; Violet Barbour, "Marine Risks and Insurance in the Seventeenth Century," *Journal of Economic and Business History* 1, no. 4 (1929): 561–96; and Meir Kohn, *The Origins of Western Economic Success: Commerce, Finance, and Government in Preindustrial Europe* (working papers, Department of Economics, Dartmouth College, Hanover, NH, 2001), http://www.dartmouth.edu/~mkohn/. Thousands of these contracts survive in the Archive of the Indies. See AGI, *Consulados*, libros 409–44, and AGI, *Consulados*, legajos 876–87. According to Lamikiz, the length of time granted to borrowers to repay their debts after arriving at port grew more generous over the course of the eighteenth century. Lamikiz, *Trade and Trust*, 90.

34. Cruz Barney, *Riesgo en el Comercio de Hispano-Indiano*, ix, 34. For the eighteenth century see Brading, *Miners and Merchants*, 97.

35. Brading, *Miners and Merchants*, 97.

36. José Joaquín Real Díaz, *Las Ferias de Jalapa* (Sevilla: Escuela de Estudios Hispano-americanos, 1959), 10–11.

37. AGI, *Consulados*, legajo 68, folios 933–34, 6 April 1771.

38. Burkholder and Johnson, *Colonial Latin America*, 169. Burkholder and Johnson is perhaps the best, most widely used college textbook on

Colonial Latin America and reflects effectively the conventional history. Also see Brading, *Miners and Merchants*, 97.

39. Testimonio del expediente sobre averiguar si hay ó no decadencia en el comercio, hallar el remedio de ella en caso de haberla, y proporcionar los auxilios mas convenientes para fomento del trafico mercantil en este ramo, Informe de Gaspar Martín Vicario, 25 June 1791, AGI, Mexico, 1554, folios 5–17.

40. Brading, *Miners and Merchants*, 97.

41. This problem is well recognized by economists. There is an incentive to break from a cartel and slightly undersell other members of the oligopoly. Any economics textbook will address this issue. See, for example, N. Gregory Mankiw, *Principles of Economics*, 4th ed. (Mason, OH: Thomson/South-Western, 2007), 359–60.

42. A good example of how such a system might have worked is provided by Avner Greif who shows how Mahgribi traders of the eleventh-century Mediterranean penalized their agents who cheated them. Organized in a loose association, these traders agreed that collectively they would ostracize any agent who deceived one of them. Furthermore, they agreed that such a cheater would be fair game to be cheated. This practice guaranteed that none would cheat, since the long-term costs (ostracism) greatly exceeded the short-term benefits. See Avner Greif, "Contract Enforceability and Economic Institutions in Early Trade: The Mahgribi Traders' Coalition," *American Economic Review* 83, no. 3 (1993): 525–48.

43. Garner and Stefanou, *Economic Growth and Change*, 168–69.

44. This data was extracted from an excellent, unpublished disseration. See George Robertson Dilg, "The Collapse of the Portobello Fairs: A Study in Spanish Commercial Reform, 1720–1740" (PhD diss., Indiana University, 1975), appendix B. While not addressing precisely market power, Dilg suggests the opposte of what Brading argued for Mexico, that in these years the Peruvian merchants were actually losing competitiveness to Peninsular counterparts. See Dilg, "Collapse of the Portobello Fairs," 220.

45. Free trade is addressed below. Many works examine the discussions over and ultimate implementation of free trade. See for examples, Brading, *Miners and Merchants*; Stanley J. Stein and Barbara H. Stein, *Silver, Trade, and War: Spain and America in the Making of Early Modern Europe* (Baltimore: Johns Hopkins University Press, 2000); Stein and Stein, *Apogee of Empire*; John Fisher, *Commercial Relations Between Spain and Spanish America in the Era of Free Trade, 1778–1796* (Liverpool: Center for Latin

American Studies, University of Liverpool, 1985); John R. Fisher, *The Economic Aspects of Spanish Imperialism in America, 1492–1810* (Liverpool: Liverpool University Press, 1997).

46. Kicza, *Colonial Entrepreneurs*, 51.

47. Archivo General de la Nación de México (AGN) Marina,Tomo 38, Exp. 6, Sobre la nulidad del embarco de granas y nombramiento de otro buque para conducir las granas sobrantes, folios 68–188,1775–77.

48. See Vila Vilar, "Poder del Consulado Sevillano," on "donativos" and the granting of concessions by the Crown.

49. AGN, Marina, Tomo 38, exp. 5, 1776, Instancia del Conde de Reparaz para poder embarcar en la Fragata Ventura y Navio San Nicolas mil y novecientos zurrones de grana fina.

50. Hundreds of these requests appear in AGI, Indiferente General, legajo 2435 and surrounding legajos.

51. P. J. Bakewell, *A History of Latin America: 1450 to the Present*, 2nd ed. (Malden, MA: Blackwell, 2004), 208.

52. Haring, *Trade and Navigation*, 8–9.

53. Ruiz Rivera, *Consulado de Cádiz*, 31–43. Antonio García-Baquero González, *Cádiz y el Atlántico: (1717–1778)*, 2 vols. (Cádiz: Diputación Provincial de Cádiz, 1988), 1:468, presents a table demonstrating the diverse origins of merchants matriculated in the Cadiz guild between 1743 and 1778.

54. AGI, *Consulados*, legajo 73, doc. 12, folio 71, 23 November 1787. This document is reproduced in Antonio García-Baquero González, *El Libre Comercio a Examen Gaditano: Crítica y Opinión en el Cádiz Mercantil de Fines del Siglo XVIII* (Cádiz: Universidad de Cádiz Servicio de Publicaciones, 1998), doc. 12.

55. Martínez del Cerro González provides a thorough discussion of the process by which Navarrese and Basque merchants relocated and established themselves in Cadiz during the second half of the eighteenth century. See Victoria Eugenia Martinez del Cerro González, *Una Comunidad de Comerciantes: Navarros y Vascos en Cádiz (Segunda Mitad de Siglo XVIII)* (Sevilla: Consejo Económico y Social de Andalucía, 2006), chs. 2–3. Stein and Stein also discuss the migration of "young men from northern Spain" to enter the commerce of Cádiz. Stein and Stein, *Apogee of Empire*, 179.

56. On his origins see AGI, *Consulados*, legajo 72, exp. 11, folio 220; his date of matriculation is cited in Ruiz Rivera, *Consulado de Cádiz*, 181.

57. Stein and Stein, *Apogee of Empire*, 24. Foreign penetration of the Indies trade occupies considerable attention of Stein and Stein.

58. Haring, *Trade and Navigation*, 96.

59. See Nuala Zahedieh, *The Capital and the Colonies: London and the Atlantic Economy, 1660–1700* (New York: Cambridge University Press, 2010), 36–38. For a good analysis of the economic and political impacts of the Navigation Acts on the thirteen colonies, see Larry Sawers, "The Navigation Acts Revisited," *Economic History Review* 45, no. 2 (1992): 262–84; for a general discussion of the philosophy of British mercantilism that led to the adoption of the Navigation Acts, see Curtis P. Nettels, "British Mercantilism and the Economic Development of the Thirteen Colonies," *Journal of Economic History* 12, no. 2 (1952): 105–14.

60. Zahedieh, *Capital and the Colonies*, 292.

61. Fisher, *Commercial Relations*, 64.

62. This argument is also made by David R. Ringrose, *Spain, Europe and the "Spanish Miracle," 1700–1900* (Cambridge: Cambridge University Press, 1996), 126–27. Ironically, in the very same work, Ringrose also stresses the development of Barcelona after 1778 as a competitor to Cadiz, a competitive level that no other Spanish Mediterranean city could match. Catalan merchants centered in Barcelona controlled the export to America of commodities produced between Barcelona and Málaga. Primary were Catalan textiles that enjoyed a productive surge following the commercial reforms. Ringrose, *Spain, Europe and the "Spanish Miracle,"* 207–12.

63. Many works have explored the politics surrounding Spanish imperial trade reform, but none is as comprehensive as Stein and Stein, *Silver, Trade, and War*. Also see Brading, *Miners and Merchants*, 95–97; Geoffrey J. Walker, *Spanish Politics and Imperial Trade, 1700–1789* (London: Macmillan, 1979), 13–14; Haring, *Trade and Navigation*, 136–45; Kicza, *Colonial Entrepreneurs*, 55, 61; Lawrence Clayton, "Trade and Navigation in the Seventeenth-Century Viceroyalty of Peru," *Journal of Latin American Studies* 7, no. 1 (1975): 1–21; and Stein and Stein, *Apogee of Empire*.

63. Many scholars have examined the role of the *consulados* in resisting reform of the commercial system, especially during the era of the "Bourbon Reforms." The most thorough discussions are the recent volumes by Stanley J. Stein and Barbara H. Stein. See Stein and Stein, *Silver, Trade, and War*; Stein and Stein, *Apogee of Empire*; and Barbara H. Stein and Stanley J. Stein, *Edge of Crisis: War and Trade in the Spanish Atlantic, 1789–1808* (Baltimore: Johns Hopkins University Press, 2009). Other interesting works on this theme include: Vila Vilar, "Poder del Consulado Sevillano"; Allan J. Kuethe, "El Fin del Monopolio: los Borbones y el Consulado Andaluz," in *Relaciones de Poder y Comercio Colonial: Nuevas Perspectivas*, ed. Enriqueta Vila Vilar, Allan J. Kuethe, and Carlos Alvarez Nogal (Madrid:

Consejo Superior de Investigaciones Científicas, 1999); Brading, *Miners and Merchants*, discusses commercial reform and the guilds' responses. See especially 114–21. The responses of Cadiz merchants to a Crown questionnaire on reform appear in García-Baquero González, *Libre Comercio*. These latter are examined in detail below.

64. France, England, and the Netherlands each created chartered trading companies during this era. The French formed the French India Company and the Royal African Company; the Dutch established Dutch East India Company and the Dutch West India Company; the English chartered the East India Company and the Hudson's Bay Company.

65. Niels Steensgaard, "Dutch East India Company as an Institutional Innovation," in *Trade in the Pre-Modern Era, 1400–1700*, ed. Douglas A. Irwin (Cheltenham, UK: Elgar Reference Collection, 1996), 446.

66. Ibid.

67. Ibid.

68. Philip Lawson, *The East India Company: A History* (London: Longman, 1993), 21–22; see also K. N. Chaudhuri, *The English East India Company: The Study of an Early Joint-Stock Company, 1600–1640* (New York: Reprints of Economic Classics, 1965); and K. N. Chaudhuri, *The Trading World of Asia and the English East India Company, 1660–1760* (Cambridge: Cambridge University Press, 1978).

69. Peter Musgrave, "The Economics of Uncertainty: The Structural Revolution in the Spice Trade, 1480–1640," in *Spices in the Indian Ocean World*, ed. M. N. Pearson, An Expanding World (Brookfield, VT: Variorum, 1996), 347.

70. Ann M. Carlos and Stephen Nicholas, "'Giants of an Earlier Capitalism': The Chartered Trading Companies as Modern Multinationals," *Business History Review* 62, no. 3. (Autumn 1988): 407. These historians, and the others cited immediately above, contributed significantly to the revisionist interpretations of early modern joint-stock companies. For an alternative perspective see S. R. H. Jones and P. Ville Simon, "Efficient Transactors or Rent-Seeking Monopolists? The Rationale for Early Chartered Trading Companies," *Journal of Economic History* 56, no. 4 (1996): 898–915, and the ensuing debate: Ann M. Carlos and Stephen Nicholas, "Theory and History: Seventeenth-Century Joint-Stock Chartered Trading Companies," *Journal of Economic History* 56, no. 4 (1996): 916–24; and S. R. H. Jones and P. Ville Simon, "Theory and Evidence: Understanding Chartered Trading Companies," *Journal of Economic History* 56, no. 4 (1996): 925–26.

71. There were several monopoly companies established by grant of the Spanish Crown for lesser areas. The most important was the la Compañía Guipúzcoana de Caracas, formed in 1728 to foster trade with Venezuela. The Habana Company created to trade with Cuba in 1740 and the Barcelona Company established in 1755 to trade with several of the smaller Caribbean isles had limited impact. See Roland Dennis Hussey, *The Caracas Company, 1728–1784: A Study in the History of Spanish Monopolistic Trade*, Harvard Historical Studies 37 (Cambridge: Harvard University Press, 1934); Raquel Rico Linage, *Las Reales Compañías de Comercio Con América: los Órganos de Gobierno*, Publicaciones de la Excma, Diputación Provincial de Sevilla, Sección Historia, Ser. 1a, No. 24 (Sevilla: Excma. Diputación Provincial de Sevilla: Escuela de Estudios Hispano-Americanos de Sevilla, 1983). On the Real Compañía de Filipinas see Carmen Yuste López, *El Comercio de la Nueva España Con Filipinas, 1590–1785* (México: Instituto Nacional de Antropología e Historia Departamento de Investigaciones Históricas, 1984).

72. Roland D. Hussey, "Antecedents of the Spanish Monopolistic Overseas Trading Companies (1624–1728)," *Hispanic American Historical Review* 9, no. 1 (1929): 7.

73. Haring, *Trade and Navigation*, 138. Colin MacLachlan argues that Spain's failure to follow the Dutch and English example is partially attributable to the different nature of Spain's monarchy. Hapsburg rule depended on the "royal jurisdiction" embodied in the "structure of viceroys, Audiencias, and other institutions." The privatization of power vested in such a monopoly company would have challenged this authority unacceptably. Indeed, one proponent of chartered companies suggested that in the 1660s "the Council of Indies would prefer to ruin the empire rather than risk infringement on its jurisdiction." Colin M. MacLachlan, *Spain's Empire in the New World: The Role of Ideas in Institutional and Social Change* (Berkeley: University of California Press, 1988), 92.

74. Extracto y minuta de la consulta del consejo de indias sobre comercio libre, 14 July 1777, AGI, Indiferente General, 2409, folio 13.

75. Haring, *Trade and Navigation*, 22–24; J. H. Elliott, *Imperial Spain, 1469–1716* (New York: St. Martins, 1963), 179; Murdo MacLeod, "Spain and America: The Atlantic Trade, 1492–1720," in *The Cambridge History of Latin America*, ed. Leslie Bethell (Cambridge: Cambridge University Press, 1984), 289, 350. For a highly readable recent account of this period, see Hugh Thomas, *Rivers of Gold: The Rise of the Spanish Empire, from Columbus to Magellan* (New York: Random House, 2005). J. H. Parry, *The Spanish*

Seaborne Empire (London: Hutchinson, 1966), 54–59, provides a convincing discussion as to why the *Casa de Contratación* was located in Seville.
76. Haring, *Trade and Navigation*, 138.
77. Veitia Linage, *Norte de la Contratación*, book 2, chapter 4, paragraph 3.
78. Haring, *Trade and Navigation*, 71; Parry, *Spanish Seaborne Empire*, 134; Smith, *Spanish Guild Merchant*, 91. See also Kenneth R. Andrews, *The Spanish Caribbean: Trade and Plunder, 1530–1630* (New Haven, CT: Yale University Press, 1978), 64–66.
79. The fleet system operated until it was temporarily suspended in 1739 in favor of *registros*, ships licensed to sail individually. Fleets were resurrected for Mexico in 1757 and continued until the 1778 promulgation of *comercio libre* initiated the phasing out of fleets. See Brading, *Miners and Merchants*, 95–96.
80. The most thorough description of the voyage is Haring, *Trade and Navigation*, 223–30; Another clear description is Bakewell, *History of Latin America*, 207.
81. Lutgardo García Fuentes, *El Comercio Español Con América, 1650–1700*, Publicaciones de la Excma, Diputación Provincial de Sevilla, Sección Historia, ser. 1a, no. 16 (Sevilla: Escuela de Estudios Hispano-Americanos Consejo Superior de Investigaciones Científicas, 1980), 164. The explanation for this decline is debated. Some scholars attribute the drop to an alleged depression in the leading sector of the American economy, mining. According to this line of reasoning, decreased silver output in Potosí, Peru, and the mines of northern New Spain resulted in declining exports of silver and a concomitant fall in shipping. Other scholars explain the decline in silver exports as an indication of the maturation of the colonial economy and its reduced dependence on primary exports to the mother country. On the so-called seventeenth-century depression thesis as applied to Mexico see Woodrow Wilson Borah, *New Spain's Century of Depression* (Berkeley: University of California Press, 1951); P. J. Bakewell, *Silver Mining and Society in Colonial Mexico: Zacatecas, 1546–1700*, Cambridge Latin American Studies 15 (1971; repr., Cambridge: Cambridge University Press, 2002); John J. Tepaske and Herbert Klein, "The Seventeenth-Century Crisis in New Spain: Myth or Reality?," *Past and Present* 90 (1981): 116–36; J. I. Israel, "Mexico and the 'General Crisis' of the Seventeenth Century," *Past and Present* 63 (May 1974): 33–57; Richard Boyer, "Mexico in the Seventeenth Century: Transition of a Colonial Society," *Hispanic American Historical Review* 57, no. 3 (1977): 455–78. On the Viceroyalty of

Peru, see Kenneth J. Andrien, *Crisis and Decline: The Viceroyalty of Peru in the Seventeenth Century* (Albuquerque: University of New Mexico Press, 1985).

82. This argument dominates the historiography. For examples, see Brading, *Miners and Merchants*, 95–97; Walker, *Spanish Politics*, 13–14; Haring, *Trade and Navigation*,136–45; Kicza, *Colonial Entrepreneurs*, 55, 61; Stein and Stein, *Silver, Trade, and War*, 13–19; Garner and Stefanou, *Economic Growth and Change*, 164–69; Clayton, "Trade and Navigation," 176. Stein and Stein, *Apogee of Empire*.

83. Many scholars have examined the role of the *consulados* in resisting reform of the commercial system, especially during the era of the "Bourbon Reforms." Perhaps the most thorough discussions are two recent books by Stanley J. Stein and Barbara H. Stein. See Stein and Stein, *Silver, Trade, and War*, and *Apogee of Empire*. Other interesting works on this theme include: Vila Vilar, "Poder del Consulado Sevillano," Kuethe, "Fin del Monopolio." Brading, *Miners and Merchants*, discusses commercial reform and the guilds' responses; see especially 114–21.

84. This quotation was selected from Peter Bakewell's authoritative and decidedly economically informed textbook; one could choose a comparable quote from most works on the subject. Bakewell, *History of Latin America*, 208.

85. The *consulado* de Cargadores a Indias and the Casa de Contratación were relocated from Seville to Cadiz by Royal Decree in 1717. This move reflected, in part, the de facto shift of commerce to Cadiz as a result of the increased silting of the bar at San Lucar de Barameda, the mouth of the Guadalquivir River, which prevented the passage of larger vessels. See Allan J. Kuethe, "Traslado del Consulado de Sevilla a Cádiz: Nuevas Perspectivas," in *Relaciones de Poder y Comercio Colonial: Nuevas Perspectivas*, ed. Enriqueta Vila Vilar, Allan J. Kuethe, and Carlos Alvarez Nogal (Madrid: Consejo Superior de Investigaciones Científicas, 1999).

86. García Fuentes, *Comercio Español Con América*, 159.

87. AGI, *Consulados*, legajo 68, folio 933–34, 6 April 1771.

88. A *palmo* was a cubic measure based, as the word suggests, on the number of "palms" (hands) that a cargo measured.

89. Sobre que exponga su dictamen con la posible brevedad, en punto al numero de toneladas a que podrá extenderse el cargamento de la proxima flota teniendo presente las noticias de Nueva España, 13 September 1775, AGI, Mexico, 2985.

90. Haring, *Trade and Navigation*, 214.

91. AGI, *Consulados*, legajo 61a.

92. Stein and Stein, *Apogee of Empire*, 130.

93. Testimonio de la representación hecha por la diputación del comercio de España sobre que por el excelentísimo Señor Virrey de este reyno se informe á S.M. los perjuicios que se infieren á ámbos comercios verificadose la llegada de flota á Veracruz el proximo año de 64, AGI, Mexico, 2503.

94. See García-Baquero González, *Cádiz y el Atlántico*, 2:102.

95. Fernando de Bustillo a Tómas Ruiz de Apodaca, Veracruz, 13 December 1763, AGI, *Consulados*, legajo 405, folios 78, 80–82.

96. One source estimates that the *consulado*'s payments to the Crown in the seventeenth century alone totaled a minimum of twenty-five million pesos. See Vila Vilar, "Poder del Consulado Sevillano," 23; García Fuentes, *Comercio Español Con América*, 109–10.

97. Lamikiz, *Trade and Trust*, 81.

98. García-Baquero González, *Cádiz y el Atlántico*, 161–73.

99. Susan Migden Socolow, "Economic Activities of the Porteño Merchants: The Viceregal Period," *Hispanic American Historical Review* 55, no. 1 (1975): 1. Of course, the Atlantic coast of South America was unimportant to Spain early in the colonial era, Mesoamerica and the Andes monopolizing its focus. But even after the Rio de la Plata region began to develop and become populated, it remained marginalized by mercantile regulations. The arrival of the first register ships in 1721 began a trade that would truly explode only after 1778 and the promulgation of free trade.

100. Quoted in Lamikiz, *Trade and Trust*, 86. Lamikiz points specifically to the trading house's conservativism in granting permits to register ships.

101. See the discussion of the differences between risk and uncertainty in this book's introduction. This distinction was first emphasized in the seminal work of Frank Hyneman Knight, *Risk, Uncertainty and Profit*, Hart, Schaffner & Marx Prize Essays 31 (Boston: Houghton Mifflin, 1921), ch. 5.

102. North, *Institutions*, 12.

103. Several earlier historians recognized the parallels of Spain's regulated trade to the joint stock companies. Haring, *Trade and Navigation*, 137, suggests that "in practice, if not in theory, they resembled the exclusive trading companies of the same period in England and Holland." This point is reiterated by Smith, *Spanish Guild Merchant*, 110.

104. Chaudhuri, *Trading World of Asia*, 37. Chaudhuri refers specifically to the English East India Company, but his point is equally applicable to the others.

Chapter 4

1. Throughout the seventeenth and eighteenth centuries, Spain's economic philosophers proposed reforms to modify the country's commercial system. The best study of these efforts are the three monumental recent works by Stanley Stein and Barbara Stein. See Barbara H. Stein and Stanley J. Stein, *Edge of Crisis: War and Trade in the Spanish Atlantic, 1789–1808* (Baltimore: Johns Hopkins University Press, 2009); Stanley J. Stein and Barbara H. Stein, *Silver, Trade, and War: Spain and America in the Making of Early Modern Europe* (Baltimore: Johns Hopkins University Press, 2000); Stanley J. Stein and Barbara H. Stein, *Apogee of Empire: Spain and New Spain in the Age of Charles III, 1759–1789* (Baltimore: Johns Hopkins University Press, 2003). Analysis of the impact of *comercio libre* has generated a large historiography, much of which is cited in this book. Important works on the subject, but by no means an exhaustive list, include: José Maria Delgado Ribas, "Libre Comercio: Mito y Realidad," in *Mercado y Desarollo Económico en la España Contemporánea*, ed. Tomas Martinez Vara (Madrid: Siglo Veintiuno de España, 1986); Josep M. Delgado Ribas, *Dinámicas Imperiales (1650–1796): España, América y Europa en el Cambio Institucional del Sistema Colonial Español*, Serie General Universitaria 63 (Barcelona: Edicions Bellaterra, 2007); Josep Fontana i Làzaro, *El Comercio Libre Entre España y America Latina: 1765–1824*, 2nd ed., Colección Seminarios y Cursos (Madrid: Fundación Banco Exterior, 1987); Antonio García-Baquero González, *Cádiz y el Atlántico: (1717–1778)*, 2 vols. (Cádiz: Diputación Provincial de Cádiz, 1988); Antonio García-Baquero González, *El Libre Comercio a Examen Gaditano: Crítica y Opinión en el Cádiz Mercantil de Fines del Siglo XVIII* (Cádiz: Universidad de Cádiz Servicio de Publicaciones, 1998); Antonio García-Baquero González, *El Comercio Colonial en la Época del Absolutismo Ilustrado: Problemas y Debates* (Granada: Universidad de Granada, 2003); Xabier Lamikiz, *Trade and Trust in the Eighteenth-Century Atlantic World: Spanish Merchants and Their Overseas Networks*, ed. the Royal Historical Society (Rochester, NY: Boydell and Brewer, 2010); Geoffrey J. Walker, *Spanish Politics and Imperial Trade, 1700–1789* (London: Macmillan, 1979). The actual promulgation is published in Bibiano Torres Ramírez and Javier Ortiz de la Tabla, *Reglamento y Aranceles Reales para el Comercio Libre de España a Indias de 12 de Octubre de 1778* (Seville: Escuela de Estudios

Hispano-Americanos, 1978). For important published primary sources related to the promulgation, see Enrique Florescano and Fernando Castillo, eds., *Controversia Sobre la Libertad de Comercio en Nueva España, 1776–1818*, 2 vols., Serie Fuentes y Estadísticas del Comercio Exterior de México 1 (México: Instituto Mexicano de Comercio Exterior, 1975); García-Baquero González, *Libre Comercio*.

2. A facsimile copy can be consulted online at http://www.archive.org /details/reglamentoyaranc00spai; or see Torres Ramírez and Ortiz de la Tabla, *Reglamento y Aranceles Reales*.

3. On the expansion of slavery in Cuba following the British occupation, see Franklin W. Knight, *Slave Society in Cuba During the Nineteenth Century* (Madison: University of Wisconsin Press, 1977), ch. 1.

4. The Steins point to the Seven Years' War as an immediate catalyst but emphasize that given the decades of discussion about regulated commerce, the ultimate decision "must be seen in long-term perspective." See Stein and Stein, *Apogee of Empire*, 147, 58. Also see John Fisher, *Commercial Relations Between Spain and Spanish America in the Era of Free Trade, 1778–1796* (Liverpool: Center for Latin American Studies, University of Liverpool, 1985), ch. 1; D. A. Brading, *Miners and Merchants in Bourbon Mexico, 1763–1810* (Cambridge: Cambridge University Press, 1971), 114–17.

5. Fisher, *Commercial Relations*, 14–15. The *reglamento* did not explicitly terminate the flota, but, in fact, the final flota returned to Spain in 1778.

6. Lamikiz, *Trade and Trust*, 87.

7. Fisher, *Commercial Relations*, 15, 87.

8. Ibid., 88–89.

9. See data in appendix C2 of Fisher, *Commercial Relations*, 115–16.

10. John H. Coatsworth, "The Mexican Mining Industry in the Eighteenth Century," in *The Economies of Mexico and Peru During the Late Colonial Period, 1760–1810*, ed. Nils Jacobsen and Hans-Jürgen Puhle (Berlin: Colloquium Verlag, 1986), 28. Actually Fisher conducted an additional study of trade during the bellicose era following 1796. See John R. Fisher, *Trade, War and Revolution: Exports from Spain to Spanish America 1797–1820* (Liverpool: Center for Latin American Studies, University of Liverpool, 1992).

11. See silver production graph in Enrique Tandeter, *Coercion and Market: Silver Mining in Colonial Potosí, 1692–1826* (Albuquerque: University of New Mexico Press, 1993), 2.

12. Richard L. Garner and Spiro E. Stefanou, *Economic Growth and Change in Bourbon Mexico* (Gainesville: University Press of Florida, 1993), 159. The quote within the quote comes from Fisher, *Commercial Relations*, 54.

13. The first to challenge Fisher's findings was Delgado Ribas, "Libre Comercio," 81. According to Delgado Ribas, Fisher's data for 1778 is abnormally low, and so it exaggerates the subsequent growth. The most complete discussion of the data's potential distortions as well as a convincing alternative statistical assessment is García-Baquero González, *Comercio Colonial*, 187–216. Garner and Stefanou, *Economic Growth and Change*, 161, further propose the possibility that Fisher's data set is "distorted" by the lack of data from 1779–81 as well as the "relatively low export figures for the years 1778, 1782, and 1783."

14. Delgado Ribas, "Libre Comercio," 81. Also see García-Baquero González, *Comercio Colonial*, 190.

15. Representacion hecha por los Individuos del comercio de España al Excelentísimo Señor Virrey de Nueva España, Xalapa, 24 September 1778, AGI, *Consulados*, legajo 68, folios 651–62. A week later they submitted a similar report to the *consulado*; see Los Individuos de ese comercio residentes en este Pueblo de Xalapa a los Srs. Prior y Consules, 29 September 1778, AGI, *Consulados*, legajo 68.

16. Stein and Stein, *Apogee of Empire*, 153. One needs to be very careful to distinguish between figures for Spanish-American exports and Spanish peninsular imports since the value of the latter is considerably greater than the former due to value added from the transatlantic voyage. While it is unclear whether the 35 million peso figure noted here is its American or Spanish value, Fisher's figure is definitely the higher Spanish import figure. In other words, the mid-century annual figure is at least nearly ten times greater than Fisher's 1778.

17. Garner distinguishes between transfers of bullion made by private merchants and the Crown, a distinction which is ignored here since Fisher's figures are the aggregate of the two. See Garner and Stefanou, *Economic Growth and Change*, 159; and D. A. Brading, review of *Commercial Relations between Spain and Spanish America in the Era of Free Trade, 1778–1796*, by John Fisher, *Journal of Latin American Studies* 19, no. 2 (1987): 419–21.

18. García-Baquero González, *Comercio Colonial*, 195. García-Baquero also cites a document seemingly corroborating his revised figure.

19. Ibid., 204.

20. Ibid., 204–9. His classic study is García-Baquero González, *Cádiz y el Atlántico.*

21. Javier Cuenca-Esteban, "Statistics of Spain's Colonial Trade, 1747–1820: New Estimates and Comparisons with Great Britain," *Revista de Historia Económica/Journal of Iberian and Latin American Economic History* 26, no. 3 (2008): 326–30 and appendices.

312

Notes to Chapter 4

22. García-Baquero González, *Comercio Colonial*, 212–14. Table 4-2 presented here suggests a decline of 18 percent rather than García-Baquero's 16 percent. The difference lies in the methodology employed. García-Baquero added the base year into his calculation of decline. My calculations consider only the years 1782–96. In any event the difference is small.

23. See María Dolores Herrero Gil, "García Baquero Versus Fisher: Las Estadísticas del Puerto de Cádiz en 1778," in *X Reunión Científica de la F.E.H.M* (Santiago de Compostela, 2008).

24. Correspondencia y documentos de don Juan José Puch (1777–1819), Ygnacio Xavier Yanze a Juan José Puch, Cadiz to Montevideo, late 1777, AGI, *Consulados*, legajo 429.

25. Ibid., Ygnacio Xavier Yanze a Juan José Puch, Cadiz, 24 September 1778.

26. Cartas a Francisco Sierra desde España, Europa y América, 1785–88, Francisco de Paula Carballeda a Francisco de Sierra, Veracruz, 31 January 1785, AGI, *Consulados*, legajo 428 (unpaginated), exp. 1785a.

27. Ibid., Sebastian Fernández de Bobadilla a Francisco de Sierra, Veracruz, 1 March 1785 and 1 April 1785, exp. 1785b.

28. Ibid., Francisco de Paula Carballeda a Francisco de Sierra, Veracruz, 31 August 1785 and 3 September 1785, exp. 1785a. The August letter was attached to the September one as a duplicate of an earlier missive.

29. Quoted in Delgado Ribas, *Dinámicas Imperiales*, 464.

30. Expedientes de los cinco gremios mayores de Madrid y sus negociaciones, AGI, Indiferente General, 1623, folios 217–27, 1791.

31. Ibid., folio 481.

32. Cartas a Francisco Sierra desde Espana, Europa y America, 1785–88, Francisco García de Gazetta a Francisco de Sierra, Buenos Aires, 10 January 1786, AGI, *Consulados*, legajo 428, (unpaginated).

33. Ibid., Joaquín Sorauren a Francisco de Sierra, Lima, 5 June 1786.

34. Ibid., Joaquín Sorauren a Francisco de Sierra, Lima, 28 July 1786.

35. Dn. Mathías Hernández al Rey, 1788–91, 21 November 1788 and 23 November 1790, AGI, Indiferente General, 2316.

36. Ibid., Dn. Diego Fernández Ximénez al Rey, 28 September 1790 and January 1791.

37. Dona María Azucar y Mayo al Exceletisimo Sr. Marqués de Sonora, 19 January 1787, AGI, Indiferente General, 2435.

38. Relaciones que forman el Administrador y Contador de esta Real Aduana de Montevideo de la escasez o abundancia de géneros, frutos y efectos de Europa, 18 April 1789, 4 May 1789, 1 July 1789, 1 September 1789, AGI, Indiferente General, 2435.

39. Gaspar de Santa Coloma to Manuel Antonio del Moral, 1 January 1789. Quoted in Susan Migden Socolow, *The Merchants of Buenos Aires, 1778–1810: Family and Commerce,* Cambridge Latin American Studies 30 (Cambridge: Cambridge University Press, 1978), 162.

40. Miguel Jacinto de Marticorena a Juan Vicente de Marticorena, Veracruz, 13 March 1790, AGI, *Consulados,* legajo 433, folios 748–49.

41. Ibid., folios 768–70.

42. Ibid., 14 July 1790, folio 870.

43. Ibid., 31 July 1790, folios 870–71.

44. Nicolás de la Cruz y Bahamonde, *De Cádiz y Su Comercio: Tomo Xiii del Viaje de España, Francia e Italia,* ed. Manuel Ravina Martín (Cádiz: Servicio de Publicaciones, Universidad de Cádiz, 1997), 283–85.

45. Delgado Ribas, *Dinámicas Imperiales,* 466–67.

46. Ibid., 461.

47. Echenique Sánchez and Company to Francisco de Sierra, Amsterdam, 29 April 1784, AGI, *Consulados,* legajo 427 (unpaginated).

48. Ibid., 15 April 1784.

49. Correspondencia General del *consulado, consulado* al Rey, 2 March 1784, AGI, *Consulados,* libro 92 (unpaginated), folio 61.

50. N. W. Posthumus, *Inquiry into the History of Prices in Holland* (Leiden: Brill, 1946), 1:420–23.

51. Thomas Tooke, William Newmarch, and T. E. Gregory, *A History of Prices and of the State of the Circulation from 1792 to 1856* (New York: Adelphi, 1928), 2:400.

52. Echenique Sánchez and Company to Francisco de Sierra, Amsterdam, 13 March 1783 and 4 December 1783, AGI, *Consulados,* legajo 424 (unpaginated).

53. Ibid., 20 May 1784, AGI, *Consulados,* legajo 427 (unpaginated).

54. Ibid., 12 August 1784.

55. Ibid., 13 May 1784.

56. Ibid., 13 December 1784.

57. There has been some pioneering work on the price history of colonial Latin America, although sadly these important efforts were largely abandoned in the 1990s. The best example is Lyman L. Johnson and Enrique Tandeter, *Essays on the Price History of Eighteenth-Century Latin America* (Albuquerque: University of New Mexico Press, 1990). Undoubtedly hoping to rekindle interest, Richard Garner has produced a very useful webpage with downloadable colonial price data at http://www.insidemydesk.com/hdd.html/. Unfortunately, none of the substantial data compiled by Garner is ideally suited for the task at hand.

58. The century-long debates over *comercio libre* are beyond the scope of this book. These debates have been especially well studied in Stein and Stein, *Silver, Trade, and War*; and Stein and Stein, *Apogee of Empire*. Also see the interpretations of these debates in Colin M. MacLachlan, *Spain's Empire in the New World: The Role of Ideas in Institutional and Social Change* (Berkeley: University of California Press, 1988).

59. Report of Cadiz merchant Miguel Rodríguez Carasa. García-Baquero González, *Libre Comercio*, 115. This is a reproduction of AGI, *Consulados*, legajo 73, folios 1–3.

60. These sources have been examined by many historians, among them Brading, *Miners and Merchants*; Garner and Stefanou, *Economic Growth and Change*; Clara Elena Suárez Argüello, "El Parecer de la Élite de Comerciantes del Consulado de la Ciudad de México Ante la Operación del Libre Comercio (1791–1793)," in *Comercio y Poder en América Colonial: los Consulados de Comerciantes, Siglos XVII–XIX*, ed. Bernd and Antonio Ibarra Hausberger (Madrid, Frankfurt am Main, México, D.F.: Iberoamerica, Vervuert Verlag, Instituto Mora, 2003); and Stein and Stein, *Edge of Crisis*. That these sources are important and valuable is further evidenced by the fact that García-Baquero González transcribed and published the Cadiz *informes* of 1787. See García-Baquero González, *Libre Comercio*. Some of the Mexican reports are published in Florescano and Castillo, *Controversia Sobre la Libertad de Comercio*.

61. Quoted in Stein and Stein, *Apogee of Empire*, 63. Hyperbole perhaps, but to some degree this is the argument made by Jeremy Adelman in a recent monograph. Adelman argues that there existed an interdependence between the Crown and the merchant guild in which the former granted trade privileges in exchange for the latter providing the bulk of the state's revenues through taxes and other transfers. See Adelman, *Sovereignty and Revolution in the Iberian Atlantic* (Princeton, NJ: Princeton University Press, 2006), 34–35.

62. Correspondencia General del *consulado, consulado* al Rey, 27 March 1778, AGI, *Consulados*, libro 89, folios 7–14v.

63. García-Baquero González, *Libre Comercio*, The original is deposited in AGI, *Consulados*, legajo 73.

64. García-Baquero González, *Libre Comercio*, 115. This is a reproduction of AGI, *Consulados*, legajo 73, doc. 1.

65. García-Baquero González, *Libre Comercio*, 116–20. Original document is AGI, *Consulados*, legajo 73, doc. 2.

66. García-Baquero González, *Libre Comercio*, 126–29. Copy of original document deposited as AGI, *Consulados*, legajo 73, doc. 5.

67. García-Baquero González, *Libre Comercio*, 121–23. Reproduction of AGI, *Consulados*, legajo 73, doc. 3.

68. García-Baquero González, *Libre Comercio*, 158–64. Original document is AGI, *Consulados*, legajo 73, doc. 11.

69. AGI, *Consulados*, legajo 73, doc. 13, folio 90v–92, 23 November 1787. Reproduced in García-Baquero González, *Libre Comercio*.

70. Carta Reservadas #627, El Conde Revillagigedo hace un difuso informe sobre averiguar si hay decadencia en el comercio de aquellos reynos y en caso de haberla, hallar las causas de ella y sus remedios, 31 August 1793, AGI, Mexico, 1554, folios 1–2. A copy of this document can be consulted at BNM, Manuscritos, ms1398, pp 324–402, 31 August 1793; it is reproduced in Florescano and Castillo, *Controversia Sobre la Libertad de Comercio*, Tomo II, 11–58.

71. John E. Kicza, *Colonial Entrepreneurs, Families and Business in Bourbon Mexico City* (Albuquerque: University of New Mexico Press, 1983), 35; Suárez Argüello, "Parecer de la Élite," 117.

72. Testimonio del expediente sobre averiguar si hay ó no decadencia en el comercio, hallar el remedio de ella en caso de haberla, y proporcionar los auxilios mas convenientes para fomento del trafico mercantil en este ramo, Informe de Ysidro Ycaza, 4 July 1791, AGI, Mexico 1554, folios 23–29.

73. Ibid., Informe de Gaspar Martín Vicario, 25 June 1791, AGI, Mexico 1554, folios 5–17. At about the same time as his report, Gaspar Martín Vicario was involved in a disastrous investment in the Vetagrande silver mine in Zacatecas in which he lost close to ninety thousand pesos. See Brading, *Miners and Merchants*, 205.

74. Testimonio del expediente sobre averiguar si hay ó no decadencia en el comercio, hallar el remedio de ella en caso de haberla, y proporcionar los auxilios mas convenientes para fomento del trafico mercantil en este ramo, Informe de Lorenzo de Angulo Guardamino, AGI, Mexico 1554, folios 42–48.

75. On the Cinco Gremios de Madrid, see J. Pinto Rodriguez, "Los Cinco Gremios Mayores de Madrid y el Comercio en el Siglo XVIII," *Revista de Indias* 192 (1991): 292–326.

76. Testimonio del expediente sobre averiguar si hay ó no decadencia en el comercio, hallar el remedio de ella en caso de haberla, y proporcionar los auxilios mas convenientes para fomento del trafico mercantil en este ramo, Informe de Manuel García Herreros, 8 July 1791, AGI, Mexico 1554, folios 33–43.

77. Ibid., Informe de Diego de Agreda, 12 July 1791, AGI, Mexico 1554, folios 48–56.

78. Ibid., Informe de Fernando de Meoqui, 14 July 1791, AGI, Mexico 1554, folios 56–60.

79. Ibid., Informe de Antonio Bassoco, 22 July 1791, AGI, Mexico, 1554, folios 60–65. Brading, *Miners and Merchants*, 126, consulted in Mexico a different copy of Bassoco's response to the Viceroy, AGI, *Consulados*, legajo 123.

80. As an example of the commercially detrimental tax structure, Yraeta referred to a new practice of demanding that merchants pay an 8 percent *alcabala* (sales tax) upon the furnishing of goods on credit to *viandantes*, traveling peddlers, rather than paying this tax only after the *viandantes* sold the merchandise.

81. Testimonio del expediente sobre averiguar si hay ó no decadencia en el comercio, hallar el remedio de ella en caso de haberla, y proporcionar los auxilios mas convenientes para fomento del trafico mercantil en este ramo, Informe de Francisco Ignacio de Yraeta, 1 July 1791, AGI, Mexico 1554, folios 17–23.

82. Delgado Ribas, *Dinámicas Imperiales*, 477.

83. Javier Ortiz de la Tabla Ducasse, *Comercio Exterior de Veracruz, 1778–1821: Crisis de Dependencia* (Sevilla: Escuela de Estudios Hispano-Americanos, 1978), 9–10.

84. El Conde Revillagigedo hace un difuso informe sobre averiguar si hay decadencia en el comercio de aquellos reynos y en caso de haberla, hallar las causas de ella y sus remedios, 31 August 1793, AGI, Mexico, 1554, Carta Reservadas #627, folios 1–2. The same manuscript can be consulted at BNM, Manuscritos, ms1398, 324–402, 31 August 1793; it has been reproduced several times including Florescano and Castillo, *Controversia Sobre la Libertad de Comercio*, Tomo II, 11–58.

85. AGI, México El Conde Revillagigedo hace un difuso informe sobre averiguar si hay decadencia en el comercio de aquellos reynos y en caso de haberla, hallar las causas de ella y sus remedios, 31 August 1793, AGI, Mexico, 1554, Carta Reservadas #627, folios 2–3.

86. Ibid.

87. Ibid.

88. Adelman, *Sovereignty and Revolution*, 40.

89. Ibid., 39.

90. Don Juan Gálvez Diputado del Comercio Marítimo de la Ciudad de Malaga suplica a V.M., 29 March 1768, AGI, Indiferente General, 2410, folios 3v–4v.

91. Oliver E. Williamson, *The Economic Institutions of Capitalism: Firms, Markets, Relational Contracting* (New York: Free Press, 1985). Douglass North

pioneered the use of institutions to explain economic history. See his classic, Douglass Cecil North, *Institutions, Institutional Change, and Economic Performance*, Political Economy of Institutions and Decisions (Cambridge: Cambridge University Press, 1990).

92. Lamikiz, *Trade and Trust*, 181.

93. Correspondencia y documentos de don Juan José Puch (1777–1819), Pedro Gil de Texada to Juan José Puch, 27 February 1798, AGI, *Consulados*, legajo 429 (letter is unsigned).

94. Stein and Stein, *Apogee of Empire*, 194.

95. Cited in Ibid., 221n150.

96. Delgado Ribas, *Dinámicas Imperiales*, 467–68.

97. Patricia H. Marks, *Deconstructing Legitimacy: Viceroys, Merchants, and the Military in Late Colonial Peru* (University Park: Pennsylvania State University Press, 2007), 100.

98. Juan Miguel de Marticorena a Juan Vicente de Marticorea, Lima, 30 August 1789, AGI, *Consulados*, legajo 433, folio 491.

99. Marks, *Deconstructing Legitimacy*, 100–103. Also see Patricia H. Marks, "Confronting a Mercantile Elite: Bourbon Reformers and the Merchants of Lima, 1765–1796," *The Americas* 60, no. 4 (2004), 537.

100. Gaspar de Santa Coloma to Bernardo Sancho Larrea, 18 May 1790. Quoted in Socolow, *Merchants of Buenos Aires*, 155.

101. Socolow, *Merchants of Buenos Aires*, 158.

102. In accordance with the Law of Indies, bankruptcies sustained by *consulado* merchants or their factors had to be adjudicated by the *consulado* tribunals. In June 1780, the *consulado* reminded the king of this requirement and urged the Crown to expressly forbid any attempts by interested parties to seek the intercession of other tribunals or settle their accounts in the offices of private lawyers. See AGI, *Consulados*, libro 90, folios 125–27, 13 June 1780.

103. On the origin and function of the Spanish *consulados*, consult Robert S. Smith, *The Spanish Guild Merchant: A History of the Consulado, 1250–1700* (New York: Octagon Books, 1972), esp. ch. 1. According to Haring, in 1543 the *consulado* took over from the *Casa de Contratación* responsibility for overseeing bankruptcy proceedings. Clarence Henry Haring, *Trade and Navigation Between Spain and the Indies in the Time of the Hapsburgs* (Cambridge: Cambridge University Press, 1918), 43–44.

104. Sebastian Pérez a Francisco de Sierra, Veracruz, 26 August 1782, AGI, *Consulados*, legajo 423 (unpaginated).

105. Correspondencia general del *consulado*, Al Rey Nuestro Señor por mano del exmo. Sr. D. Antonio Valdes de Juan Francisco de Vea Murguía,

Ruperto López García, y Francisco Ángel y Laraviera, AGI, *Consulados*, libro 93, folios 258–259v.

106. Sobre la quiebra de Don Domingo Labady, 15 March 1791 and 14 June 1791, AGI, Indiferente General, 2316.

107. Lic. D. Francisco Xavier Peñaranda y Castañeda, "Informe Jurídico por Don Maríano Bernabe de Frías, Vecino de Cadiz, Comerciante Matriculado en la Universidad de Cargadores a Indias, en los Autos de Su Inculpable Atraso," Publicado por Don Blas Roman, Impressor de la Real Academia de Derecho Español y Público, 16 April 1790, deposited in Sobre la quiebra de Dn. Maríano Bernabe de Frías del comercio de Cadiz, 1787–91, AGI, Indiferente General, 2316.

108. Correspondencia general del *consulado*, El *consulado* de la ciudad de Cadiz al Rey sobre la quiebra de Dn. Maríano Bernabe de Frías, Yndividuo de la carrera a indias, 23 March 1787, AGI, *Consulados*, libro 93, folios 277v–284. Stein and Stein, whose reference directed me to this document, seem to agree with the creditors claiming that "now [the *consulado*] stood publicly accused of gross negligence in handling the illegal actions of a prominent Gaditano shipper and *consulado* member with manifest partiality." Stein and Stein, *Apogee of Empire*, 195.

109. A few of the 159 were second *concursos* for the same individual, perhaps to complete unfinished business or to alter the original agreement. These are ignored since there are just a few.

110. Notas y apuntes en borrador y jusificantes de los interesados en varias quiebras, 1787–91, AGI, *Consulados*, legajo 522, exp. 9, folios 897–1130.

111. Ibid., folio 916. The junta held for the Conde de Repáraz predated all of others in the document by more than a year. As a consequence, it was left off of Figure 4.3.

112. Antonio-Miguel Bernal, *La Financiación de la Carrera de Indias (1492–1824): Dinero y Crédito en el Comercio Colonial Español Con América* (Sevilla: Fundación el Monte, 1992), 454–56, explains the commercial origins of the prominent Uztáriz family.

113. Hananel Jacob Mendes da Costa a Francisco de Sierra, London, 20 June 1786, AGI, *Consulados*, legajo 428 (unpaginated).

114. Notas y apuntes en borrador y jusificantes de los interesados en varias quiebras, AGI, *Consulados*, legajo 522, exp. 9, folio 922. Sierra's private records are deposited at the AGI. See Cartas a Francisco de Sierra desde España, Europa y America, AGI, *Consulados*, legajos 420–28. Also see Libro de cartas del dueño del navío el Jasón a particulares, desde Veracruz, Cadiz, Buenos Aires, etc. (1772–76), AGI, *Consulados*, libro 157.

115. In a number of cases it was impossible to know whether, for example, the bankrupted Juan Martínez was one of the several *consulado* merchants with the same name, in which case it was simply excluded from the list provided in Table 4.3. Even for those included in the table, it is possible that the bankrupted person is not the same as the guild member with an identical name. The spelling of names was anything but consistent in the era.

116. *Notas y apuntes en borrador y jusificantes de los interesados en varias quiebras*, AGI, *Consulados*, legajo 522, exp. 9, folio 1026. The date of Jardin's proceedings was not listed.

117. Ibid., folios 926 and 945.

118. Ibid., folio 1062.

119. Ibid., folio 954.

120. Ibid., folio 986.

121. *Lista de los concursos que ha havido ante el tribunal de comercio desde el año de 1808*, Cadiz, 5 April 1816, AGI, *Consulados*, legajo 522, folio 1131.

122. Bernal, *Financiación de la Carrera de Indias*, 466.

123. Cruz y Bahamonde, *De Cádiz y Su Comercio*, 283–85.

124. *Correspondencia general del consulado*, Suplemento a este coPíador, Cadiz, 9 December 1786, dictamen de Lic. Don Juan de Mora y Morales, AGI, *Consulados*, libro 93, folios 265–72.

125. *Correspondencia general del consulado*, Cadiz, 31 March 1789, Francisco del Valle, Juan Francisco de Vea Murguía y Ruperto López García al Rey Nuestro Señor, AGI, *Consulados*, libro 93, folios 228–230.

126. Delgado Ribas, *Dinámicas Imperiales*, 468–69.

127. AGI, México *El Conde Revillagigedo hace un difuso informe sobre averiguar si hay decadencia en el comercio de aquellos reynos y en caso de haberla, hallar las causas de ella y sus remedios*, 31 August 1793, AGI, México, 1554, Carta Reservadas #627, folios 2–3.

128. See García-Baquero González, *Comercio Colonial*; Fisher, *Commercial Relations*; Cuenca-Esteban, "Statistics of Spain's Colonial Trade,"; Herrero Gil, "García Baquero Versus Fisher,"

129. In the past several decades, historians have examined the impact of Spain's colonial taxation policies. Without exception, they have noted the rise in tax collection as a result of late century Bourbon policies, although the growing fiscal receipts were not primarily taxes on international commerce. The starting point for examinations of Spanish American public finance is the work of John TePaske and Herbert Klein who, along with a team of archivists, assembled in the 1970s and 1980s a monumental

collection of colonial treasury records. The raw data is published in John TePaske and Herbert Klein, *Ingresos y Egresos de la Real Hacienda de Nueva España*, 2 vols. (Mexico City: Instituto Naciónal de Antropología e Historia, 1986), and John Jay TePaske et al., *The Royal Treasuries of the Spanish Empire in America*, 4 vols. (Durham, NC: Duke University Press, 1982, 1990). Compilation of this data spawned a number of studies, many by Klein and TePaske themselves. For examples, see Herbert S. Klein, *The American Finances of the Spanish Empire: Royal Income and Expenditures in Colonial Mexico, Peru, and Bolivia, 1680–1809* (Albuquerque: University of New Mexico Press, 1998); Herbert Klein, "Origin and Volume of Remission of Royal Tax Revenues from the Viceroyalties of Peru and New Spain," in *Dinero, Moneda y Crédito en la Monarquía Hispánica*, ed. Antonio-Miguel Bernal (Madrid: Marcial Pons, 2000); Jacques Barbier and Herbert Klein, "Recent Trends in the Study of Spanish American Colonial Public Finance," *Latin American Research Review* 23, no. 1 (1988): 35–62; John TePaske, "General Tendencies and Secular Trends in the Economies of Mexico and Peru, 1750–1810: The View from the Cajas of Mexico and Lima," in *The Economies of Mexico and Peru During the Late Colonial Period, 1760–1810*, ed. Nils Jacobsen and Hans-Jürgen Puhle (Berlin: Colloquium Verlag, 1986). Several other studies that examine colonial taxation are Kenneth J. Andrien, *The Kingdom of Quito, 1690–1830: The State and Regional Development*, Cambridge Latin American Studies 80 (Cambridge: Cambridge University Press, 1995), 195–210; and especially Carlos Marichal, *Bankruptcy of Empire: Mexican Silver and the Wars between Spain, Britain, and France, 1760–1810*, Cambridge Latin American Studies 91 (New York: Cambridge University Press, 2007).

130. Stein and Stein, *Apogee of Empire*, 204–9.

131. D. A. Brading, "Bourbon Spain and Its American Empire," in *The Cambridge History of Latin America*, ed. Leslie Bethell (Cambridge: Cambridge University Press, 1984), 413–14, oddly refers to this interwar period as a "golden age," even while simultaneously noting that "throughout the empire prices tumbled and profits dwindled as markets were saturated with imports. Many merchants went bankrupt and others cut their losses by withdrawing from transatlantic trade."

Chapter 5

1. AGI, *Consulados*, 61a, sobre el comercio libre con América, anonymous and undated.

2. Marichal is somewhat ambivalent on whether the tax system should be considered regressive. Carlos Marichal, *Bankruptcy of Empire: Mexican*

Silver and the Wars between Spain, Britain, and France, 1760–1810, Cambridge Latin American Studies 91 (New York: Cambridge University Press, 2007),14, 54–55, 74–75.

3. On the *repartimiento de comercio* in Mexico see Brian R. Hamnett, *Politics and Trade in Southern Mexico, 1750–1821* (Cambridge: Cambridge University Press, 1971); Arij Ouweneel, *Shadows over Anáhuac: An Ecological Interpretation of Crisis and Development in Central Mexico, 1730–1800* (Albuquerque: University of New Mexico Press, 1996); Marcello Carmagnani, *El Regreso de los Dioses: el Proceso de Reconstitución de la Identidad Étnica en Oaxaca, Siglos XVII y XVIII*, Sección de Obras de Historia (México: Fondo del Cultura Económica, 1988); and Jeremy Baskes, *Indians, Merchants, and Markets: A Reinterpretation of the Repartimiento and Spanish-Indian Economic Relations in Colonial Oaxaca, 1750–1821* (Stanford, CA: Stanford University Press, 2000).

4. El Conde Revillagigedo hace un difuso informe sobre averiguar si hay decadencia en el comercio de aquellos reynos y en caso de haberla, hallar las causas de ella y sus remedios, 31 August 1793, AGI, Mexico, 1554, Carta Reservadas #627. The viceroy's lengthy analysis appears in folios 14–55. The quote comes from folios 28–30.

5. European imports consisted overwhelmingly of luxury goods consumed by a small fraction of Mexico's population. Mexico's indigenous majority had limited need for most items imported from Spain, producing directly the bulk of its subsistence. Certainly European textiles, the leading import, enjoyed scant demand among Mexico's Indian population. Even if such goods were coveted, most Indians could not have purchased them unless provided with credit.

6. Marie Francois, "Cloth and Silver: Pawning and Material Life in Mexico City at the Turn of the Nineteenth Century," *The Americas* 60, no. 3 (2004): 325–27. See also Marie Francois, *A Culture of Everyday Credit: Housekeeping, Pawnbroking, and Governance in Mexico City, 1750–1920* (Lincoln: University of Nebraska Press, 2006), ch. 1.

7. Jane Mangan found that even elites in silver-rich Potosí sometimes resorted to pawning items to permit consumption. Jane E. Mangan, *Trading Roles: Gender, Ethnicity, and the Urban Economy in Colonial Potosí*, Latin America Otherwise (Durham, NC: Duke University Press, 2005), 120.

8. D. A. Brading, *Miners and Merchants in Bourbon Mexico, 1763–1810* (Cambridge: Cambridge University Press, 1971), 100.

9. Stanley J. Stein and Barbara H. Stein, *Apogee of Empire: Spain and New Spain in the Age of Charles III, 1759–1789* (Baltimore: Johns Hopkins University Press, 2003), 15–16.

10. On the use of *libranza*, see Jacques A. Barbier, "Venezuelan 'Libran-zas,' 1788–1807: From Economic Nostrum to Fiscal Imperative," *The Americas* 37, no. 4 (1981); and Pedro Pérez Herrero, *Plata y Libranzas: la Articulación Comercial del México Borbónico / Pedro Pérez Herrero* (México: Centro de Estudios Históricos, Colegio de México, 1988).

11. The example described is quite simple. In reality, however, the pro-cess could become far more complex. Mendes da Costa might pay Sierra's libranza by drawing a libranza against yet another party with which the commercial house had credit, and the latter party might do the same. The result was a credit network that encompassed numerous parties, likely crossing imperial borders as well. Ideally, this system allowed all parties the greatest liquidity, but it did entail risks. If any party were to go bank-rupt, there resulted a potential domino effect that would reach many merchants, including some who were only distantly connected to the insolvent party.

12. Hananel and Jacob Mendes da Costa and Company to Francisco de Sierra, London, 23 March 1784, AGI, *Consulados*, legajo 427 (unpaginated).

13. Ibid.

14. Several works have examined the sea loan in Spanish commerce. See Antonio-Miguel Bernal, *La Financiación de la Carrera de Indias (1492–1824): Dinero y Crédito en el Comercio Colonial Español Con América* (Sevilla: Fundación el Monte, 1992); and Oscar Cruz Barney, *El Riesgo en el Com-ercio de Hispano-Indiano: Préstamos y Seguros Maritimos Durante los Siglos XVI a XIX* (Mexico City: UNAM, 1998). For non-Spanish areas see Meir Kohn, *The Origins of Western Economic Success: Commerce, Finance, and Gov-ernment in Preindustrial Europe* (Working papers, Department of Economics, Dartmouth College, Hanover, NH, 2001), http://www.dartmouth.edu /~mkohn/, ch. 12; and Florence Edler de Roover, "Early Examples of Marine Insurance," *Journal of Economic History* 5, no. 2 (1945): 172–200. Thousands of these contracts survive in the Archive of the Indies. See, for example, AGI, *Consulados*, libros 409–44, and AGI, *Consulados*, legajos 876–87. For an eighteenth-century discussion of the legal obligations of both parties in these *préstamos*, see José María Quirós, *Guía de Negociantes: Compendio de la Legislación Mercantil de España e Indias*, ed. Pedro Pérez Herrero (México: Universidad Nacional Autonoma de México, 1986), 304–8. The characteristics of these contracts are also spelled out in Uni-versidad y Casa de Contratación de la M.N. y M.L. Villa de Bilbao. *Or-denanzas de la Ilustre Universidad y Casa de Contratacion de la M. N. y M. L. Villa de Bilbao Aprobadas, y Confirmadas por el Rey Nuestro Señor Don Phelipe Quinto (Que Dios Guarde) Año de 1737*. Madrid :: Viuda de D. M. Fernan-

dez, 1769, ch. 23, 212–22. Originally published in 1737, these trade ordinances were reprinted at several later dates. For a 1775 facsimile, consulted here, see http://books.google.com/books?id=k7pDAAAAcAAJ &printsec=frontcover&source=gbs_ge_summary_r&cad=0#v=onepage &q&f=false.

15. Bernal, *Financiación de la Carrera de Indias*, 420–24; M. Guadalupe Carrasco González, "El Negocio de los Seguros Marítimos en Cádiz a Finales del Siglo XVIII," *Hispania, Revista Española de Historia* Vol. 59:, no. 201 (1999): 298.

16. Figures extracted from Bernal, *Financiación de la Carrera de Indias*, appendix 4, 592–651.

17. This is the central argument of John E. Kicza, "Consumption and Control: The Mexico City Business Community and Commodity Marketing in the Eighteenth Century," *Estudios de Historia Novohispana* 12 (1992): 159–69.

18. Baskes, *Indians, Merchants, and Markets*, esp. ch. 2.

19. Kicza, "Consumption and Control," 162, 167–68.

20. Susan Deans-Smith, *Bureaucrats, Planters, and Workers: The Making of the Tobacco Monopoly in Bourbon Mexico* (Austin: University of Texas Press, 1992), 124–34.

21. Brading, *Miners and Merchants*, 149–52.

22. Richmond F. Brown, "Profits, Prestige, and Persistence: Juan Fermín de Aycinena and the Spirit of Enterprise in the Kingdom of Guatemala," *Hispanic American Historical Review* 75, no. 3 (1995): 414, 419–21.

23. Testimonio del expediente sobre averiguar si hay ó no decadencia en el comercio, hallar el remedio de ella en caso de haberla, y proporcionar los auxilios mas convenientes para fomento del trafico mercantil en este ramo, Informe de Fernando de Meoqui, 14 July 1791, AGI, Mexico, 1554, folios 56–60.

24. John E. Kicza, *Colonial Entrepreneurs, Families and Business in Bourbon Mexico City* (Albuquerque: University of New Mexico Press, 1983), esp, ch. 4; Brading, *Miners and Merchants*, 97–99; P. J. Bakewell, *Silver Mining and Society in Colonial Mexico: Zacatecas, 1546–1700*, Cambridge Latin American Studies 15 (1971; repr., Cambridge: Cambridge University Press, 2002), 110–15; Eric Van Young, *Hacienda and Market in Eighteenth-Century Mexico: The Rural Economy of the Guadalajara Region, 1675–1820* (Berkeley: University of California Press, 1981), 144–45; Enrique Florescano, "The Hacienda in New Spain," in *Colonial Spanish America*, ed. Leslie Bethell, Cambridge History of Latin America (New York: Cambridge University Press, 1987), 275–81.

25. Stanley J. Stein, "Tending the Store: Trade and Silver at the Real de Huatla, 1778–1781," *Hispanic American Historical Review* 77, no. 3 (1997): 384.

26. Jorge Silva Riquer, *La Estructura y Dinámica del Comercio Menudo en la Ciudad de Valladolid, Michoacán a Finales del Siglo XVIII* (Mexico City: INAH, 2007), 102–4.

27. Susan Migden Socolow, *The Merchants of Buenos Aires, 1778–1810: Family and Commerce*, Cambridge Latin American Studies 30 (Cambridge: Cambridge University Press, 1978), 14, 58.

28. Stein, "Tending the Store," 381.

29. Kicza, *Colonial Entrepreneurs*, 96–97.

30. On the *repartimiento* in Mexico see Baskes, *Indians, Merchants, and Markets*; Hamnett, *Politics and Trade*; Carmagnani, *Regreso de los Dioses*; Ouweneel, *Shadows over Anáhuac*.

31. Compañía establecida por el manejo de repartimientos por D. Ildefonso Ma. Sánchez Solache, electo A.M. de la jurisdiccion de Chicicapa y Zimatlan, y D. Manuel Ramón de Goya del comercio de México, BNM, ms58, 147–49.

32. R. Douglas Cope, *The Limits of Racial Domination: Plebeian Society in Colonial Mexico City, 1660–1720* (Madison: University of Wisconsin Press, 1994), 112–18.

33. Mangan, *Trading Roles*, ch. 4.

34. Kicza, *Colonial Entrepreneurs*, 55.

35. Brown, "Profits, Prestige, and Persistence," 417.

36. See "carta para Señor don José Fernández Gil a Guatemala," México, 2 December 1778 in Maria Cristina Torales Pacheco, ed., *La Compañia de Comercio de Francisco Ignacio de Yraeta (1767–1797)* (México: Instituto Mexicano de Comercio Exterior con la colaboraciâon de la Universidad Iberoamericana, 1985), 2:222.

37. Louisa Schell Hoberman, *Mexico's Merchant Elite, 1590–1660: Silver, State, and Society* (Durham, NC: Duke University Press, 1991), 54.

38. Ibid., 58–59.

39. Brown, "Profits, Prestige, and Persistence," 415, figures derived from tables 2 and 3.

40. For a recent treatment of the importance of reputation to merchants in the Spanish world, see Xabier Lamikiz, "Un 'Cuento Ruidoso': Confidencialidad, Reputación, y Confianza en el Comercio del Siglo XVIII," *Obradoiro de Historia Moderna* 16 (2007): 115–24. More generally see, Nuala Zahedieh, "Credit, Risk and Reputation in Late Seventeenth-Century Colonial Trade," in *Merchant Organization and Maritime Trade in the North*

Atlantic, 1660–1815, ed. Olaf Uwe Janzen (St. John's, Newfoundland: International Maritime Economic History Association, 1998), 53–74; Peter Mathias, "Risk, Credit, and Kinship in Early Modern Enterprise," in *The Early Modern Atlantic Economy*, ed. John J. and Kenneth Morgan McCusker (Cambridge: Cambridge University Press, 2000). According to Clé Lesger, "The 'Visible Hand': Views on Entrepreneurs and Entrepreneurship in Holland, 1580–1850," in *Small Business Entrepreneurs in Asia and Europe: Towards a Comparative Perspective*, ed. Mario Rutten and Carol Upadhya (Thousand Oaks, CA: Sage, 1997), 270, there was an "almost obsessive preocccupation with reputation in early modern society."

41. Jeremy Adelman, *Sovereignty and Revolution in the Iberian Atlantic* (Princeton, NJ: Princeton University Press, 2006), 81.

42. Quaderno de Representaciones echas en Jalapa por los comerciantes de España al excelentísimo Sr. Virrey el Baylio Don Antonio María Bucareli y Ursua desde 13 November 1773 to 20 January 1774, AGI, *Consulados*, legajo 68, folio 632v.

43. Compañía de comercio establecida en esta plaza entre Don Pedro Antonio de Aguirre, y Don Joséf y Don Juan Bautista de Vea Murguía bajo la denominacion de Aguirre y Vea Murguía Hijos, por tiempo de cinco anos, 7 January 1803, AGI, *Consulados*, legajo 78, doc. #85.

44. Pedro Mártir Coll y Alsina, *Tratado Elemental Teorico y Práctico de Comercio: en Que Se Presentan Varias Formulas de Contratas de Fletamentos, Conocimientos, Pólizas de Seguros . . . Que para Gobierno de Un Hijo Suyo Joven Comerciante Compusó, y Ha Corregido y Aumentado en Esta Edición, Pedro Martir Coll, y Alsina* (Barcelona: M. y T. Gaspar, 1818), 167, available online at: http://books.google.com.mx/books?id=2dXB2D0aiu8C&printsec=frontcover&source=gbs_ge_summary_r&cad=0#v=onepage&q&f=false.

45. Juan Vicente de Martricorena a José Gabriel Arozarena, Cadiz, 5 November 1802, AGI, *Consulados*, legajo 438, folio 716.

46. On honor in colonial Latin America, see Lyman L. Johnson and Sonya Lipsett-Rivera, *The Faces of Honor: Sex, Shame, and Violence in Colonial Latin America* (Albuquerque: University of New Mexico Press, 1998). While none of the essays in this book directly addresses honor and credit, the introduction mentions the connection in passing. The authors suggest that honor and credit were more closely associated among plebians who "did not enjoy the reputational insulation provided by great wealth" (11). This seems logical, but there is no question that wealthy merchants imagined that their wealth and creditworthiness reflected strongly on their claims to honor.

47. Pedro Fermín de Córdoba a Juan Vizente de Marticorena, Cadiz, 28 September 1798, AGI, *Consulados*, legajo 437, folio 566.

48. Antonio Manuel de Oviedo a Juan Vicente de Marticorena, Sevilla, 6 October 1798, AGI, *Consulados*, legajo 437, folio 583. It is not entirely clear when the Casa de Viuda de Oviedo, Hermano e Hijos declared bankruptcy. In July 1798, Antonio Oviedo, the firm's director, advised Juan Vicente that the firm had been granted a "paso" from the *consulado* "so as not be inconvenienced by our creditors," but Oviedo assured Juan Vicente that this was not to be seen as a declaration of bankruptcy. Antonio Oviedo de la casa Viuda de Oviedo, Hermano e hijos a Juan Vicente de Marticorena, 25 July 1798, AGI, *Consulados*, legajo 437, folio 441. Antonio-Miguel Bernal and Antonio García-Baquero González, *Tres Siglos del Comercio Sevillano, 1598–1860: Cuestiones y Problemas* (Sevilla: Camara Oficial de Comercio Industria y Navegación de Sevilla, 1976), 153, 252, make reference to the firm's bankruptcy but the authors are uncertain of the year, suggesting 1800 but surrounding the date with question marks (i.e., ¿1800?).

49. AGI, *Consulados*, legajo 73, Doc. 12, 23 November 1787, folio 72. This report is reproduced in Antonio García-Baquero González, *El Libre Comercio a Examen Gaditano: Crítica y Opinión en el Cádiz Mercantil de Fines del Siglo XVIII* (Cádiz: Universidad de Cádiz Servicio de Publicaciones, 1998), doc. 12.

50. Sobre la quiebra de Dn. Maríano Bernabe de Frías del comercio de Cadiz, 1787–91, Frías al Rey, 6 April 1791, AGI, Indiferente General, 2316.

51. Mateo Bernal al Rey, 14 December 1789, AGI, Indiferente General, 2314.

52. Sobre la quiebra de Dn. Maríano Bernabe de Frías del comercio de Cadiz, 1787–91. Lic. D. Francisco Xavier Peñaranda y Castañeda, "Informe Jurídico por Don Maríano Bernabe de Frías, Vecino de Cadiz, Comerciante Matriculado en la Universidad de Cargadores a Indias, en los Autos de Su Inculpable Atraso," Publicado por Don Blas Roman, Impressor de la Real Academia de Derecho Español y Público, 16 April 1790, AGI, Indiferente General, 2316, folio 7.

53. Correspondencia y documentos de don Juan José Puch (1777–1819), copy of letter attached to another dated 1 August 1778, AGI, *Consulados*, legajo 429.

54. Hananel and Jacob Mendes da Costa and Company to Francisco de Sierra, London, 8 February 1785, AGI, *Consulados*, legajo 428 (unpaginated).

55. Ibid., 8 March 1785 (unpaginated).
56. Ibid., 5 April 1785 (unpaginated).
57. Ibid., 8 April 1785 (unpaginated).
58. Ibid., 29 April 1785 (unpaginated).
59. Ibid., 2 December 1785 (unpaginated).
60. Ibid., 20 June 1786 (unpaginated).
61. The important role of the *consulado* in maintaining trust in the marketplace is stressed by Lamikiz, "Un 'Cuento Ruidoso,'" 8–9.
62. Correspondencia general del *consulado*, Francisco del Valle, Juan Francisco de Vea Murguía y Ruperto López García al Rey Nuestro Señor, Cadiz, 31 March 1789, AGI, *Consulados*, libro 93, folios 228–30.
63. Pedro Fermín de Córdoba a Juan Vicente de Marticorena, Cadiz, 1 January 1798, AGI, *Consulados*, legajo 437, folios 1–2.
64. Ibid., San Sebastian, 21 December 1798, folio 723.
65. For the Anglo-American Transatlantic trade, this point is made by Sheryllynne Haggerty, *The British-Atlantic Trading Community,1760–1810: Men, Women, and the Distribution of Goods* (Leiden: Brill, 2006), 213.
66. "Carta para Señor don José Fernández Gil a Guatemala," México, 2 December 1778, in Torales Pacheco, *Compañia de Comercio*, 2:221–22. The comparative advantage enjoyed by wealthier merchants was, of course, universal within Atlantic world trade. In the early eighteenth century, British trader Stephen Girard boasted to the London comercial empire of Baring Brothers that "my comercial capital enables me to sell my goods on credit, and to carry on my maritime business throughout, cash in Hand, without the aid of discount." His point was that he commanded capital sufficient to engage in business deals that poorer merchants could not. See Norman Sydney Buck, *The Development of the Organisation of Anglo-American Trade, 1800–1850* (New Haven, CT: Yale University Press, 1925), 115.
67. The practice of selling goods on credit at inflated prices rather than charging interest explicitly was designed to avoid charges of usury. Catholic doctrine limited interest rates to 5 percent, often well below the actual cost of obtaining credit. For a discussion of merchants' pricing merchandise so as to avoid accusations of usury, see Baskes, *Indians, Merchants, and Markets*, 74–75.
68. Long-distance commerce in the early modern era moved slowly. Business deals took a long time to be completed. This characteristic was universal in the Atlantic world; it was by no means unique to the Spanish imperial trade system. Much of the delay stemmed from the need to finance transactions. In 1808 the British parliament collected testimonies

328 Notes to Chapter 5

from merchants to improve its understanding of the inner workings of long-distance commerce. Asked about the "average period for which credit is given" in the American trade, one merchant, a Mr. Wood, explained that "my house does not receive its remittances from America, on the average, at less than eighteen months." He added that his house might have been more forgiving than most but that the average overall for such commerce was fifteen months. See Buck, *Development of the Organisation*, 114.

69. Compañía de comercio establecida en esta plaza entre Don Pedro Antonio de Aguirre, y Don Joséf y Don Juan Bautista de Vea Murguía bajo la denominacion de Aguirre y Vea Murguía Hijos, por tiempo de cinco anos, 7 January 1803, AGI, *Consulados*, legajo 78, doc. #85.

70. On the feria de Jalapa see José Joaquín Real Díaz, *Las Ferias de Jalapa* (Sevilla: Escuela de Estudios Hispano-americanos, 1959). On the Portobello, Panama, fair that supplied the viceroyalty of Peru until replaced in the 1730s by direct voyages through the straits of Magellan, see George Robertson Dilg, "The Collapse of the Portobello Fairs: A Study in Spanish Commercial Reform, 1720–1740" (PhD diss., Indiana University, 1975).

71. Borrador de cartas de Villa Alta, 1776–77, BNM, ms84 [1553], folio 123.

72. Brading, *Miners and Merchants*, 270–71.

73. Testimonio del expediente sobre averiguar si hay ó no decadencia en el comercio, hallar el remedio de ella en caso de haberla, y proporcionar los auxilios mas convenientes para fomento del trafico mercantil en este ramo, Informe de Gaspar Martín Vicario, 25 June 1791, AGI, Mexico, 1554, folios 5–17.

74. Richard L. Garner and Spiro E. Stefanou, *Economic Growth and Change in Bourbon Mexico* (Gainesville: University Press of Florida, 1993), 169.

75. Christopher Ward, *Imperial Panama: Commerce and Conflict in Isthmian America, 1550–1800* (Albuquerque: University of New Mexico Press, 1993), 81.

76. Brading, *Miners and Merchants*, 97.

77. José María Quirós, member and secretary of the Veracruz *consulado*, noted that sea loans were made "under the condition that upon arriving to the port of the destination the lenders are freed of any risk and [have] the option to collect the principal and interest at the stipulated times." Quirós, *Guía de Negociantes*, 304. Most often this term was brief, perhaps just twenty-four hours after items were disembarked. Cruz Barney, *Riesgo en el Comercio de Hispano-Indiano*, 34. The loans sometimes gave the borrower a

bit lengthier period following safe arrival to liquidate his cargo. See Bernal, *La Financiación de la Carrera de Indias*, 48.

78. British merchants carrying cargo to America also discounted their wares to cash-paying customers. For the very same reasons addressed above, these traders viewed as appealing the opportunity to avoid extending credit and incurring the associated risks. See Buck, *Development of the Organisation*, 115.

79. Representacion hecha por los Individuos del comercio de España al Excelentísimo Señor Virrey de Nueva Espana, Xalapa, 24 September 1778, AGI, *Consulados*, legajo 68, folio 652v.

80. See "Carta para Señor don José Fernández Gil a Guatemala," México, 12 January 1780, in Torales Pacheco, *Compañia de Comercio*, 2:237.

81. Garner and Stefanou, *Economic Growth and Change*, 169.

82. Kohn, *Origins of Western Economic Success*.

83. Representacion hecha por los Individuos del comercio de España al Excelentísimo Señor Virrey de Nueva España, Xalapa, 24 September 1778, AGI, *Consulados*, legajo 68, folio 652v.

84. Ibid., 24 September 1778, folio 656v–657.

85. Los individuos de ese comercio residentes en este Pueblo de Xalapa a los Srs. Prior y Consules, 29 September 1778, AGI, *Consulados*, legajo 68. This document sent to the *Consulado* largely reiterates what the seventy-seven commercial agents wrote to the viceroy five days earlier.

86. Representacion hecha por los Individuos del comercio de España al Excelentísimo Señor Virrey de Nueva España, Xalapa, 24 September 1778, AGI, *Consulados*, legajo 68, folio 656.

87. Miguel Jazinto de Marticorena a Juan Vizente de Marticorena, Veracruz, 30 August 1789, AGI, *Consulados*, legajo 433, folio 483.

88. Testimonio del expediente sobre averiguar si hay ó no decadencia en el comercio, hallar el remedio de ella en caso de haberla, y proporcionar los auxilios mas convenientes para fomento del trafico mercantil en este ramo, Informe de Fernando de Meoqui, 14 July 1791, AGI, Mexico, 1554, folios 56–60.

89. Ibid., Informe de Manuel García Herreros, 8 July 1791, folios 33–43.

90. Juan Ignacio de Ezcurray a Juan Vicente de Marticorena, Bueno Aires, 18 March 1789, AGI, *Consulados*, legajo 433, folio 279.

91. Benito Lorenzo Lavaque a Juan Vizente de Marticorena, Nueva Guatemala, 2 September 1789, AGI, *Consulados*, legajo 433, folios 500–501.

92. Francisco García de Gazetta a Francisco de Sierra, Buenos Aires, 10 January 1786, AGI, *Consulados*, legajo 428 (unpaginated).

93. Cartas a Francisco Sierra desde Espana, Europa y America, 1785–88, Joaquín Sorauren a Francisco de Sierra, Lima, 20 August 1786, AGI, *Consulados*, legajo 428 (unpaginated).

94. Juan Bautista de Marticorena a Juan Vicente de Marticorena, Nueva Guatemala, 2 January 1790, AGI, *Consulados*, legajo 433, folios 648–52.

95. Ibid., 2 June 1790, folio 775.

96. Miguel Jacinto de Marticorena a Juan Vicente de Marticorena, Veracruz, 1 October 1790, AGI, *Consulados*, legajo 433, folio 958.

97. Francisco García de Gazetta a Francisco de Sierra, Buenos Aires, 10 January 1786, AGI, *Consulados*, legajo 428 (unpaginated).

98. See "Carta para Alonso Magro a Oaxaca," 19 December 1787, in Torales Pacheco, *Compañia de Comercio*, 2:256.

99. Antonio Saenz de Tejada a Francisco de Sierra, Lima, 5 October 1784, AGI, *Consulados*, Legajo 426 (unpaginated).

100. The practice of incorporating the interest charge into the price to deflect church criticism was very common in medieval Europe. See Kohn, *Origins of Western Economic Success*, ch. 6. I make a similar argument to explain pricing within the *repartimiento de bienes*. See Baskes, *Indians, Merchants, and Markets*, 74–75.

101. Mercantile records often expressed items in *reales de vellón*. There were twenty *reales de vellón* in one peso fuerte.

102. Documentos correspondientes a la quiebra de Pedro Martínez de la Junquera, 1809, AGI, *Consulados*, legajo 522, folios 774–81. Martínez de la Junquera is not listed as a matriculated member of the *consulado*, but three other merchants with the surname Martínez Junquera are recorded, all of whom originated from Burgos and matriculated in the mid-eighteenth century. See Julián Bautista Ruiz Rivera, *El Consulado de Cádiz: Matrícula de Comerciantes, 1730–1823* (Cádiz: Diputación Provincial de Cádiz, 1988), 182.

103. An anonymous reader selected by Stanford University Press proposed that "violent means" meant the actual employment of "leg-breakers." But, as the reader further noted, their rejection of such means only strengthens the case that debt collection was difficult.

104. Tomás de Balenzattegui a Juan Vicente de Marticorena, Bueno Aires, 18 November 1788, AGI, *Consulados*, legajo 433, folio 191.

105. Antonio de Neira a Juan Vizente de Marticorena, 3 December 1802, AGI, *Consulados*, legajo 438, folio 767.

106. Tomás de Balenzattegui a Juan Vicente de Marticorena, Buenos Aires, 6 August 1802, AGI, *Consulados*, legajo 438, folio 624.

107. Juan Felipe de Laurnaga a Juan Vicente de Marticorena, Veracruz, 16 April 1798, AGI, *Consulados*, legajo 437, folio 239.

108. Juan Miguel de Marticorena a Juan Vicente de Marticorena, Lima, 16 April 1788, AGI, *Consulados*, legajo 433, folio 63.

109. "54 tercios 3 cajones arpilldos y 30 medias marquetas de cera."

110. Juan Miguel de Marticorena a Juan Vicente de Marticorena, Lima, 20 June 1788, AGI, *Consulados*, legajo 433, folios 109–17.

111. Ibid.

112. Juan Miguel de Marticorena a Juan Vicente de Marticorena, Lima, 20 June 1788, AGI, *Consulados*, legajo 433, folios 109–17.

113. Ibid.

114. Ibid.

115. Ibid.

116. Ibid.

117. Xabier Lamikiz, *Trade and Trust in the Eighteenth-Century Atlantic World: Spanish Merchants and Their Overseas Networks*, ed. Royal Historical Society (Rochester, NY: Boydell and Brewer, 2010), 175. On the issue of Peru's massive oversupply, also see Patricia H. Marks, "Confronting a Mercantile Elite: Bourbon Reformers and the Merchants of Lima, 1765–1796." *The Americas* 60, no. 4 (2004): 536–38.

118. Juan Miguel de Marticorena a Juan Vicente de Marticorena, Lima, 20 June 1788, AGI, *Consulados*, legajo 433, folios 109–17.

119. Ibid., 20 November 1788, folios 196–97.

120. Ibid., 16 July 1789, folio 426.

121. Antonio Álvarez de Villar a Juan Vicente de Marticorena, Lima 26 June 1793, AGI, *Consulados*, legajo 434, folio 1140.

122. Robert S. Smith, "Indigo Production and Trade in Colonial Guatemala," *Hispanic American Historical Review* 39, no. 2 (1959): 193.

123. Miguel Jacinto de Marticorena a Pedro Fermín de Córdoba, Nueva Guatemala, 3 June 1803, AGI, *Consulados*, legajo 438, folio 961. Pedro Fermín de Córdoba was Juan Vicente de Marticorena's assisstant in Cadiz as well as a cousin. This letter was sent by Juan Vicente's brother, Miguel Jacinto de Marticorena, who had recently moved to Guatemala from Veracruz.

124. Ibid.

125. Joséph Ritton, y Juan Joséf Sáenz de la Calle a Juan Vicente de Marticorena, 12 July 1803, AGI, *Consulados*, legajo 438, folio 998.

126. AGI, *Consulados*, legajo 438, folio 1000.

127. Alzueta y Beratarrechea a Juan Vicente de Marticorena, Cadiz, 20 August 1806, AGI, *Consulados*, legajo 439, folios 240–42.

128. Miguel Jacinto de Marticorena a Pedro Fermín de Córdoba, Guatemala, 3 June 1803, AGI, *Consulados*, legajo 438, folio 961. In this letter Miguel Jacinto notes that Juan Bautista always paid in cash any letters drawn against him by his brother, even when Juan Vicente had no credits on his account.

129. Juan Bautista de Marticorena a Pedro Fermín de Córdoba, Guatemala, 3 August 1800, AGI, *Consulados*, legajo 438, folio 168.

130. Juan Bautista de Marticorena a Juan Vizente de Marticorena, 3 December 1802, AGI, *Consulados*, legajo 438, folio 772.

131. Miguel Jazinto de Marticorena a Juan Vizente de Marticorena, 3 January 1805, AGI, *Consulados*, Llegajo 438, folio 1266.

132. Gabriel de Yturbe e Yraeta married his uncle's (Francisco Ignacio de Yraeta's) daughter, thus being both Francisco Ignacio de Yraeta's nephew and son-in-law.

133. See "Finiquito de compañía entre Francisco Ignacio de Yraeta y Gabriel de Yturbe e Yraeta. 1797," in Torales Pacheco, *Compañia de Comercio*, 2:150–57. These figures are summarized in a table in 1:145.

134. Their case is discussed in detail in Lamikiz, "Un 'Cuento Ruidoso,'" and Lamikiz, *Trade and Trust*, 153–61.

135. Sobre deuda de Don Blas Benito Ximenez y Don Juan de Eguino, 1774–76, AGI, Indiferente General, 2432.

136. Rafael José Facio a Juan José de Puch, 31 August and 30 September 1802, AGI, *Consulados*, legajo 429.

137. Juan Phelipe de Lauranaga a Juan Vizente de Marticorena, Veracruz, 24 September 1802, AGI, *Consulados*, legajo 438, folio 674.

138. Brown, "Profits, Prestige, and Persistence," 415, tables 2 and 3.

139. Miguel Jazinto de Marticorena a Pedro Fermín de Córdoba, Guatemala, 3 June 1803, AGI, *Consulados*, legajo 438, folio 961. Several Larrains were engaged in business with their cousins, the Marticorena brothers. Juan Bernardo Larrain lived in Caracas in 1797. More prominent in the correspondence was Juan Bautista de Larrain, who lived in Cadiz. Indeed, in 1794 he shared a house with Juan Vicente de Marticorena and Pedro Fermín de Córdoba, which was located at Calle San Gines 21 in the Barrio Nuestra Señora de Pilar.

140. AGI, *Consulados*, legajo 522, exp. 11, folios 1144–1268. The document is undated but seems to be from late 1804 or 1805. Also see folios 1269–78.

141. Joseph Ritton y Juan Josef Saenz de la Calle a Juan Vizente de Marticorena, 12 July 1803, AGI, *Consulados*, legajo 438, folio 998.

Chapter 6

1. Freight rates on ships belonging to the Royal Armada were set by Royal edict but nonetheless responded to conditions of war-related risk. In 1773, the *consulado* petitioned the Crown for a reduction in freight rates due to the fact that they had been raised during previous years of war but never lowered with the return of peace, to the detriment of commerce. See AGI, *Consulados*, libro 86, folio 76v–77v, 14 May 1773.

2. José Ignacio de Pombo, *Comercio y Contrabando en Cartagena de Indias, 2 de Junio de 1800*, Nueva Biblioteca Colombiana de Cultura, Serie Breve, Historia (Bogotá, Colombia: Procultura, 1986), "Informe del real tribunal del *consulado* de Cartagena de Indias al Sr. Virrey del reyno sobre el origen y causas del contrabando, sus perjuicios, los medios de evitarlo, y de descubrir los fraudes, 2 de junio de 1800," 13–14. Pombo's appeal to the viceroy recommended opening the port of Cartagena to ships of all nationalities. Pombo argues that such a reform would help eradicate the high levels of illicit commerce.

3. Ibid., 37.

4. Antonio Narváez y la Torre, José Ignacio de Pombo, and Sergio Elías Ortiz, *Escritos de Dos Economistas Coloniales: Don Antonio de Narváez y la Torre, y Don José Ignacio de Pombo*, Archivo de la Economía Nacional 29 (Bogotá: Banco de la República, Archivo de la Economía Nacional, 1965), XX.

5. On *comercio neutro* see Barbara H. Stein and Stanley J. Stein, *Edge of Crisis: War and Trade in the Spanish Atlantic, 1789–1808* (Baltimore: Johns Hopkins University Press, 2009), ch. 8.

6. Fairly complete price series exist for cochineal, making it ideal for such analysis. Prices for Oaxaca have been published several times. See, for example, Jeremy Baskes, *Indians, Merchants, and Markets: A Reinterpretation of the Repartimiento and Spanish-Indian Economic Relations in Colonial Oaxaca, 1750–1821* (Stanford, CA: Stanford University Press, 2000), appendix B, 203–4. The northern European prices displayed in this figure are actually a composite of prices from two sources. From 1758 to 1781, the price utilized was that quoted in the Amsterdam commodity exchange and published in N. W. Posthumus, *Inquiry into the History of Prices in Holland* (Leiden: Brill, 1946), 1:420–23. For 1803 to 1821, I used the London commodity exchange price, which was extracted from Thomas Tooke, William Newmarch, and T. E. Gregory, *A History of Prices and of the State of the Circulation from 1792 to 1856* (New York: Adelphi, 1928), 2:400. Both sources listed prices for the intervening years, 1782–1802. For

these years, the average of the Dutch and English prices was used in the construction of the European price series. English pounds sterling were converted to Spanish pesos at the exchange rate £1 = 5 pesos. Dutch guilders were converted at the rate of 1 guilder = 0.45 pesos. For fuller discussion and justification of the methodology employed, see Baskes, *Indians, Merchants, and Markets*, 139–40.

7. Pombo, *Comercio y Contrabando*, 21. Pombo continues by suggesting that price convergence in the other direction (European goods in America) will not result from peace since, as his report seeks to argue, contraband has resulted in continued entry of smuggled goods (originating primarily in Jamaica) brought by the enemy or other illicit traders.

8. Manuel de Arana a Antonio de Artechea, Buenos Aires, 24 December 1796, AGI, *Consulados*, legajo 440.

9. José Ramon de Ugarteche a Antonio de Artechea, Buenos Aires, 24 December 1796, AGI, *Consulados*, legajo 440.

10. Francisco Valdovinos a Antonio de Artechea, Buenos Aires, 9 September 1797, AGI, *Consulados*, legajo 440.

11. Nicolás de la Cruz y Bahamonde and Sergio Martínez Baeza, *Epistolario de Don Nicolás de la Cruz y Bahamonde, Primer Conde de Maule*, 1st ed., Fuentes para el Estudio de la Colonia 2 (Santiago de Chile: Dirección de Bibliotecas Archivos y Museos Centro de Investigaciones Diego Barros Arana, 1994), Doc. 3, 42–43, Conde de Maule a don Juan Manuel de la Cruz, Cadiz, 2 December 1794.

12. On the Nootka affair, see William R. Manning, *The Nootka Sound Controversy* (Washington, DC: American Historical Association, 1904).

13. Miguel Jacinto de Marticorena a Juan Vicente de Marticorena, Veracruz, 31 July 1790, AGI, *Consulados*, legajo 433.

14. Juan Felipe Laurnaga a Juan Vicente de Marticorena, Veracruz, 4 June 1793, AGI, *Consulados*, legajo 434, folio 1113.

15. Juan Felipe Laurnaga and Miguel Jacinto de Marticorena a Juan Vicente de Marticorena, Veracruz, 8 November 1796, AGI, *Consulados*, legajo 436, folio 607.

16. Rafael José Facio a Juan José de Puch, 2 November 1797 and 30 April 1798, AGI, *Consulados*, legajo 429.

17. Rafael José Facio a Juan José de Puch, 26 November 1803, AGI, *Consulados*, legajo 429.

18. A price inelastic commodity is one whose demand is not severely affected by price. Had prices skyrocketed, consumers would have still purchased wine. In truth, some poorer consumers might have switched to a cheaper, locally produced, substitute alcoholic beverage such as pulque.

19. Miguel Jacinto de Marticorena a Juan Vicente de Marticorena, Veracruz, 6 and 20 December 1790, AGI, *Consulados*, legajo 433, folios 977–78, 1032.

20. Correspondencia y documentos de don Juan José Puch (1777–1819), 30 April 1798, AGI, *Consulados*, legajo 429 (unpaginated).

21. Spain declared war on England on 7 October 1796. News of the war took several months to reach Górriz in Guatemala.

22. Pedro José de Górriz a Juan Vicente de Marticorena, Nueva Guatemala, 3 January 1797, AGI, *Consulados*, legajo 436, folio 637.

23. Ibid.

24. Ibid.

25. Antonio Saenz de Tejada a Francisco de Sierra, Lima, 5 August 1784, AGI, *Consulados*, legajo 426.

26. Juan Bautista de Marticorena a Juan Vicente de Marticorena, Nueva Guatemala, 2 May 1793, AGI, *Consulados*, legajo 434, folio 1043.

27. Ibid., 2 August 1793, folio 1230. On Pedro José de Górriz, see Pedro José de Górriz a Juan Vicente de Marticorena, Nueva Guatemala, 3 January 1797, AGI, *Consulados*, legajo 436, folio 637.

28. Juan Bautista de Marticorena a Juan Vizente de Marticorena, Nueva Guatemala, 2 January 1796, AGI, *Consulados*, legajo 436, folio 1.

29. Miguel Jacinto de Marticorena a Juan Vicente de Marticorena, Nueva Guatemala, 3 July 1798, AGI, *Consulados*, legajo 437, folio 330.

30. Ibid., 3 July 1798, folio 388.

31. Juan Bautista de Marticorena a Juan Vicente de Marticorena, Nueva Guatemala, 17 May 1793, AGI, *Consulados*, legajo 434, folio 1046.

32. El Virrey de Buenos Aires, El Marqués de Loreto, contextando la Superior Orden del Excelentísimo Sr. Bo. Fr. Don Antonio Valdes sobre el comercio marítimo y terrestre, 30 September 1789, AGI, Indiferente General, 2435.

33. Rafael José Facio a Juan José de Puch, Mexico, 30 April 1798, AGI, *Consulados*, legajo 429.

34. Cartas de *Consulados*, diputados de comercio y de flotas desde America (1796–1799), año 1798, Relacion del consulado de Mexico sobre los atrasos que sufre el comercio del reyno por consequencia de la guerra y si combendria franquear el comercio de licita introduccion de Havana, Mexico, 19 October 1798, AGI, *Consulados*, legajo 340.

35. Hananel and Jacob Mendes da Costa to Francisco de Sierra, London, 24 January 1783, AGI, *Consulados*, legajo 424 (unpaginated).

36. Ibid., 14 March 1783.

37. Ibid., 6 May 1783.

38. Ibid., 30 May 1783.

39. Josep M. Delgado Ribas, *Dinámicas Imperiales (1650–1796): España, América y Europa en el Cambio Institucional del Sistema Colonial Español*, Serie General Universitaria 63 (Barcelona: Edicions Bellaterra, 2007), 455–60.

40. Miguel Jacinto de Marticorena a Juan Vicente de Marticorena, Nueva Guatemala, 3 July 1798, AGI, *Consulados*, legajo 437, folios 330, 388.

41. See "Discurso del Mariscal de Campo de los Reales Exercitios don Antonio de Narváez y la Torre," 5 June 1805, in Narváez y la Torre, Pombo, and Ortiz, *Escritos de Dos Economistas Coloniales*, 88.

42. Quoted in Geoffrey Clark, "Insurance as an Instrument of War in the 18th Century," *Geneva Papers on Risk and Insurance* 29, no. 2 (2004): 247.

43. Oscar Cruz Barney, *El Régimen Jurídico del Corso Marítimo: El Mundo Indiano y el México del Siglo XIX*, 1st ed., Serie C–Estudios Históricos 64 (México: Universidad Nacional Autónoma de México, 1997), 144–47; Robert Greenhalgh Albion and Jennie Barnes Pope, *Sea Lanes in Wartime: The American Experience, 1775–1942* (New York: Norton, 1942), 23. On privateering and piracy in the Spanish empire, especially the ealier colonial period, also see: Kris E. Lane, *Pillaging the Empire: Piracy in the Americas, 1500–1750*, Latin American Realities (Armonk, NY: M. E. Sharpe, 1998); Kenneth R. Andrews, *The Spanish Caribbean: Trade and Plunder, 1530–1630* (New Haven, CT: Yale University Press, 1978).

44. Oscar Cruz Barney, *El Riesgo en el Comercio de Hispano-Indiano: Préstamos y Seguros Maritimos Durante los Siglos XVI a XIX* (Mexico City: UNAM, 1998), 155–60.

45. AGI, *Consulados*, libro 90, folios 15v–16.

46. A "cannon of 24" was a long gun used to fire twenty-four-pound cannon balls. Similarly, a howitzer or "obus of 12" shot twelve-pound balls. So *El Buen Vasallo* had "a single 24 pounder long gun, probably mounted midship on a turntable to fire over the bulwarks, two 12 pound boat howitzers, probably mounted on truck carriages to fire through ports in the gunwales abaft the beam, and two considerably smaller pedreros, probably swivel guns. A small vessel like this suitable for the *guerre de course* would have likely carried all of its ordnance on the upper deck." I am grateful to Dr. Joseph Guilmartin of Ohio State University for helping me to understand (via email, 22 June 2006) how this ship was armed.

47. Poliza del Armamento del Corsario Español nombrado *El Buen Vasallo*, 12 February 1805, AGI, *Consulados*, legajo 72, folios 244–48. It is not clear why the contract described the allocation so oddly, granting the

captain and crew 2 percent and then one-third of the remaining 98 pe-
cent, instead of simply awarding them 34.3 percent, which was the share
that they actually received.

48. The Alboran Sea is the westernmost portion of the Mediterranean
Sea and is bordered on the west by the Straits of Gibraltar.

49. Instrucciones de Corso para el capitan del corsario Español nombrado *El Buen Vasallo* armado por Juan Vicente de Marticorena, 12 March
1805, AGI, *Consulados*, legajo 72, folios 242–43.

50. Condiciones para los interesados del corsario *"El Buen Vasallo,"*
Cadiz, July 1805, AGI, *Consulados*, legajo 72, folios 240–41.

51. Juan Vicente de Marticorena a Miguel Jacinto de Marticorena,
Cadiz, 22 July 1806, AGI, *Consulados*, legajo 439, folio 203.

52. Ibid.

53. Relacion de lo acaecido sobre el Laud nombrado Amborou, February
1806, AGI, *Consulados*, legajo 439, folio 26.

54. The online Diccionario de la Lengua Española of the Real Aca-
demica Española defines a *místico* as a "coastal vessel of three masts, and
sometimes of two, with Latin sails, used in the Mediterranean." See http://
www.rae.es/.

55. The online Diccionario de la Lengua Española of the Real Aca-
demica Española defines a *falucho* as a "coastal vessel with one Latin sail."
See http://www.rae.es/.

56. Nota de la carga del falucho español nombrado la Virgen de Europa
procedente de Gibraltar para Tavira y apresado por el corsario español *El
Buen Vasallo*, Tarifa, 10 April 1806, AGI, *Consulados*, legajo 439, folio 102.

57. Juan Vicente de Marticorena a Miguel Jacinto de Marticorena,
Cadiz, 22 July 1806, AGI, *Consulados*, legajo 439, folio 203.

58. A corvette is a small, highly mobile, lightly armed warship.

59. AGI, *Consulados*, legajo 439, 1 June 1806, folio 145; and 2 June 1806,
folio 147.

60. Juan Vicente de Marticorena a Miguel Jacinto de Marticorena,
Cadiz, 22 July 1806, AGI, *Consulados*, legajo 439, folio 203.

61. Gabriel de Ybarreche a Juan Vicente de Marticorena, 9 September
1806, AGI, *Consulados*, legajo 439, folios 273–75.

62. Roque Manuel de Artiaga a Juan Vicente de Marticorena, 24 October 1806, AGI, *Consulados*, legajo 439, folio 373.

63. A Jabeque (Xebec in English) was a three-masted Mediterranean
vessel.

64. Juan Vicente de Marticorena a Francisco Xavier Ramos, Algeciras,
17 August 1807, AGI, *Consulados*, legajo 439, folio 601.

65. Correspondencia y documentos de don Juan José Puch (1777–1819), Rafael José Facio a Juan José de Puch, 31 July 1803, AGI, *Consulados*, legajo 429.

66. Comerciantes de Jalapa al Virrey Bucareli, AGI, *Consulados*, legajo 808.

67. Jesús Turiso Sebastián, *Comerciantes Españoles en la Lima Borbónica: Anatomía de Una Élite de Poder, 1701–1761*, Serie Historia y Sociedad (Valladolid: Universidad de Valladolid, 2002), 228.

68. A *zurron* was a sack that could hold 7 to 9 *arrobas* of cochineal, 175 to 225 pounds. Nineteen hundred *zurrones* of cochineal was an enormously valuable cargo, likely worth in excess of 800,000 pesos in Mexico in 1776, given that the dye was valued at the time at 17 *reales* per pound.

69. Instancia del Conde de Repáraz para poder embarcar en la Fragata Ventura y Navío San Nicolás mil y novecientos zurrones de grana fina, AGN, Marina, Tomo 38, exp. 5, 1776.

70. Sobre la nulidad del embarco de granas y nombramiento de otro buque para conducir las granas sobrantes, AGN, Marina, Tomo 38, exp. 6, folios 68–188, 1775–77.

71. Pedro José de Górriz a Juan Vicente de Marticorena, Nueva Guatemala, 3 October 1798, AGI, *Consulados*, legajo 437, folio 575.

72. AGI, *Consulados*, legajo 429, Rafael José Facio a Juan José de Puch, 30 April 1799.

73. Michael P. Costeloe, "Barcelona Merchants and the Latin American Wars of Independence," *The Americas* 38, no. 4 (1982): 436.

74. See Victoria Eugenia Martinez del Cerro González, *Una Comunidad de Comerciantes: Navarros y Vascos en Cádiz (Segunda Mitad de Siglo XVIII)* (Sevilla: Consejo Económico y Social de Andalucía, 2006), 374, table 46.

75. Correspondencia General del Consulado, 90–97, 12 May 1793 and 17 May 1793, AGI, *Consulados*, libro 95.

76. Ibid., 171, 174–75.

77. Correspondencia general del consulado, 395–96, 24 January 1804, AGI, *Consulados*, libro 99.

78. Cruz Barney, *Riesgo en el Comercio de Hispano-Indiano*, 149–50.

79. Pedro Fermín de Córdoba a Juan Vizente de Marticorena, Cadiz, 29 June 1798, AGI, *Consulados*, legajo 437, folio 379.

80. James Stephen, *War in Disguise; or, the Frauds of the Neutral Flags*, 4th ed. (London: Printed by C. Whittingham and sold by J. Hatchard and J. Butterworth, 1806), 9.

81. AGI, Indiferente General, 2419, 1781.

82. Joséf Carbo a Juan José Puch, 30 June 1798, AGI, *Consulados,* legajo 429. Due to the British blockade of Spanish ships, on 18 November 1797 the Crown had issued a Royal Order temporarily permitting the entry of ships flying the flag of neutral nations into the legal Spanish American ports. Carbo's plan to use a Genoese vessel was thus legal.

83. Joséf Carbo a Juan José Puch, 14 July 1798, AGI, *Consulados,* legajo 429.

84. John R. Fisher, *Trade, War and Revolution: Exports from Spain to Spanish America 1797–1820* (Liverpool: Center for Latin American Studies, University of Liverpool, 1992), 57.

85. Brian R. Hamnett, *Politics and Trade in Southern Mexico, 1750–1821* (Cambridge: Cambridge University Press, 1971), 101.

86. Pombo, *Comercio y Contrabando,* 34–35.

87. See John H. Coatsworth, "American Trade with European Colonies in the Caribbean and South America, 1790–1812," *William and Mary College Quarterly Historical Magazine* 24, no. 2 (1967): 252; Javier Cuenca-Esteban, "The United States Balance of Payments with Spanish America and the Philippine Islands, 1790–1819," in *The North American Role in the Spanish Imperial Economy, 1760–1819,* ed. Jacques and Allan Kuethe Barbier (Manchester: Manchester University Press, 1984), 32; Peggy K. Liss, "Creoles, the North American Example and the Spanish American Economy, 1760–1810," in *The North American Role in the Spanish Imperial Economy, 1760–1819,* ed. Jacques and Allan Kuethe Barbier (Manchester: Manchester University Press, 1984), 20.

88. Donald R. Adams Jr., "American Neutrality and Prosperity, 1793–1808: A Reconsideration," *Journal of Economic History* 40, no. 4 (1980): 732–33. Also see Alexander de Conde, *The Quasi-War: Politics and Diplomacy of the Undeclared War with France, 1797–1801* (New York: Scribner, 1966).

89. Costeloe, "Barcelona Merchants," 433–34.

90. Echenique y Sánchez a Francisco de Sierra, Amsterdam, 10 September 1781, AGI, *Consulados,* legajo 421 (unpaginated).

91. Testimonio literal de la Real Cedula en que S.M. establece las reglas con que deben comerciarse en las Indias los efectos y manufacturas Ynglesas que se introduzcan en virtud del permiso concedido, AGI, Indiferente General, 2418. Spanish merchants were granted six months to dispense of any British merchandise that they then held.

92. Fermín de Tastet y Compañía a Francisco de Sierra, London, 22 May 1781, AGI, *Consulados,* legajo 421 (unpaginated).

93. Hananel y Jacob Mendes da Costa y Compañía a Francisco de Sierra, London, 4 September 1781, AGI, *Consulados*, legajo 421 (unpaginated).

94. Ibid., 25 December 1781.

95. Fermín de Tastet y Compañía a Francisco de Sierra, London, 22 May 1781, AGI, *Consulados*, legajo 421 (unpaginated).

96. See, for example, ibid., 20 July 1781. Sierra's experience undoubtedly justified his faith that the English insurance industry would respect any losses he sustained despite the Anglo-Spanish war. In a similar case, the Cadiz industry cast doubts on its reliability. In March 1795 the *consulado*, at the request of several of that city's insurance firms, inquired about the possibility of annulling all policies that were currently underwritten to French nationals. In the end, the *consulado* recommended the cancellation of all policies of French nationals for which the insurers had not already received a premium or whose premiums had not been totally financed prior to the start of the war. There is no evidence that this policy was ever implemented. Correspondencia general del *consulado*, AGI, *Consulados*, libro 96, folios 238–39.

97. Juan Felipe Laurnaga a Juan Vicente de Marticorena, 15 April 1793, AGI, *Consulados*, legajo 434.

98. Virrey Revillagigedo a Don Diego de Gardoqui sobre los fletes de caudales en buques de Real Armada, 1793, AGI, Audiencia de Mexico, 1554, no. 20.

99. Rafael José Facio a Juan José de Puch, 30 September 1798, AGI, *Consulados*, legajo 429.

100. Ibid., 1 October 1799.

101. Expedientes del *Consulado* y Comercio, 1800–2, Los diputados del comercio de Oaxaca piden que los buques de guerra se franquean para hacer el comercio de grana y añil, AGI, Audiencia de Mexico, 2509.

102. El *Consulado* de Guatemala representa los perjuicios que se le siguen al comercio de que no salgan de la Havana las tintas que conduxeron a ella el Bergantín San Rafael y la Fragata Placentina y suplica S.M se sirva mandar se trasladen a España en buques de guerra, 3 February 1800, AGI, *Consulados*, legajo 341. Reagrding the eventual arrival of some of this indigo, see AGI, *Consulados*, legajo 438, folio 541, Cadiz, 26 May 1802.

103. Pólizas de seguros del concurso de don Antonio de Artechea, AGI, *Consulados*, legajo 518, exp. 12, folio 193. Insurance is discussed in great detail in chapters 7–9.

104. Manuel Ravina Martin, "Participación Extranjera en el Comercio Indiano: El Seguro Marítimo a Fines del Siglo XVII," *Revista de Indias* 43 (1983): 502.

105. Hananel and Jacob Mendes da Costa a Francisco de Sierra, London, 20 February 1784, AGI, *Consulados*, legajo 427 (unpaginated).

106. Antonio Sáenz de Tejada a Francisco de Sierra, Lima, 5 March 1781, AGI, *Consulados*, legajo 421 (unorganized).

107. Pio de Elizalde a Juan Vizente de Marticorena, Septiembre 1798, AGI, *Consulados*, legajo 437, folio 552–54. Elizalde wrote Marticorena hoping that the latter could recommend a trustworthy agent in Veracruz. Despite the fact that the partnership was "entirely filled," Elizalde offered to let Marticorena purchase a share or two. Marticorena, despite his virtual insolvency at the time, indeed acquired a share but failed to pay for it, leading Elizalde to later strip him of his interest in the venture.

108. Clarence Henry Haring, *Trade and Navigation Between Spain and the Indies in the Time of the Hapsburgs* (Cambridge: Cambridge University Press, 1918), 237–39.

109. Pablo Amorós a Juan Vicente de Marticorena, Tarifa, 23 November 1806, AGI, *Consulados*, legajo 439, folio 416.

110. AGI, *Consulados*, libro 90, folios 40–40v, 13 October 1779.

111. AGI, *Consulados*, legajo 336 (unpaginated), Mexico, 9 October 1780.

112. *Consulado* al Rey Nuestro Senor, 27 November 1781, AGI, *Consulados*, libro 91, folios 52v–54v.

113. Fermín de Tastet y Compañía a Francisco de Sierra, London, 31 July1781, AGI, *Consulados*, legajo 421 (unpaginated).

114. Correspondencia General del Consulado, El Consulado al Senor Don Luis de Cordova, Director de la Real Armada, 18 September 1784, AGI, *Consulados*, libro 92, 135v–136v.

115. For many more examples and discussion of the central importance placed on convoys during wartime, see AGI, *Consulados*, legajo 336.

116. Joséf Ignacio Pavón y Muñoz a Juan José Puch, Jalapa, 29 November 1799, AGI, *Consulados*, legajo 429.

117. Manuel de Arana a Antonio de Artechea, Buenos Aires, 24 December 1796, AGI, *Consulados*, legajo 440.

118. Pedro José de Górriz a Juan Vicente de Marticorena, Nueva Guatemala, 3 January 1797, AGI, *Consulados*, legajo 436, folio 637.

119. Antonio García-Baquero González, *Comercio Colonial y Guerras Revolucionarias: La Decadencia Económica de Cádiz a Raíz de la Emancipación Americana*, 1st ed. (Sevilla: Escuela de Estudios Hispano-Americanos Consejo Superior de Investigaciones Científicas, 1972), 134.

120. Representacion hecha a Su Magestad por el Real *Consulado* y Diputacion de Comercio de esta Plaza, 23 December, 1817, AGI, *Consulados*, legajo 81.

121. Correspondencia General del *Consulado*, Al ministerio de hacienda, 14 April 1818, AGI, *Consulados*, libro 108, folios 460–62.

122. Costeloe, "Barcelona Merchants," 433.

123. Juan Bautista de Marticorena a Juan Vicente de Marticorena, Nueva Guatemala, 28 August 1793, AGI, *Consulados*, legajo 434, folio 1265.

124. Many factors went into calculating the rate of insurance, so it is really quite impossible to extrapolate with any precision from a premium rate how frequently ships were anticipated to be captured. Obviously, the higher the rate, the greater the expected risk of seizure, assuming other factors held constant. In the particular case noted above, seizure by French corsairs was the principle risk factor that had caused the elevated rates.

125. Juan Miguel de Marticorena a Juan Vicente de Marticorena, Cadiz, 9 May 1780, AGI, *Consulados*, legajo 432, folios 31–32.

126. Ibid., folios 41–42.

Chapter 7

1. If the ventures themselves were pooled, then many of the uncertainties that plagued the individual merchants would have been reduced. Specifically, the formation of the modern corporation was somewhat inspired by the value of concentrating decisions under a single entity. This pooling of decisions reduces the uncertainty of market fluctuations, for example, because a large firm can better regulate the flow of commodities. Indeed, this is one of the prime reasons why the trading companies of northern Europe were founded.

2. This is well explained in Frank Hyneman Knight, *Risk, Uncertainty and Profit*, Hart, Schaffner & Marx Prize Essays 31 (Boston: Houghton Mifflin, 1921), 213.

3. In Spanish these loans are called *préstamos a riesgo maritime, préstamos a la gruesa ventura*, and *escrituras de riesgo*. In English they were frequently termed bottomry loans since they were often extended to shipowners who pledged as collateral the keels (bottoms) of their vessels.

4. Several studies have focused on sea loans in the Spanish empire. The most comprehensive study is Antonio-Miguel Bernal, *La Financiación de la Carrera de Indias (1492–1824): Dinero y Crédito en el Comercio Colonial Español Con América* (Sevilla: Fundación el Monte, 1992). Also see Oscar Cruz Barney, *El Riesgo en el Comercio de Hispano-Indiano: Préstamos y Seguros Maritimos Durante los Siglos XVI a XIX* (Mexico City: UNAM, 1998). For other areas see Florence Edler de Roover, "Early Examples of Marine Insurance," *Journal of Economic History* 5, no. 2 (1945): 172–200; Violet Barbour,

"Marine Risks and Insurance in the Seventeenth Century," *Journal of Economic and Business History* 1, no. 4 (1929): 582–84, and Meir Kohn, *The Origins of Western Economic Success: Commerce, Finance, and Government in Preindustrial Europe* (Working papers, Department of Economics, Dartmouth College, Hanover, NH, 2001), http://www.dartmouth.edu/~mkohn/, ch. 12. Thousands of these contracts survive in the Archive of the Indies. See, for examples, AGI, *Consulados*, libros 409–44, and AGI, *Consulados*, legajos 876–87.

5. Bernal, *Financiación de la Carrera de Indias*, 389–90.

6. Of course, marine insurance was far from new. It had existed in Europe for centuries. A good starting point for the history of maritime insurance is de Roover, "Early Examples of Marine Insurance."

7. See, for example, M. Guadalupe Carrasco González, "El Negocio de los Seguros Marítimos en Cádiz a Finales del Siglo XVIII," *Hispania, Revista Española de Historia* 59:1, no. 201 (1999): 269–304; Bernal, *Financiación de la Carrera de Indias*; and Cruz Barney, *Riesgo en el Comercio de Hispano-Indiano*. By far the best study of maritime insurance is Spooner's study of the late eighteenth-century Amsterdam insurance market. See Frank Spooner, *Risks at Sea: Amsterdam Insurance and Maritime Europe, 1766–1780* (Cambridge: Cambridge University Press, 1983).

8. The company charters are deposited in AGI, *Consulados*, legajo 78.

9. See citations throughout text for specific locations of policies.

10. A. H. John, "The London Assurance Company and the Marine Insurance Market of the Eighteenth Century," *Economica* 25, no. 98 (1958): 136. Clark notes that in the eighteenth century Parliament prohibited trade between England and its enemies during wartime but normally permitted the extention of insurance due to its profitability. Geoffrey Clark, "Insurance as an Instrument of War in the 18th Century," *Geneva Papers on Risk and Insurance* 29, no. 2 (2004): 251, 256.

11. Bernal devised his own system to determine the importance of the creditors, a measure that considered both the number of loans as well as their total value. Bernal, *Financiación de la Carrera de Indias*, 459–60, table 6.52.

12. Lara Arroyo, "Redes de Influencia: Relaciones Privilegiados en el Comercio Colonial a Finales del Siglo XVIII: los Marticorena y Su Correspondencia Epistolar," *Nuevo Mundo Mundos Nuevos*, January 30, 2007, http:\\nuevomundo.revues.org\index3213.html (accessed September 20, 2010).

13. Cadiz's continued dominance is amply demonstrated by John Fisher, *Commercial Relations Between Spain and Spanish America in the Era of*

Free Trade, 1778–1796 (Liverpool: Center for Latin American Studies, University of Liverpool, 1985), 64.

14. AGI, *Consulados*, libro 90, folio 178, 15 August 1780.

15. AGI, *Consulados*, legajo 61A, exp. 15.

16. The legajo actually contains eighty-four insurance company charters, but one dates from 1814 and is excluded from the analysis that follows here. Another document in this legajo (see "Nota de algunas compañías de seguros que no han pasado a esta contaduria para la toma de razón") refers to seven companies that failed to deliver their charters as requested. These companies had 37, 26, 33, 40, 30, 30, and 50 shareholders respectively. Unfortunately, the dates on which these seven firms were established are available for only two and the length of time that they were to operate is not noted. As a result, these were included only partially in the analysis. Last, this file also contains a number of commercial companies organized at the time in which the partners agreed to pool resources for their transatlantic ventures. Several of these companies proposed underwriting insurance policies if they deemed it desirable. These companies are excluded from the analysis, which focuses exclusively on companies chartered to underwrite insurance alone. AGI, *Consulados*, legajo 78.

17. Ibid., docs. #26 and #31.

18. Ibid., doc. #39. All of the companies placed themselves under the protection of a Catholic patron, most often the Virgin Mary or Jesus.

19. Noticia extractada de los Directores de Compañías de Seguros establecidos en esta plaza y registradas en esta contaduria del *consulado* del tiempo en que empezó a correr el termino de ellas y del en que deben concluir, segun escripturas, AGI, *Consulados*, legajo 78. This legajo also contains the charters establishing most of these partnerships. Antonio García-Baquero González, *Comercio Colonial y Guerras Revolucionarias: La Decadencia Económica de Cádiz a Raíz de la Emancipación Americana*, 1st ed. (Sevilla: Escuela de Estudios Hispano-Americanos Consejo Superior de Investigaciones Científicas, 1972), 47, notes that there were seventy-five insurance companies listed in the 1795 Cadiz "commercial guide."

20. Correspondencia general del *consulado*, AGI, *Consulados*, libro 97, folios 182–89.

21. Compañía establecida bajo la dirección de Nicolás María de Alva, 30 March 1792, AGI, *Consulados*, legajo 78, doc. #13.

22. AGI, *Consulados*, legajo 78, doc. #86, article 3, 24 December 1803.

23. Ibid., doc. #74, 30 March 1797.

24. Ibid., doc. #3.

25. Ibid., doc. #28.

26. Ibid., doc. #86, folio 4v.

27. Correspondencia general del *consulado*, AGI, *Consulados*, libro 97, folios 380–82.

28. Ibid., folio 474.

29. Juan Manuel de Arzubialde a Juan Vizente de Marticorena, 5 March 1799, AGI, *Consulados*, legajo 437, folio 851. Marticorena's reluctance to attend the meetings stemmed from the fact that he was very near to the category of insolvent.

30. This book focuses on the insurance industry in Cadiz, but there were a few firms organized during this era in the colonies as well. This paragraph discusses a partnership formed in Havana in 1795. See Compañía de Seguros establecida en la Havana en que la Real Cia de Comercio de la misma plaza tiene una accion de 5000 pesos, 24 January 1795, AGI, Ultramar, 273. Ortiz de la Tabla cites Miguel Lerdo de Tejada who noted that two firms existed in Veracruz, one founded in 1789 and the other in 1802. See Javier Ortiz de la Tabla Ducasse, *Comercio Exterior de Veracruz, 1778–1821: Crisis de Dependencia* (Sevilla: Escuela de Estudios Hispano-Americanos, 1978), 29. Insurance firms were also underwriting policies in Río de la Plata. See Enrique Wedovoy, *La Evolución Económica Rioplatense a Fines del Siglo XVIII y Princípios del Siglo XIX, a la Luz de la História del Seguro* (La Plata: Universidad Nacional de la Plata, 1967). There is also mention of a Buenos Aires firm established in the mid-1790s in Cartas a Dn. Antonio de Artechea desde distintos puntos de España y America, 1786–99, Dn. José Ramon de Ugarteche a Artechea, Buenos Aires, 24 December 1796, AGI, *Consulados*, legajo 440.

31. Compañía de Seguros establecida en la Havana en que la Real Cia de Comercio de la misma plaza tiene una accion de 5000 pesos, 24 January 1795, AGI, Ultramar, 273.

32. Documentos relativos a las quiebras y liquidaciones de las compañías de seguros, AGI, *Consulados*, legajo 522, folios 847–48, 868. Also see the company's charter at AGI, *Consualdos*, legajo 78, doc. #3. Marticorena purchased his share under his initials, JVM.

33. AGI, *Consulados*, legajo 78, doc. #42.

34. Ibid., doc. #77.

35. Noticia extractada de los Directores de Compañías de Seguros establecidos en esta plaza y registradas en esta contaduria del *consulado* del tiempo en que empezó a correr el termino de ellas y del en que deben concluir, segun escripturas, AGI, *Consulados*, legajo 78.

36. To compute this figure I simply took the sum of the companies' total share subscriptions for each year. See online Appendix B.

37. Correspondencia general del consulado, 2 August 1796, AGI, *Consulados*, libro 96, folios 168–71.

38. John, "London Assurance Company," 127. The exchange rate used was just over 4.65 Spanish pesos per pound sterling. The computation was done on the historical currency converter calculator at http://www. pierre-marteau.com/currency/converter/eng-spa.html (accessed 16 July 2010).

39. For the operations of this company see AGI, *Consulados*, legajo 522, exp. 8, 18 February 1799, folio 850. Estado de la Compañía de Seguros a la direccion de Don Juan Estevan de Thellechea Marca M desde Diciembre de 1793, en que dió principio, hasta 31 de diciembre de 1796. For its capital structure see Noticia extractada de los Directores de Compañías de Seguros establecidos en esta plaza y registradas en esta contaduria del *consulado* del tiempo en que empezó a correr el termino de ellas y del en que deben concluir, segun escripturas, AGI, *Consulados*, legajo 78.

40. In one case (AGI, *Consulados*, legajo 78, doc. #82) only one of three directors could be linked by family name to other shareholders.

41. This rate seems to have been fairly universal. See, for example, AGI, *Consulados*, legajo 78, doc. #6, 24 November 1791, which established an insurance company under the directorship of Don Antonio Lasqueti and called Compañía Española de Seguros bajo la proteción de Nuestra Madre y Señora de las Angustias y San Antonio de Padua. Also see ibid., doc. #7, 1 December 1791.

42. Ibid., doc. #86, article 4, 24 December 1803.

43. Ibid., doc. #79.

44. Robert S. Smith, *The Spanish Guild Merchant: A History of the Consulado, 1250–1700* (New York: Octagon Books, 1972), 26–27, 78–80.

45. AGI, *Consulados*, legajo 78, doc. #6.

46. Ibid.

47. Ibid., doc. #2.

48. Ibid., doc. #1.

49. AGI, *Consulados*, legajo 518, exp. 6, folio 78, 6 November 1789. A line is an insurance term referring to the proportion of a risk covered by a particular underwriter. Policies were signed by representatives of the

firms underwriting the risk who in addition specified the amount of coverage and the premium rate. Each entry represents an individual line.

50. AGI, *Consulados*, legajo 889, varias Tomás de razón.

51. AGI, *Consulados*, legajo 78, doc. #3.

52. Ibid., doc. #7.

53. See, for instance, ibid., doc. #39; doc. #42; and doc. #77.

54. See, for instance, ibid., doc. #39; doc. #42; and doc. #77.

55. Compañía de Seguros Marca JPH, AGI, *Consulados*, legajo 78.

56. AGI, *Consulados*, legajo 78, doc. #6. The figure of 8000 pesos comes from 200×40, the number of subscribed shares in the company.

57. Compañía de Seguros Marca JPH, AGI, *Consulados*, legajo 78.

58. AGI, *Consulados*, legajo 78, doc. #73. Spooner, *Risks at Sea*, 153, refers to a 1779 policy written at Rotterdam that included a "clause" on slaves lost overboard or via a riot.

59. See AGI, *Consulados*, legajo 518, folios 549 and 563. The ship *La Pieded* was originally destined to Lima with a possible stop in Cuba for which the premium was to be 15 percent if the ship went directly to Lima and 22 percent if it also stopped in Cuba. The *Nuevo Pajaro* was charged a premium of 16 percent to Puerto Rico and 22 percent if it continued on to Havana.

60. AGI, *Consulados*, legajo 499, exp. 12, poliza #41, 20 April 1778. Spanish functionaries paid their own expenses to assume government posts in America, including the considerable costs of paying ocean passage and relocating. Until the sale of government posts was largely terminated in the 1750s, officials also had to buy the office itself. On the sales of office, see Kenneth J. Andrien, "The Sale of Fiscal Offices and the Decline of Royal Authority in the Viceroyalty of Peru, 1633–1700," *Hispanic American Historical Review* 62, no. 1 (1982): 49–71; Jeremy Baskes, *Indians, Merchants, and Markets: A Reinterpretation of the Repartimiento and Spanish-Indian Economic Relations in Colonial Oaxaca, 1750–1821* (Stanford, CA: Stanford University Press, 2000); Brian R. Hamnett, *Politics and Trade in Southern Mexico, 1750–1821* (Cambridge: Cambridge University Press, 1971).

61. *Avería* translates literally to "average," which is an insurance term that means loss. This term should not be confused with the *Derecho de Avería*, which was an *ad valorem* tax collected on shipped merchandise to be used to defray the costs of the armada that accompanied the flota.

62. This class of losses is today called "particular average."

63. This type of loss is today termed "general average."

64. José María Quirós, *Guía de Negociantes: Compendio de la Legislación Mercantil de España e Indias*, ed. Pedro Pérez Herrero (México: Universidad

Nacional Autonoma de México, 1986), 265. Also see *Ordenanzas de Bilbao*, http://books.google.com/books?id=k7pDAAAAcAAJ&printsec=front cover&source=gbs_ge_summary_r&cad=0#v=onepage&q&f=false., chs. 20–21, 172–87.

65. AGI, *Consulados*, legajo 78, doc. #78.

66. Ibid., doc. #79.

67. See Quirós, *Guía de Negociantes*, 265–75. And *Ordenanzas de Bilbao*, chs. 21–21, 172–87. The treatment of *averías gruesas* is also described in Joséph de Veitia Linage, *Norte de la Contratación de las Indias Occidentales* (Buenos Aires: Comisión argentina de fomento interamericano, 1945), Libro II, Capítulo XIX. Originally written in 1672, Veitia Linage's guide is an invaluable source to understanding Spain's commercial legislation.

68. This practice was apparently common in other insurance markets of the era. Spooner, *Risks at Sea*, 152, refers to the exclusion of "average below 3 percent" in the insurance industry of Middleburg, Netherlands. In other words, claims that did not exceed 3 percent of the value of the insured cargo were not admissible.

69. AGI, *Consulados*, legajo 78, doc. #39.

Chapter 8

1. AGI, *Consulados*, legajo 78, doc. #42.

2. Ibid., doc. #74.

3. Nuevas Ordenanzas de Corredores, Cadiz, 1782, AGI, *Consulados*, legajo 1757, exp. a, article 32. These and other responsibilities of a *corredor* are delineated in the *Ordenanza de Bilbao* of 1737, which can be consulted at http://biblio.juridicas.unam.mx/libros/5/2260/25.pdf.

4. Nuevas Ordenanzas de Corredores, Cadiz, 1782, AGI, *Consulados*, legajo 1757, exp. a, article 33. The role of the *corredor* is also described in M. Guadalupe Carrasco González, "El Negocio de los Seguros Marítimos en Cádiz a Finales del Siglo XVIII," *Hispania, Revista Española de Historia* 59:1, no. 201 (1999): 281.

5. Specifically, the ship had to have been lost far enough away that news could not have arrived to the policyholder in the intervening time, assuming movement of the information at one league (2.6 miles) per hour. Joseph de Veitia Linage, *Norte de la Contratación de las Indias Occidentales* (Buenos Aires: Comisión argentina de fomento interamericano, 1945), book 2, ch. 9.

6. Viuda de Oviedo, Hermano e Hijos a Juan Vizente de Marticorena, Sevilla, 19 January 1797, AGI, *Consulados*, legajo 436, folio 703.

7. Correspondencia general del *consulado*, 7 February 1797, AGI, *Consulados*, libro 96, folio 223.

8. Viuda de Oviedo, Hermano e Hijos a Juan Vizente de Marticorena, Sevilla, 21 March 1797, AGI, *Consulados*, legajo 436, folio 785.

9. Juan Bautista de Marticorena to Juan Vicente de Marticorena, Guatemala, 3 June 1797, AGI, *Consulados*, legajo 436, folio 911.

10. AGI, *Consulados*, legajo 518, exp. 18, folio 340.

11. Modern insurance companies also make a substantial profit (or loss) from investing premiums collected from policyholders in current or past years. Naturally, such sums can be enormous. It is not clear whether the Cadiz firms invested their revenues in any way; regardless, it is ignored in this discussion. Importantly, the size of the capital holdings of the Spanish insurance firms was limited due to their short-term existence. At the end of the firm's tenure, four to six years, the earnings were paid out to shareholders and the partnership dissolved.

12. AGI, *Consulados*, legajo 78, doc. #39.

13. Ibid., doc. #42. This firm was originally chartered in 1794 but suspended its underwriting during the war. In 1801 it renewed its operations.

14. Frank Spooner, *Risks at Sea: Amsterdam Insurance and Maritime Europe, 1766–1780* (Cambridge: Cambridge University Press, 1983), 120–26; A. H. John, "The London Assurance Company and the Marine Insurance Market of the Eighteenth Century," *Economica* 25, no. 98 (1958): 137.

15. AGI, *Consulados*, legajo 78, doc. #3.

16. Ibid., doc. #8.

17. See Christopher W. Landsea, "A Climatology of Intense (or Major) Atlantic Hurricanes," *Monthly Weather Review* 121 (1993): 1707, table 3.

18. Tilly's actual words were *tiempos benignos*, which could also be translated as "benign times," the Spanish word *tiempo* meaning both "time" and "weather." Either way, the meaning is identical. El Marques de Casa Tilly acompaña un pliego de las observaciones particulares y reparos que ha hecho durante el comando de la flota de su cargo, por si se contemplan dignos de alguna atencion, 10 August 1770, AGI, Audiencia de México, legago 2985.

19. Tomás Ruiz de Apodaca a su esposa, Eusebia María de Eliza, Veracruz, 2 October 1759, AGI, *Consulados*, legajo 405, folios 9–10.

20. Clarence Henry Haring, *Trade and Navigation Between Spain and the Indies in the Time of the Hapsburgs* (Cambridge: Cambridge University Press, 1918), 207. Veitia Linage, *Norte de la Contratación*, book II, ch. IV, paragraph 8.

21. Alejandro de la Fuente, César García del Pino, and Bernardo Iglesias Delgado, *Havana and the Atlantic in the Sixteenth Century*, Envisioning Cuba (Chapel Hill: University of North Carolina Press, 2008), 16.

22. Antonio García-Baquero González, *Cádiz y el Atlántico: (1717–1778)*, 2 vols. (Cádiz: Diputación Provincial de Cádiz, 1988), 1:278–81.

23. Importantly, one should not conclude from this data that these routes were necessarily the most traveled or most insured. The policies used in this study were simply those located in the archive and were by no means complete sets representing the total business of any single company. Most were discovered deposited in the personal papers of individual merchants and thus might simply reflect the individual's peculiar business practices.

24. Libro de operaciones de la Compañía de seguros por Don Antonio Ramírez desde 9 de Mayo 1788 a 12 de Agosto de 1795 con esperacion de los llegados a su destino los que han retornado y los perdidos, AGI, *Consulados*, libro 444b, folio 15.

25. Ibid., folio 30.

26. AGI, *Consulados*, legajo 518, exp. 29, folio 576.

27. Spooner, *Risks at Sea*, 117, 128.

28. Ibid., 129. Spooner reports r^2 to be 0.887.

29. These calculations were carried out with data extracted from the online Appendix C.

30. See Spooner, *Risks at Sea*, 129.

31. For example, Amsterdam to London is 211 miles, and to Smyrna 3,030 miles.

32. AGI, *Consulados*, legajo 518, exp. 16, folio 223.

33. AGI, *Consulados*, legajo 78, doc. #5.

34. Ibid., doc. #39.

35. La Compañía de Seguros Marca JPH, 1 December 1801, AGI, *Consulados*, legajo 78.

36. AGI, *Consulados*, legajo 78, doc. #1, folio 17.

37. Ibid., doc. #2, clause 14.

38. For López García's firm see ibid., doc. #5. For the company directed by Lasqueti see ibid., doc. #6.

39. Ibid., doc. #39. The revised 1801 charter is contained within.

40. Ibid., doc. #42.

41. Ibid., doc. #79.

42. Ibid., doc. #4. Sacra Familia was directed by Joséf Salvador de Valverde, Joséf Augustin de Valverde, and Matias Rafael Davila.

43. Ibid., doc. #72.

44. Ibid., doc. #26 and #31.

45. Spooner, *Risks at Sea*, 31. Christopher Kingston, "Marine Insurance in Britain and America, 1720–1844: A Comparative Institutional Analysis," *Journal of Economic History* 67, no. 2 (2007): 389.

46. Testimonio del expediente sobre dificultades ocurridas a los matriculados del comercio de España, Mexico, 9 March 1782, AGI, *Consulados*, legajo 337, folio 5.

47. AGI, Indiferente General, 2417a, 2 March 1779.

48. Correspondencia general del *consulado*, El *consulado* a Pedro de Varela, 7 February 1797, AGI, *Consulados*, libro 96, folio 223. The breakdown of relations between Spain and England really began with Spain's 19 August 1796 signing of the Treaty of Ildefonso with Revolutionary France. War with England was not officially declared until October 7. Dates taken from Miguel Artola, *Enciclopedia de Historia de España*, 7 vols. (Madrid: Alianza, 1988), vol. 6.

49. Correspondencia general del *consulado*, El *consulado* a Diego de Gardoqui, 12 May 1793, AGI, *Consulados*, libro 95, folios 90–91.

50. Cartas a Don Antonio de Artechea desde distintos puntos de España y America, 1786–99, Don José Ramon de Ugarteche a Artechea, fechas varias, 24 December 1796, AGI, *Consulados*, legajo 440.

51. Correspondencia general del *consulado*, El *consulado* al Vice consul de su magestad en Lagos, 12 December 1804, AGI, *Consulados*, libro 100, folio 81.

52. Correspondencia general del *consulado*, AGI, *Consulados*, libro 100, folios 168–69.

53. See "Discurso del Mariscal de Campo de los Reales Exercitios don Antonio de Narváez y la Torre," 5 June 1805, in Antonio Narváez y la Torre, José Ignacio de Pombo, and Sergio Elías Ortiz, *Escritos de Dos Economistas Coloniales: Don Antonio de Narváez y la Torre, y Don José Ignacio de Pombo*, Archivo de la Economía Nacional 29 (Bogotá: Banco de la República, Archivo de la Economía Nacional, 1965), 72.

54. AGI, *Consulados*, legajo 499, exp. 12, folio 50.

55. AGI, *Consulados*, libro 437, folios 560–61.

56. Ibid., folios 564–65.

57. AGI, *Consulados*, legajo 499, exp. 12, folio 47.

58. Ibid., folio 56.

59. See AGI, *Consulados*, legajos 420–28. Legajos 421–23 contain Sierra's correspondence for the years 1781–82.

60. AGI, *Consulados*, legajo 72, exp. 26, 285, 286, 291, and 295.

61. See online Appendix C.

62. Rates were sometimes made conditional on whether or not the ship arrived safely, a higher rate applying when ships were lost or seized. On conditional rates, see discussion in this chapter.

63. Francisco Valdovinos to Antonio de Artechea, Buenos Aires, 1 January 1797, AGI, *Consulados*, legajo 440.

64. AGI, *Consulados*, legago 518, exp. 13, folio 197, and AGI, *Consulados*, libro 889.

65. See *Correo Mercantil de España y sus Indias*, 26 March 1798, 210, available online at http://hemerotecadigital.bne.es.

66. AGI, *Consulados*, legajo 518, exp. 18, folio 344.

67. Ibid., folio 340.

68. See online Appendix C.

69. John Fisher, *Commercial Relations Between Spain and Spanish America in the Era of Free Trade, 1778–1796* (Liverpool: Center for Latin American Studies, University of Liverpool, 1985), 61.

70. AGI, *Consulados*, legajo 772, exp. 2.

71. AGI, *Consulados*, legajo 499, exp. 12, folio 17.

72. AGI, *Consulados*, legajo 499, exp. 12, folio 31. Perhaps unimportant, these merchants ultimately cancelled this policy for unspecified reasons. Whenever polices were *extrornada* (returned), the insured paid a small fee, perhaps 0.5 perecent.

73. AGI, *Consulados*, legajo 518, exp. 12, folio 186.

74. Ibid., folio 247.

75. Archivo Histórico Nacional (hereafter AHN), Consejos, 20214, exp. 7. Available online at http://pares.mcu.es/ (accessed 6 June 2008).

76. Correspondencia general del *consulado*, Sres. Ruiz, Araurra, y Murguía a Pedro Varela, 7 April 1797, AGI, *Consulados*, libro 96, folios 238–39. For a summary of the *consulado* debate that led to this decision, see AGI, *Consulados*, libro 20, 5 April 1797.

77. Correspondencia general del *consulado*, Sres. Murguía y Ramos a Pedro Varela, 23 May 1797, AGI, *Consulados*, libro 97, folios 17–18.

78. Correspondencia general del *consulado*, Cadiz, 5 April 1799, AGI, *Consulados*, libro 97, folios 482–85. It is not evident why the premium collected was only 13.8 percent.

79. Correspondencia general del *consulado*, Cadiz, 20 March 1800, AGI, *Consulados*, libro 98.

80. Agi, *Consulados*, libro 434, folios 766–67.

81. See AGI, *Consulados*, legajo 499, exp. 12, folio 39; AGI, *Consulados*, legajo 499, exp. 12, folio 34; and AGI, *Consulados*, libro 437, folios 560–61.

82. See online Appendix C.

83. Juan Bautista de Marticorena a Juan Vicente de Marticorena, Nueva Guatemala, 28 August 1793, AGI, *Consulados*, legajo 434, folio 1265.

84. Libro de cartas del dueño del navío el Jasón a particulares, desde Veracruz, Cadiz, Buenos Aires, etc., Francisco de Sierra to Juan Joséf Vizarron, Cadiz, 18 August 1773, AGI, *Consulados*, libro 157, folio 21v.

85. AGI, *Consulados*, legajo 499, exp. 12, folio 27.

86. AGI, *Consulados*, legajo 518, exp. 12, folio 247.

87. The markup of 200 percent (three times) was chosen merely for illustrative purposes. The formula used for the calculation of net returns was gross revenues minus original value minus insurance premium. So, if gross revenues $= 2,300 \times 3 = 6,900$ pesos, then estimated nominal net profitss $= 6,900 - 2,300 - (2300 \times 50.25\%) = 3,455.75$. If the Sally were captured, Sierra would have simpy lost his premium or 1,155.75 pesos.

88. Relacion del *consulado* de Mexico sobre los atrasos que sufre el comercio del reyno por consequencia de la guerra y si combendria franquear el comercio de licita introduccion de Havana, 19 October 1798, AGI, *Consulados*, legajo 340.

89. Expedientes del *Consulado* y Comercio, 1800–1802, Remite los citados del comercio de entrada y salida de Veracruz el ano de 1799, AGI, Audiencia de Mexico, legajo 2509.

90. El *Consulado* de Guatemala representa los perjuicios que se le siguen al comercio de que no salgan de la Havana las tintas que conduxeron a ella el Bergantín San Rafael y Fragata Placentina y suplica Su Magestad se sirva mandar se trasladen a España en buques de guerra, año de 1800, AGI, *Consulados*, libro 341.

91. AGI, *Consulados*, legajo 72, exp. 26, folio 291.

92. Ibid., folio 289.

93. AGI, *Consulados*, legajo 518, exp. 15, folios 205, 207, 209, and 211.

94. AGI, *Consulados*, libro 434, folios 766–67.

95. AGI, *Consulados*, legajo 518, exp. 16, folio 249.

96. Pio de Elizalde a Juan Vizente de Marticorena, September 1798, AGI, *Consulados*, legajo 437, folio 552–54, and 7 December 1798, folio 699.

97. On the concept of moral hazard, see Kenneth Joseph Arrow, *Essays in the Theory of Risk-Bearing* (Chicago: Markham, 1971), 142–43. For the referenced passages of the *Ordenanza de Bilbao*, see http://www.biblioju ridica.org/libros/libro.htm?l=2260, ch. 22, sections VII and IX, 191–92. These sections were largely reproduced in José María Quirós, *Guía de Negociantes: Compendio de la Legislación Mercantil de España e Indias*, edited

by Pedro Pérez Herrero (México: Universidad Nacional Autonoma de México, 1986), article 9, sections 8 and 10, 289–90.

98. Arrow, *Essays in the Theory of Risk-Bearing*, 143.

99. Oscar Cruz Barney, *El Riesgo en el Comercio de Hispano-Indiano: Préstamos y Seguros Maritimos Durante los Siglos XVI a XIX* (Mexico City: UNAM, 1998), 31.

100. AGI, *Consulados*, libro 90, folio 116v, 9 May 1780.

101. AGI, *Consulados*, legajo 499, exp. 12, folio 66. Policies actually stated this in reverse. This particular policy, for example, stipulated a rate of 25.5 percent with a reduction to 20.25 percent if the vessel arrived safely. I have chosen to express it differently than the policies did since the actual rate charged under normal circumstances would have been the safe arrival rate, not the captured rate. By using the safe arrival rate, the "normal" rate, I can more effectively compare premium rates between policies.

102. AGI, *Consulados*, legajo 518, exp. 10, folio 153.

103. Ibid., exp. 11, folio 171.

104. AGI, *Consulados*, legajo 889.

105. AGI, *Consulados*, legajo 518, exp. 18, folios 344 and 340 respectively.

106. Ibid., exp. 29, folio 582.

107. Ibid., exp. 28, folio 571.

108. Pedro Mártir Coll y Alsina, *Tratado Elemental Teorico y Práctico de Comercio: en Que Se Presentan Varias Formulas de Contratas de Fletamentos, Conocimientos, Pólizas de Seguros . . . Que para Gobierno de Un Hijo Suyo Joven Comerciante Compusó, y Ha Corregido y Aumentado en Esta Edición, Pedro Martir Coll, y Alsina* (Barcelona: M. y T. Gaspar, 1818), 19. This book can be consulted online at: http://books.google.com.mx/books?id=2dXB2D0aiu8C&printsec=frontcover&source=gbs_ge_summary_r&cad=0#v=onepage&q&f=false.

109. See lengthier discussion in Chapter 3 above.

110. On the heyday of piracy in the Spanish empire see, for example, Kris E. Lane, *Pillaging the Empire: Piracy in the Americas, 1500–1750*, Latin American Realities (Armonk, NY: M. E. Sharpe, 1998); and Kenneth R. Andrews, *The Spanish Caribbean: Trade and Plunder, 1530–1630* (New Haven, CT: Yale University Press, 1978).

111. Pablo Amorós a Juan Vicente de Marticorena, Tarifa, 23 November 1806, AGI, *Consulados*, legajo 439, folio 416.

112. Joséf Ignacio Pavón y Muñoz a Juan José Puch," 29 November 1799, AGI, *Consulados*, legajo 429.

113. AGI, *Consulados*, legajo 499, exp. 12, folio 26.
114. AGI, *Consulados*, libro 437, folio. 530.
115. Ibid., folio 536.
116. AGI, *Consulados*, legajo 499, exp. 12, folio 56.
117. Fermín de Tastet y Compañia to Francisco de Sierra, 10 August 1781, AGI, *Consulados*, legajo 421 (unpaginated).
118. AGI, *Consulados*, legajo 518, exp. 9, folio 127.
119. Ibid., exp. 10, folio 139.
120. Ibid., exp. 20, folio 348.
121. Manuel Ravina Martin, "Participación Extranjera en el Comercio Indiano: El Seguro Marítimo a Fines del Siglo XVII," *Revista de Indias* 43 (1983): 490 and appendix 1.
122. John, "London Assurance Company," 137–38. Clark cites a source indicating that nonconvoyed ships paid four times the premium of convoyed vessels. This seems to overstate the normal surcharge. See Geoffrey Clark, "Insurance as an Instrument of War in the 18th Century," *Geneva Papers on Risk and Insurance* 29, no. 2 (2004): 249.
123. Harrold Edgar Gillingham, *Marine Insurance in Philadelphia, 1721–1800, with a List of Brokers and Underwriters as Shown by Old Policies and Books of Record, Including an Appendix of Marine Insurance of Archibald Mccall, 1809–1811* (Philadelphia: Patterson & White, 1933), 72, 101.
124. Spooner, *Risks at Sea*, 106, 130.
125. Ibid., 105–6.
126. Meir Kohn, *The Origins of Western Economic Success: Commerce, Finance, and Government in Preindustrial Europe* (Working papers, Department of Economics, Dartmouth College, Hanover, NH, 2001), available online at http://www.dartmouth.edu/~mkohn/.
127. Francisco Paula Carballeda a Francisco de Sierra, Guarico, 24 February 1782 AGI, *Consulados*, legajo 423, (unpaginated legajo).
128. Correspondencia general del *consulado*, Cadiz, 19 April 1793, AGI, *Consulados*, libro 95, folios 72–74.
129. Ibid., 7 May 1793, folios 85–86.
130. See the multiple requests in AGI, *Consulados*, libros 95–100. Numerous requests for convoys also appear in AGI, *Consulados*, libro 20.
131. Contextacion del *Cadiz consulado* al Ynterrogatorio que de Real Orden le dirigio el Excelentisimo Señor Ministro de Hacienda con fecha 17 del proximo pasado més de febrero, 30 March 1819, AGI, *Consulados*, legajo 81.
132. A multiple regression is a statistical method used to measure the relationship between a dependent variable and several independent

variables. In the multiple regression performed above, the goal was to assess the impact of multiple factors (independent variables) on the premium rate (dependent variable) charged.

133. An F-test was performed to test if it was possible that none of the independent variables had an effect on the premium. The calculated F-statistic was 22.5, permitting the rejection of the idea that none of the variables had an effect.

134. The five categories were ship, precious metals, all other goods, combination, and miscellaneous. The category of combination was used whenever the insured items consisted of both precious metals and other goods. The miscellaneous category was a catchall of unusual items that did not fit anywhere else.

135. To reject the idea that an individual variable (factor) had no effect at the standard 5 percent level, the absolute value of the t-statistic needed to be greater than 1.96.

136. AGI, *Consulados*, legajo 78, doc. #39. See also AGI, *Consulados*, Legajo 78, doc. #42.

137. AGI, *Consulados*, legajo 78, doc. #42.

138. Ibid., doc. #77.

139. AGI, *Consulados*, legajo 72, exp. 26, folio 322.

140. AGI, *Consulados*, legajo 518, exp. 3, folio 31.

141. Informe del *consulado* de Sevilla sobre comercio libre Seville, 1788, BNM, Manuscritos, ms1397, folios 261–308,

142. Informe reservado de don Tomás Murphy, dirigido al Virrey, sobre el Estado que guarda el comercio de la Nueva España, Veracruz, 20 April 1793. Published in Enrique Florescano and Fernando Castillo, eds., *Controversia Sobre la Libertad de Comercio en Nueva España, 1776–1818*, Serie Fuentes y Estadísticas del Comercio Exterior de México 1 (México: Instituto Mexicano de Comercio Exterior, 1975), Tomo 1, 389.

143. These three figures show "effective rates," defined here as the presumed actual rates charged for a voyage. Whenever a policy stipulated a surcharge in the event of war, for example, the effective rate used for this analysis includes this surcharge only when Spain was actually engaged in war. So if Spain was not at war when the policy was underwritten, the peacetime rate was deemed to be the effective rate. If war was already in process, then the surcharge was included. For the purposes of examining general trends, this methodology seems reasonable. But it should be noted that there are at least several reasons why this method might not accurately capture the actual rates that would have applied. For one, insurance policies were often, but not always, underwritten well before the vessel was

launched. This is, of course, one reason why rates were expressed conditionally. A policy might be taken out in January even though the the ship did not embark until June. During the interim war might erupt requiring the payment of wartime rates, the regular peacetime rate plus the surcharge. For the discussion that follows, the January peacetime rate is assumed, not the latter, and actual, wartime rate. A second possible problem arises from the uncertainty of determining precisely when insurers began charging the elevated wartime rates. As discussed above, insurers and insured hotly debated this date. The insurance companies argued for the earliest date possible; the insured parties hoped a later date would allow them to avoid payment of the surcharges. It fell to the consulado to determine the date to be used for the outbreak of war for insurance purposes. Because this ambiguity had to be minimized for this exercise, it was decided to employ the dates on which Spain declared war against its enemies. Again, any discrepancy is minimal and certainly does not affect the general conclusions of the analysis that follows.

144. The routes included were, in either direction, Cadiz–La Guaira; Northern Spain–La Guaira; Cadiz–Havana; Northern Spain–Havana; Cadiz–Cartagena; Cadiz–Central America; Cadiz–Veracruz; Cadiz–Río de la Plata; Barcelona–Veracrruz; Northern Spain–Río de la Plata; and Cadiz–Lima. The ports classified as "Northern Spain" consisted of Santander, La Coruña, and Bilbao, and, to a lesser extent, San Sebastian and Vigo. Río de la Plata included both Monevideo and Buenos Aires. Central America entailed overwhelmingly the ports of Honduras.

145. A simple example can illustrate. If a data set consisted of three years and the variable moved from 1 to 10 to 100 units over the period, growth between year 2 and year 3 would appear much greater in a standard figure than change between year 1 and year 2. A logarithmic figure would show these as identical changes (a straight line) since in both cases growth was of a magnitude of ten. The logarithmic scale illustrates *relative* change.

146. For the French port of La Rochelle, see John G. Clark, "Marine Insurance in Eighteenth-Century La Rochelle," *French Historical Studies* 10, no. 4 (1978): 583–84; for Amsterdam, see Spooner, *Risks at Sea*, 56–58; and regarding London, consult Jacob M. Price, "Transaction Costs: A Note on Merchant Credit and the Organization of Private Trade," in *The Political Economy of Merchant Empires: State Power and World Trade, 1350–1750*, ed. James D. Tracy (Cambridge: Cambridge University Press, 1991), 288–89.

147. See Douglass North, "Ocean Freight Rates and Economic Development 1750–1913," *Journal of Economic History* 18, no. 4 (1958): 541–42;

and Douglass C. North, "Sources of Productivity Change in Ocean Shipping, 1600–1850," *Journal of Political Economy* 76, no. 5 (1968): 954. There is some challenge to North's conclusions. Employing a different methodology, Harley concludes that freight rates rose moderately from 1740 to the mid-nineteenth century. See C. Knick Harley, "Ocean Freight Rates and Productivity, 1740–1913: The Primacy of Mechanical Invention Reaffirmed," *Journal of Economic History* 48, no. 4 (1988): 853.

148. Noticia extractada de los Directores de Compañías de Seguros establecidos en esta plaza y registradas en esta contaduria del *consulado* del tiempo en que empezó a correr el termino de ellas y del en que deben concluir, segun escripturas, AGI, *Consulados*, legajo 78. Also see Table 8.1.

149. France and Britain resumed fighting in May 1803 but Spain actually remained neutral until 14 December 1804. The peacetime rates used for this comparison consider only the months leading up to the resumption of hostilities between Spain's neighbors. This seems prudent since Spanish merchants must have concluded after May 1803 that their nation's reentry into the war was inevitable.

150. Data extracted from online Appendix C.

151. Correspondencia y documentos de don Juan José Puch (1777–1819), Rafael José Facio a Juan José de Puch, 26 November 1803, AGI, *Consulados*, legajo 429. Most historians of the Napoleonic wars view Amiens as a temporary truce, an orchestrated break in hostilities so that each side could recover and redouble their efforts for the following round of war. For an alternative view, see John D. Grainger, *The Amiens Truce: Britain and Bonaparte, 1801–1803* (Rochester, NY: Boydell, 2004).

152. The Crown was adequately concerned about the rise of this "piracy" that it initiated an investigation into what could be done to address the related commercial decay. See Contestación del *Cadiz consulado* al Ynterrogatorio que de Real Orden le dirigió el Excelentísimo Señor Ministro de Hacienda con fecha 17 del próximo pasado mes de febrero, 30 March 1819, AGI, *Consulados*, legajo 81.

153. Data extracted from online Appendix C.

Chapter 9

1. Antonio-Miguel Bernal, *La Financiación de la Carrera de Indias (1492–1824): Dinero y Crédito en el Comercio Colonial Español Con América* (Sevilla: Fundación el Monte, 1992), 474–75. Unfortunately, the reference to the source used by Bernal was not sufficiently clear to permit its location and consultation. This large number of firms eclipses the quantity identified and discussed in Chapter 7. In contrast, eighty-seven firms is close to the

total number of firms identified in Chapter 7 as having been established throughout the 1790s. Perhaps this is where Bernal's figure originates.

2. Nicolás de la Cruz y Bahamonde, *De Cádiz y Su Comercio: Tomo Xiii del Viaje de España, Francia e Italia*, edited by Manuel Ravina Martín (Cádiz: Servicio de Publicaciones, Universidad de Cádiz, 1997), 69. This multivolume work was originally published from 1806 to 1813.

3. Correspondencia general del *consulado*, AGI, *Consulados*, libro 98, folios 123–28.

4. Pedro Fermín de Córdoba a Juan Vicente de Marticorena, Cadiz, 12 March 1799, AGI, *Consulados*, legajo 437, folio 863.

5. The *livres tournois* was an imaginary coin used to record French commercial transactions. In this regard it was the same as the Spanish *real de maravedí*, which by the eighteenth century had ceased to circulate but was still often employed in accounting.

6. Estado general de los seguros de La Compañía Gaditana a la dirección de don Juan Payan, 31 October 1784, AGI, *Consulados*, legajo 428 (unpaginated).

7. AGI, *Consulados*, libro 444B.

8. This commission rate is unusually low, as the industry standard, discussed above, was 0.5 percent. What is likely is that the directors had not yet collected their entire commission, perhaps awaiting the collection of premiums still outstanding. Indeed it was customary for the directors to charge their commission only upon the receipt of premiums. Although this issue is ignored for purposes of analysis, it would only increase further the company's financial woes.

9. The figures shown in the table come directly from the ledger, converted from *reales* to pesos. The numbers mysteriously leave 437 pesos unaccounted. This was ignored because it seemed preferable to present the figures as they appear in the records rather than guess from where the error arose.

10. Libro de operaciones de la compañía de seguros por Don Antonio Ramírez desde 9 de Mayo 1788 a 12 de Agosto de 1795 con expresión de los llegados a su destino, los que han retornados, y los perdidos, AGI, *Consulados*, libro 444B.

11. Source: AGI, *Consulados*, legajo 522, exp. 8, folio 850.

12. Estado de la Compañía de Seguros a la dirección de Don Juan Esteban de Tellechea Marca M desde Diciembre de 1793, en que dió principio, hasta 31 de diciembre de 1796 a 18 February 1799, AGI, *Consulados*, legajo 522, exp. 8, folio 850.

13. AGI, *Consulados*, legajo 522, exp. 8, folio 857, 16 June 1796.

14. Juan Vicente de Marticorena al Rey, 24 August 1801, AGI, *Consulados*, legajo 72, folio 443v.

15. AGI, *Consulados*, legajo 437, folio 696. AGI, *Consulados*, legajo 522, folios 844 and 896 are slightly different versions of the same list, snapshots of Marticorena's debts at different moments. These lists, which were little more than marginal scribbles, were clearly prepared by Marticorena for his own eyes only. Unfortunately, Marticorena's lists are undated, but seem to be from the last year or so of the century.

16. Noticia extractada de los Directores de Compañías de Seguros, AGI, *Consulados*, legajo 78, docs. 3, 19, 28, 34, 50, and 66. More detail on Marticorena's insurance shares and especially the demands made that Marticorena pay his share of losses can be examined in Documentos relativos a las quiebras y liquidaciones de las compañías de seguros (1793–1804), AGI, *Consulados*, legajo 522.

17. Correspondencia general del *consulado*, AGI, *Consulados*, libro 97, folios 182–89.

18. Ibid.

19. Ibid., folios 191–93.

20. Ibid., folios 209–10.

21. Ibid., folios 182–89.

22. Ibid., folios 310–15.

23. Ibid.

24. Ibid.

25. Pedro Fermín de Córdoba a Juan Vicente de Marticorena, Cadiz, 5 February 1799, AGI, *Consulados*, legajo 437, folio 782.

26. Ximénez Perez Padre y Hijo a Juan Vicente de Marticorena, Cadiz, 12 December 1797, AGI, *Consulados*, legajo 436, folio 1201.

27. Ximénez Perez Padre y Hijo a Pedro Fermín de Córdoba, 11 July 1798, AGI, *Consulados*, legajo 437, folio 409.

28. Pedro Fermín de Córdoba a Juan Vicente de Marticorena, Cadiz, 31 July 1798, AGI, *Consulados*, legajo 437, folio 452.

29. Juan Francisco de Alzueta a Juan Vicente de Marticorena, 3 July 1798, AGI, *Consulados*, legajo 437, folio 393.

30. Joaquin de Ezcurra a Juan Vicente de Marticorena, Cadiz, 4 December 1798, AGI, *Consulados*, legajo 437, folio 695.

31. Noticia extractada de los Directores de Compañías de Seguros establecidos en esta plaza y registradas en esta contaduría del *consulado* del tiempo en que empezó a correr el termino de ellas y del en que deben concluir, según escrituras, AGI, *Consulados*, legajo 78, doc. 53.

32. Victoria Eugenia Martinez del Cerro González, *Una Comunidad de Comerciantes: Navarros y Vascos en Cádiz (Segunda Mitad de Siglo XVIII)* (Sevilla: Consejo Económico y Social de Andalucía, 2006), 180.

33. Correspondencia general del *consulado*, Cadiz, 5 April 1799, AGI, *Consulados*, libro 97, folios 482–85.

34. These estimated profits seems very low. Had this truly been an investment of 10,000 pesos, then a 500 peso profit over five years would have been less than 1 percent compounded. Of course, the issue here is a bit more complicated since the "investors" did not really put up any funds; they just guaranteed to deposit funds in the event of losses.

35. Correspondencia general del *consulado*, AGI, *Consulados*, libro 98, folios 123–28.

36. Pedro Fermín de Córdoba a Juan Vicente de Marticorena, Cadiz, 5 August 1800, AGI, *Consulados*, legajo 438, folio 169.

Chapter 10

1. Jeremy Adelman, *Sovereignty and Revolution in the Iberian Atlantic* (Princeton, NJ: Princeton University Press, 2006), 8.

2.. The role of government in providing the protection that merchants need to profit is one of the central themes of Frederic Chapin Lane, *Profits from Power: Readings in Protection Rent and Violence-Controlling Enterprises* (Albany: State University of New York Press, 1979).

3. Ynforme de los Señores Terry y Aguirre sobre la observancia de las leyes de Indias en el comercio de America contra la solicitud de los Americanos de hacerlo libremente para Reinos extraños en derechura satisfaciendo el decretro de 12 de Noviembre de 1816 . . . Julio 1817, AGI, *Consulados*, legajo 81, folios 1–2.

Adams, Donald R., Jr. "American Neutrality and Prosperity, 1793–1808: A Reconsideration." *Journal of Economic History* 40, no. 4 (1980): 713–37.

Adelman, Jeremy. *Republic of Capital: Buenos Aires and the Legal Transformation of the Atlantic World*. Stanford, CA: Stanford University Press, 1999.

———. *Sovereignty and Revolution in the Iberian Atlantic*. Princeton, NJ: Princeton University Press, 2006.

Ahonen, Kalevi. *From Sugar Triangle to Cotton Triangle: Trade and Shipping Between America and Baltic Russia, 1783–1860*. Jyvaskyla: University of Jyvaskyla, 2005.

Albion, Robert Greenhalgh, and Jennie Barnes Pope. *Sea Lanes in Wartime: The American Experience, 1775–1942*. New York: Norton, 1942.

Andrews, Kenneth R. *The Spanish Caribbean: Trade and Plunder, 1530–1630*. New Haven, CT: Yale University Press, 1978.

Andrien, Kenneth J. "The Sale of Fiscal Offices and the Decline of Royal Authority in the Viceroyalty of Peru, 1633–1700." *Hispanic American Historical Review* 62, no. 1 (1982): 49–71.

———. *Crisis and Decline: The Viceroyalty of Peru in the Seventeenth Century*. Albuquerque: University of New Mexico Press, 1985.

———. *The Kingdom of Quito, 1690–1830: The State and Regional Development*. Cambridge Latin American Studies 80. Cambridge: Cambridge University Press, 1995.

———. "The Spanish Atlantic System." In *Atlantic History: A Critical Appraisal*, edited by Jack P. Greene and Philip D. Morgan, 55–80. Oxford: Oxford University Press, 2009.

Archivo General de Indias (AGI), Seville. Foreign archives.

Archivo General de la Nación de México (AGN), Mexico City, Foreign archives.

Archivo Histórico Nacional (AHN), Madrid. Foreign archives.

Armitage, David, and M. J. Braddick. *The British Atlantic World, 1500–1800*. New York: Palgrave Macmillan, 2002.

Arrow, Kenneth Joseph. *Essays in the Theory of Risk-Bearing*. Chicago: Markham, 1971.

———. *Limits of Organization*. Fels Lectures on Public Policy Analysis. New York: Norton, 1974.

Arroyo, Lara. "Redes de Influencia: Relaciones Privilegiados en el Comercio Colonial a Finales del Siglo XVIII: los Marticorena y Su Correspondencia Epistolar." *Nuevo Mundo Mundos Nuevos*. January 30, 2007. Accessed September 20, 2010. http:\\nuevomundo.revues.org\index3213 .html.

Artola, Miguel. *Enciclopedia de Historia de España*. 7 vols. Madrid: Alianza, 1988.

Bailyn, Bernard. "Braudel's Geohistory—A Reconsideration." *Journal of Economic History* 11, no. 3 (1951): 277–82.

———. "Communications and Trade: The Atlantic in the Seventeenth Century." *Journal of Economic History* 13, no. 4 (1953): 378–87.

———. *Atlantic History: Concept and Contours*. Cambridge, MA: Harvard University Press, 2005.

Bakewell, P. J. *Silver Mining and Society in Colonial Mexico: Zacatecas, 1546–1700*. Cambridge Latin American Studies 15. 1971. Reprint, Cambridge: Cambridge University Press, 2002.

———. *Miners of the Red Mountain: Indian Labor in Potosí, 1545–1650*. Albuquerque: University of New Mexico Press, 1984.

———. *A History of Latin America: 1450 to the Present*. 2nd ed. Malden, MA: Blackwell, 2004.

Barbier, Jacques A. "Venezuelan 'Libranzas,' 1788–1807: From Economic Nostrum to Fiscal Imperative." *The Americas* 37, no. 4 (1981): 457–78.

Barbier, Jacques, and Herbert Klein. "Recent Trends in the Study of Spanish American Colonial Public Finance." *Latin American Research Review* 23, no. 1 (1988): 35–62.

Barbour, Violet. "Marine Risks and Insurance in the Seventeenth Century." *Journal of Economic and Business History* 1, no. 4 (1929): 561–96.

Baskes, Jeremy. *Indians, Merchants, and Markets: A Reinterpretation of the Repartimiento and Spanish-Indian Economic Relations in Colonial Oaxaca, 1750–1821*. Stanford, CA: Stanford University Press, 2000.

Benjamin, Thomas. *The Atlantic World: Europeans, Africans, Indians and Their Shared History, 1400–1900*. New York: Cambridge University Press, 2009.

Bernal, Antonio-Miguel. *La Financiación de la Carrera de Indias (1492–1824): Dinero y Crédito en el Comercio Colonial Español Con América*. Sevilla: Fundación el Monte, 1992.

Bernal, Antonio-Miguel, and Antonio García-Baquero González. *Tres Siglos del Comercio Sevillano, 1598–1860: Cuestiones y Problemas*. Sevilla: Camara Oficial de Comercio Industria y Navegación de Sevilla, 1976.

Biblioteca Nacional de México (BNM). Mexico City. Foreign Archives.

Bleichmar, Daniela, Paula De Vos, Kristin Huffine, and Kevin Sheehan, eds. *Science in the Spanish and Portuguese Empires, 1500–1800*. Stanford, CA: Stanford University Press, 2009.

Borah, Woodrow Wilson. *New Spain's Century of Depression*. Berkeley: University of California Press, 1951.

Boyer, Richard. "Mexico in the Seventeenth Century: Transition of a Colonial Society." *Hispanic American Historical Review* 57, no. 3(1977): 455–478.

Brading, D. A. *Miners and Merchants in Bourbon Mexico, 1763–1810*. Cambridge: Cambridge University Press, 1971.

———. "Bourbon Spain and Its American Empire." In *The Cambridge History of Latin America*, edited by Leslie Bethell, 1:389–439. Cambridge: Cambridge University Press, 1984.

———. Review of *Commercial Relations between Spain and Spanish America in the Era of Free Trade, 1778–1796*, by John Fisher. *Journal of Latin American Studies* 19, no. 2 (1987): 419–21.

Brading, D. A., and Harry E. Cross. "Colonial Silver Mining: Mexico and Peru." *Hispanic American Historical Review* 52, no. 4 (1972): 545–79.

Braudel, Fernand. *The Mediterranean and the Mediterranean World in the Age of Philip II*. New York: Harper & Row, 1972.

Brown, Richmond F. "Profits, Prestige, and Persistence: Juan Fermín de Aycinena and the Spirit of Enterprise in the Kingdom of Guatemala." *Hispanic American Historical Review* 75, no. 3 (1995): 405–40.

———. *Juan Fermín de Aycinena: Central American Colonial Entrepreneur, 1729–1796*. Norman: University of Oklahoma Press, 1997.

Buck, Norman Sydney. *The Development of the Organisation of Anglo-American Trade, 1800–1850*. New Haven, CT: Yale University Press, 1925.

Burkholder, Mark A., and Lyman L. Johnson. *Colonial Latin America*. 6th ed. New York: Oxford University Press, 2008.

Cañizares-Esguerra, Jorge. *How to Write the History of the New World: Histories, Epistemologies, and Identities in the Eighteenth-Century Atlantic World.* Cultural Sitings. Stanford, CA: Stanford University Press, 2001.

————. *Puritan Conquistadors: Iberianizing the Atlantic, 1550–1700.* Stanford, CA: Stanford University Press, 2006.

Cañizares-Esguerra, Jorge, and Erik R. Seeman. *The Atlantic in Global History, 1500–2000.* Upper Saddle River, NJ: Pearson Prentice Hall, 2007.

Cardoso, Fernando Henrique, and Enzo Faletto. *Dependency and Development in Latin America.* Berkeley: University of California Press, 1979.

Carlos, Ann M. "Principal-Agent Problems in Early Trading Companies: A Tale of Two Firms." *American Economic Review* 82, no. 2 (1992): 140–45.

Carlos, Ann M., and Stephen Nicholas. "'Giants of an Earlier Capitalism': The Chartered Trading Companies as Modern Multinationals." *Business History Review* 62, no. 3 (Autumn 1988): 398–419.

————. "Agency Problems in Early Chartered Companies: The Case of the Hudson's Bay Company." *Journal of Economic History* 50, no. 4 (1990): 853–75.

————. "Theory and History: Seventeenth-Century Joint-Stock Chartered Trading Companies." *Journal of Economic History* 56, no. 4 (1996): 916–24.

Carmagnani, Marcello. *El Regreso de los Dioses: el Proceso de Reconstitución de la Identidad Étnica en Oaxaca, Siglos XVII y XVIII.* Sección de Obras de Historia. México: Fondo del Cultura Económica, 1988.

Carrasco González, M. Guadalupe. "El Negocio de los Seguros Marítimos en Cádiz a Finales del Siglo XVIII." *Hispania, Revista Española de Historia* 59:1, no. 201 (1999): 269–304.

Chaudhuri, K. N. *The English East India Company: The Study of an Early Joint-Stock Company, 1600–1640.* New York: Reprints of Economic Classics, 1965.

————. *The Trading World of Asia and the English East India Company, 1660–1760.* Cambridge: Cambridge University Press, 1978.

Clark, Geoffrey. "Insurance as an Instrument of War in the 18th Century." *Geneva Papers on Risk and Insurance* 29, no. 2 (2004): 247–57.

Clark, John G. "Marine Insurance in Eighteenth-Century La Rochelle." *French Historical Studies* 10, no. 4 (1978): 572–98.

Clayton, Lawrence. "Trade and Navigation in the Seventeenth-Century Viceroyalty of Peru." *Journal of Latin American Studies* 7, no. 1 (1975): 1–21.

Coatsworth, John H. "American Trade with European Colonies in the Caribbean and South America, 1790–1812." *William and Mary College Quarterly Historical Magazine* 24, no. 2 (1967): 243–66.

———. "The Mexican Mining Industry in the Eighteenth Century." In *The Economies of Mexico and Peru During the Late Colonial Period, 1760–1810*, edited by Nils Jacobsen and Hans-Jürgen Puhle, 26–45. Berlin: Colloquium Verlag, 1986.

Cope, R. Douglas. *The Limits of Racial Domination: Plebeian Society in Colonial Mexico City, 1660–1720*. Madison: University of Wisconsin Press, 1994.

Costeloe, Michael P. "Barcelona Merchants and the Latin American Wars of Independence." *The Americas* 38, no. 4 (1982): 431–48.

Crosby, Alfred W. *The Columbian Exchange: Biological and Cultural Consequences of 1492*. Westport, CT: Greenwood, 1972.

———. *Ecological Imperialism: The Biological Expansion of Europe, 900–1900*. Studies in Environment and History. Cambridge: Cambridge University Press, 1986.

Cruz Barney, Oscar. *El Régimen Jurídico del Corso Marítimo: el Mundo Indiano y el México del Siglo XIX*. Serie C—Estudios Históricos 64. México: Universidad Nacional Autónoma de México, 1997.

———. *El Riesgo en el Comercio de Hispano-Indiano: Préstamos y Seguros Maritimos Durante los Siglos XVI a XIX*. Mexico City: UNAM, 1998.

Cruz y Bahamonde, Nicolás de la. *De Cádiz y Su Comercio: Tomo Xiii del Viaje de España, Francia e Italia*. Edited by Manuel Ravina Martín. Cádiz: Servicio de Publicaciones, Universidad de Cádiz, 1997.

Cruz y Bahamonde, Nicolás de la, and Sergio Martínez Baeza. *Epistolario de Don Nicolás de la Cruz y Bahamonde, Primer Conde de Maule*. Fuentes para el Estudio de la Colonia 2. Santiago de Chile: Dirección de Bibliotecas Archivos y Museos Centro de Investigaciones Diego Barros Arana, 1994.

Cuenca-Esteban, Javier. "Statistics of Spain's Colonial Trade, 1747–1820: New Estimates and Comparisons with Great Britain." *Revista de Historia Económica/Journal of Iberian and Latin American Economic History* 26, no. 3 (2008): 323–54.

———. "The United States Balance of Payments with Spanish America and the Philippine Islands, 1790–1819." In *The North American Role in the Spanish Imperial Economy, 1760–1819*, edited by Jacques and Allan Kuethe Barbier. Manchester: Manchester University Press, 1984.

Curtin, Philip D. *The Atlantic Slave Trade: A Census*. Madison: University of Wisconsin Press, 1969.

Davis, David Brion. *The Problem of Slavery in the Age of Revolution, 1770–1823*. Ithaca, NY: Cornell University Press, 1975.

————. *Inhuman Bondage: The Rise and Fall of Slavery in the New World.* New York: Oxford University Press, 2008.

de Conde, Alexander. *The Quasi-War: Politics and Diplomacy of the Undeclared War with France, 1797–1801.* New York: Scribner, 1966.

de Roover, Florence Edler. "Early Examples of Marine Insurance." *Journal of Economic History* 5, no. 2 (1945): 172–200.

Deans-Smith, Susan. *Bureaucrats, Planters, and Workers: The Making of the Tobacco Monopoly in Bourbon Mexico.* Austin: University of Texas Press, 1992.

Delgado Ribas, José Maria. "Libre Comercio: Mito y Realidad." In *Mercado y Desarollo Económico en la España Contemporánea*, edited by Tomas Martinez Vara, 69–83. Madrid: Siglo Veintiuno de España, 1986.

Delgado Ribas, Josep M. *Dinámicas Imperiales (1650–1796): España, América y Europa en el Cambio Institucional del Sistema Colonial Español.* Serie General Universitaria 63. Barcelona: Edicions Bellaterra, 2007.

Diamond, Jared M. *Guns, Germs and Steel: The Fates of Human Societies.* London: Jonathan Cape, 1997.

Dilg, George Robertson. "The Collapse of the Portobello Fairs: A Study in Spanish Commercial Reform, 1720–1740." PhD diss., Indiana University, 1975.

Dosman, Edgar J. *The Life and Times of Raúl Prebisch, 1901–1986.* Montreal: McGill-Queen's University Press, 2008.

Dym, Jordana, and Christophe Belaubre. *Politics, Economy, and Society in Bourbon Central America, 1759–1821.* Boulder: University Press of Colorado, 2007.

Egerton, Douglas R., Alison Games, Jane G. Landers, Kris Lane, and Donald R. Wright. *The Atlantic World: A History, 1400–1888.* Wheeling, IL: Harlan Davidson, 2007.

Elliott, J. H. *Imperial Spain, 1469–1716.* New York: St. Martins, 1963.

Elliott, John Huxtable. *Empires of the Atlantic World: Britain and Spain in America, 1492–1830.* New Haven, CT: Yale University Press, 2006.

Eltis, David. *The Rise of African Slavery in the Americas.* Cambridge: Cambridge University Press, 2000.

Eltis, David, James Walvin, and Svend E. Green-Pedersen. *The Abolition of the Atlantic Slave Trade: Origins and Effects in Europe, Africa, and the Americas.* Madison: University of Wisconsin Press, 1981.

Fisher, John. *Commercial Relations Between Spain and Spanish America in the Era of Free Trade, 1778–1796.* Liverpool: Center for Latin American Studies, University of Liverpool, 1985.

Fisher, John R. *Trade, War and Revolution: Exports from Spain to Spanish America 1797–1820.* Liverpool: Center for Latin American Studies, University of Liverpool, 1992.

———. *The Economic Aspects of Spanish Imperialism in America, 1492–1810.* Liverpool: Liverpool University Press, 1997.

Florescano, Enrique. "The Hacienda in New Spain." In *Colonial Spanish America*, edited by Leslie Bethell, Cambridge History of Latin America, 250–85. New York: Cambridge University Press, 1987.

Florescano, Enrique, and Fernando Castillo, eds. *Controversia Sobre la Libertad de Comercio en Nueva España, 1776–1818.* Serie Fuentes y Estadísticas del Comercio Exterior de México 1. México: Instituto Mexicano de Comercio Exterior, 1975.

Fontana i Làzaro, Josep. *El Comercio Libre Entre España y America Latina: 1765–1824.* 2nd ed. Colección Seminarios y Cursos. Madrid: Fundación Banco Exterior, 1987.

Francois, Marie. "Cloth and Silver: Pawning and Material Life in Mexico City at the Turn of the Nineteenth Century." *The Americas* 60, no. 3 (2004): 325–62.

———. *A Culture of Everyday Credit: Housekeeping, Pawnbroking, and Governance in Mexico City, 1750–1920.* Lincoln: University of Nebraska Press, 2006.

Frank, Andre Gunder. *Capitalism and Underdevelopment in Latin America: Historical Studies of Chile and Brazil.* New York: Monthly Review Press, 1967.

Fuente, Alejandro de la, César García del Pino, and Bernardo Iglesias Delgado. *Havana and the Atlantic in the Sixteenth Century.* Envisioning Cuba. Chapel Hill: University of North Carolina Press, 2008.

Furtado, Celso, and Ricardo W. de Aguiar. *Development and Underdevelopment.* Berkeley: University of California Press, 1964.

Gallardo, Diego Maria. *Almanak Mercantil Ó Guia de Comerciantes para el Año de 1802.* Madrid: Vega y Compañía, 1802.

Games, Alison. "Atlantic History: Definitions, Challenges, and Opportunities." *American Historical Review* 111, no. 3 (2006): 741–57.

García-Baquero González, Antonio. *Comercio Colonial y Guerras Revolucionarias: La Decadencia Económica de Cádiz a Raíz de la Emancipación Americana.* Sevilla: Escuela de Estudios Hispano-Americanos Consejo Superior de Investigaciones Científicas, 1972.

———. *Cádiz y el Atlántico: (1717–1778).* 2 vols. Cádiz: Diputación Provincial de Cádiz, 1988.

——. *El Libre Comercio a Examen Gaditano: Crítica y Opinión en el Cádiz Mercantil de Fines del Siglo XVIII.* Cádiz: Universidad de Cádiz Servicio de Publicaciones, 1998.

——. *El Comercio Colonial en la Época del Absolutismo Ilustrado: Problemas y Debates.* Granada: Universidad de Granada, 2003.

García Fuentes, Lutgardo. *El Comercio Español Con América, 1650–1700.* Publicaciones de la Excma. Diputación Provincial de Sevilla. Sección Historia, ser. 1a, no. 16. Sevilla: Escuela de Estudios Hispano-Americanos Consejo Superior de Investigaciones Científicas, 1980.

Garner, Richard L., and Spiro E. Stefanou. *Economic Growth and Change in Bourbon Mexico.* Gainesville: University Press of Florida, 1993.

Gillingham, Harrold Edgar. *Marine Insurance in Philadelphia, 1721–1800, with a List of Brokers and Underwriters as Shown by Old Policies and Books of Record, Including an Appendix of Marine Insurance of Archibald Mccall, 1809–1811.* Philadelphia: Patterson & White, 1933.

Grainger, John D. *The Amiens Truce: Britain and Bonaparte, 1801–1803.* Rochester, NY: Boydell, 2004.

Greene, Jack P., and Philip D. Morgan. *Atlantic History: A Critical Appraisal.* Oxford: Oxford University Press, 2009.

Greif, Avner. "Reputations and Coalitions in Medieval Trade: Evidence on the Maghribi Traders." *Journal of Economic History* 49, no. 4 (1989): 857–82.

——. "Contract Enforceability and Economic Institutions in Early Trade: The Mahgribi Traders' Coalition." *American Economic Review* 83, no. 3 (1993): 525–48.

——. "On the Political Foundations of the Late Medieval Commercial Revolution: Genoa During the Twelfth and Thirteenth Centuries." *Journal of Economic History* 54, no. 2 (1994): 271–87.

——. "Microtheory and Recent Developments in the Study of Economic Institutions Through Economic History." In *Advances in Economics and Econometrics: Theory and Applications: Seventh World Congress,* edited by David M. Kreps and Kenneth Frank Wallis, Vol. 2. 79–113. Econometric Society Monograph 27. Cambridge: Cambridge University Press, 1997.

Haggerty, Sheryllynne. *The British-Atlantic Trading Community,1760–1810: Men, Women, and the Distribution of Goods.* Leiden: Brill, 2006.

Hamnett, Brian R. *Politics and Trade in Southern Mexico, 1750–1821.* Cambridge: Cambridge University Press, 1971.

Haring, Clarence Henry. *Trade and Navigation Between Spain and the Indies in the Time of the Hapsburgs.* Cambridge: Cambridge University Press, 1918.

Harley, C. Knick. "Ocean Freight Rates and Productivity, 1740–1913: The Primacy of Mechanical Invention Reaffirmed." *Journal of Economic History* 48, no. 4 (1988): 851–76.

Hejeebu, Santhi. "Contract Enforcement in the English East India Company." *Journal of Economic History* 65, no. 2 (2005): 496–523.

Herrero Gil, María Dolores. "García Baquero Versus Fisher: Las Estadísticas del Puerto de Cádiz en 1778." In *X Reunión Científica de la F.E.H.M.* Santiago de Compostela, 2008.

Hoberman, Louisa Schell. *Mexico's Merchant Elite, 1590–1660: Silver, State, and Society.* Durham, NC: Duke University Press, 1991.

Hussey, Roland D. "Antecedents of the Spanish Monopolistic Overseas Trading Companies (1624–1728)." *Hispanic American Historical Review* 9, no. 1 (1929): 1–30.

Hussey, Roland Dennis. *The Caracas Company, 1728–1784: A Study in the History of Spanish Monopolistic Trade.* Harvard Historical Studies 37. Cambridge: Harvard University Press, 1934.

Inikori, J. E., and Stanley L. Engerman. *The Atlantic Slave Trade: Effects on Economies, Societies, and Peoples in Africa, the Americas, and Europe.* Durham, NC: Duke University Press, 1992.

Israel, J. I. "Mexico and the 'General Crisis' of the Seventeenth Century." *Past and Present* 63 (May 1974): 33–57.

John, A. H. "The London Assurance Company and the Marine Insurance Market of the Eighteenth Century." *Economica* 25, no. 98 (1958): 126–41.

Johnson, Lyman L., and Sonya Lipsett-Rivera. *The Faces of Honor: Sex, Shame, and Violence in Colonial Latin America.* Albuquerque: University of New Mexico Press, 1998.

Johnson, Lyman L., and Enrique Tandeter. *Essays on the Price History of Eighteenth-Century Latin America.* Albuquerque: University of New Mexico Press, 1990.

Jones, S. R. H., and P. Ville Simon. "Efficient Transactors or Rent-Seeking Monopolists? The Rationale for Early Chartered Trading Companies." *Journal of Economic History* 56, no. 4 (1996): 898–915.

———. "Theory and Evidence: Understanding Chartered Trading Companies." *Journal of Economic History* 56, no. 4 (1996): 925–26.

Kicza, John E. *Colonial Entrepreneurs, Families and Business in Bourbon Mexico City.* Albuquerque: University of New Mexico Press, 1983.

———. "Consumption and Control: The Mexico City Business Community and Commodity Marketing in the Eighteenth Century." *Estudios de Historia Novohispana* 12 (1992): 159–69.

Kingston, Christopher. "Marine Insurance in Britain and America, 1720–1844: A Comparative Institutional Analysis." *Journal of Economic History* 67, no. 2 (2007): 379–409.

Klein, Herbert. "Origin and Volume of Remission of Royal Tax Revenues from the Viceroyalties of Peru and New Spain." In *Dinero, Moneda y Crédito en la Monarquía Hispánica*, edited by Antonio-Miguel Bernal. Proceedings, Simposio Internacional, Dinero, moneda y crédito: De la Monarquía Hispánica al Integración Monetaria Europea, Madrid, 1999, 269–292. Madrid: Marcial Pons, 2000.

Klein, Herbert S. *The American Finances of the Spanish Empire: Royal Income and Expenditures in Colonial Mexico, Peru, and Bolivia, 1680–1809.* Albuquerque: University of New Mexico Press, 1998.

Klein, Herbert S., and Ben Vinson. *African Slavery in Latin America and the Caribbean.* 2nd ed. Oxford: Oxford University Press, 2007.

Knight, Frank Hyneman. *Risk, Uncertainty and Profit.* Hart, Schaffner & Marx Prize Essays 31. Boston: Houghton Mifflin, 1921.

Knight, Franklin W. *Slave Society in Cuba During the Nineteenth Century.* Madison: University of Wisconsin Press, 1977.

Knight, Franklin W., and Peggy K. Liss. *Atlantic Port Cities: Economy, Culture, and Society in the Atlantic World 1650–1850.* Knoxville: University of Tennessee Press, 1991.

Kohn, Meir. *The Origins of Western Economic Success: Commerce, Finance, and Government in Preindustrial Europe.* Working papers, Department of Economics, Dartmouth College, Hanover, NH, 2001. http://www.dartmouth.edu/~mkohn/.

Kuethe, Allan J. "El Fin del Monopolio: los Borbones y el Consulado Andaluz." In *Relaciones de Poder y Comercio Colonial: Nuevas Perspectivas*, edited by Enriqueta Vila Vilar, Allan J. Kuethe, and Carlos Alvarez Nogal, 35–66. Madrid: Consejo Superior de Investigaciones Científicas, 1999.

———. "Traslado del Consulado de Sevilla a Cádiz: Nuevas Perspectivas." In *Relaciones de Poder y Comercio Colonial: Nuevas Perspectivas*, edited by Enriqueta Vila Vilar, Allan J. Kuethe, and Carlos Alvarez Nogal, 67–82. Madrid: Consejo Superior de Investigaciones Científicas, 1999.

Lamikiz, Xabier. "Patrones de Comercio y Flujo de Información Comercial Entre España y América Durante el Siglo XVIII." *Revista de Historia Económica/Journal of Iberian and Latin American Economic History* 25, no. 2 (2007): 231–58.

———. "Un 'Cuento Ruidoso': Confidencialidad, Reputación, y Confianza en el Comercio del Siglo XVIII." *Obradoiro de Historia Moderna* 16 (2007): 113–42.

————. *Trade and Trust in the Eighteenth-Century Atlantic World: Spanish Merchants and Their Overseas Networks.* Edited by the Royal Historical Society. Rochester, NY: Boydell and Brewer, 2010.

Landsea, Christopher W. "A Climatology of Intense (or Major) Atlantic Hurricanes." *Monthly Weather Review* 121 (1993): 1703–13.

Lane, Frederic Chapin. *Profits from Power: Readings in Protection Rent and Violence-Controlling Enterprises.* Albany: State University of New York Press, 1979.

Lane, Kris. "Gone Platinum: Contraband and Chemistry in Eighteenth-Century Colombia." *Colonial Latin American Review* 20, no. 1 (2011): 61–79.

Lane, Kris E. *Pillaging the Empire: Piracy in the Americas, 1500–1750.* Latin American Realities. Armonk, NY: M. E. Sharpe, 1998.

Lawson, Philip. *The East India Company: A History.* London: Longman, 1993.

Lesger, Clé. "The 'Visible Hand': Views on Entrepreneurs and Entrepreneurship in Holland, 1580–1850." In *Small Business Entrepreneurs in Asia and Europe: Towards a Comparative Perspective,* edited by Mario Rutten and Carol Upadhya, 255–77. Thousand Oaks, CA: Sage, 1997.

Liss, Peggy K. *Atlantic Empires: The Network of Trade and Revolution, 1713–1826.* Johns Hopkins Studies in Atlantic History and Culture. Baltimore: Johns Hopkins University Press, 1983.

————. "Creoles, the North American Example and the Spanish American Economy, 1760–1810." In *The North American Role in the Spanish Imperial Economy, 1760–1819,* edited by Jacques and Allan Kuethe Barbier. Manchester: Manchester University Press, 1984.

MacLachlan, Colin M. *Spain's Empire in the New World: The Role of Ideas in Institutional and Social Change.* Berkeley: University of California Press, 1988.

MacLeod, Murdo. "Spain and America: The Atlantic Trade, 1492–1720." Vol. 1 of *The Cambridge History of Latin America,* edited by Leslie Bethell. Cambridge: Cambridge University Press, 1984.

Mangan, Jane E. *Trading Roles: Gender, Ethnicity, and the Urban Economy in Colonial Potosí.* Latin America Otherwise. Durham, NC: Duke University Press, 2005.

Mankiw, N. Gregory. *Principles of Economics.* 4th ed. Mason, OH: Thomson /South-Western, 2007.

Manning, William R. *The Nootka Sound Controversy.* Washington, DC: American Historical Association, 1904.

Marichal, Carlos. *Bankruptcy of Empire: Mexican Silver and the Wars between Spain, Britain, and France, 1760–1810.* Cambridge Latin American Studies 91. New York: Cambridge University Press, 2007.

Marks, Patricia H. "Confronting a Mercantile Elite: Bourbon Reformers and the Merchants of Lima, 1765–1796." *The Americas* 60, no. 4 (2004): 519–58.

————. *Deconstructing Legitimacy: Viceroys, Merchants, and the Military in Late Colonial Peru.* University Park: Pennsylvania State University Press, 2007.

Martinez del Cerro González, Victoria Eugenia. *Una Comunidad de Comerciantes: Navarros y Vascos en Cádiz (Segunda Mitad de Siglo XVIII).* Sevilla: Consejo Económico y Social de Andalucía, 2006.

Mártir Coll y Alsina, Pedro. *Tratado Elemental Teorico y Práctico de Comercio: en Que Se Presentan Varias Formulas de Contratas de Fletamentos, Conocimientos, Pólizas de Seguros . . . Que para Gobierno de Un Hijo Suyo Joven Comerciante Compusó, y Ha Corregido y Aumentado en Esta Edición, Pedro Martir Coll, y Alsina.* Barcelona: M. y T. Gaspar, 1818.

Mathias, Peter. "Strategies for Reducing Risk by Entrepreneurs in the Early Modern Period." In *Entrepreneurs and Enterpreneurship in Early Modern Times: Merchants and Industrialists within the Orbit of the Dutch Staple Market,* edited by Clé Lesger and L. Noordegraaf, 5–24. Den Haag: Stichting Hollandse Historische Reeks, 1995.

————. "Risk, Credit, and Kinship in Early Modern Enterprise." In *The Early Modern Atlantic Economy,* edited by John J. and Kenneth Morgan McCusker, 15–35. Cambridge: Cambridge University Press, 2000.

Matson, Cathy. "Introduction: The Ambiguities of Risk in the Early Republic." *Business History Review* 78, no. 4 (2004): 595–606.

McCusker, John J. "The Demise of Distance: The Business Press and the Origins of the Information Revolution in the Early Modern World." *American Historical Review* 110, no. 2 (2005): 295–321.

McNeill, William Hardy. *Plagues and Peoples.* Garden City, NY: Anchor /Doubleday, 1976.

Musgrave, Peter. "The Economics of Uncertainty: The Structural Revolution in the Spice Trade, 1480–1640." In *Spices in the Indian Ocean World,* edited by M. N. Pearson, *An Expanding World: The European Impact on World History 1450-1800,* Vol. 11:337–49. Brookfield, VT: Variorum, 1996.

Narváez y la Torre, Antonio, José Ignacio de Pombo, and Sergio Elías Ortiz. *Escritos de Dos Economistas Coloniales: Don Antonio de Narváez y la Torre, y Don José Ignacio de Pombo.* Archivo de la Economía Nacional 29. Bogotá: Banco de la República, Archivo de la Economía Nacional, 1965.

Nettels, Curtis P. "British Mercantilism and the Economic Development of the Thirteen Colonies." *Journal of Economic History* 12, no. 2 (1952): 105–14.

"The New British History in Atlantic Perspective." *American Historical Review* 104, no. 2 (1999): 426–500.

North, Douglass. "Ocean Freight Rates and Economic Development 1750–1913." *Journal of Economic History* 18, no. 4 (1958): 537–55.

North, Douglass C. "Sources of Productivity Change in Ocean Shipping, 1600–1850." *Journal of Political Economy* 76, no. 5 (1968): 953–70.

North, Douglass Cecil. *Institutions, Institutional Change, and Economic Performance.* The Political Economy of Institutions and Decisions. Cambridge: Cambridge University Press, 1990.

Ortiz de la Tabla Ducasse, Javier. *Comercio Exterior de Veracruz, 1778–1821: Crisis de Dependencia.* Sevilla: Escuela de Estudios Hispano-Americanos, 1978.

Ouweneel, Arij. *Shadows over Anáhuac: An Ecological Interpretation of Crisis and Development in Central Mexico, 1730–1800.* Albuquerque: University of New Mexico Press, 1996.

Paquette, Gabriel. *Enlightenment, Governance, and Reform in Spain and Its Empire, 1759–1808.* New York: Palgrave Macmillan, 2008.

Parry, J. H. *The Spanish Seaborne Empire.* London: Hutchinson, 1966.

Pérez Herrero, Pedro. *Plata y Libranzas: la Articulación Comercial del México Borbónico / Pedro Pérez Herrero.* México: Centro de Estudios Históricos, Colegio de México, 1988.

Pike, Ruth. *Aristocrats and Traders: Sevillian Society in the Sixteenth Century.* Ithaca, NY: Cornell University Press, 1972.

Pinto Rodriguez, J. "Los Cinco Gremios Mayores de Madrid y el Comercio en el Siglo XVIII." *Revista de Indias* 192 (1991): 292-326.

Pombo, José Ignacio de. *Comercio y Contrabando en Cartagena de Indias, 2 de Junio de 1800.* Nueva Biblioteca Colombiana de Cultura, Serie Breve, Historia. Bogotá, Colombia: Procultura, 1986.

Posthumus, N. W. *Inquiry into the History of Prices in Holland.* Leiden: Brill, 1946.

Prebisch, Raúl. *The Economic Development of Latin America and Its Principal Problems.* New York: United Nations, 1962.

Price, Jacob M. "Transaction Costs: A Note on Merchant Credit and the Organization of Private Trade." In *The Political Economy of Merchant Empires: State Power and World Trade, 1350–1750,* edited by James D. Tracy, 276–97. Cambridge: Cambridge University Press, 1991.

Quirós, José María. *Guía de Negociantes: Compendio de la Legislación Mercantil de España e Indias.* Edited by Pedro Pérez Herrero. México: Universidad Nacional Autonoma de México, 1986.

Ravina Martin, Manuel. "Participación Extranjera en el Comercio Indiano: El Seguro Marítimo a Fines del Siglo XVII." *Revista de Indias* 43 (1983): 481–513.

Real Díaz, José Joaquín. *Las Ferias de Jalapa.* Sevilla: Escuela de Estudios Hispano-americanos, 1959.

Rico Linage, Raquel. *Las Reales Compañías de Comercio Con América: los Órganos de Gobierno.* Publicaciones de la Excma, Diputación Provincial de Sevilla, Sección Historia, Ser. 1a, No. 24. Sevilla: Excma. Diputación Provincial de Sevilla: Escuela de Estudios Hispano-Americanos de Sevilla, 1983.

Ringrose, David R. *Spain, Europe and the "Spanish Miracle," 1700–1900.* Cambridge: Cambridge University Press, 1996.

Ruiz Rivera, Julián Bautista. *El Consulado de Cádiz: Matrícula de Comerciantes, 1730–1823.* Cádiz: Diputación Provincial de Cádiz, 1988.

Sawers, Larry. "The Navigation Acts Revisited." *Economic History Review* 45, no. 2 (1992): 262–84.

Schwartz, Stuart B. *Sugar Plantations in the Formation of Brazilian Society: Bahia, 1550–1835.* Cambridge Latin American Studies 52. Cambridge: Cambridge University Press, 1985.

Silva Riquer, Jorge. *La Estructura y Dinámica del Comercio Menudo en la Ciudad de Valladolid, Michoacán a Finales del Siglo XVIII.* Mexico City: INAH, 2007.

Smith, Robert S. "Indigo Production and Trade in Colonial Guatemala." *Hispanic American Historical Review* 39, no. 2 (1959): 181–211.

———. *The Spanish Guild Merchant: A History of the Consulado, 1250–1700.* New York: Octagon Books, 1972.

Socolow, Susan Migden. "Economic Activities of the Porteño Merchants: The Viceregal Period." *Hispanic American Historical Review* 55, no. 1 (1975): 1–24.

———. *The Merchants of Buenos Aires, 1778–1810: Family and Commerce.* Cambridge Latin American Studies 30. Cambridge: Cambridge University Press, 1978.

Spooner, Frank. *Risks at Sea: Amsterdam Insurance and Maritime Europe, 1766–1780.* Cambridge: Cambridge University Press, 1983.

Steensgaard, Niels. "Dutch East India Company as an Institutional Innovation." In *Trade in the Pre-Modern Era, 1400–1700,* edited by Douglas A. Irwin, 1:443–65. Cheltenham, UK: Elgar Reference Collection, 1996.

Stein, Barbara H., and Stanley J. Stein. *Edge of Crisis: War and Trade in the Spanish Atlantic, 1789–1808.* Baltimore: Johns Hopkins University Press, 2009.

Stein, Stanley, J. "Tending the Store: Trade and Silver at the Real de Huatla, 1778–1781." *Hispanic American Historical Review* 77, no. 3 (1997): 377–408.

Stein, Stanley J., and Barbara H. Stein. *The Colonial Heritage of Latin America: Essays on Economic Dependence in Perspective.* New York: Oxford University Press, 1970.

———. *Silver, Trade, and War: Spain and America in the Making of Early Modern Europe.* Baltimore: Johns Hopkins University Press, 2000.

———. *Apogee of Empire: Spain and New Spain in the Age of Charles III, 1759–1789.* Baltimore: Johns Hopkins University Press, 2003.

Stephen, James. *War in Disguise: Or, the Frauds of the Neutral Flags.* 4th ed. London: Printed by C. Whittingham and sold by J. Hatchard and J. Butterworth, 1806.

Suárez Argüello, Clara Elena. "El Parecer de la Élite de Comerciantes del Consulado de la Ciudad de México Ante la Operación del Libre Comercio (1791–1793)." In *Comercio y Poder en América Colonial: los Consulados de Comerciantes, Siglos XVII–XIX,* edited by Bernd and Antonio Ibarra Hausberger, 103–30. Madrid,: Iberoamerica, 2003.

Sunderland, David. "Principals and Agents: The Activities of the Crown Agents for the Colonies, 1880–1914." *Economic History Review* 52, no. 2 (1999): 284–306.

Tandeter, Enrique. *Coercion and Market: Silver Mining in Colonial Potosí, 1692–1826.* Albuquerque: University of New Mexico Press, 1993.

TePaske, John. "General Tendencies and Secular Trends in the Economies of Mexico and Peru, 1750–1810: The View from the Cajas of Mexico and Lima." In *The Economies of Mexico and Peru During the Late Colonial Period, 1760–1810,* edited by Nils Jacobsen and Hans-Jürgen Puhle, 316–39. Berlin: Colloqium Verlag, 1986.

Tepaske, John J., and Herbert Klein. "The Seventeenth-Century Crisis in New Spain: Myth or Reality?" *Past and Present* 90 (1981): 116–36.

TePaske, John Jay, Herbert S. Klein, Kendall W. Brown, and Alvaro Jara. *The Royal Treasuries of the Spanish Empire in America.* 4 vols. Durham, NC: Duke University Press, 1982, 1990.

TePaske, John, and Herbert Klein. *Ingresos y Egresos de la Real Hacienda de Nueva España.* 2 vols. Mexico City: Instituto Naciónal de Antropología e Historia, 1986.

Thomas, Hugh. *Rivers of Gold: The Rise of the Spanish Empire, from Columbus to Magellan.* New York: Random House, 2005.

Tooke, Thomas, William Newmarch, and T. E. Gregory. *A History of Prices and of the State of the Circulation from 1792 to 1856*. New York: Adelphi, 1928.

Torales Pacheco, Maria Cristina, ed. *La Compañia de Comercio de Francisco Ignacio de Yraeta (1767–1797)*. México: Instituto Mexicano de Comercio Exterior con la colaborariâon de la Universidad Iberoamericana, 1985.

Torres Ramírez, Bibiano, and Javier Ortiz de la Tabla. *Reglamento y Aranceles Reales para el Comercio Libre de España a Indias de 12 de Octubre de 1778*. Seville: Escuela de Estudios Hispano-Americanos, 1978.

Townsend, Camilla. *Tales of Two Cities: Race and Economic Culture in Early Republican North and South America: Guayaquil, Ecuador, and Baltimore, Maryland*. Austin: University of Texas Press, 2000.

Turiso Sebastián, Jesús. *Comerciantes Españoles en la Lima Borbónica: Anatomía de Una Élite de Poder, 1701–1761*. Serie Historia y Sociedad. Valladolid: Universidad de Valladolid, 2002.

Universidad y Casa de Contratación de la M.N. y M.L. Villa de Bilbao. *Ordenanzas de la Ilustre Universidad y Casa de Contratacion de la M. N. y M. L. Villa de Bilbao Aprobadas, y Confirmadas por el Rey Nuestro Señor Don Phelipe Quinto (Que Dios Guarde) Año de 1737*. Madrid: Viuda de D. M. Fernandez, 1775. http://books.google.com/books?id=k7pDAAAAcAAJ &printsec=frontcover&source=gbs_ge_summary_r&cad=0#v=onep age&q&f=false.

Van Young, Eric. *Hacienda and Market in Eighteenth-Century Mexico: The Rural Economy of the Guadalajara Region, 1675–1820*. Berkeley: University of California Press, 1981.

Veitia Linage, Joseph de. *Norte de la Contratación de las Indias Occidentales*. Buenos Aires: Comisión argentina de fomento interamericano, 1945.

Vila Vilar, Enriqueta. "El Poder del Consulado Sevillano y los Hombres del Comercio en el Siglo XVII: Una Aproximación." In *Relaciones de Poder y Comercio Colonial: Nuevas Perspectivas*, edited by Enriqueta Vila Vilar, Allan J. Kuethe, and Carlos Alvarez Nogal, 3–34. Madrid: Consejo Superior de Investigaciones Científicas, 1999.

Walker, Geoffrey J. *Spanish Politics and Imperial Trade, 1700–1789*. London: Macmillan, 1979.

Wallerstein, Immanuel Maurice. *The Modern World-System*. 3 vols. Studies in Social Discontinuity. New York: Academic Press, 1974.

Ward, Christopher. *Imperial Panama: Commerce and Conflict in Isthmian America, 1550–1800*. Albuquerque: University of New Mexico Press, 1993.

Wedovoy, Enrique. *La Evolución Económica Rioplatense a Fines del Siglo XVIII y Princípios del Siglo XIX, a la Luz de la História del Seguro.* La Plata: Universidad Nacional de la Plata, 1967.

Williamson, Oliver E. *The Economic Institutions of Capitalism: Firms, Markets, Relational Contracting.* New York: Free Press, 1985.

Woodward, Ralph Lee. *Class Privilege and Economic Development: The Consulado de Comercio of Guatemala, 1793–1871.* Chapel Hill: University of North Carolina Press, 1966.

Yuste López, Carmen. *El Comercio de la Nueva España Con Filipinas, 1590–1785.* México: Instituto Nacional de Antropología e Historia Departamento de Investigaciones Históricas, 1984.

Zahedieh, Nuala. "Credit, Risk and Reputation in Late Seventeenth-Century Colonial Trade." In *Merchant Organization and Maritime Trade in the North Atlantic, 1660–1815,* edited by Olaf Uwe Janzen, Research in Maritime History, Vol. 15, 53–74. St. John's, Newfoundland: International Maritime Economic History Association, 1998.

———. *The Capital and the Colonies: London and the Atlantic Economy, 1660–1700.* New York: Cambridge University Press, 2010.

INDEX

accounts receivable, 117; at time of
death, 142–143
agents: cheating by, 292n33, 293n39,
301n42; correspondence from, 22;
demand estimates by, 37; dependence
on, 27, 292n32; foreign, 29;
information gathering by, 18;
management of, 292n33; monitoring
of, 28; principal-agent problem and,
27–30, 292n33; trust in, 28
Agreda, Diego de, 92
aguardiente, 39, 222, 235–236
alcabala, 316n80
alcaldes emayores: credit provided by,
115–117, 126
almaceneros: cash purchases by, 126–128;
credit use by, 116; monopoly position
of, 45–54, 127 *See also mercaderes*
American Revolutionary War: armed
convoys during, 174–175, 240;
commercial expansion after, 70–86,
159; competition increase after, 184;
end of, 79; insurance during,
223–224, 230, 250; mail transit time
during, 24–25; market saturation
after, 39, 77–86, 160; prices and, 36
Amiens, Peace and Treaty of, 153, 158,
167, 169, 193, 218, 221, 224, 237,
253–254, 358n151. *See also* Treaty of
Amiens

Amsterdam: cacao price in, 84–85;
cochineal price in, 22, 83–85;
commodity exchange, 333n6; hide
price in, 84–85; indigo price in, 22,
84–85; insurance in, 213–215; market
saturation in, 82
Andalusia, 6
Andes: trade to, 308n99; wool from,
83–84
Ángel, El, 31
Angulo Guardamino, Lorenzo de,
91–92
antitrust laws, 299n19
arbitristas, 69
armament: of corsairs, 162, 171, 336n46;
of merchant vessels, 62
Argentina, *see* Rio de la Plata
Artechea, Antonio de, 236–238
Atlantic world, 1–2, 11–14; and
Columbian exchange, 285n19;
sources on, 286n25, 287n26
avería, 202–203, 347n61
Aycinena, Juan Fermín de, 117–118,
142–143, 145

Baltic ports, 289n2
bankruptcy: in Cadiz, 99, 102–107; *Casa
de Contratación* oversight of, 317n103;
consulado oversight of, 14–15, 99–101,
317n102; Council of Indies oversight

Icaza, Isidro Antonio de, 91
Imaña, Ventura de, 88, 211
Import Substituting Industrialization, 285n20
imports: to Mexico, 321n5; to Spain, 74–75, 91, 107, 311n16
incarceration, 102–103
indefinidos, 216–217
indigenous people: cochineal harvest by, 13; consumption of imports by, 111–112, 321n5; taxation of, 111
indigo: from Guatemala, 84–85, 156, 172, 208, 231; price of, 22, 36, 84–85; production of, 116, 139
inelasticity, 334n18
information, 4, 17; agent gathering of, 18; asymmetry, 292n33; from correspondence, 17, 22–27, 41; on demand, 34–35; distance and, 288n2; imperfect, 4–5; from *lonja*, 106, 123; on market conditions, 21, 33–37; movement of, 26, 348n5; from newspapers, 34; political, 30–33; on prices, 17; public exchange of, 106, 123; trading company, 60; on treaties, 153; on war, 220–222. *See also* correspondence
informes: of Cadiz *consulado*, 15; on *comercio libre*, 88–90; Spanish Crown requests for, 88–90, 94–96
institutions: in Cadiz, 6, 57; convoys and fleet system as risk-reducing institution, 44, 58, 65–68; 86, 97–98, 107–109, 184, 244; and economic activity, 5, 43, 67, 97, 275–277, 316n91; oceanic commerce, 58–59; purpose of, 296n1; risk management and, 5, 28, 43–44, 68, 86, 97–98, 107, 184, 275–276
insurance, 3, 179–180, 182–183; during American Revolutionary War, 223–224, 230, 250; in Amsterdam, 213–215; average in, 347n61; *avería* types in, 202–203; British laws on, 184–185; broker, 206–207; cancelled, 352n72; claims, 11, 220–221, 261, 348n68; coinsurance, 234–238;

commodity of, 200–202, 246–248; with convoys, 238–244, 355n122; coverage duration, 206; deductibles, 203; in Europe, 343n6; during French Revolution, 223, 250; international, 340n96; life, 201–202; marine, 9, 343n6; and Marticorena, Juan Bautista de, 230; and Marticorena, Juan Vicente de, 208–209, 258, 262–263; multivariate regression analysis of, 245, 355n132; partial, 232–233; of precious metals, 246; profitability of, 184, 190, 219, 223, 255–256, 259–260, 283n6; risk and, 197–199, 271–272; routes and, 212–217, 249–250, 350n23; season and, 210–212; of ships, 199–200, 234; Sierra purchases of, 223, 225–226, 230, 236, 239–240; of slaves, 200–201, 347n58; supply of, 219–220; war claims, 11, 220–221; of warships, 173; weather conditions and, 210–212
insurance industry: of Buenos Aires, 345n30; of Havana, 345n30; income of, 258–260; losses of, 258–260; merchants in, 184; oversight of, 267, 270; reforms to, 270; of Río de la Plata, 345n30; of Veracruz, 345n30. *See also* Cadiz insurance industry; London insurance industry
insurance partnerships, 9–10; bankruptcy and, 191; charters of, 183, 196–198, 217–219; clients of, 193; compensation systems in, 196; coverage from, 195; directors of, 195–197, 219, 359n8; dissolution of, 188; divine protection for, 197; foreign, 340n96; formation of, 187–188; investment in, 269; liability in, 192; number of, 188–189; patrons of, 344n18; risk estimates by, 257, 283n6; shareholders of, 185–186, 190, 195, 266–267; size of, 193–195; structure of, 346n49. *See also* Appendix C (on-line)
insurance policies, 183, 204–206; boilerplate language of, 206;

SOCIAL SCIENCE HISTORY

Moramay López-Alonso, *Measuring Up: A History of Living Standards in Mexico 1850–1950*

Yovanna Pineda, *Industrial Development in a Frontier Economy: The Industrialization of Argentina, 1890–1930*

John P. Enyeart, *The Quest for "Just and Pure Law": Rocky Mountain Workers and American Social Democracy, 1870–1924*

Paul W. Drake, *Between Tyranny and Anarchy: A History of Democracy in Latin America, 1800–2006*

Armando Razo, *Social Foundations of Limited Dictatorship: Networks and Private Protection During Mexico's Early Industrialization*

Stephen Haber, Douglass C. North, and Barry R. Weingast, editors, *Political Institutions and Financial Development*

David W. Brady and Mathew D. McCubbins, *Party, Process, and Political Change in Congress, Volume 2: Further New Perspectives on the History of Congress*

Anne G. Hanley, *Native Capital: Financial Institutions and Economic Development in São Paulo, Brazil, 1850–1920*

Fernando Rocchi, *Chimneys in the Desert: Industrialization in Argentina During the Export Boom Years, 1870–1930*

J. G. Manning and Ian Morris, *The Ancient Economy: Evidence and Models*

Daniel Lederman, *The Political Economy of Protection: Theory and the Chilean Experience*

William Summerhill, *Order Against Progress: Government, Foreign Investment, and Railroads in Brazil, 1854–1913*

Samuel Kernell, *James Madison: The Theory and Practice of Republican Government*

Francisco Vidal Luna and Herbert S. Klein, *Slavery and the Economy of Sao Paulo, 1750–1850*

Noel Maurer, *The Power and the Money: The Mexican Financial System, 1876–1932*

David W. Brady and Mathew D. McCubbins, *Party, Process, and Political Change in Congress: New Perspectives on the History of Congress*

Jeffrey Bortz and Stephen Haber, *The Mexican Economy, 1870–1930: Essays on the Economic History of Institutions, Revolution, and Growth*

Edward Beatty, *Institutions and Investment: The Political Basis of Industrialization in Mexico Before 1911*

Jeremy Baskes, *Indians, Merchants, and Markets: A Reinterpretation of the Repartimiento and Spanish-Indian Economic Relations in Colonial Oaxaca, 1750–1821*

Lightning Source UK Ltd.
Milton Keynes UK
UKHW010342070722
405476UK00002B/79

9 780804 785426